The Curriculum:

Context, Design
and Development

The Curriculum: context, design and development course team in the Faculty of Educational Studies at The Open University.

John Merritt (course team chairman)
Robert Bell
Judith Fage
Alan Harris
Donald Holms
Richard Hooper
Martin Lawn
George Low
Bill Prescott
Michael Price
Gwynn Pritchard
John Raynor
David Seligman

The Curriculum:

Context, Design and Development

*Readings edited by Richard Hooper for
the course team at The Open University*

*Oliver & Boyd, Edinburgh
in association with
The Open University Press*

First published 1971 by

Oliver & Boyd
Tweeddale Court
14 High Street
Edinburgh EH1 1YL
(A Division of Longman Group Ltd)
in association with
The Open University Press

ISBN 0 05 002464 7

Set in 'Linotype' 10/12pt Pilgrim
and 'Monotype' Univers series.
Printed in Great Britain by
Richard Clay (The Chaucer Press) Ltd
Bungay, Suffolk

Contents

PART II: Design of the curriculum

General Introduction

This book of readings has been prepared by members of an Open University course team and forms part of a second-level course in the Faculty of Educational Studies called: *The curriculum: context, design and development*. An interdisciplinary approach has been taken to the study of curriculum with contributions by historians, sociologists, psychologists, philosophers, curriculum designers and educational technologists. The main aim of the course is to develop the teacher's own judgement concerning the kinds of curricula which schools could provide and to develop the teacher's ability to design and implement new curricula.

The course and the Reader are divided into three parts—

     I   context of the curriculum
    II   design of the curriculum
   III   development of the curriculum

In the first part, the relationship between curriculum and society is examined, drawing on examples from different countries What are the historical and cultural roots of present-day British curricula? What does the curriculum do *to* people and *for* society—other than transmit certain types of knowledge?

The second part explores problems of curriculum design. What sort of models are useful in the design of curriculum? What is the relationship between different elements of the curriculum—for example, objectives and methods? How are curriculum objectives formulated? What is the relationship between theories of knowledge and curriculum design? What does learning theory tell us about the design of conditions of learning to reach curriculum objectives?

The third part of the Reader surveys the problems of curriculum development. What are the constraints on implementing new curricula? Why does innovation fail? What sorts of strategies of innovation can and are being employed?

This Reader has been produced as a component of a multi-media course, which also includes correspondence texts, radio and television programmes, and a wide range of student activities and assignments. Taken on its own, however, the Reader provides a very useful collection of material for teachers in both in- and pre-service training. Articles and excerpts from books on curriculum have been selected, ranging from the theoretical to the practical, with short summaries provided at the head of each for ease of access.

The last few years have seen in the United Kingdom what amounts almost to a curriculum revolution. As with all revolutions in education, there is an urgent need for careful scrutiny of claims made for the various new curricula. There is an urgent need for teachers in the classroom to be able to evaluate and adapt curricula developed nationally, and to be provided with the time, resources and encouragement to invent and organize local curriculum resources. There is much controversy today about comprehensive reorganization, streaming, the future shape of higher education. Given this controversy, it is important for everyone in education to be aware of the far-reaching implications of decisions made about the curriculum. The study of curriculum is no longer a narrow and esoteric discussion of pure content, uncontaminated by such matters as teaching method, school organization and selection, and social class. In one sense the study of curriculum is the study of education. Decisions about which curricula for which groups of children are decisions about the shape and future of society. For these reasons, the Reader should be of value to a wider audience of teachers, students and parents.

Part I
Context of the curriculum

Introduction

At a time of educational controversy, 'tradition' is quoted as defence against change. An important way of setting the context within which curriculum can be studied is to analyse 'tradition'. '...the phrase "the English tradition of education", not infrequently used in arguing against further rapid change in the character of secondary education, has a very limited validity. It can scarcely apply to the public system which, even during its brief history, has greatly altered in respect of objectives, structure and methods of selection. Nor, in the sense of a centuries-old persistence of character, is the term really applicable to the private sectors, whether secondary or university' (David Glass, I : 3). Writing about the growth of the modern university, Robert Bell (I : 6) argues that assumptions about the 'traditional role' of the university are historically invalid and dangerously misleading.

The curriculum is socially and historically located, and culturally determined. Curriculum does not develop in a vacuum but proceeds on the basis of beliefs—seldom made explicit—about how people learn, what human beings should be like, what society is. 'The curriculum is ... interwoven with the social fabric that sustains it' (Smith *et al.*, I : 2). The shape of modern British education and the curriculum embedded in it were largely determined in the nineteenth century, with the coming of education for all. Education developed along two fairly distinct tracks—one for the mass of the people, one for the middle classes—and this dualism has dominated British education ever since. William Taylor (I : 5) examines the dualism found in the secondary curriculum during the last sixty years. The Hadow Report of 1926 '... made clear that the academic, bookish curriculum suitable for the selected minority in the Grammar schools was not suitable for the majority of pupils attending Modern schools'. David Glass (I : 3) notes that the 1956 White Paper *Technical Education* introduces dualism into higher education by placing '...higher technical education in about the same relationship to university education as junior technical schools were to grammar schools before the war—necessary and worthy, but of inferior status'.

The existence of different types of education, with different types of curricula, for different groups of people within a population, is at the centre of the modern educational debate. Smith *et al.* (1:2), make a useful distinction between *common education* and *special education*. Common education is '...based upon the universal elements of the culture and ... is concerned with the problem of maintaining the society as a closely-knit and well-integrated unit'. Special education is '...based largely upon the dominant specialties of the culture ... designed to train the individual for a particular social or vocational position. ... In societies having a recognized social élite, it will be found that instruments of education will be set aside for training the immature members of the élite group in the special points of view and patterns of conduct of these privileged adults. The presence of *exclusive* private or finishing schools is evidence of the existence of an élite class having particular outlooks, polite manners and behavioral patterns which it wishes to maintain. Indeed, the existence of such classes has led in some nations to the creation of dual educational systems—one for the folk and another for the upper classes. For this reason higher forms of education, including secondary as well as higher schools, have tended historically to be designed for the privileged few. Even in the more democratically inclined countries, where a single educational ladder has been adopted, the curriculum of the upper rungs reflects a privileged origin.'

Nigel Grant (1:7) analyses the dilemma of special versus common education in the communist countries of Eastern Europe where the dominant ideology clearly requires common education—uniform curriculum for all—yet the school tradition inherited from pre-communist times is, like in Western Europe, academically élitist. Some specialization in the curriculum is occurring, because pupils do have differing abilities and because an advanced industrial economy demands it—but how much specialization is permissible before the notion of *common* education is lost?

The move towards common and away from special education in the United Kingdom would tend to be associated with the left wing of the political spectrum. But the move can on occasion come from a more conservative position—with a very different motivation.

Taylor (I:5) gives an example from recent developments in the secondary modern curriculum. Child-centred project work, with its roots in the progressive movement of A. S. Neill and Dewey, is giving way in a number of schools to emphasis on basic literacy, the need to pass external exams, and a generally more 'tough-minded' approach on the part of teachers and headmasters. This move towards subject-centred, grammar school-type education is traced back by Taylor to statements such as the following in the Spens Report on Secondary Education, 1938: '...in our opinion the "project method" in the full sense of the term has a very useful place in the teaching of young children. We recognize, moreover, the great value of occasions ... which invite the application and synthesis of a considerable range of acquired knowledge and skills. But our general doctrine forbids us to go much further than this; for its essence is that the school "subjects" stand for traditions of practical, aesthetic and intellectual activity, each having its own distinctive individuality; and we hold that the profit a pupil derives from them does not come from casual or episodical contacts, but by his being, so to speak, put to school to them, and so getting to make their outstanding characters part of the equipment and habit of his mind.' Views similar to this about the secondary school curriculum are supported in Part II by Paul Hirst (II:8) and John White (II:11)— for very different reasons.

The existence of different curricula for different people should make the curriculum designer consider the implications of decisions made about curriculum. These decisions are far from neutral. There is a tendency to believe that the sole function of education is to transmit to children via the curriculum certain amounts of value-free knowledge and objective Truth. Not only is the knowledge carried by the curriculum highly value-laden and relative, as a quick glance at textbooks written in different countries about the same event will demonstrate, but education also of course fulfils other functions. One aim in the nineteenth century, David Glass points out (I:3), was to gentle the masses. According to the 1858 Newcastle Commission: 'A set of good schools civilizes a whole neighbourhood.' Paul Goodman (I:11) describes a modern American version: 'Whatever the deliberate intention, schooling today serves mainly for policing and for taking up the slack in youth unemployment.' Education, and by implication curriculum, has a major function for society—it sorts people out. '...the question "Who should go to college?" translates itself into the more compelling question "Who is going to manage the society?" ' (John Gardner, I : 8). The extent of the selection process is quantified by R. K. Harker's research (I : 9) into the effects of streaming in a New Zealand comprehensive school. As with similar studies undertaken in the United Kingdom by Halsey, Floud and Douglas, Harker's research demonstrates conclusively that the selection mechanisms of education—for example, tests of verbal ability—discriminate against working-class children. As a result the top streams are full of middle-class children opting to do academic subjects, the bottom streams full of working-class children opting to do book-keeping and metalwork. The streaming of pupils in the New Zealand comprehensive school performs the same function as the tripartite selection carried out on secondary school children by many English education authorities.

With the gradual ending of 11-plus and tripartite selection, Martin Shipman (I : 10) warns that some of the recent curriculum innovations in Britain, for example the Schools Council Humanities Project, may be dividing education into two systems in the 1970s as effectively as selection at 11-plus has done in the past. 'It may be that in a technological society a minority educated to administer and a majority educated to enjoy leisure and reconciled to a superfluous role will be appropriate. But an élite schooled in academic disciplines and the rest knowledgeable about clothes, pop culture, the local environment and family life around the world will not be a just division of culture and was not the objective of those who have been pressing home the changes that are creating this separation.' It is paradoxical that Paul Goodman (I : 11), a leading radical of the Left in American education, should argue for separate public (English usage : state) schools for the academically minded just when the Left in the United Kingdom is pushing comprehensive reorganization modelled on American high-school lines.

The context of the curriculum is always changing. Changes in society bring about, in time, changes in the educational system— and vice versa. Beliefs alter about how people learn, what human beings should be like, what society is. For example, a popular psychological theory about intelligence—that human beings possess fixed immutable quantities of IQ—has for years been used '. . . to ratify graded systems of education . . . in the final interest of a particular model of the social system' (Raymond Williams, I : 4). This theory has in recent years been shown to be inaccurate, yet it is still quoted in defence of existing educational structures. At the basis of so much thinking about curriculum is the belief that '. . . the essence of true education is timelessness. It is something that endures through changing conditions like a solid rock standing squarely and firmly in the middle of a raging torrent' (I : I). It is the timelessness of curriculum that 'The saber-tooth curriculum' (I : I) satirizes.

Harold Benjamin

I:1 The saber-tooth curriculum

This is a chapter from a famous satire on curriculum published in the United States in 1939. It tells the story of a prehistoric tribe which decided to introduce systematic education for its children. The curriculum was specifically designed to meet particular survival needs in the local environment and so included such subjects as saber-tooth-tiger-scaring-with-fire. But the climate of the region changes and the saber-tooth tigers perish. Attempts to change the curriculum to meet new survival needs encounter stern opposition.

The first great educational theorist and practitioner of whom my imagination has any record was a man of Chellean times whose full name was *New-Fist-Hammer-Maker* but whom, for convenience, I shall hereafter call *New-Fist*.

New-Fist was a doer, in spite of the fact that there was little in his environment with which to do anything very complex. You have undoubtedly heard of the pear-shaped, chipped-stone tool which archeologists call the *coup-de-poing* or fist hammer. New-Fist gained his name and a considerable local prestige by producing one of these artifacts in a less rough and more useful form than any previously known to his tribe. His hunting clubs were generally superior weapons, moreover, and his fire-using techniques were patterns of simplicity and precision. He knew how to do things his community needed to have done, and he had the energy and will to go ahead and do them. By virtue of these characteristics he was an educated man.

New-Fist was also a thinker. Then, as now, there were few lengths to which men would not go to avoid the labor and pain of thought. More readily than his fellows, New-Fist pushed himself beyond those lengths to the point where cerebration was inevitable. The same quality of intelligence which led him into the socially approved activity of producing a superior artifact also led him to engage in the socially disapproved practice of thinking. When other men gorged themselves on the proceeds of a successful hunt and vegetated in dull stupor for many hours thereafter, New-Fist ate a little less heartily, slept a little less stupidly, and arose a little earlier than his comrades to sit by the fire and think. He would stare moodily at the flickering flames and wonder about various parts of his environment until he finally got to the point where he became strongly dissatisfied with the accustomed ways of his tribe. He began to catch glimpses of ways in which life might be made better for himself, his family, and his group. By virtue of this development, he became a dangerous man.

This was the background that made this doer and thinker hit upon the concept of a conscious, systematic education. The immediate stimulus which put him directly into the practice of education came from watching his children at play. He saw these children at the cave entrance before the fire engaged in activity with bones and sticks and brightly colored pebbles. He noted that they seemed to have no purpose in their play beyond immediate pleasure in the activity itself. He compared their activity with that of the grown-up members of the tribe. The children played for fun; the adults worked for security and enrichment of their lives. The children dealt with bones, sticks, and pebbles; the adults dealt with food, shelter, and clothing. The children protected themselves from boredom; the adults protected themselves from danger.

'If I could only get these children to do the things that will give more and better food, shelter, clothing, and security,' thought New-Fist, 'I would be helping this tribe to have a better life. When the children became grown, they would have more meat to eat, more skins to keep them warm, better caves in which to sleep, and less danger from the striped death with the curving teeth that walks these trails by night.'

Having set up an educational goal, New-Fist proceeded to construct a curriculum for teaching that goal. 'What things must we tribesmen know how to do in order to live with full bellies, warm backs, and minds free from fear?' he asked himself.

To answer this question, he ran various activities over in his mind. 'We have to catch fish with our bare hands in the pool far up the creek beyond that big bend,' he said to himself. 'We have to catch fish with our bare hands in the pool right at the bend. We have to catch them in the same way in the pool just this side of the bend. And so we catch them in the next pool and the next and the next.

Always we catch them with our bare hands.'

Thus New-Fist discovered the first subject of the first curriculum —fish-grabbing-with-the-bare-hands.

'Also we club the little woolly horses,' he continued with his analysis. 'We club them along the bank of the creek where they come down to drink. We club them in the thickets where they lie down to sleep. We club them in the upland meadow where they graze. Wherever we find them we club them.'

So woolly-horse-clubbing was seen to be the second main subject in the curriculum.

'And finally, we drive away the saber-tooth tigers with fire,' New-Fist went on in his thinking. 'We drive them from the mouth of our caves with fire. We drive them from our trail with burning branches. We wave firebrands to drive them from our drinking hole. Always we have to drive them away, and always we drive them with fire.'

Thus was discovered the third subject—saber-tooth-tiger-scaring-with-fire.

Having developed a curriculum, New-Fist took his children with him as he went about his activities. He gave them an opportunity to practice these three subjects. The children liked to learn. It was more fun for them to engage in these purposeful activities than to play with colored stones just for the fun of it. They learned the new activities well, and so the educational system was a success.

As New-Fist's children grew older, it was plain to see that they had an advantage in good and safe living over other children who had never been educated systematically. Some of the more intelligent members of the tribe began to do as New-Fist had done, and the teaching of fish-grabbing, horse-clubbing, and tiger-scaring came more and more to be accepted as the heart of real education.

For a long time, however, there were certain more conservative members of the tribe who resisted the new, formal educational system on religious grounds. 'The Great Mystery who speaks in thunder and moves in lightning,' they announced impressively, 'the Great Mystery who gives men life and takes it from them as he wills—if that Great Mystery had wanted children to practice fish-grabbing, horse-clubbing, and tiger-scaring before they were grown up, he would have taught them these activities himself by implanting in their natures instincts for fish-grabbing, horse-clubbing, and tiger-scaring. New-Fist is not only impious to attempt something the

Great Mystery never intended to have done; he is also a damned fool for trying to change human nature.'

Whereupon approximately half of these critics took up the solemn chant, 'If you oppose the will of the Great Mystery, you must die,' and the remainder sang derisively in unison, 'You can't change human nature.'

Being an educational statesman as well as an educational administrator and theorist, New-Fist replied politely to both arguments. To the more theologically minded, he said that, as a matter of fact, the Great Mystery had ordered this new work done, that he even did the work himself by causing children to want to learn, that children could not learn by themselves without divine aid, that they could not learn at all except through the power of the Great Mystery, and that nobody could really understand the will of the Great Mystery concerning fish, horses, and saber-tooth tigers unless he had been well grounded in the three fundamental subjects of the New-Fist school. To the human-nature-cannot-be-changed shouters, New-Fist pointed out the fact that paleolithic culture had attained its high level by changes in human nature and that it seemed almost unpatriotic to deny the very process which had made the community great.

'I know you, my fellow tribesmen,' the pioneer educator ended his argument gravely, 'I know you as humble and devoted servants of the Great Mystery. I know that you would not for one moment consciously oppose yourselves to his will. I know you as intelligent and loyal citizens of this great cave-realm, and I know that your pure and noble patriotism will not permit you to do anything which will block the development of that most cave-realmish of all our institutions—the paleolithic educational system. Now that you understand the true nature and purpose of this institution, I am serenely confident that there are no reasonable lengths to which you will not go in its defense and its support.'

By this appeal the forces of conservatism were won over to the side of the new school, and in due time everybody who was anybody in the community knew that the heart of good education lay in the three subjects of fish-grabbing, horse-clubbing, and tiger-scaring. New-Fist and his contemporaries grew old and were gathered by the Great Mystery to the Land of the Sunset far down the creek. Other men followed their educational ways more and more, until at last all the children of the tribe were practiced systematically in the three fundamentals. Thus the tribe prospered and was happy in the possession of adequate meat, skins, and security.

It is to be supposed that all would have gone well forever with this good educational system if conditions of life in that community had remained forever the same. But conditions changed, and life which had once been so safe and happy in the cave-realm valley became insecure and disturbing.

A new ice age was approaching in that part of the world. A great glacier came down from the neighboring mountain range to the north. Year after year it crept closer and closer to the headwaters of the creek which ran through the tribe's valley, until at length it reached the stream and began to melt into the water. Dirt and gravel which the glacier had collected on its long journey were dropped into the creek. The water grew muddy. What had once been a crystal-clear stream in which one could see easily to the bottom was now a milky stream into which one could not see at all.

At once the life of the community was changed in one very important respect. It was no longer possible to catch fish with the bare hands. The fish could not be seen in the muddy water. For some years, moreover, the fish in this creek had been getting more timid, agile, and intelligent. The stupid, clumsy, brave fish, of which originally there had been a great many, had been caught with the bare hands for fish generation after fish generation, until only fish of superior intelligence and agility were left. These smart fish, hiding in the muddy water under the newly deposited glacial boulders, eluded the hands of the most expertly trained fish-grabbers. Those tribesmen who had studied advanced fish-grabbing in the secondary school could do no better than their less well-educated fellows who had taken only an elementary course in the subject, and even the university graduates with majors in ichthyology were baffled by the problem. No matter how good a man's fish-grabbing education had been, he could not grab fish when he could not find fish to grab.

The melting waters of the approaching ice sheet also made the country wetter. The ground became marshy far back from the banks of the creek. The stupid woolly horses, standing only five or six hands high and running on four-toed front feet and three-toed hind feet, although admirable objects for clubbing, had one dangerous characteristic. They were ambitious. They all wanted to learn to run on their middle toes. They all had visions of becoming powerful and aggressive animals instead of little and timid ones. They

dreamed of a far-distant day when some of their descendants would
be sixteen hands high, weigh more than half a ton, and be able to
pitch their would-be riders into the dirt. They knew they could
never attain these goals in a wet, marshy country, so they all went
east to the dry, open plains, far from the paleolithic hunting
grounds. Their places were taken by little antelopes who came
down with the ice sheet and were so shy and speedy and had so
keen a scent for danger that no one could approach them closely
enough to club them.

The best-trained horse-clubbers of the tribe went out day after
day and employed the most efficient techniques taught in the school,
but day after day they returned empty-handed. A horse-clubbing
education of the highest type could get no results when there were
no horses to club.

Finally, to complete the disruption of paleolithic life and education, the new dampness in the air gave the saber-tooth tigers pneu-
monia, a disease to which these animals were peculiarly susceptible
and to which most of them succumbed. A few moth-eaten speci-
mens crept south to the desert, it is true, but they were pitifully few
and weak representatives of a once numerous and powerful race.

So there were no more tigers to scare in the paleolithic community, and the best tiger-scaring techniques became only academic
exercises, good in themselves, perhaps, but not necessary for tribal
security. Yet this danger to the people was lost only to be replaced
by another and even greater danger, for with the advancing ice
sheet came ferocious glacial bears which were not afraid of fire,
which walked the trails by day as well as by night, and which could
not be driven away by the most advanced methods developed in the
tiger-scaring courses of the schools.

The community was now in a very difficult situation. There was
no fish or meat for food, no hides for clothing, and no security from
the hairy death that walked the trails day and night. Adjustment to
this difficulty had to be made at once if the tribe was not to become
extinct.

Fortunately for the tribe, however, there were men in it of the old
New-Fist breed, men who had the ability to do and the daring to
think. One of them stood by the muddy stream, his stomach
contracting with hunger pains, longing for some way to get a fish to
eat. Again and again he had tried the old fish-grabbing technique
that day, hoping desperately that at last it might work, but now in
black despair he finally rejected all that he had learned in the

schools and looked about him for some new way to get fish from that stream. There were stout but slender vines hanging from trees along the bank. He pulled them down and began to fasten them together more or less aimlessly. As he worked, the vision of what he might do to satisfy his hunger and that of his crying children back in the cave grew clearer. His black despair lightened a little. He worked more rapidly and intelligently. At last he had it—a net, a crude seine. He called a companion and explained the device. The two men took the net into the water, into pool after pool, and in one hour they caught more fish—intelligent fish in muddy water—than the whole tribe could have caught in a day under the best fish-grabbing conditions.

Another intelligent member of the tribe wandered hungrily through the woods where once the stupid little horses had abounded but where now only the elusive antelope could be seen. He had tried the horse-clubbing technique on the antelope until he was fully convinced of its futility. He knew that one would starve who relied on school learning to get him meat in those woods. Thus it was that he too, like the fish-net inventor, was finally impelled by hunger to new ways. He bent a strong, springy young tree over an antelope trail, hung a noosed vine therefrom, and fastened the whole device in so ingenious a fashion that the passing animal would release a trigger and be snared neatly when the tree jerked upright. By setting a line of these snares, he was able in one night to secure more meat and skins than a dozen horse-clubbers in the old days had secured in a week.

A third tribesman, determined to meet the problem of the ferocious bears, also forgot what he had been taught in school and began to think in direct and radical fashion. Finally, as a result of this thinking, he dug a deep pit in a bear trail, covered it with branches in such a way that a bear would walk out on it unsuspectingly, fall through to the bottom, and remain trapped until the tribesmen could come up and despatch him with sticks and stones at their leisure. The inventor showed his friends how to dig and camouflage other pits until all the trails around the community were furnished with them. Thus the tribe had even more security than before and in addition had the great additional store of meat and skins which they secured from the captured bears.

As the knowledge of these new inventions spread, all the members of the tribe were engaged in familiarizing themselves with the new ways of living. Men worked hard at making fish nets, setting

antelope snares, and digging bear pits. The tribe was busy and pros-
perous.

There were a few thoughtful men who asked questions as they
worked. Some of them even criticized the schools.

'These new activities of net-making and operating, snare-setting,
and pit-digging are indispensable to modern existence,' they said.
'Why can't they be taught in school?'

The safe and sober majority had a quick reply to this naïve
question. 'School!' they snorted derisively. 'You aren't in school
now. You are out here in the dirt working to preserve the life and
happiness of the tribe. What have these practical activities got to do
with schools? You're not saying lessons now. You'd better forget
your lessons and your academic ideals of fish-grabbing, horse-clubbing, and tiger-scaring if you want to eat, keep warm, and have
some measure of security from sudden death.'

The radicals persisted a little in their questioning. 'Fishnet-making
and using, antelope-snare construction and operation, and bear-
catching and killing,' they pointed out, 'require intelligence and
skills—things we claim to develop in schools. They are also activities we need to know. Why can't the schools teach them?'

But most of the tribe, and particularly the wise old men who
controlled the school, smiled indulgently at this suggestion. 'That
wouldn't be *education*,' they said gently.

'But why wouldn't it be?' asked the radicals.

'Because it would be mere training,' explained the old men
patiently. 'With all the intricate details of fish-grabbing, horse-clubbing, and tiger-scaring—the standard cultural subjects—the school
curriculum is too crowded now. We can't add these fads and frills
of net-making, antelope-snaring, and—of all things—bear-killing.
Why, at the very thought, the body of the great New-Fist, founder of
our paleolithic educational system, would turn over in its burial
cairn. What we need to do is to give our young people a more
thorough grounding in the fundamentals. Even the graduates of the
secondary schools don't know the art of fish-grabbing in any complete sense nowadays, they swing their horse clubs awkwardly too,
and as for the old science of tiger-scaring—well, even the teachers
seem to lack the real flair for the subject which we oldsters got in
our teens and never forgot.'

'But, damn it,' exploded one of the radicals, 'how can any person
with good sense be interested in such useless activities? What is the
point of trying to catch fish with the bare hands when it just can't

be done any more. How can a boy learn to club horses when there are no horses left to club? And why in hell should children try to scare tigers with fire when the tigers are dead and gone?'

'Don't be foolish,' said the wise old men, smiling most kindly smiles. 'We don't teach fish-grabbing to grab fish; we teach it to develop a generalized agility which can never be developed by mere training. We don't teach horse-clubbing to club horses; we teach it to develop a generalized strength in the learner which he can never get from so prosaic and specialized a thing as antelope-snare-setting. We don't teach tiger-scaring to scare tigers; we teach it for the purpose of giving that noble courage which carries over into all the affairs of life and which can never come from so base an activity as bear-killing.'

All the radicals were silenced by this statement, all except the one who was most radical of all. He felt abashed, it is true, but he was so radical that he made one last protest.

'But—but anyway,' he suggested, 'you will have to admit that times have changed. Couldn't you please *try* these other more up-to-date activities? Maybe they have *some* educational value after all?'

Even the man's fellow radicals felt that this was going a little too far.

The wise old men were indignant. Their kindly smiles faded. 'If you had any education yourself,' they said severely, 'you would know that the essence of true education is timelessness. It is something that endures through changing conditions like a solid rock standing squarely and firmly in the middle of a raging torrent. You must know that there are some eternal verities, and the saber-tooth curriculum is one of them!'

**B. O. Smith, W. O. Stanley
and J. H. Shores**

I:2 Cultural roots
of the curriculum

*The curriculum is interwoven with the social fabric that
sustains it. Every society distinguishes between the
curriculum of common education—the universal elements
of the culture—and the curriculum of special education
—the requirements of special groups within society.
When a society passes from a class to a classless system,
the special education for the upper classes in the earlier
phase tends to persist in the later phase, under the guise
of common education. The authors draw their examples
from American education.*

If an observer looks at the curriculum of the school in any society,
he will find, either stated or implied, a set of educational objectives,
a body of subject matter, a list of exercises or activities to be performed, and a way of determining whether or not the objectives
have been reached by the students. He will find also some kind of
control which the teacher is required to exercise over the learners.
These things comprising the curriculum are always, in every
society, derived from the culture. The objectives stressed will be
those that reflect the controlling ideas and sentiments contained in
the universals. The subject matter will tend to be that which is
believed to embrace the most significant ideas and most generally
used knowledges and skills. The way in which the learners are controlled will reflect the prevailing methods of social control of the
society at large. As the instrument of society for the education of
the young, the curriculum will reflect the ideals, knowledges, and
skills that are believed to be significant, or that are related to the
common activities of the members of society. The curriculum is,
therefore, interwoven with the social fabric that sustains it.

In every society a distinction is made between the curriculum of
common education and that of special education. Common education will be based upon the universal elements of the culture and

such aspects of the specialties as are of general concern. Special education will be based largely upon the dominant specialties of the culture. It will be designed to train the individual for a particular social or vocational position.

Common education based upon cultural universals

Common education is concerned with the problem of maintaining the society as a closely knit and well-integrated unit. It is only natural, therefore, that the rules and knowledges by which the people as a whole regulate their conduct and anticipate the behavior of one another should be its principal content. Not all the universals, however, will be contained in the common curriculum. It will ordinarily not incorporate such superficial elements as the method of greeting friends or the way to tie shoes. As a rule, these things are left to the individual to acquire informally and often unconsciously through participation in the common life of the people. Instead, the curriculum will tend to emphasize the more fundamental universals, or cultural core, such as the values, sentiments, knowledges, and skills that provide society with stability and vitality and individuals with the motivations and deep-lying controls of conduct.

The heart of the universals, as already pointed out, is the standards and knowledges by which the people decide what is right and wrong, good and evil, beautiful and ugly, true and false, appropriate and inappropriate in all sorts of activities—political, economic, aesthetic, educational, or what not. These standards constitute the moral content of the society. Next to them in importance are the knowledges and skills that have to do with the control and improvement of the common activities of the people such as their political and economic behavior. Together these constitute the subject matter of common education.

Special education related to the specialties of the culture

Returning now to special education, it is to be remembered that the specialties of a culture are usually those ways of thinking and acting associated either with vocational groups or social classes, or both. Hence special education may follow the interests of either one or both of these special groups. In societies having a recognized social elite, it will be found that instruments of education will be set aside for training the immature members of the elite group in the special points of view and patterns of conduct of these privileged adults. The presence of *exclusive* private or finishing schools is evidence of the existence of an elite class having particular outlooks, polite manners, and behavioral patterns which it wishes to maintain. Indeed, the existence of such classes has led in some nations to the creation of dual educational systems—one for the folk and another for the upper classes. For this reason higher forms of education, including secondary as well as higher schools, have tended historically to be designed for the privileged few. Even in the more democratically inclined countries, where a single educational ladder has been adopted, the curriculum of the upper rungs reflects a privileged origin.

Education for vocational purposes is always correlated with the needs of persons of particular socio-economic level. Hence it is sometimes difficult to distinguish from that form of special education designed to equip the individual to occupy a particular position in society. The sons of upper-class families in western nations who go to private schools, or to publicly supported schools specially designed for them, in order to pursue the so-called 'cultural' subjects—not to mention programs leading to 'higher' professions—are thereby being trained for upper-class vocations. This type of training usually is just as vocational for them as the study of how to read blueprints would be for a prospective plumber, because the so-called 'cultural' courses prepare them for domestic governmental positions, for foreign diplomatic service, or for positions in industrial bureaucracies. In any case, the display of relatively useless knowledge, information, and skills, marking their possessor as a member of the leisure class, will be of inestimable value, for it gains admission to the polite circles of other countries as well as his own.

The point of this discussion is not that all vocational education is class education. Only in societies where certain vocations are associated with particular social classes will this tend to be true. Social systems that emphasize an open-door policy for all occupations—making it possible for every individual irrespective of race, creed, or social background to acquire the knowledges and skills he is capable and desirous of obtaining—will reduce the chances that some occupations will be monopolized by privileged classes. In these societies vocational education will be least associated with class education.

Class education sometimes confused with common education

Not only is there a tendency for class education to be confused with vocational training, but also with common education. When a society passes from a class to a classless system (or to one in which classes exist only in a loose sense), the educational ideals and programs designed in the earlier phase for the education of the upper classes tend to persist in the later phase, under the guise of general or common education. It is for this reason that the curriculum of the American high schools, as well as that of American colleges, has been so slow to adjust to the demands of mass education. Thorstein Veblen, about fifty years ago, made it clear that remnants of the leisure class educational program persisted in schools and colleges.[1] These remnants may still be detected today.

Moreover, the colleges tend on the whole to continue to provide vocational programs under the banner of liberal education. A former president of Harvard University—James B. Conant—has aptly phrased this point.

By and large, the general education which our conventional four-year liberal arts colleges provide in one form or another is given as a background for two vocations—the learned professions and the managerial positions in business. This type of education, however much it may be improved (and it will be improved greatly in the coming years, I feel sure), cannot be considered apart from the vocations for which it prepares. In short, it has no over-all general validity for it cannot be considered apart from the clientele for which it has been developed over the years.[2]

It is disturbing that in the United States, where the prevailing social creed denies the desirability of social classes, there should be social groups trying to reinstate and bolster up outworn systems of class education in the name of general or liberal education. Few things have encumbered thinking about the development of a more adequate program of common education in the United States, as well as in other countries, so much as adherence to educational ideas brought over from the class system of past cultural phases.

References

1 Thorstein Veblen, *The theory of the leisure class.*
2 James Bryant Conant, 'Public education and the structure of American society.' *Teachers College Record*, vol. 47, no. 3 (December 1945), pp. 164–165. By permission.

David V. Glass

I:3 Education and social change in modern England

By placing English education in its social and historical context, the British sociologist David Glass argues that the idea of an 'English tradition of education' has limited validity. Much of the 'tradition' is barely a century old. The one underlying continuity beneath the surface of educational change is the influence of the class structure of England on the images of education and its function. Glass examines this influence and its consequences in nineteenth- and twentieth-century English education.

Those who have read Dicey's *Lectures* will remember that he has very little to say on the development of educational policy. He was concerned with the growth of collectivism—with that 'combination of socialistic and democratic legislation' which, in his view, threatened 'the gravest danger of the country.'[1] Educational objectives as such, and their relation to the needs and structure of society, did not form part of his inquiry. Hence his brief comments on the then recent history of public elementary education were designed only to show that the new system was a 'monument to the increasing predominance of collectivism.' In that respect the Education (Provision of Meals) Act of 1906 drew some of his sharpest criticism. 'No one can deny,' he said, 'that a starving boy will hardly profit much from the attempt to teach him the rules of arithmetic. But it does not necessarily follow that a local authority must provide every hungry child at school with a meal; still less does it seem morally right that a father who first lets his child starve, and then fails to pay the price legally due from him for a meal given to the child at the expense of the ratepayers should ... retain the right of voting for a Member of Parliament.'[3] It would not be too difficult to envisage Dicey's attitude to present-day public expenditure of about £20 millions a year in subsidising school milk and meals.[4]

Whether or not it is appropriate to attach the label 'collectivist' to the whole complex of educational change in England since the nineteenth century, the label itself provides no explanation of that change. Nor does the enunciation of the principle of the 'Equalisation of Advantages among individuals possessed of unequal means for their attainment'[5]—a principle upon which Dicey calls in discussing the growth of State support of education—take us very much further. Educational policy, like all social policy, is rarely single-minded. To understand the final compromise of policy means tracing the main strands of ideas and influences which have been woven into it. First, however, it is necessary to draw attention to the time-scale on which educational change has taken place, for that has a bearing upon the present situation and upon future possibilities.

Education for the mass of children and young people, financed to the greatest extent by public money, has a short history in England. Though private philanthropy and governmental subventions joined together to support a considerable number of primary schools from the 1830s, it was not until 1870 that the law assured public primary education to children who did not have access to private schools. Compulsory attendance came afterwards—in 1880, up to the age of ten; in 1893, up to the age of eleven; and not until 1918 up to a minimum age of fourteen.[6] Substantial provision of secondary education began even later. The numbers of pupils in the boys' 'public schools' had never been large, and by the early nineteenth century those schools had ceased to draw, to any appreciable extent, upon the general population. Nor did the endowed grammar schools cover more than a small fraction of children. Even after the work of the Endowed School Commissioners, by 1895, the total number of children in endowed and proprietary secondary schools was not, apparently, much above 100,000.[7] It was under the 1902 Act that responsibility for elementary education came to be laid on the local authorities, who were also given power to assist or provide secondary or other higher education. To the now subsidised endowed schools were added others maintained by the local education authorities. By the eve of the First World War the number of pupils in secondary schools recognised by the Board of Education was over 200,000, and by 1937 almost 560,000, of whom not far short of 90 per cent were in schools aided or maintained by public funds.[8] Secondary education for all was not, however, provided until the 1944 Act, under which the minimum school-leaving age was immediately raised to fifteen years. The numbers of children in local education authority secondary schools alone now exceed two million.[9]

Moving along a different route, central and local government support of university education has been equally recent. Public funds were first granted to the universities in 1882, but relatively large-scale financing dates only from 1920. Since that time British university income, which has grown more than eightfold, has become increasingly supplied from taxation. Today, the universities, autonomous institutions protected by the Treasury from parliamentary control, neither created nor maintained by the devices applied to primary or secondary education, receive about three-quarters of their income from parliamentary and local authority grants.[10] And in addition, aid from public funds is given to some 80 per cent of university students.[11] Since 1920, the numbers of full-time students have risen from 46,000 to nearly 90,000.[12] Thus, in less than forty years—that is, from the end of the First World War—secondary school populations have been multiplied by six and university populations have been doubled.

I have begun with this historical outline in order to emphasise two points. First, that in the late nineteenth century England was still educationally a very underdeveloped society. It would, of course, be both incorrect and unjust to minimise the part which religious and philanthropic bodies had already played in establishing schools. The incidence of illiteracy could not have been as high as it is in some underdeveloped countries today. Even so, a third of the men marrying in 1840 in England and Wales, and half of the women, signed the registers by a mark; the proportions in 1870 were still 20 per cent and 27 per cent.[13] The rate of change in the provision of education since 1870 has been so rapid that it must be taken into account when considering present-day educational deficiencies.

Secondly, it must be equally clear that the phrase 'the English tradition of education', not infrequently used in arguing against further rapid change in the character of secondary education, has a very limited validity. It can scarcely apply to the public system which, even during its brief history, has greatly altered in respect of objectives, structure and methods of selection. Nor, in the sense of a centuries-old persistence of character, is the term really applicable to the private sectors, whether secondary or university. It is true that, as an institution, the grammar school 'has a thousand years of history behind it'.[14] But the present character of grammar schools derives from action taken during the nineteenth and twentieth centuries, action originally taken because, however deeply rooted the grammar school idea may have been, the schools themselves had ceased to be effective as educational institutions. In any case, most grammar schools today are not private. They are maintained by the local education authorities; they are thus part of the public system; and they have been exposed to powerful pressures for change in the curriculum, in the universe from which pupils are drawn, and in the qualifications of teachers. The public schools, too—the schools belonging to the Headmasters' Conference and the most firmly imbedded and 'traditionalist' part of the private system—bear little resemblance to their original form. They were, on the contrary, the first schools to be reconstructed in the nineteenth century. Indeed, it was the reforms introduced by Arnold and others which, as G. M. Young has said, 'reconciled the serious classes to the public school',[15] and which encouraged the establishment of additional schools; fifty-one out of the present 116 independent public boarding schools were founded in the nineteenth century.[16] The curriculum has also changed, though more slowly, and half the present public schools specialise in science and mathematics.[17] The process of change has applied equally to the universities. The history of university reform is too well known to need documenting here. But it is evident that Trevelyan's description of Oxford and Cambridge in the days of decay as 'little more than comfortable monastic establishments for clerical sinecurists with a tinge of letters'[18] would scarcely apply now. Moreover, the larger part of the university complex is itself the creation of the nineteenth century, and almost two-thirds of today's university students are studying in institutions established since the 1830s.[19]

Much of the present educational system is thus not traditional. Moreover, many of its characteristics are not particularly English. Even during the first half of the nineteenth century, once the memory of the French Revolution had become a little clouded, educational reformers in England drew markedly upon the experiments which were being conducted on the Continent.[20] And this was just as well, for the new influences helped to replace the more specifically British contributions of Lancaster's mutual system and Bell's 'Madras' system, which appeared to require a school to be a combination of factory and of Bentham's Panopticon. Later in the century Matthew Arnold imported from France the term 'secondary education' and with it the objective of a reorganised and comprehensive system. Technical education, too, especially in its shifting emphasis from craftsmanship to general principles and their application, was influenced both by foreign competition and by foreign models. All this has clearly been to the good. But along with these innovations there has been one underlying continuity—the influence of the class structure on the images of education and its function. It is this continuity and its consequences which I should now like to discuss.

During the nineteenth century, educational developments reflected two fairly distinct sets of considerations, one relating to the mass of the population and the other to the middle classes. Public concern with elementary education was in large measure concern to meet certain minimum requirements in a changing society—the need to ensure discipline, and to obtain respect for private property and the social order, as well as to provide that kind of instruction which was indispensable in an expanding industrial and commercial nation. Though many individuals and groups showed a far broader vision, these minimal considerations are evident in the very limited objectives of the system which grew up at that time. In the earliest period, the Bible and the catechism were sufficient, Hannah More thought; she would 'allow no writing for the poor'. Later, the sights were set a little higher. Speaking of the working-class child, James Fraser, subsequently Bishop of Manchester, told the 1858 Newcastle Commission that: 'we must make up our minds to see the last of him, as far as the day school is concerned, at ten or eleven ... and I venture to maintain that it is quite possible to teach a child soundly and thoroughly, in a way that he shall not forget it, all that is necessary for him to possess in the shape of intellectual attainment, by the time that he is ten years old'. The Commission accepted the fact that most children would go to work at the age of ten or eleven.[21] A similar assumption underlies the 1870 Act. It is not surprising the H. G. Wells referred to it as 'an Act to educate the lower classes for employment on lower class lines, and with specially trained, inferior teachers ...'.[22]

To gentle the masses was another explicit purpose. 'A set of good schools civilises a whole neighbourhood,' said the Newcastle Commission,[23] and Forster, when he introduced his 1870 bill in Parliament, spoke of 'removing that ignorance which we are all aware is pregnant with crime and misery, with misfortune to individuals and danger to the community ...'. And he continued, 'I am one of those who would not wait until the people were educated before I would trust them with political power. If we had thus waited we might have waited long for education; but now that we have given them political power, we must not wait any longer to give them education.'[24] Some of these notions were changed when the 1902 Act provided a framework for both elementary and secondary education. But the civilisation motive had a longer currency, and even in 1929 Sir Cyril Norwood argued that it was largely elementary education which had prevented 'Bolshevism, Communism, and theories of revolt and destruction from obtaining any real hold upon the people of this country'. 'I hope,' he added, 'that those who attribute the scarcity of domestic servants to the unreasonable institution of elementary education, by which they are made to pay for the teaching of other people's children, will lay in the other scale this other service, which has made of Bolshevism only a bogy which sits by their pillows and frightens them in the night....'[25]

Concern with secondary education sprang from different motives. The effectiveness of the public schools and the endowed grammar schools as educational institutions for those groups who could afford to make use of them was the main issue. In the early part of the century an attempt had been made to compel the public schools to give the local poor the rights to entry provided by the founders' statutes. But the attempt failed, and the place of the public schools in the national system of secondary education was not again discussed by a Government committee until 1942.[26] Instead, in 1861 a Royal Commission was appointed to study the quality of the education in what have ever since been known as the 'Clarendon schools' —nine schools with 2,815 pupils. And the Clarendon Commission was immediately followed by the Taunton Commission, which inquired into the education given in the endowed grammar schools. Though expressing some disquiet at existing class distinction in education, the Taunton Commission in the main accepted the situation as they found it, and their recommendations were drawn up for the benefit of the middle classes by whom the schools were being used. What is particularly interesting is the emergence at this stage of a fresh criterion of the effectiveness of secondary education, the criterion of providing an avenue to the universities; and there were unfavourable references to the fact that 550 grammar schools sent no boys to universities, in sharp contrast to the large numbers now going from the nine Clarendon schools and from some of the recently founded proprietary schools.[27]

For university education, like secondary education, was coming to have a new meaning. The changing society needed individuals of greater educational maturity and tested qualifications. The old and the new middle classes needed avenues of employment which would provide both prestige and relatively high income for their sons. Considerations of both scientific and social status were causing the existing professions to raise their standards of entry, and additional professions, including the higher civil service, were beginning to develop, also demanding considerable educational attainments. In earlier days, when Fellows of the Royal College of Physicians were practising medicine in the intervals between their active social life rather than practising medicine in order to live, the College restricted its Fellowship to graduates of Oxford, Cambridge and Trinity College, Dublin. These were men of good breeding, and some of them earned substantial incomes. Their background and their style of living conferred prestige upon the profession. As one eighteenth-century pamphleteer wrote 'the very sight of a handsome dress is restorative and comes like a good prognostick ... a sordid surface is not only unpromising, but prejudicial...', and 'poverty ... in any profession is but a bad sign of qualification and ability'.[28] The nineteenth-century objective went further : it was not simply to recruit members who would confer distinction upon the profession, but also to have a profession which would confer social prestige upon its members. And by the time the Taunton Commission was sitting, even Miss Marrable, Anthony Trollope's conservative old spinster, who entirely rejected the notion that wealth by itself might confer social distinction, was beginning to admit that medicine, surgery, the civil service and possibly civil engineering might offer suitable employment for the sons of gentlemen.[29]

Miss Marrable was in fact a little ahead of her time. It took State intervention to add the final touches to some of the professions and to intensify their social homogeneity. For the higher civil service, it was the application of the Northcote–Trevelyan reforms which, as the Permanent Secretary of the Board of Trade said at the time, involved the selection of individuals who had had 'an expensive education in high subjects in early years, which only the rich can afford'.[30] In medicine, as Professor Titmuss has suggested, it required the 1911 Health Act, which raised the income of the general practitioner; while the increasing spread of State medical aid also helped by narrowing the field of action of the unlicensed practitioner. Nevertheless, by the time of the Taunton Commission, secondary and university education were ceasing to be largely the concomitants of relatively high social status. They were becoming the means whereby, for the middle classes, status might be preserved or improved. The Commission clearly had this in mind in referring to the particular needs of 'the great body of professional men, especially the clergy, medicine men and lawyers', who 'have nothing to look to but education to keep their sons on a high social level'.[31]

Though the grammar schools improved after the Taunton Commission, and though elementary education became far more widespread after the 1870 Act, in neither case was the rate of progress adequate. But change was in the air. Two further commissions were appointed, one of which, the Bryce Commission, not only laid the foundations of the 1902 Act, but also defined secondary education in terms not accepted until 1944. On the social and economic side there were stimuli equivalent to those which generated a more acute concern for public health. Foreign industrial competition was one such stimulus, and particularly competition by industries based upon the new chemical technology. The need for science teaching and for the training of technicians was acknowledged. Shortages of other kinds of trained manpower were also visible. The Boer War, which showed up physical defects in the working classes also revealed deficiencies in the education of the officers. Comparable education deficiencies lower in the social scale were such that, it was said, 'city offices were forced to employ so many thousands of German clerks for want of a home-grown substitute'.[32] When he was introducing the 1870 Bill, Forster spoke of the relation between education and national power, and he argued that 'we must make up for the smallness of our numbers by increasing the intellectual force of the individual'.[33] Now the slogan became 'sea power and school power' as the essential basis of the Empire. The validity of assistance to the working classes was also being reviewed. Preston's pamphlet, *The Bitter Cry of Outcast London*—read and commented upon by Robert Morant when he was an undergraduate[34]—and Booth's encyclopedia of London poverty, had shown that, for a large proportion of urban workers, self-help was not a precept which could be followed. The total combination of influences made possible the 1902 Education Act, providing a national system in which public funds were to be used to assist secondary, in addition to providing elementary, education. Middle-class as well as working-class children were to benefit. The inclusion of the former perhaps helps to explain the otherwise curious fact that Dicey, though he criticises the granting of free school meals, makes no reference to the supply of subsidised secondary education.[35]

How did the national system work out in practice? The very great quantitative changes which occurred after the 1902 Act have already been indicated, but it is equally important to emphasise the general improvement in the quality of the education given. In particular, the aims of elementary education were entirely redefined by Morant. To 'make the best use of the school years available,' was now the purpose, not to provide the 'minimum mental equipment' required for the mass of the children, as Lowndes put it for the school board days.[36] With the educational objective thus changed, the middle classes, too, came increasingly to use the public elementary schools for their children—especially as the spread of suburbs lead to the building of new schools for populations which, socially, were relatively homogeneous.[37] Publicly aided and maintained secondary education experienced similar improvements, and the proportions of children going from an elementary to a secondary school more than doubled between the wars. Further, a new scholarship route was established between the elementary and the secondary school. So far as the middle classes were concerned, the Taunton Commission had already envisaged the need for a ladder, allowing able children to reach the higher grades of secondary school. The Bryce Commission extended the ladder to working-class children, and from 1907 onward increasing numbers of scholarships were provided out of public funds. To the surprise of some grammar school head teachers, who had envisaged the free-placer as a 'fearsome wild beast', working-class scholarship winners behaved well, scholastically and socially, and one of the major pressures during the inter-war period was for more and more scholarships.[38] New links between school and university were also created by central and local government scholarships and the proportion of boys proceeding from secondary grammar schools to universities increased by about a third.

At the same time, it is clear from these percentages of growth in secondary and university education, that, though the situation was changed under the 1902 Act, it was by no means transformed. In fact, speaking now not in terms of growth, but of the actual position of boys born between 1910 and 1929, less than a fifth of the generation (17·6 per cent) reached a secondary school; and of those reaching a secondary school, about a seventh (14·3 per cent) went on to university.[39] Moreover, the relative position of middle-class and working-class children remained substantially different. Again, taking the generation of boys born between 1910 and 1929, two-fifths (39 per cent) of those from the middle class, as compared with one-tenth of those from the working class, went to a secondary school, a ratio of 4:1; and for the universities the ratio was 6:1; the proportions being 8·5 and 1·4 per cent. There is no doubt, then, that the middle classes benefited greatly from the expansion of secondary and university education between the wars, and that they were aided in this by the more generous public provision after the 1902 Act. But why it is that the working classes profited so much less than might have been expected?

In part, of course, the explanation is an economic one. Thus, for example, the provision of scholarships did not catch up with the demand for them. Already in 1923, the President of the Board of Education was reporting so strong a pressure by parents for scholarships, that he doubted whether 'even in normal times, with money easy, we could have been able adequately to cope with the demand'.[41] But for most working-class parents, the scholarship road to the secondary school was the only one they could use. For middle-class parents, on the other hand, paying the relatively low, publicly subsidised fees at the grammar school was by no means impossible and there were thus two access roads. Ability to pay became, relatively, still more important during the financial stringency of the 1930s, with the introduction of 'special places' for which partial fees might be demanded on the basis of a means test. In 1938, children for whom full or partial fees were being paid were over half (53 per cent) of all the pupils in grant-earning secondary schools.[42] Ability to forgo the wages that a child might otherwise begin to earn at the age of fourteen years was another economic factor. When reference is made nowadays to the 'deferred gratification pattern' of the middle classes, in contrast to the 'live for the present' pattern of the working classes, it is important to remember that poverty and malnutrition—which were amply with us until the Second World War—are not the best bases for forethought or abstinence.

Measured intelligence, commonly referred to as I.Q., is also part of the explanation. But it is only one part, for even leaving aside the cultural components in intelligence tests, equal access to grammar schools between the wars would have produced a social class distribution, similar to, though not exactly the same as that found in, the grammar schools today, following the 1944 Act. That is, some

60 per cent of all the pupils would have been the children of skilled, semi-skilled and unskilled workers.[43]

A third factor, and one which I should like to emphasise, is the social class image of the secondary school and its purpose. The inter-war secondary school was a grammar school. The Bryce Commission, when it defined secondary education, took the revolutionary view that 'secondary' and 'technical' education were in large measure interchangeable concepts. They claimed that 'no definition of technical instruction is possible that does not bring it under the head of Secondary Education, nor can Secondary Education be so defined as absolutely to exclude from it the idea of technical instruction...'.[44] The experiments which were being made by various school boards with higher grade schools—experiments possible because increasing numbers of parents were prepared to have their children continue at school beyond the minimum school-leaving age—certainly came under the category of secondary education as defined by the Bryce Commission. But with the 1902 Act, these schools were removed from the elementary sector, where they had been located, and absorbed in the new system of secondary schools. Technical education as such was henceforth put on a separate limb—in the central schools, which were higher elementary schools for purposes of administration; and in the junior technical schools. Though valuable work was done in both these types of school, and though the junior technical schools came to challenge more orthodox secondary education, the official view was that their status was, and should be, below that of a secondary school; that at best they were vocational schools, geared up with local employment possibilities.[45] In that sense a child had to choose a specific occupation when entering one of these schools at the age of thirteen.

Whether or not it was Morant who was responsible for imposing the pattern of the public school and of the grammar school upon the new system of secondary education, is not really important. The important point is that there was a powerful demand for just such a type of secondary school. For many middle-class parents, as well as for those working-class parents anxious to see their children rise in the social scale, a grammar school education was the kind which they wanted but to which they had not hitherto had access. It was the way to the black-coated job, respectable and secure. Conceivably, it might also be the way to the university and a profession, still more respectable and secure. And this impression must have been heightened by the emphasis which came to be laid on passing those external examinations—matriculation and the higher school certificate—which were the keys to higher education and higher social status. In many respects, the possibilities of social advance were rather limited. Sir George Kekewich was not entirely wrong when he said, as early as 1909, that the over-supply of clerks, depressing wages and conditions of work, was the result of that 'national system of education that we are so abominably proud of. It is a bad system, directed at turning out a nation of clerks'.[46] But for the lower middle class and aspiring working-class parents, a clerk's job was at least better than that of a manual worker—rightly so, if thought of in terms of the vista of security in a highly insecure world. In 1931 unemployment among male clerks amounted to less than half of that in the labour force as a whole (5·3 per cent as compared with 12·7 per cent). Among some groups of clerical workers there was hardly any unemployment and in general the higher ranks had the smallest proportions of dismissals.[47]

Since secondary education was focused upon black-coated employment, working-class parents who wished their sons to go to a grammar school had to accept the fact that they would move out of the parental 'class'. Some parents did accept this fact—indeed, they positively wished for it. But many did not. Today, some of the differences between the classes are less striking—differences in clothing and housing, for example; and the educational gap between the generations in working-class families is a little narrower. In the mid-thirties, it should be remembered, working-class fathers with children of secondary school age would themselves have ended their education at the age of twelve or thirteen in a not very greatly reformed schoolboard school. Even now, working-class fathers still do not show a strong drive towards black-coated employment for their sons.[48] In the thirties, moving out of one's class might well have involved a much sharper break between parents and children. And at the same time, clerical work, which constituted a large share of the available black-coated employment opportunities has not been held in very high regard by the working class as a whole.[49] If secondary education had led directly to supervisory or technical posts in industry, posts closely related to industrial production but nevertheless carrying social prestige, working-class attitudes to secondary education might have been somewhat different. But until the late thirties, apprenticeship regulations were not very helpful in that respect, for in general the age of entry was rather low. There were better opportunities for boys from the junior technical schools.

Beginning as craftsmen, they were often promoted to technical or junior staff positions in factories. But there were not many of these schools, and this may help to account for their relative success.

Looking back over the inter-war years, it is obvious that 'collectivism' is hardly the appropriate term for the kind of educational policy which was carried out, or for the results of that policy. Certainly the working classes benefited. But so far as secondary education was concerned, the middle classes benefited still more. Their wider use of publicly supported or provided secondary schools sprang from the same motives which, in the case of the working classes, acted in the contrary direction—from a desire to keep their sons in their own class, which in the case of the middle classes meant especially saving their sons from becoming manual workers. For such a purpose the new system worked fairly well, for the association between education and jobs carrying prestige became tighter during the period. University graduates, in particular, began to enter new fields, helped by the efforts made by university appointment boards to persuade industry to establish management traineeships. Recent studies have shown that, among managers, the proportions educated in a grammar or in a public school increased fairly steadily, and that the proportions with university degrees rose rather more steeply.[50] Those sections of the middle classes who sent their boys to boarding schools showed their realisation of this tighter operative relationship between university education and socially acceptable employment. Of their sons born between 1910 and 1929, almost a third went to universities, as against less than a fifth of the generation of boarding school boys born before 1910. A similar trend applied to the middle classes as a whole.[51] The university now began to be their target, perhaps made all the more attractive in that, with still relatively small numbers of students, Britain did not have an academic proletariat, as other countries did during the depression of the 1930s.[52] And in the late thirties the middle classes were being increasingly helped to reach their target by public expenditure on secondary and university education.

Finally, I should like to refer to the most recent changes—to the 1944 Education Act and its background, and to the way in which secondary and university education have developed since the Second World War. To those who believe that the demand for universal secondary education came from the Labour Party, the 1944 Act might appear the ultimate vindication of Dicey's forecast. But there were at least two sets of pressures working in the same direction, one political and the other specifically educational. It is true that the political pressures were very largely those of the Labour Party and its associated bodies. As Mrs Banks has pointed out in her book, from at least the 1890s on, the Trade Union Movement was demanding equality of opportunity in secondary education; and from the end of the First World War, secondary education for all was the centre of Labour Party educational policy. The Conservative Party, though it acknowledged the need for additional free places, continued to regard secondary education as necessarily selective. Secondary education, said Lord Eustace Percy in 1933, should act as 'a lift or stairway to the higher storeys of the social structure'. His criticism of the existing system was that this function was not being adequately fulfilled.[53] But the educational pressures for universal secondary education were also strong. They came from teachers who saw their attempts to experiment in meeting the different needs of different children frustrated by the existing regulations; from educational associations; and from expert committees appointed by government. From 1926, when the Hadow Committee reported, the idea of primary education as a first stage, to be followed by secondary education as a second stage for all, became accepted educational currency. It was to be a differentiated system. The Hadow Committee proposed two kinds of school, grammar and modern.[54] Later, in 1939, the Spens Committee suggested three, adding the technical school. When in the atmosphere of the Second World War, the Government issued its proposals for educational reconstruction, they incorported the Spens Committee's recommendations for grammar, modern and technical schools.[55] And shortly afterwards this idea of tripartism was supported by the Norwood Committee on the grounds of historical reality and on the basis of a typology of children which psychologists have not accepted.[56] Though tripartism was not specified in the 1944 Act itself, it was clearly intended by the Government, and this intention has been carried out in most subsequent practice. The link with the earlier conception of selective secondary education is evident. If the ladder between elementary and secondary education as a whole has been abandoned, it has been replaced by a ladder from the primary school to the grammar school. And the nineteenth-century social class homogeneity of the grammar school has been replaced by a homogeneity of measured intelligence, the upper 20 per cent on the I.Q. scale.[57]

Secondary education since the 1944 Act has become not only the subject of persistent wrangles between experts, but also one of the major topics of general conversation and general concern.[58] Parents promise their children costly gifts if they obtain grammar school places. Children's papers advertise textbooks designed to improve their chances. For middle-class parents, in particular, eleven-plus day is a day of national mourning. Like King Aegeus they sit on the cliffs, waiting to see if the returning sails are white or black. And if the incidence of neurosis among frustrated middle-class parents has not risen significantly, it is largely because the independent secondary schools, giving education of a grammar school variety, offer parents a possible alternative in the struggle to maintain or improve the social status of their children by the way of education. That is one of the reasons why the popularity of public schools has not diminished and why, as was said recently, 'the average middle-class parent still regards a public school education as the best investment for his child's future'.[59] Standing outside the general system, and protected by a cordon of preparatory schools, the public school has tightened its link with the university,[60] and in so doing it has helped to reinforce the widely held views that the ideal type of secondary school is the public school and that the main function of the university is to staff the professions and to supply the administrators. In my opinion, the social consequences of these views are even more important than the results of public school exclusiveness.[61]

So far as State-provided secondary education is concerned, the present situation has been aptly described in a governmental report. Speaking of the effect of examinations, the report argues that 'there is nothing to be said in favour of a system which subjects children at the age of eleven to the strain of a competitive examination on which, not only their future schooling, but their future careers may depend'. And referring to the grammar school, it adds, 'too many of the nation's abler children are attracted into a type of education which prepares primarily for the university, and for the administrative and clerical professions; too few find their way into schools from which the design and craftsmanship sides of industry are recruited'. I should explain, however, that the governmental report in question is the White Paper on educational reconstruction, and that the defects referred to are those which the 1944 Act was designed to remove.[62] It is sometimes a little difficult to distinguish the new cure from the old disease. But the present system is new, and it is neither completely uniform nor fixed throughout the country. In one important respect the situation today has no pre-war parallel.

There is now a recognition that secondary education is a proper subject for discussion and for study. This is in striking contrast to the pre-war position, when attempts to investigate access to the various stages of education tended to be looked at by the Government as attacks on the class structure. And indeed they were, for, as I have indicated, secondary and higher education were in large measure tied to the middle classes. Since the 1944 Act, however, there has been a wealth of fresh inquiries into the working out of the new secondary education, one of the most illuminating having been sponsored by the Government itself.[63] The very acceptance of the principle of secondary education for all, however ambivalent the practice may be, is provoking a further review of the objectives of that education and of the kinds of institution in which it might best be obtained.

At the same time I do not see how a thorough review of the objectives and possibilities of secondary education can be undertaken unless the purposes of university education are also reviewed. And this is still largely to be done. There have, of course, been special studies of the needs for particular types of trained manpower, such as doctors, scientists and technologists. The further employment of arts graduates in industry has been investigated. The anatomy of Redbrick has been displayed and the 'crisis in the university' has been ventilated on the Third Programme. Less public consideration has, however, been given in recent years to the objectives of universities, to the way in which those objectives may be regarded by potential students, and to the kind of student population that may in consequence be recruited. But in a society in which universal secondary education has in principle become the accepted goal, these are questions of major importance.

Since 1938–39, the number of full-time university students have increased from 50,000 to over 85,000.[64] Most of the students are British—about 90 per cent of them—and about four-fifths of British students receive financial assistance. much of it considerably more substantial than was the case in pre-war days. In addition, the universities themselves are heavily supported by public funds and are thereby enabled to pass on a further subsidy to students, in the sense that tuition fees probably do not cover more than one-seventh of the total cost of tuition. With this more solid basis of public financing, paralleling the more extensive financing of secondary education, how far does the composition of the student body reflect the statement of the White Paper on educational reconstruction, that 'the aim of a national policy must be to ensure that high ability is not handicapped by the accidents of place of residence or lack of means in securing a university education.'[65] Unfortunately, our knowledge of changes in the composition of the student body is quite inadequate, for the recent inquiry undertaken for the Vice-Chancellors' Committee was the first of its kind. But a comparison with our own, much smaller sample inquiries into education and social mobility does not suggest that there has been any basic change in recent years. It is very probable that there have been shifts within the middle classes, with a larger proportion of students coming from families of less wealthy black-coated workers. But of the undergraduates and diploma students admitted in October 1955, only a quarter were the sons and daughters of manual workers.[66] It is clear from the Vice-Chancellors' inquiry that this low proportion is not explained by a failure of working-class boys and girls to obtain university places when they apply for them, but by a failure to apply for places. So far it has been the middle classes who have made the most use of the increased public financing of university education.[67]

The Ministry of Education report on *Early Leaving* has shown how the school side of this situation works out. Within the grammar school, working-class children tend to perform less well than middle-class children as they pass through the school, they also leave earlier; and, when they leave, they go directly into employment rather than into further full-time education. In explaining these findings, the report emphasises the importance of the child's home background—both his physical and economic environment and 'the different social assumptions which affect not only a child's parents but the whole society in which he is brought up.'[68] Of course, those assumptions include the views of society on the purposes of further education. And it is here that the dominant view of the vocational objectives of a university education may act as a constraint, as grammar school objectives acted as a constraint on the entry to secondary education between the wars.

Sir Alexander Carr-Saunders once said : 'in England a university is just a place where by paying so much you prepare yourself for a certain career...'.[69] The careers contemplated are in the main the professions, and these do not as yet include employment for which higher technical education is required. On the contrary, the proposals of the recent White Paper would place higher technical education in about the same relationship to university education as junior technical schools were to grammar schools before the war—necessary and worthy, but of inferior status.[70] Most students who entered the universities in 1955 had in mind a professional occupation as their goal. Thus, in the eyes of the beholder, the university, whatever its intellectual function may be, is also to a great extent a device for achieving or maintaining social status.[71] That being so, for many working-class boys and girls the university route may mean a sharp break with their family and class environment, and one which neither they nor their parents can contemplate with unalloyed approval.

It is unlikely that the status aspect of university education could be entirely removed. But it is neither necessary nor desirable that undergraduate education should be as dominated as it is now by the expectations of employment with relatively high social status. The present dominance is a reflection of that continuity of attitude which associates secondary and university education with the middle classes, and which imposes middle-class needs and aspirations upon the education pattern.[72] Whatever may have been the position a century ago, when the professions were seeking to provide objective criteria of ability and training, it is no longer in the social or economic interest of the country for the image of undergraduate education in the university to be that of education for the small proportion of men and women who will enter professional or quasi-professional occupations. The wider needs of industry and of citizenship must be considered, and the range of undergraduate possibilities and objectives extended. Changing the objectives of undergraduate studies would not necessarily mean a lowering of standards; and at the same time, to postpone to the graduate stage those kinds of studies more closely connected with employment in the professions would raise professional standards and might well expand professional employment.[73] To effect the changes suggested would involve a reappraisal of both secondary and university education as a whole. But it is just such a reappraisal which is needed if we are to give real meaning to the aims of the 1943 White Paper on educational reconstruction: to combine diversity of educational provision with equality of educational opportunity; but so to combine them as to attain greater social unity within the educational system, and thereby to help in the creation of a more closely knit society.[74]

Notes and References

1 A. V. Dicey, *Lectures on the relation between law and public opinion ...*, 2nd ed. reprint (London, 1926), p. xc.

2 *Ibid.*, p. 279.

3 *Ibid.*, p. 1.

4 England and Wales, 1954–1955, after deducting parents' contributions.

5 Dicey, *op. cit.*, pp. 260 and 275–279.

6 For the history of primary and secondary education in England and Wales since the early nineteenth century, I have drawn mainly upon J. W. Adamson, *English education 1789–1902* (Cambridge, 1930); R. L. Archer, *Secondary education in the nineteenth century* (Cambridge, 1921); G. A. N. Lowndes, *The silent social revolution* (Oxford, 1937); and H. C. Dent, *Secondary education for all* (London, 1949).

7 Lowndes, *op. cit.*, pp. 45–50.

8 Board of Education, *Report of the Consultative Committee on Secondary Education* (Spens Committee) (London, 1938), pp. 81–92.

9 See Ministry of Education, *Education in 1956*, Cmd. 223 (London, 1957), pp. 94–95, 111 and 119.

10 In 1955–1956, 73·3 per cent of the published income came from parliamentary and local authority grants. Fees (forming 11·2 per cent of income) also include local and central authority payments in respect of students, and the figures suggest that such payments must represent a very substantial part of the total. Overall public aid must therefore amount to considerably more than 73 per cent of published income. But the published totals do not include Oxford and Cambridge college income used for specifically college purposes.

11 See R. K. Kelsall, *Applications for admission to universities* (London, 1957), Tables 16a and 16b and p. 11.

12 Autumn 1956—includes graduates and overseas students. See U.G.C., *University development: interim report on the years 1952 to 1956*, Cmd. 79 (London, 1957), p. 8.

13 *Eighth annual report ... of the Registrar-General* (London, 1848), p. lvii; *Thirty-third annual report* (London, 1872), p. vii.

14 W. O. Lester Smith, *Education: an introductory survey* (London, 1957), p. 105.

15 G. M. Young, *Victorian England* (Oxford, 1936), p. 97.

16 See G. C. Leybourne and K. White, *Education and the birth-rate* (London, 1940), p. 45 n. 1. citing E. L. Clarke; and R. Williams. *Whose public schools?* (London, 1957), p. 7 (Bow Group Publication).

17 R. Williams, *op. cit.*, p. 61.

18 G. M. Trevelyan, *British history in the nineteenth century*, cited by Leybourne and White, *op. cit.*, p. 40.

19 Autumn 1956.

20 H. M. Pollard, *Pioneers of popular education 1760–1850* (Cambridge, Mass., 1957), Chap. 22.

21 Adamson, *op. cit.*, pp. 209 and 221.

22 Lowndes, *op. cit.*, p. 5.

23 Adamson, *op. cit.*, p. 210.

24 National Education Union, *A verbatim report ... of the debate in Parliament during the progress of the Elementary Education Bill, 1970 ...* (Manchester, n.d.). pp. 5 and 18.

25 C. Norwood, *The English tradition of education* (London, 1929), pp. 171–172.

26 See E. C. Mack, *Public schools and British public opinion 1780 to 1860* (London, 1938), pp. 132–137.

27 Archer. *op. cit.*, p. 167

28 B. Holt-Smith, *Some aspects of the medical profession in eighteenth century England*, Ph.D. Thesis, University of London (1952), p. 176.

29 *The vicar of Bullhampton*, which began to appear in parts in July 1869. (The reference is to the World's Classics edition, pp. 60–61.)

30 Thomas Farrer. See J. D. Kingsley, *Representative bureaucracy* (Yellow Springs, Ohio, 1944), pp. 76–77.

31 O. Banks, *Parity and prestige in English secondary education* (London, 1955), pp. 2–3.

32 Lowndes, *op. cit.*, pp. 89–90.

33 *Op. cit.*, p. 18.

34 B. M. Allen, *Sir Robert Morant* (London, 1934), p. 25.

35 The 1902 Act was passed at one of the major crossroads of policy making. Theoretically, secondary education might have been provided for all children—in effect, in line with the Bryce Commission views on the nature of secondary education. That it was not, and that, instead, existing endowed schools were subsidised, are explicable in terms of the dominant middle-class views on the nature and purpose of secondary education.

36 *Op. cit.*, p. 141.

37 See Tables 3 and 4, pp. 126–127, in J. Floud, 'The educational experience of the adult population of England and Wales as at July 1949', in D. V. Glass, ed., *Social mobility in Britain* (London, 1954).

38 There were, of course, scholarships before 1907. On the impact of these in London, and on the judgment of head teachers as regards the scholarship winners, see F. Campbell, *Eleven-plus and all that* (London, 1956), pp. 70–76. See also O. Banks, *op. cit.*, p. 67.

39 All the statistics given here on inter-war changes in educational opportunity are, unless otherwise specified, from J. Floud. *op. cit.*

41 O. Banks, *op. cit.*, p. 69.

42 J. Floud, *op. cit.*, p. 140, Appendix Table 1.

43 The proportion of working-class children in maintained and direct-grant grammar schools in England in the Ministry of Education sample inquiry, carried out in 1953, was 64·6 per cent. Ministry of Education, *Early Leaving* (London, 1954), p. 17, Table J. It should be also noted that, in recent years, the use of I.Q. tests for selection has been increasingly queried by educational psychologists and so, too, has selection at the age of eleven years in general. In view of the acknowledged cultural components in the tests, an I.Q. test, in addition to other defects, acts in some degree as a self-fulfilling prophecy.

44 H. C. Dent, *op. cit.*, pp. 32–33.

45 O. Banks, *op. cit.*, Chap. 8.

46 Cited in D. Lockwood, *The black coated worker* (London, 1958), p. 117.

47 D. Lockwood, *op. cit.*, p. 55.

48 See F. M. Martin, in Glass, *Social mobility*, pp. 68–69.

49 In our studies of occupational prestige, routine clerks were ranked about halfway down the scale of status. The attraction of clerical work to the lower middle class and aspiring working class was its combination of security and 'respectability.' Further, like teaching, it appeared to provide a springboard for additional social ascent in the next generation.

50 Acton Society Trust (Rosemary Stewart), *Management Succession* (London, 1956). pp. 13–18.

51 The figures for boarding-school boys are 30·6 per cent and 19·0 per cent, respectively. For boys who went to secondary grammar schools the corresponding figures are 11·4 and 9·0 per cent. See J. Floud, *op. cit.*, p. 119.

52 See W. M. Kotschnig, *Unemployment in the learned professions* (London, 1937), pp. 121–125.

53 O. Banks, *op. cit.*, p. 124, citing *Hansard*.

54 This was, however, only the broad classification. The Committee distinguished, under the category of modern schools, between selective and non-selective (equivalent to the existing central schools) and the 'senior classes' of public elementary schools, 'providing post-primary education for children who do not go to any of the three previous types of schools . . .'. See Board of Education, *The education of the adolescent* (London, 1926), pp. 172–175.

55 Board of Education, *Educational reconstruction*, Cmd. 6458 (London, 1943), p. 10, para. 31. The Spens Committee's recommendations are given in Board of Education, *Secondary education* (London, 1938), pp. xvii–xviii and xxvi–xxxiii.

56 Board of Education, *Curriculum and examinations in secondary schools* (London, 1943), pp. 2–4.

57 Secondary school selection procedures are now widely based on I.Q. tests. The proportion of 20 per cent in grammar schools is that given in the Ministry of Education report, *Early leaving*, p. 14, as applying to England as a whole (excluding Wales), though there is considerable local variation.

58 See, for example, R. Pedley, *Comprehensive education* (London, 1956), Chap. 2.

59 This was the comment of the chartered surveyor who carried out the recent valuation (for rating purposes) of the buildings of Uppingham School. See *The Times*, 29 October 1927.

60 According to R. Williams, *op. cit.*, p. 39 (citing the Public Schools Appointments Bureau), 42·4 per cent of the public school leavers in 1954–1955 were going to a university.

61 And, in addition, the view not infrequently expressed that the public school type of education is the best preparation for the university.

62 *Educational reconstruction*, pp. 6 and 9.

63 The report on *Early leaving*, referred to previously.

64 In Autumn 1956, 88,701 students. See U.G.C., *University development: interim report on the years 1952 to 1956*, Cmd. 79 (London. 1957), p. 22.

65 *Op. cit.*, p. 25.

66 Kelsall, *op. cit.*, pp. 9–10, and Tables 14, 16a and 16b.

67 Students of all major categories of social origin are receiving assistance. Among the 1955 entrants, the proportions of male students receiving financial assistance were 73 per cent for those whose fathers were in the Registrar-General's classes 1 and 2 (professional, employers, managers, executives and similar occupations), and over 90 per cent for the students with routine clerical or manual backgrounds. (Kelsall, Table 16a.)

68 See pp. 56 and 34–41.

69 In Kotschnig, *op. cit.*, p. 124.

70 See *Technical education*, Cmd. 9703 (London, 1956).

71 Of the male entrants to British universities in October 1955, 23 per cent had no classifiable occupation in mind—usually because they did not answer the question or because they had no particular occupation in view. But of the rest, over 90 per cent contemplated a professional occupation including teaching, research and the civil service, and only 10 per cent envisaged industrial or commercial occupations. For men of manual origin, industry and commerce were even less in view. (See Kelsall, *op. cit.*, Table 17g.)

72 Consider, for example, the statement of a former Chairman of the University Grants Committee, Sir Walter Moberly, in 1939: 'If the chief object of going to the university was to secure a satisfactory niche in professional life, the universities could not afford greatly to increase their present intake, and the present social distribution of students could not with advantage be fundamentally modified. On a purely vocational basis something like saturation point had been reached.' Moberly was replying to Professor Major Greenwood's argument that university education should be regarded as a preparation for life and leisure, not as a training for better jobs, and it is only fair to note that Moberly continued: 'On the other hand, if university education was regarded as primarily an education for life rather than for livelihood, quite a different conclusion was indicated, though time did not permit him to develop it.' (*J.R.S.S.*, Vol. CII, Part 3 (1939), p. 381.)

73 With our present system. students tend either to have had so general a course that they are not professional in the sense of being able to show specific competence; or else to have concentrated upon a limited range of subjects in a professional or near professional course which cannot be broadened because there is not sufficient time. In preparing for professional work there is much to be said for a combination of a first degree and a more intensive graduate course, involving systematic, advanced training and, where appropriate, evidence of capacity to undertake research. In the social sciences, my own experience suggests that it is this systematic, advanced training which is particularly necessary if there is to be a rise in standards and an increase in the use of social scientists in professional employment.

74 In order to simplify the references and the citation of statistics, most of the discussion in this paper has been restricted to boys. The general argument and conclusions apply equally to girls, though there have been important qualitative and quantitative differences in their effective access to secondary and higher education, reflecting the different emphasis in our society on the education and careers of girls.

Raymond Williams

I:4 The long revolution

*Nineteenth-century Britain saw a major reorganization of
elementary, secondary and higher education, along lines
which are still generally followed today. The revolutionary
idea of 'education for all' got its impetus from the rise
of an organized working class demanding education, and
from the pressures of a changing economy. These
economic pressures led to a complex argument about
the nature of the curriculum. The curriculum that evolved
was a compromise between the public educators, the
industrial trainers, and the old humanists—with the
industrial trainers predominant. In the twentieth
century the public educators' idea of education for all
has been extended but the 'shadow of class thinking'
remains.*

The nineteenth-century achievement is evidently a major reorganization of elementary, secondary, and university education, along
lines which in general we still follow. Both in kinds of institution,
and in the matter and manner of education, it shows the reorganization of learning by a radically changed society, in which the
growth of industry and of democracy were the leading elements,
and in terms of change both in the dominant social character and in
types of adult work. At no time in England have the effects of these
influences on the very concept of education been clearer, but, precisely because this was so, a fundamental argument about the purposes of education was the century's most interesting contribution.
Two strands of this argument can be separated: the idea of education for all, and the definition of a liberal education. The former, as
we have seen, was fiercely argued, and the history of the century
represents the victory of those who, in the early decades, had been a
minority. Two major factors can be distinguished: the rise of an
organized working class, which demanded education, and the needs
of an expanding and changing economy. In practice, these were
closely interwoven, in the long debate, and the victory of the reformers rested on three elements: a genuine response to the growth
of democracy, as in men like Mill, Carlyle, Ruskin, and Arnold;

Williams, R., *The long revolution*, 1958. (Pelican Books, 1965, pp. 161–168.)
Reprinted by permission of the author and Chatto and Windus Ltd.

protective response, the new version of 'moral rescue', very evident
in the arguments for the 1870 Education Act in relation to the
franchise extensions of 1867—'our future masters ... should at least
learn their letters'; and the practical response, perhaps decisive,
which led Forster in 1870 to use as his principal argument: 'upon
the speedy provision of elementary education depends our industrial
prosperity'. In the growth of secondary education this economic
argument was even more central.

The democratic and the industrial arguments are both sound, but
the great persuasiveness of the latter led to the definition of education in terms of future adult work, with the parallel clause of
teaching the required social character—habits of regularity, 'self-
discipline', obedience, and trained effort. Such a definition was challenged from two sides, by those with wider sympathies with the
general growth of democracy, and by those with an older conception of liberal education, in relation to man's health as a spiritual
being. This interesting alliance is broadly that which I traced as a
tradition in Culture and Society, and the educational argument was
always near the centre of this continuing tradition. On the one hand
it was argued, by men with widely differing attitudes to the rise of
democracy and of working-class organization, that men had a
natural human right to be educated, and that any good society
depended on governments accepting this principle as their duty. On
the other hand, often by men deeply opposed to democracy, it was
argued that man's spiritual health depended on a kind of education
which was more than a training for some specialized work, a kind
variously described as 'liberal', 'humane', or 'cultural'. The great
complexity of the general argument, which is still unfinished, can be
seen from the fact that the public educators, as we may call the first
group, were frequently in alliance with the powerful group which
promoted education in terms of training and disciplining the poor,
as workers and citizens, while the defenders of 'liberal education'
were commonly against both: against the former because liberal
education would be vulgarized by extension to the 'masses'; against
the latter because liberal education would be destroyed by being
turned into a system of specialized and technical training. Yet the
public educators inevitably drew on the arguments of the defenders
of the old 'liberal' education, as a way of preventing universal
education being narrowed to a system of pre-industrial instruction.
These three groups—the public educators, the industrial trainers,
and the old humanists—are still to be distinguished in our own

time. . . . . In general, the curriculum which the nineteenth century evolved can be seen as a compromise between all three groups, but with the industrial trainers predominant. The significant case is the long controversy over science and technical education. If we look at the range of scientific discovery between the seventeenth and the end of the nineteenth centuries, it is clear that its importance lies only in part in its transformation of the techniques of production and communication; indeed lies equally in its transformation of man's view of himself and of his world. Yet the decisive educational interpretation of this new knowledge was not in terms of its essential contribution to liberal studies, but in terms of technical training for a particular class of men. The old humanists muddled the issue by claiming a fundamental distinction between their traditional learning and that of the new disciplines, and it was from this kind of thinking that there developed the absurd defensive reaction that all real learning was undertaken without thought of practical advantage. In fact, as the educational history shows, the classical linguistic disciplines were primarily vocational, but these particular vocations had acquired a separate traditional dignity, which was refused to vocations now of equal human relevance. Thus, instead of the new learning broadening a general curriculum, it was neglected, and in the end reluctantly admitted on the grounds that it was of a purely technical kind. The pressure of the industrial trainers eventually prevailed, though not with any general adequacy until the Technical Instruction Act of 1889, and even here, significantly, it was 'instruction' rather than 'education'. This history was damaging both to general education and to the new kinds of vocational training, and yet it was only an exceptional man, such as Huxley, who could see this at the time and consequently argue in the only adequate way : that science must become a part of general education and of liberal culture, and that, as a further provision, there must be an adequate system of specific professional training, in all kinds of scientific and technical work, on the same principle as the further professional training of doctors, lawyers, teachers, artists, and clergy. We can take only a limited satisfaction in the knowledge that the industrial trainers won, inert and stupid as the old humanists were and have continued to be. Huxley was a public educator, in the full sense, and it was only in this tradition that the problem might have been solved.

The shadow of class thinking lies over this as over so much other nineteenth-century educational thinking. The continued relegation of trade and industry to lower social classes, and the desire of successful industrialists that their sons should move into the now largely irrelevant class of gentry, were alike extremely damaging to English education and English life. As at the Reformation, a period of major reconstruction of institutions was undertaken largely without reference to the best learning of the age, and without any successful redefinition of the purposes of education and of the content of a contemporary liberal culture. The beginnings of technical instruction in the Mechanics' Institutes might have developed into a successful redefinition, but again it was the training of a specific class, whereas in fact the new sciences were radical elements in the society as a whole: a society which had changed its economy, which under pressure was changing its institutions, but which, at the centres of power, was refusing to change its ways of thinking. And then to the new working class, the offered isolation of science and technical instruction was largely unacceptable, for it was precisely in the interaction between techniques and their general living that this class was coming to its new consciousness. Politics, in the wide sense of discussing the quality and direction of their living, was excluded from these Institutes, as it was to remain largely excluded from the whole of nineteenth-century education. It was only very slowly, and then only in the sphere of adult education, that the working class, drawing indeed on very old intellectual traditions and on important dissenting elements in the English educational tradition, made its contribution to the modern educational debate. This contribution—the students' choice of subject, the relation of disciplines to actual contemporary living, and the parity of general discussion with expert instruction—remains important, but made little headway in the general educational organization. Like the individual public educators, their time was not yet.

* * * * *

In the twentieth century, the framework inherited from the nineteenth century has been greatly expanded and improved. Elementary education has been redefined as primary education, ending at eleven, and from this definition, since 1944, it has been possible to provide secondary education for all. A greatly expanded system of combined first-grade and second-grade secondary schools has been brought into being, and arrangements for a substantial minority to pass from primary schools into this system, and for a much smaller minority to pass on to higher education, have been if not completely

at least effectively established. A large number of third-grade secondary schools, with limited connexions to the minority system, are in
process of creation, and vary considerably in quality. In primary
education, a notable expansion of the curriculum is perhaps the
century's major achievement; it is mainly here that the influence of
the public educators has been effective. The universities, if unevenly
and at times without clear definition, have expanded their curricula
in vitally important ways. It is at the level of secondary education,
whether 'grammar' or 'modern', that the essential argument continues, in terms that reveal again the close relationship between
curriculum and organization.

In theory, the principles of the public educators have been
accepted: that all members of the society have a natural right to be
educated, and that any good society depends on governments
accepting this principle as a duty. In practice the system is still
deeply affected by other principles, as a few examples will show.
The continued existence of a network of private education, in the
preparatory and public schools, may or may not be socially desirable, but in any case it shows the kind of education, and the
necessary level of investment in it, which a particular social group
accepts as adequate for itself. The large class, for example, has
haunted public education from the beginning: from Lancaster's
1,000 children under one master, through the 60–80 of the urban
board schools, to the still common 40–50 of our own day. In the
private network, very much smaller classes, and the necessary investment to ensure them, have been accepted as a private duty, in a
quite different way from the interpretation of public duty in the
national system. Similarly, by the same social group, the necessary
minimum level of education of all its members has been set as at
least the second-grade school, usually followed by further professional training, whereas the public definition, for the members of
other social groups, is at the lower minimum of what is still very
much the old third grade. Again, the minimum level, for the limited
social group, is set to include subjects which are only available to a
minority of the society as a whole. It is not easy to argue that this
limited social group has no right to provide the education it thinks
fit for its own members, but the contrasts between this and the
general provision show very clearly the survival of a familiar kind
of class thinking, which has limited the practical execution of a
formally accepted public duty. In the analysis of our present educational system, this point is usually neglected in favour of an argu-

ment in terms of levels of intelligence, and it is often argued that we face wholly new problems, in the education of the 'masses', because levels of measured intelligence vary so widely. There are problems indeed, but in fact the education of this limited social class has throughout its history had to deal with this same kind of mental variation, and it has been the level of education required by a member of this class, rather than the level thought appropriate to a particular mental measurement, that has in fact governed its organization. If we put the matter in this way, that because a child will be this kind of adult, he must be brought to a given degree of education, we can begin to see the pattern more clearly.

Differences in learning ability obviously exist, but there is great danger in making these into separate and absolute categories. It is right that a child should be taught in a way appropriate to his learning ability, but because this itself depends on his whole development, including not only questions of personal character growth but also questions of his real social environment and the stimulation received from it, too early a division into intellectual grades in part creates the situation which it is offering to meet. The effect of stimulation on intellectual performance has been interestingly described, in our present context, by Professor Vernon:

'After 11, in Britain, we do get bigger divergences in environmental stimulation. Children are now at an age when they should be acquiring complex concepts and modes of thought, and the different kinds of schooling provided in grammar, modern and other schools, together with the different intellectual levels of their homes, may well affect their growth. At 15 the majority leave school and enter jobs which do little to exercise their "brains", and their leisure pursuits are mostly non-stimulating. But a privileged minority continue to receive intellectual stimulation to 17, 18, 21 or later, and are more likely to enter jobs where they use their minds, and to indulge in cultural leisure-time pursuits. Hence we would expect, as has been clearly proved, that education during the teens does affect the ultimate adult intelligence level. The man with full secondary and university education has on the average a 12 IQ point advantage over the man who was equally intelligent at 15 but has had no further education since then.'

This is the reality behind the confident use of mental measurement to ratify graded systems of education. To take intelligence as a fixed quantity, from the ordinary thinking of mechanical materialism, is a denial of the realities of growth and of intelligence itself, in the final interest of a particular model of the social system. How else can we explain the very odd principle that has been built into modern English education: that those who are slowest to learn should have the shortest time in which to learn, while those who learn quickly will be able to extend the process for as much as seven years beyond them? This is the reality of 'equality of opportunity', which is a very different thing from real social equality. The truth is that while for children of a particular social class we have a conception, however imperfect, of a required minimum of general education whatever their measured intelligence might be, we have no such conception, or a much lower conception, for the majority of those outside this class. This fact in itself, together with other social processes, magnifies natural inequalities, in a persistent way. For of course there is no absolute correlation between intelligence and membership of a particular occupational group. The mean I.Q. of children of such groups varies, but the differences within groups are greater than those between the groups. And then, if longer education can be bought by a few, and if more favourable learning environments are perpetuated by the social inequality resulting from previous inequalities of real opportunity, natural inequalities are again magnified and take on a direct social relevance. If one is asked, at any point in this process, to 'stop being utopian and consider the hard facts about educating the masses', it is very difficult to be patient. While we shall always be faced with substantial differences in learning ability among all children, we have to face the really hard fact that we are now meeting this problem in a particular way which serves in the end to magnify the differences and then pass them off as a natural order. We can only change this way if we get rid of conscious or unconscious class thinking, and begin considering educational organization in terms of keeping the learning process going, for as long as possible, in every life. Instead of the sorting and grading process, natural to a class society, we should regard human learning in a genuinely open way, as the most valuable real resource we have and therefore as something which we should have to produce a special argument to limit rather than a special argument to extend. We will perhaps only get to this when we have learned to think of a genuinely open culture.

William Taylor

I:5 A secondary curriculum for the average child

*An analysis is made of the social functions of the British
secondary modern curriculum and the social factors that
influence the day-to-day work of the schools, with a view
to putting in context the new courses being propounded
for the 'average child'. Taylor identifies two main
historical influences—the 1926 Hadow Report's
recommendation for a practical curriculum for modern
school pupils because the academic curriculum for the
select minority in grammar schools was not suitable; the
ideas of the progressive movement—Summerhill, Dewey,
Montessori. Recently, there has been a reaction in favour
of a more tough-minded approach to education, with
emphasis on basic literacy and the desire in many
secondary modern schools to enter children for external
examinations.*

There is a depressing similarity about much of the literature on the
curriculum of the Modern school, and the sentiments and even
wording of some of the official reports and memoranda that have
influenced the practice of the schools are commonly echoed and
restated. What follows is concerned primarily with the social functions of the curriculum and the social factors that influence the day-
to-day work of the schools, with a view to establishing a background against which the advanced and extended courses which are
characteristic of the 'new concept' of the Modern school can be
evaluated.

The basic timetable

It is true that the work of the Modern school today is very different
from that of the Senior departments and the Higher Elementary
schools of sixty years ago, but changes in theory and attitudes have
been greater than changes in the distribution of subjects and the

Taylor W., *The secondary modern school*, Faber, 1964, pp. 82–102. Reprinted
by permission of Faber and Faber Ltd.

structure of the timetable. The greatest alteration has occurred in the peripheral subjects: cooking and manual training have developed into the specialized disciplines of domestic science, needlework, light craft, woodwork, and metalwork; 'drill' has become physical education and games; and so on. The central core of the curriculum, based on the 'Three R's', and the requirements of a knowledge of basic number and of literacy, has undergone development within the 'subjects' themselves: in the greater degree of practical work in arithmetic and geography, for example; the changed attitude to the purposes and methods of art teaching; the greater breadth in the teaching of English, as opposed to the older 'reading and writing'. Method and content have changed a great deal, and the teaching force has become far more specialized. There is, however, a considerable element of continuity in the curriculum, determined in large part by the demands of society for adaptable and literate individuals, able to fit themselves to a variety of vocational roles within the limits of the range of occupations served by a particular type of school. This absence of rigidly vocational specialization has been, until recent times, an important factor in shaping the curriculum of the post-primary schools for the mass of the population. It has to a large extent kept out subjects which are required for qualifying purposes—such as Latin and French—and has prevented any large measure of specialization in the upper reaches of the three- or four-year course. If the extended courses, quasi-vocational specialization and examination work of the Modern school are left out of account, it is possible to outline a basic curriculum which is common to the large majority of English Modern schools.

Some schools operate a thirty-five period week, whilst others have forty rather shorter periods. Some schools have a seven- or eight-day instead of a five-day timetable, but within these different systems the apportionment of time is roughly as follows: English and arithmetic or mathematics still receive pride of place, and each has an allocation of some five to eight periods a week. Usually, but not always, a class has all its English periods with a single teacher—often the form teacher—who is responsible for dividing the time available between language, literature, drama, and poetry. History and geography—sometimes 'social studies'—receive two periods each, as do religious education, music, art and science; sometimes biology has two additional periods. A whole afternoon or morning is frequently devoted to metalwork, woodwork or domestic science, with, very often, a further two periods given over to gardening, needlework, light craft and other practical activities. Three or more periods are usually devoted to physical education and games. In addition to the subjects mentioned, others, such as technical drawing and rural science, have a place in many schools.

One interesting feature of this basic curriculum is the extent to which it has withstood the onslaughts of educational ideas which at one time might have seemed likely to alter substantially the 'subject-centred' timetable in favour of projects, centres of interest, individual assignments, and subject groups. Schools in which the work is based on such approaches are objects of comment and clearly exceptional in the general run of Modern schools. It appears that what the Consultative Committee on Secondary Education, 1938, had to say about the subjects of the Grammar school applies equally to the subjects taught in the Modern school : '... we attach much importance to the "problem method" which is akin to the "project method", and in our Report on *The Primary School* have stated that in our opinion the "project method" in the full sense of the term has a very useful place in the teaching of young children. We recognize, moreover, the great value of occasions ... which invite the application and synthesis of a considerable range of acquired knowledge and skill. But our general doctrine forbids us to go much further than this; for its essence is that the school "subjects" stand for traditions of practical, aesthetic and intellectual activity, each having its own distinctive individuality; and we hold that the profit a pupil derives from them does not come from casual or episodical contacts, but by his being, so to speak, put to school to them, and so getting to make their outstanding characters part of the equipment and habit of his mind.'[1]

The committee went on to suggest that the subjects of the timetable must be regarded as institutions in their own right, not simply as logical classification of material. During recent years the timetable of the Modern school has displayed signs of reflecting something of this academic attitude towards subject-matter, and this has been associated with a more rigorous and systematic form of teaching.

'Practical', 'Vocational' and the Hadow Report

The philosophy of the Secondary Modern school that manifested itself in official statements after 1944, and was so strong a feature of the Hadow Report, with its stress on equality, parity of esteem, non-vocational aims, and the writing down of many relevant considerations of social class and occupation, was hardly perceptible at the beginning of this century. The education beyond the elementary stage that was demanded and approved by large sections of the population was scientific and academic, rather than practical. It led to recognized qualifications and, whether concerned with the humanities or with science and mathematics, was academic in nature and taught in a 'bookish' manner. This was the type of curriculum provided not only by the existing Secondary (Grammar) schools, but also by many of the Higher Grade and Higher Elementary schools prior to 1902. After 1902 this academic type of work became the prerogative of the new Secondary schools, with the result that the work of other types of post-primary school became regarded as of somewhat inferior status. The attendance at these schools of the mass of the working population confirmed the label and committed the schools to a curriculum that appeared to have no easily ascertainable aim and led to no generally recognized qualification. Such a situation could only continue if a number of requirements were fulfilled. In the first place, there needed to be enough outlets for selective secondary education to satisfy the demands of lower middle-class parents who were willing to pay for it, and to provide for the needs of the most able sons and daughters of the working classes who were capable of winning scholarships. Secondly, there needed to be some psychological rationale for educating a minority of the most able in separate institutions, and making a selection for these institutions at an 'appropriate' age; this was provided by tradition, and justified by the growth of successful psychological investigations of difference in ability.

To an increasing extent after 1907, when the free place system was introduced, these requirements for the perpetuation of two types of curricula were fulfilled. The working out of the tendencies that began with the early factory legislation, however, by which the concept of childhood was extended upward in terms of age, brought with it further problems. The old elementary school, with its orientation towards basic literacy, was no longer, by the nineteen-twenties, able to satisfy the educational requirements of the children of thirteen and fourteen for whom it was called upon to cater. Many authorities had been providing separate schools for older children since before 1902; many more began to do so after the impetus provided by the Fisher Act of 1918, though greatly hindered within a year or two by the economic difficulties of the country as a whole.

In these new senior schools the timetables reflected the developing practice of the previous thirty years, and in many cases separate provision for craft subjects, for gardening, domestic science and so on, was made. The Consultative Committee that began its work in 1925 under the chairmanship of Sir Henry Hadow was thus considering measures to rationalize and universalize existing practice and promote and inspire further change.

The report of the Consultative Committee dealt extensively with the history and development of post-primary education, and its curricular recommendations and suggestions have been the basis of much that has been written subsequently on the subject. The committee recognized frankly that the curricular requirements of Modern schools would be determined partly by conditions of economic necessity, but seemed to accept these conditions as given factors in planning the structure of post-primary education. It was suggested that any classification of children that 'implies that a child who leaves school at fifteen or younger is "of a different kind" from one that stays to a later age, is to be deprecated. The relevance of the leaving age to the curriculum is simply a matter of practical convenience'.[2]

The Committee went on to state the case for considering the curriculum of the Modern school as an organic whole, to be planned as a continuous course from eleven to fifteen. It was recognized that the average age of attendance would probably rise, as had happened in the case of Secondary (Grammar) schools, where the length of school life had increased from 2 years 7 months in 1909–10 to 3 years 7 months in 1923–4. Individual pupils who might want to stay on at Modern schools should be catered for, but children who wished to continue their education for any considerable period should be transferred to another type of school providing an appropriate course.

The curricular orientation that ran through the whole of the Hadow Report, and for which it is best known, is summed up in its statement that a 'humane or liberal education is not one given through books alone, but one which brings children into contact with the larger interests of mankind',[3] and it was suggested that the aim of Modern schools and senior classes should be to provide 'such an education by means of a curriculum containing large opportunities for practical work and related to living interests...'.[4] It was made clear that the academic, bookish curriculum suitable for the selected minority in the Grammar schools was not suitable for the majority of pupils attending Modern schools. A large measure of practical work was advocated, not for its own sake, nor for vocational purposes, but as a *means* of intellectual training.... It would seem possible to classify the reasons for the employment of practical subjects in schools in three categories. First, there is the motivational : the use of practical activities to enlist the pupil's interest and enthusiasm, especially in the later years of full-time attendance at school. Secondly, there is the cultural factor : the view that the teaching of practical subjects embodies techniques and the acquisition of habits of mind which help in communicating the cultural heritage to the pupil. Thirdly, there is the principle of *relevance*, by which the teaching of practical subjects is related to the pupil's future occupation. It is clear that all three factors played their part in the recommendations of the Hadow Committee. The first, the motivational factor, can be said to have been dominant; it was naturally closely allied to the third, the principle of relevance; but the sociological conclusions in terms of occupational class and status, that had to be drawn if the vocational aspects of the 'practical subjects' were pursued to their logical conclusion, were not given the attention they deserved because of the need to stress equality and play down social differences.[5]

The progressive influence

The content of the 'Hadow' curriculum thus represented a continuation of the established practice of 'Central' and 'Senior' schools, and included an emphasis upon the need for an approach to 'subjects' that was both practical and realistic. In this stress upon the practical the report reflected some of the more revolutionary ideas about the construction of the curriculum that were beginning to influence the practice of the schools, ideas derived from Rousseau, Dewey and Montessori, and the example of 'progressive' schools like Bedales and Summerhill. The main parts of the curricular recommendations of the Hadow Committee were traditional enough, however; no mention can be found of the 'project', the centre of interest, or the plans for the integration of subjects that feature largely in the report of the Spens Committee twelve years later. The importance of the progressive movement on the curriculum of the Modern school must not be underestimated. Untrammelled by the requirements of external examinations; officially encouraged to experiment and find its own way; the Modern school was particularly open to the influence

of progressive ideas. These had so many manifestations, were represented by so many different associations, and sometimes appeared to be united only by their own unorthodoxy, that it is
difficult to categorize in simple terms their most prominent concepts. Without doing an injustice to the range of notions represented. it is fair to say that most of the 'progressives' were of a
radical social and political persuasion, and saw the future of education and society as requiring much less competition and more co-
operation, attempting to place the child, instead of the curriculum
or the subject, in the centre of the educational stage and critical of
'tradition'. Ideas such as these were embodied or implied in much of
the writing of educational thinkers, and obtained a firm hold on
many of those concerned with the training of teachers in colleges
and universities. In turn, these teachers took with them some aspects
of the new approach into the schools, and signs of this are easily
found in existing practice. The emphasis on the value of play and
activity in the infant and junior school; new methods of teaching
the basic skills; a new attitude towards the spontaneous expressive
activities of the child; the introduction of composite subjects such as
'social studies', of new and more 'natural' crafts, such as clay model-
ling; the attention given to the practical subjects and education
through the senses rather than the intellect; and a change in the
attitude towards information and facts and a recognition of the
importance of experience : all are manifestations of the spirit of the
'new education' as it has worked out in contact with the existing
elements of the curriculum....

The influence of radical progressive ideas such as these was destined to be made greater by their being incorporated in the thinking
that inspired the spirit of change and reform of the years prior to
the passing of the 1944 Education Act. This influence is reflected in
the educational literature of the period, and, in turn, in the official
pamphlets and pronouncements of the Ministry of Education in the
immediately post-war years.[6]

From the 1944 Act to the extended course

Thus, by the beginning of the nineteen-forties, the Modern school,
which did not yet exist as an administrative type, had to help to
determine its purposes the experience of post-primary education
that had been built up during the inter-war period; the influence of a
good deal of new thinking about educational aims and the content

and method of the curriculum, largely 'progressive' in nature; the suggestions of the Hadow Committee of 1926; and the implied suggestions of the Spens Committee of 1938; its 'objective' position as the institution in which all children from eleven plus who were not selected for other forms of secondary education were educated; and the expectation that it would have an important part to play in the post-war pattern of educational provision. With the passing of the Education Act of 1944, and the provision of 'Secondary education for all', the Modern school became a part of the tripartite structure of secondary education that was adopted in most local authority areas. . . .

The functions of the Modern school, and the type of educational programme it was to adopt, were set out in a number of official pamphlets. . . . *The new secondary education* echoed many of the progressives' ideals regarding the child-centred curriculum,[7] and in *The nation's schools* the project method, encouraged by the Spens Report, was strongly supported. The curriculum of the Secondary Modern school was, then, to be very general; neither vocational nor directed towards examinations; nor determined by the requirements of the traditional subject divisions. At the same time, the other types of secondary schools were to continue to provide broadly the educational diet that had come to be associated with them during the previous decades of the present century, except that to an increasing extent the Grammar school course was to be thought of as a connected whole up to and including sixth-form work.

. . . to propose a curriculum of this type for the Modern school was to make it impossible for it to compete with other types of secondary school in the occupational field, and to sharpen the differences between types of secondary school within the tripartite system. In fact, as we know, the type of curriculum envisaged by the Ministry at this period never became the practice of more than a minority of schools. A large number continued to teach in the way they had done during the thirties—the 'sound senior elementary work' that has been referred to elsewhere. Some began to experiment with 'modern methods', projects, centres of interest and so on. Soon, however, there arose a concern with the standards of work being achieved in the Modern schools, particularly with standards of attainment in the basic subjects, and with pupils' attitudes towards the school and their work. This concern can be accounted for partly as social protest, generally of middle-class origin, against the social doctrines that seemed to be implied by the idea of free secondary

education for all and the expenditure of large sums of money on 'working-class' schools. In this it became associated with the demand for economy, the cutting out of 'frills' and a concentration upon essentials. In addition, there were many teachers and others who were of the opinion that the inter-war revolution against formalism had had too much influence on the work of the schools, and that the time was ripe for a restatement of traditional aims. Standards of basic literacy were clearly affected by the war and its aftermath; it was very easy, however, to use progressive methods as the whipping boy for any defects that might make themselves felt. Thirdly, it became clear that economic developments were making it more than ever necessary that pupils should have a good standard of general education, and qualifications began to be relevant to more and more types of jobs.

Those concerned with standards received a certain amount of support from the Report of the Ministry of Education for 1949:

'If many modern schools are now human, civilizing places with much to offer the social and spiritual side of their pupil's development, far fewer seem to have come to grips with the problem of how to meet intellectual needs and how to stimulate fullest effort.'[8]

An objective index of how standards had been affected can be obtained from studies of changes in the standards of reading ability, initiated by the Ministry of Education, and published in two reports in 1950 and 1956. The latter report showed that a very considerable improvement had taken place since 1948,[9] and the findings of the national surveys were in large part corroborated by the survey of reading in Kent published early in 1959.[10] Although reading is not the sole accomplishment on the basis of which the standards of the schools may be assessed, it is vital to the performance of many other activities, and thus the testimony of these studies has been of some value in showing the extent to which the schools have been able to tackle the problems of basic literacy successfully. There is little concrete evidence on which a comparison between the standards of the old Senior Elementary and the Secondary Modern school can be based. In a sense, the comparison is meaningless, since the length of the course is different, and more time is now given to certain subjects. When the National Association of Schoolmasters asked their members: 'Do you consider the general level of attainment in the secondary modern school is (a) higher, (b) lower than in the old senior school?' 15 per cent of respondents considered that it was higher, 72 per cent that it was lower and 13 per cent that it varied.[11] In another survey of standards in Modern schools, the Kent County Association of the National Union of Teachers found less pessimism regarding the effects of 'broadening the curriculum' upon standards, but nearly half of their respondents felt that the Modern school could learn from the example of the best elementary schools in respect of work in the 'basic essentials'.[12] There was a good deal of support, however, for the view that 'the best modern schools can well stand comparison with the best elementary schools . . . and still have something over'.[13] Some respondents 'very much doubted the claims frequently made for the elementary schools, which, as one contributor said, "are developing with each passing year a brighter halo" '.[14]

These studies are useful in indicating the direction of teacher opinion, and it is clear that there is a desire to reiterate the claims of basic literacy and the fundamental functions of the school; this desire is perhaps made stronger by the emphasis of the universities, training colleges and inspectorate on what many teachers consider to be the less fundamental problems. It may be suggested, too, that there is in the attitude of many teachers towards curricular change something of the puritanical spirit that seems endemic in English society; the child-centred curriculum appears too soft an option, and current difficulties regarding staffing and accommodation accentuate this impression. As a result, there has been a reaction in favour of a more 'tough-minded' approach to education, a movement to rescue the word 'discipline' from the unpleasant associations that it had in the writings of some progressives. Professor Lester Smith has summed up this attitude as following along a road 'which will lead us, not back to the Lockian view that strict obedience is all-important or to the rigidities of the Victorian schoolroom, but forward to a new philosophy of education in which authority will count for rather more than it has done since the nineteen-twenties, when we were, perhaps, too ready to say "good-bye to all that" '.[15]

Much of the development in the curriculum of the Modern school that has taken place since 1947 has been initiated at humble levels of the educational hierarchy, and has only recently become official local and county policy. In the majority of cases, the impulse to enter children for external examinations and to develop bias along semi-vocational lines arose from the schools themselves. Certain features of the movement took their form from the inter-war reports and thinking on aims and methods in secondary education, and if the schools had not been given the freedom they were in 1945, such developments could hardly have taken place. On the other hand, in choosing to seek status in the same terms as those of other secondary school, many Modern school headmasters acted against most of the generally accepted ideas of what Modern school practice should be, ideas manifested in such varied statements as those of the progressives on the one hand and the Norwood Report on the other. In these new developments the Modern school is showing many signs of the same zest that inspired the head teachers of the Higher Grade schools at the end of the nineteenth century.[16] These sought to give a scientific and mathematical basis to the education of adolescents, often from comparatively humble homes, at a time when the existing secondary curricula were becoming out of touch with social and economic realities, and when the state had failed to deal with the problems of technical education. When these schools were either 'downgraded' or assimilated into the secondary system after 1902, a good deal of this technical and scientific influence remained. There was a continuing failure during the first three decades of the present century to get to grips with the problem of relating technical, scientific and general education, and it was not until the publication of the Spens Report in 1938 that technical education at the post-primary level was recognized as 'secondary'. The number of junior technical schools established during the interwar period was quite inadequate to cope with the need for this type of education, and after the war the position of the Technical school, despite its recognition as one of the main branches of the tripartite system, often remained obscure at the local level. Many authorities ceased to provide such schools, and relied instead upon the Grammar and Modern schools to make full provision for secondary education. Thus the post-war developments in the curriculum of the Modern school have been considerably affected by the fact that in many areas the tripartite system has never been a reality, and a good deal of Technical school work has come to be included in the Modern school course. This has meant an emphasis upon science, mathematics and other 'technical subjects', especially in the education of boys, that has many affinities with the type of curriculum provided by the Higher Grade schools sixty years ago.

Notes and References

1 Spens Report, H.M.S.O., 1938, p. 159.

2 Hadow Report, 1926, p. 82.

3 Hadow Report, 1926, p. 84.

4 *Ibid.*

5 There is a valuable analysis of the process by which 'Craft' found its way into the curriculum of the senior elementary school in Bramwell, R. D., *Elementary school work*, University of Durham, 1961, pp. 107–18.

6 In a widely read book, A. H. Greenough and F. Crofts, who have since been instrumental in developing specialized courses in Chesterfield's post-primary schools, referred to the characteristics of the society in which the reformed schools would find their place, and the educational methods and curricula appropriate to this society. *Theory and practice in the new secondary schools*, U.L.P., 1945, p. 38.

7 *The new secondary education*, p. 31.

8 *Education in 1949*, p. 21.

9 *Standards of reading*, 1948–56, 1956. Pamphlet No. 32.

10 Morris, J. M., *Reading in the primary school*, National Foundation for Educational Research and Newnes, 1959.

11 *The secondary modern school today—an interim study*, op. cit., National Association of Schoolmasters, 1955, p. 29

12 *Standards in the secondary modern school*, Kent County Association of the National Union of Teachers, 1956, p. 5. (Privately circulated.)

13 *Ibid.*, p. 12.

14 *Ibid.*, p. 13.

15 Lester-Smith, W. O., *Education—an introductory survey*, Penguin Books, 1958, p. 59.

16 It is interesting in this context to note the parallel between the legal difficulties encountered by the Higher Grade school movement and the fact that Modern schools are now entering pupils below the age of 16 for external examinations in apparent contravention of the spirit of the Ministry of Education 'Schools Regulations'.

Robert Bell

I:6 The growth of the modern university

The purpose of this paper by Robert Bell, an educational historian at the Open University, is to show that one of the most widely held assumptions about the modern university is both historically invalid and, at a time of controversy and change in higher education, dangerously misleading. According to this assumption, the traditional role and status of the British university is self-evident, endorsed by decades, if not centuries, of usage and experience. Drawing on evidence from Scotland and England, Bell points out that the 'tradition' is not of long standing and the 'role and status' far from unchanging.

Since the foundation of the University Grants Committee and, even more, since the general rise in university entrance requirements during the 1950s, there has been a growing tendency to regard all British universities as equal, at least in scope and function. Underlying the claims of the Black Papers, and, indeed, underlying the Robbins Report itself, is an assumption of common aims and standards that would have astonished academics even in the 1940s and an even clearer assumption that the 'traditional' role and status of the university is self-evident, endorsed by decades, if not centuries, of usage and experience. The purpose of this paper is to suggest that, in Britain at any rate, such assumptions are historically invalid and can be dangerously misleading when reference to 'traditional role' becomes an emotive ingredient in any discussion of the future pattern of the Higher Education system as a whole.

Indeed, until the 1960s both the British academic and the layman were clearly aware that 'university' was never such a unitary concept. Categorization of institutions was usually crude, as in the meaningless dichotomy of 'Oxbridge' and 'Red Brick' which lumped St Andrews with Hull, and L.S.E. with Aberystwyth and ignored the many characteristics which Oxford and Cambridge shared with other institutions (for example with Durham as a residential collegiate university, with Manchester as a centre of élitist research

Reproduced by permission of the Seminars Committee of the Faculty of Social Sciences, University of Edinburgh. A revised version of this paper will be published in a forthcoming volume by Tavistock Publications Ltd.

and with London as part of a metropolitan culture.) Equally meaningless, as it ignored functions, was the common division into
ancient and modern, with Dublin and Edinburgh uneasily occupying some chronological middle ground as models of the 'civic'
university (an equally misleading phrase).

Even the many categorizations based on subtler historical analyses such as that which posed models of 'Paris' versus 'Bologna'
depended on the naïve assumption that universities remain frozen in
polarized administrative states for long periods of time and the even
more naïve assumption that British universities have ever self-con-
sciously accepted such clear-cut foreign models without considerable local modification. Yet the old (Parisian?) picture of the dedicated scholar (research-worker?) kindly allowing a brood of young
men to sit at his feet in earnest apprenticeship is still sufficiently
flattering to academic self-esteem for it to have lost none of its
potency. However, the alternative (Bolognese?) model, believed
(probably falsely) to be perpetuated in the Scottish Rectorial system,
of a band of students employing a servile professor to teach them at
their whim seems now to have lost its earlier appeal.

Far less crude was the categorization offered by the Principal of
Edinburgh at the opening of the session of 1870–1871 when he
classified British universities as the 'collegiate' (Oxford, etc.) allowing students privileged entry into a 'traditional' community of
scholars, the 'professorial' (the Scottish universities and the new
English colleges at Manchester and London which had been modelled upon them) and the 'non-teaching' university, the university
purely as an examination board (of which the University of London
was then the prime example, but the idea of which underlay both
the future Royal University of Ireland and the Victoria University
in Lancashire and Yorkshire). Yet, even in 1870, such a threefold
categorization was becoming far from satisfactory. Trinity College,
Dublin, had characteristics both of 'collegiate' Cambridge and of
'professorial' Edinburgh. Oxford and Cambridge themselves were
already beginning to emphasize once more the importance of the
university, as opposed to the college, as a major teaching agency
with the newly active professors attracting mass audiences in true
Scottish style. It is useful also to remember that even the notion of
'university as examination board' had had its origins in Oxford,
(before the State finally broke the colleges' strangle-hold on teaching) and that Gladstone, for largely Oxonian reasons, was anxious to
impose on the Scottish universities (or 'colleges' as Edinburgh still

liked to call them) the federal structure which in his opinion could alone ensure adequate examination standards.

However, all such later nineteenth- and twentieth-century categorizations make the same assumption that, whatever their respective academic or social standing, 'universities' form a recognizable group quite separate from all other forms of educational institution, and, perhaps too glibly, we now readily assume that such Victorian notions of demarcation and of internal functioning must therefore correspond very largely to our own. In fact, however, the legal and 'traditional' bases for the universities' present exclusive functions do not always stand up well to close examination. Certainly the apparently timeless trappings of university life are, even now, far from being protected legally. Universities have, for example, no exclusive rights to the use of the term 'professor', despite the charisma which has protected its recent use in British circles.* The university cannot even challenge the use of its academic dress by outside bodies, as Aberdeen discovered when they attempted to prevent the local art college from stealing their M.A. hood. Even the right to grant 'degrees', now commonly seen as the exclusive mark of the true university, is of course available to many chartered bodies such as the Professional Colleges or the Educational Institute of Scotland, while the Council for National Academic Awards (not to mention the Archbishop of Canterbury) actually use the university nomenclature when doing so. Perhaps, however, the term least protected— until usage made it so in recent times—is the word 'university' itself which here, as it still is in North America, was for long interchangeable with 'college' and with 'school' as a description of institutions ranging from dancing academies through Glasgow's Andersonian University (which began much of modern technological education) to those institutions which have now eventually claimed exclusive right to it (though, as in Edinburgh and Aberdeen for example, some colleges had for long preferred the use of 'college' for internal purposes).

Thus, when in the 1820s, Brougham and his supporters set up their establishment in Gower Street called 'The University of London' (later University College) they did not then necessarily have in mind, as later general historians have assumed, a middle-class equivalent of Oxford; such equivalents, often educationally superior,

---

* It is, for example, used widely in Catholic secondary schools as well as in bodies such as the Royal Academy.

were already readily available in the Dissenting Academies, largely unhampered by their inability to award degrees (of little account at that time in any case). The 'University of London' offered a metro-politan centre of educational activity, free from religious tests, and its customers' wishes and nature were eventually to decide its place in a spectrum in which even the educational (as opposed to the social) status of Oxford and Cambridge remained far from clear. Brougham himself declared that he saw his new 'University' as providing for London what the Royal High School provided for Edinburgh and at no stage did he appear to see it as a degree-granting body until its Anglican rivals, King's and Durham, began to move in that direction. When a 'true' (i.e. a degree-granting) Univer-sity of London was finally established in 1836 it took the form of a government board with the staff of the various teaching colleges, of which Brougham's was but one, having little or no say, even in its examinations, until as late as 1900.

Thus before 1850, the notion of a 'university' was, in British terms, clearly a vague one and, indeed, to many fellows of Cam-bridge colleges the 'university' as such often represented the 'enemy' threatening his privileges throughout the period of reform.

Moreover, throughout the nineteenth century, the 'true' functions and style of what universities there were in Britain tended to be equally disputed even among academics themselves. Newman's *Idea of a university* written in the 1850s has come to be regarded (largely by those who have not read it carefully) as a statement of 'tradi-tional' belief, yet despite its defence of 'liberal' values, it is far from presenting a picture of any British university that existed at that time or of any likely to be present in the minds of twentieth-century defenders of academic 'standards'. It then represented an almost totally idiosyncratic position. Newman believed, for example, in the notion of the university as a living community of like-minded scholars of assorted ages at a time when almost all the Scottish universities and even many Oxford and Cambridge dons (Thomas Arnold among them) saw the drawing of young men out of the religious safeguards of the home into an artificial community as a danger to morality and, at best, a necessary evil. Indeed, during the first half of the nineteenth century (as Rothblatt has emphasized*) only in a few colleges such as Newman's own, did the college tutor become more than at best a schoolmaster and at worst a policeman,

---

* In his *The revolution of the dons* (London: Faber, 1968).

the proctor with his bulldogs, with little about him of the house-masterly, or even the scholarly figure which he later became. Not until well after 1900 did Glasgow or Edinburgh encourage students' residences and Patrick Geddes' establishment in Ramsay Garden was both disapproved of and opposed as a betrayal of Scottish tradition.

Newman also believed in a breadth of curriculum totally un-acceptable to the vested interests and superstitions of contemporary academics even in Scotland. Moreover, he was opposed to profes-sional studies, perhaps the one genuinely traditional element in the contemporary university and a major spur to nineteenth-century reform. Above all, he was totally opposed to the pursuit of scientific research within the university itself and to the modern notion of a don so continually and rightly at the frontiers of knowledge that to return to teach the undergraduate becomes an act of grace and favour. He saw his don as being principally paid to teach and the university as merely one of the many academically élitist institu-tions in the country. Clearly in the terms of 1970 this is neither the 'traditional' nor the convenient view for those who prefer the (Parisian?) myth of the charismatic research-worker gathering his eager but ignorant students around him.

Newman's lectures were originally delivered in connection with the founding of an abortive Catholic university in Dublin and this in itself reminds us that, until the late nineteenth century, the idea of the university as the imposer of a single version of religious belief did not come strangely to the Oxford don. At least until the 1850s he assumed his right to regulate not merely the religious but also on occasions the political activities of those who came into his charge. The Scottish universities' persistent refusal to accept that role, or, indeed any role 'in loco parentis', provided perhaps the greatest single contrast between the two groups of institutions. Certainly general university freedom of belief and preaching is a compara-tively recent innovation so far as England is concerned. Freedom of institutional arrangements there certainly was, freedom of speech was another matter.

In addition, Newman envisaged his potential students as coming from a much younger age group (say, 15–18) than today and, in many instances, it is clear that throughout the nineteenth century the university continued to provide, for those who wished, a general education at a standard now clearly delegated to the secondary school. Indeed, both at Edinburgh (as late as 1881) and (in mid-cen-tury) in the London colleges, local schools were often in open competition with the universities themselves for students of the same age and academic standard. At King's College, London, the pupils at its own school (ostensibly preparatory) were often said to be both older and more able than in the 'higher' institution. Both Oxford and Cambridge consciously negotiated with the public schools for the gradual handing over to them of undergraduate courses and clearly, the distinction between the nature of secondary and tertiary education was (and is) far from 'traditionally' fixed. Thomas Arnold, as a founder Senator of London University, saw its B.A. as the equivalent of sixth-form work at Rugby. Where entrance requirements to tertiary education existed, they were (until after 1900) normally of an extremely undemanding kind and, indeed, in Scotland until the 1890s the very idea of their introduction was seen as a national betrayal. It is true that Marischal College in Aberdeen had for long had entrance requirements but, on merging with King's in 1860, the latter (as the senior institution) insisted on their being abandoned, specifically in the name of 'tradition'.

Clearly there is little of current academic élitism in this picture. Even after the changes of the 1850s, the Scottish universities continued in England to be generally regarded (along with the new English colleges) as essentially secondary institutions of the German kind and an early volume of the journal *Mind* had to allow Scottish academics to defend themselves against such charges—not necessarily with great success, for Scottish and Irish honours graduates, however distinguished, continued for many decades to pass on, not to post-graduate study at Oxford and Cambridge but to the élitist undergraduate study which was seen as starting where their Scottish wide, but shallow, 'general' education had left off.

Statistically also, the Scottish universities do not suggest, nor would at least some Scottish academics have claimed, either academic or social élitism. The number of matriculated male students in Edinburgh in 1889 (almost all undergraduates) was 3,576 and while numbers dropped by 1,000 ten years later as a result of stricter entrance requirements undergraduate male entry was not to reach such a peak again until it was finally exceeded in 1962. Even as late as 1920 when the populations of England and Scotland were in the ratios of 9 : 1, the university populations were at 3 : 1. Clearly, there is a case for examining whether such institutions in the two countries were, in fact, performing similar social or academic functions and now to class them together may be both misleading and unfair to both. Scottish universities and their English imitators were clearly

major agencies of upward mobility while the older English universities catered mainly for those who had arrived already. The Scottish
universities were to a much greater extent dominated by a wide
range of professions (particularly medicine and school-teaching)
than were Oxford and Cambridge who came, once the church had
been largely set aside, to be dominated by the academic profession
itself. Indeed, the spread of the Oxford and Cambridge academic
career structure so as to include Scotland and the other English
institutions was in itself to prove a cause of tension.

George Davie* has rightly made much of the introduction of
English-style Honours degrees to Scotland after 1858. This need not,
of course, have the anti-nationalist significance which he gives it. It
may well be seen as yet another manifestation of greater social
complexity in an expanding economy. Nevertheless, such changes
must be clearly seen in context. At Glasgow, for example, though
there were always, between 1889 and 1900, some 2,000 matriculated students, the number graduating with honours in any one year
never rose above thirty-eight and in one year (1892–1893) it fell as
low as four. Moreover, throughout the nineteenth century, a major
problem in Scotland was how to persuade a student to attend whole
courses and to graduate at all.† The style and the level of attendance and aspiration for the majority of students had far more in
common with modern further education colleges than with the
modern university. The holding of D.P. (duly-performed) certificates
was sufficient of a meal ticket for most professional situations, and
élitist educational changes such as the introduction of English style
tutorials at undergraduate level could, as Jennie Lee has described,
cause, as late as 1924, actual strikes among students avid for lecture
notes. The colleges of London and Manchester, modelled on Scotland, faced similar problems.

George Davie has, of course, also rightly reminded us that there
were earlier periods of greater academic glory just as even in the
darkest periods of the eighteenth century there were both distinguished research workers, and even teachers, among Cambridge
dons. Nevertheless, such famous figures remain almost certainly the
statistical exception and one must not ignore the fact that far more
élitist researchers and teachers made their impact outside the university altogether. It remains a challenging fact that the period from

---

* In *The democratic intellect* (Edinburgh: University Press).
† A similar problem existed in the Irish institutions.

1700 to 1850, one of the greatest periods of British intellectual, industrial, and scientific development, happened also to be the period when the universities were at their lowest academic ebb. The portraits of distinguished men, the magnificent old libraries and the current activities of particular institutions must not blind us to the fact that the majority of their inhabitants, during a considerable period of their existence, were in no sense part of any academic élite and that for most of their lives, our present 'ancient' universities were, even by the standards of their own day, performing functions now performed by secondary schools or colleges of further education, while their present functions of research and technical advising were largely being performed by other bodies and institutions altogether.

Clearly this was far less true of Germany and even of the United States and, perhaps when the British academic speaks of his 'tradition' it is, not without reason, a European or an Anglo-Saxon rather than a British tradition which he has in mind. The present élitist function of the British university clearly is a late nineteenth-century innovation based upon those imported models, which prompted individuals, and eventually the State, to force what were highly resistant, socially élitist institutions into largely new patterns of behaviour.

It is remarkable, therefore, how little attention social scientists have paid to this sudden nineteenth-century change.* Clearly there is much to interest even the anthropologist in the way in which largely moribund ceremonial and examination structures suddenly achieved immense significance for those men of high intelligence who for decades had either satirized or ignored them completely. A structuralist investigation of the sudden revival of academic dress in Scotland could clearly illuminate other aspects of Victorian middle-class behaviour, such as the codification of games—again, a development in a wholly academic context. (It might also explain our continued reluctance to regularize a degree system which remains as chaotic as a hundred years ago.)

However, perhaps even more fruitful scientific investigation would involve an approach to the growth of the modern university not in terms of intellectual activity (this has far too often been attempted in isolation from other factors) as in terms of the university's market economy and all that the economist and sociologist could say about

* With the honourable exception of Glass, McPherson and Rothblatt.

it. For there is no superstitition more misleading or more clearly nonsensical than the belief that universities were once interested only in academic matters and only now in recent decades have begun to be obsessively concerned with money.

It is, of course, true that before the abolition of life-fellowships, dons in England never needed to worry about where the next meal was coming from, but their lives were still considerably dominated by matters of career, status, patronage and even pin-money. It was perfectly normal in early nineteenth-century Cambridge for the latter to be earned by College fellows, in a personal capacity, on the basis of giving private tuition to Hons. students outside the college premises and a major objection to the development of the curriculum beyond the basic subjects of elementary Classics and high-level Maths lay in the economic threat to such extra earnings which this would pose. Thus all triposes began as postgraduate courses, apparently so as not to threaten the posts and incomes of existing teachers. At the same time, because much of the special advanced coaching was given by non-university teachers, when a Classics Tripos was finally established, it could only be taken as a second postgraduate qualification after the Maths Tripos for which official college teaching existed. Hence the fanatical opposition to parliament's later removal of many financial securities in the interests of widening the curriculum. Ostensibly, of course, the objections made were academic, though it is clear that when Cambridge men taught elsewhere—at Durham or at the Anglican King's College—their objections to a wide curriculum quickly melted away, except inasmuch as certain subjects such as pedagogy and later sociology remained (for sociological reasons) generally degrading. Reform, it is true, began inside Oxford and Cambridge but, until state intervention, the reformers remained a small and ineffectual minority.

For much of the nineteenth century, Oxford and Cambridge were dominated by the needs of a career structure which embraced the Church of England and its sister churches, the public schools and their own college offices. It was even possible to combine Headmastership with benefices or Chairs (as Arnold did). Teaching in socially élitist schools was never seen as being at a lower academic level. Movement from one of these sectors to another was extremely simple and the whole structure carefully balanced. Freedom of conscience clearly did not arise except within extremely circumscribed (and purely Anglican) limits while violent scholarly activity, beyond the apprentice period, though not actually discouraged, produced

little or no dividends. In mid-century, the State, apparently awak-
ened to the threat of growing competition from countries with more
sophisticated systems of higher education and to the demands of the
Prince Consort and the reforming dons themselves, proceeded to
dismantle this whole edifice and, for the remainder of the century,
gave administrative and financial encouragement both to the more
diversified lines of academic activity already being followed in Scotland, London and Manchester, and to the provision of professional
courses, especially in medicine. It also encouraged the drawing of
the Honours examinations into undergraduate courses, as a reformed secondary sector took over the university's earlier and more
generalized educative function. This latter process is now clearly
taking place under government direction in the Irish Republic and
was, of course, begun (but only half concluded) in the case of Scotland whose professors, financially more strained, still demanded
every student they could get. Hence the present Scottish university
curriculum with its un-English mixture of Hons. specialist and
generalist education (much of which is largely 'secondary' in
nature).

In two of the few genuinely sociological investigations during this
period, McPherson has examined such Scottish changes while Rothblatt has examined Cambridge (though, strangely, Oxford not at
all). The latter's conclusion is tentative but clear: that university
teachers, having been divested by government intervention (and the
conscientious acts of some of their own members) of their earlier
prestigious, comfortable but academically non-élitist roles, began to
turn to new roles which involved the early pre-empting on traditional grounds of the most prestigious position in the newly developing spectrum of higher education—that is, the position most
likely to pay in terms of that very financial and social prestige
which was now in jeopardy. Thus, the two ancient English universities defined their new role, in Jowett's Platonic terms, as the producers of leaders (political, scientific and professional) and in order
to facilitate the adoption of this role, made it easier for their undergraduates (though they did not compel them) to reach, more rapidly,
academic levels of a clear distinction hitherto reserved only for
post-graduate students. The Scottish universities, in a less rewarding
economy, had lowlier aims—to provide high-standard courses for
entry to the professions (especially medicine and teaching) and
within these limits to follow the fashionable English to the greatest
extent possible. Those Scots seeking political leadership had, clearly,

still to go south—if necessary, as postgraduate undergraduates!

The Scottish desire to emulate the English is not only reflected in the growing tendency towards recruiting English 'beginners' as professors (thus drawing the Scottish universities into the more prestigious English career structure) but also in the great respect shown by academic selection committees to Oxford and Cambridge distinctions and in the desire of both Edinburgh and St Andrews to play up their 'medieval' picturesqueness as a suitable setting for Oxford-style academic activity. (Glasgow, alas, which in Defoe's time had been said to be even more beautiful than either of the others had, by 1850, lost that particular academic (economic?) asset. This 'English' tendency was reflected even more in the universities' eventual attempts to cater especially for the products of the new cheaper middle-class secondary schools (Heriot's, Watson's and the rest), which, after 1870, suddenly mushroomed in the major cities, so that the old 'open' procedure—of going straight from village school to university—became less and less possible.

The reform of the older establishments economically exposed their newer rivals and, without being a Marxist, one is nevertheless amused to see how readily Durham (overtly founded to protect the Dean and Chapter's finances from government attack) quickly lowered its academic requirements in order to beat off its economic rivals, offering colleges at all income levels (with consciously differing social tones) as well as lopping a year off the B.A. course, and how the London colleges tried a whole range of commercial experiments from offering military science at the time of the Crimea to the cramming of Eton boys for Oxford, as that university's demands increased. Meanwhile, in Scotland, the economically more exposed Aberdeen and St Andrews, with their comparatively small numbers, fruitlessly tried to embrace, in the one case, the socially and academically suspect activity of training school teachers and, in the other, the unsuccessful Durham game of offering the social and medieval graces of Oxford without the latter's new-found academic rigour or its metropolitan prestige.

In general, the new élitism was slower off the ground in Scotland, partly because of the 'open' national tradition, and, even more, because the institutions were poorly endowed and needed every reasonable student they could get. Thus, although the professors eventually gave up their practice of competing with schoolmasters in their teaching of pre-graduating classes and moved closer to a more academically respectable fixed salary situation so that their income did not rise and fall merely on the number of students whom they could attract (rather in the style recently advocated by the Prices and Incomes Board), they were nevertheless clearly unwilling to abolish the Ordinary Arts classes which gave the university its basic income. In order to catch the market. the Scottish universities could not afford until much later to ignore the wishes of the professional associations or the Chambers of Commerce in the way that Oxford and Cambridge had earlier ignored the (in English early nineteenth-century terms) non-élitist professions of medicine and engineering. Yet, even so, despite the fact that the Scottish secondary teachers, in particular, had achieved growing academic prestige, the teachers in particular, had achieved growing academic prestige, the internal vested interests of the university could still prevent full Scottish acceptance of modern languages as academic subjects until well into this century, while Geography and History were not even recognized as independent secondary school subjects for university entrance purposes until 1939—and this despite Scotland's legitimate boast, a century earlier, of the comparative width of her curriculum.

At the same time, the laws of commerce being what they are, even the older English universities could not overnight abandon their original, less intelligent or less prestigious clientele. Indeed, reforms at Cambridge did not prove immediately attractive in commercial terms. In 1858, the reforming master of Pembroke, for example, found himself with a total lack of any undergraduate entry. Nor did reforms automatically change the nature of such catchment as there was. Rothblatt has demonstrated that the nature of the families (principally clergy families) patronizing Sidney Sussex remained largely constant between 1815 and 1900; while the academic stimulation to the growth of meritocracy supposed to be afforded by the opening up of closed scholarships did little, immediately, to encourage a greater influx of intelligent students from schools of lower social status.

Even now, it is doubtful whether Oxford and Cambridge would have totally abandoned their residual habit of reserving college places for the academically mediocre games-player and the *filius alumni* or whether, in Scotland, universities would have screened Ordinary candidates quite so carefully as they do now, had not two quite new economic factors played an ever-increasing part in university development following 1945. The first was, of course, the enormous expansion of research grants and a growth in the availability of money on such a scale that the old economic primacy of caring for the actual teaching of the undergraduates could, except in so far as research itself needed a supply of the most able students, be largely set aside. Indeed, it is interesting to see how the departments now most given to defending the high-level teaching of undergraduate classes (as opposed to giving primacy to research) or even to defending the Scottish Ordinary courses on academically doctrinal grounds, are often those, such as Philosophy or Modern Languages, which have not such ready access to large research grants and depend for the adequate staffing of their more élitist and prestigious activities on the continual existence of a large underbelly of mediocre students.*

The second factor, of course, was the vast new provision of state aid not only in capital but also in grants to virtually any student who required help. The result was both to end, finally, any residual dependence on the social élite and to make necessary the creation of a quite new form of enforced undergraduate élitism in face of the totally new enormity of the demand for places. This new élitism is now defended by the editors of the Black Papers as the natural and 'traditional' élitism of the British university, yet it was most certainly not the élitism of Professor Cox's own undergraduate days at Cambridge during the early 1950s when the genuinely intellectual élite could still inhabit the same college with many who would now be considered 'unworthy' of a degree course or would have to be content with study in some other sector of higher education. The boundaries of 'worthiness' are remarkably shifting ones and standards are clearly related to the supply of money.

It is, therefore, perhaps, the ultimate irony that those who defend the élitist sanctum from encroachment should often see as their principal enemy that very State, which not only freed the old English universities from sectarian domination, but also freed the British academic from financial anxiety so that, whether as teacher or researcher, he could, for the first time, pursue his élitist tasks in peace, free from all those earlier economic anxieties which could cause Scottish professors to teach and mark the work of classes of 600 or cause Oxford tutors to seek out rich or prestigious games-players of no intellectual distinction in an effort to boost a college building programme.

Typically, it was the State which after 1918 suggested to univer-

---

* Hatfield was cheaper (and overtly lower class) than University College.

sities the desirability of establishing the Ph.D. in the light of the general belief (whether ill-founded or not) that Britain was yet again lagging behind America and Germany and that British universities were, as usual, taking few initiatives to move towards the centre of industrial, let alone general research activities. In an earlier period, most of those who had introduced scientific research into the university sector had, first of all, had to study in Germany or America. Roscoe and Ward had demonstrated at Manchester that a new college, which had, like London and Durham, failed to catch the market could eventually catch it by offering an exciting German-style research-based teaching almost entirely new to Britain and destined later to provide a model for tutorial teaching in Oxford and Cambridge themselves. Earlier still, Thomas Jefferson's plans for the University of Virginia, including many German notions, had provided a major model for English curricular expansion in London and elsewhere.

There is then little evidence that the modern homogeneous, academically élitist sector of higher education known as 'universities' could have come into existence without German and American examples and without the State's continuous support and financial protection. In turn the State has always made it clear that such protection has its price in supervision. As long ago as the Irish Universities Act of 1908 it made clear that when parliamentary investment in a university reached a certain level, it was necessary for the Comptroller and Auditor General to have access to its books. Given the generally low academic standards of pre-U.G.C. days in most university institutions in Britain, it is worth considering just how deep-rooted our academic independence and standards would prove to be if this protection were even gradually removed. Certainly, there is little evidence in the history of the past hundred years to suggest that university élitism is firmly established or that the boundaries between the university and the rest of higher education have been finally and convincingly drawn. We now have a group of élitist institutions enjoying parity of esteem and this group is larger than the equivalent group which existed in the 1930s, but in other ways, the position has hardly changed since then. The low-status University Colleges, taking London external degrees, have been called to higher sevice. Instead, we have the Polytechnics taking the external degrees of the CNAA, whose whole function as a statutory body supervising the work of scattered colleges, is almost exactly that of the pre-1900 University of London, though it trusts the

examining powers of the local teachers far more than that body
ever did. The Open University also clearly serves many of the categories which the London external degree once served (but with, one
hopes, more skilful techniques). The Scottish universities continue to
offer a vast number of non-honours degrees chiefly because the
different career-structure of the country's teaching profession demands it, so that tasks of general teacher education carried out
elsewhere in colleges remain firmly within the university sector.

One can therefore be excused for wondering whether the 'true'
functions of the different sectors of Higher Education are, as yet,
clear and whether firm 'decisions' by apparently autonomous academics in favour of 'centres of excellence' or other sheddings of non-
élitist tasks can ever really be effective so long as the old patterns of
economic arrangements and the old patterns of sociological development remain largely unexplored beneath the present (resented)
blanket of state protection. Certainly planning which takes account
of such patterns will be far more realistic than any based purely on a
false assertion of 'traditional' excellence and a false nostalgia for a
late nineteenth-century Imperial situation which will never return.
University freedom, like artistic freedom, has always depended on
the wealthy patron. Perhaps the State is the only really reliable and
tolerant patron we have left.

Nigel Grant

I:7 Curriculum change
in Eastern Europe

In this comparative study, Nigel Grant looks at curriculum change in Eastern Europe. He identifies five factors that have played a major part in the process of change since the Second World War: (1) the existing traditional educational systems; (2) changes in educational objectives as a result of the coming to power of communist regimes; (3) structural changes in the educational systems, particularly the move towards comprehensive reorganization; (4) changes in the content of education, for example vocational training; (5) the process of assessment and reassessment in practice, followed by further change.

As events are constantly reminding us, Eastern Europe is an extremely complex area. Varying as it does from time to time and place to place, it defies attempts to single out any one country as an exemplar for the whole.... Certainly, the East European countries share many common assumptions; but (as recent tragic developments in Czechoslovakia confirm rather than negate) the common framework of communist rule embraces wide difference of atmosphere, approach, and ways of translating theory into practice....

Again, although we are concerned here mainly with changes in the curriculum, these must be put into context by looking at changes in the structure of the school systems themselves. (This is perhaps a case of a reversal of the classic Marxist formulation—here, form can determine content.) To take one obvious example, the reorganisation of a selective system on comprehensive lines is liable to bring about changes in the kind of curriculum, whether or not this was part of the original intention.

It need hardly be said that educational changes do not occur spontaneously, but come about in response to pressures, many of which arise outside the educational system itself. Nor can they be implemented in a vacuum; the very pressures, indeed, that make felt

In *The changing school curriculum*, Report of a conference held at Bolton College of Education, 13–16 September 1968, Comparative Education Society of Europe (British Section). Reprinted by permission of the author.

the need for change frequently determine the form that the change eventually takes. The factors at work in this process are far too many and complex to attempt anything like a full analysis here; the following, however, may be regarded as the most important considerations in the process of change in Eastern Europe since the Second World War:

1 The existing traditional educational systems.
2 Changes in educational *objectives* in the immediate post-war period.
3 *Structural* changes in the educational systems.
4 Changes in the *content* of education.
5 Assessment and reassessment in practice, followed by further change.

Let us look at these in turn.

1 The existing traditional educational systems

The educational heritage of the countries of Eastern Europe was extremely varied—not only, as one might expect, from one country to another, but within the individual countries themselves. In many cases, the roots go deep, and the present regimes tend to make a great deal of this, even now. This is what one might expect in Poland and Czechoslovakia, where the Krakow and Charles Universities did much to light up the end of the Dark Ages; or in Rumania, where national fervour highlights past as well as recent achievements. But similar attitudes are widespread in Yugoslavia, Hungary and Bulgaria as well; the Bulgarians, in particular, like it to be remembered that the development of literacy (and Christianity) among the Eastern Slavs can be traced to the activities of the Bulgars Cyril and Methodos. But one should not make too much of this. The thread of continuity through the Middle Ages to the present, though real, is rather frayed in places; with the exception of a few universities and secondary schools, the general form of the modern systems can be traced with some confidence to the nineteenth century, under obvious influence from France and even more from Germany.

In an area with a better claim than Belgium to the unenviable title of 'the cockpit of Europe', it is hardly surprising that the school systems reflected national pecularities as far as possible. Amid this welter of variety, however, one can generalise to some extent. Fig. 1

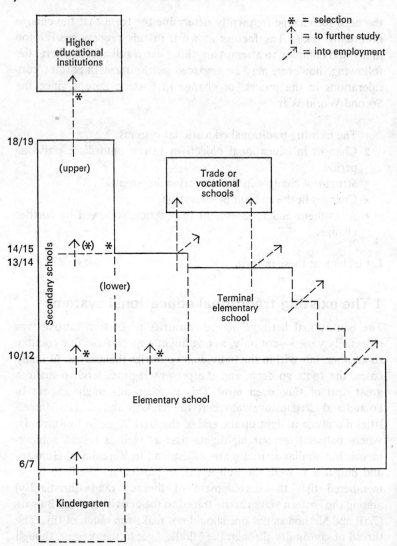

Fig. 1 The basic pattern of schooling in pre-war Eastern Europe

illustrates the basic pattern of the older school systems, which can be characterised thus:

(a) *They were highly selective.* The general rule was early selection, at the age of 10, 11 or 12, of a small minority of pupils for secondary education at the end of 4–6 years of elementary school. For the rest, the usual pattern was terminal elementary schooling up to the age of 13 or 14, from which the pupils went to work. In the more advanced areas, the rigidity of this separation was somewhat mitigated. In Czechoslovakia, for example, terminal elementary schools had been replaced by 'civic' or lower secondary schools, from which one *might* go on to the higher stages of the secondary school or *gymnasium*.

(*b*) *They were highly academic.* The scholastic standards of the *lycées* and *Gymnasien* in Bucharest and Belgrade, Budapest and Warsaw, Prague and Sofia were frequently excellent, quite as good as their western counterparts, and just as uncompromising in their commitment to the mastery of the traditional disciplines. The present-day *lycées* in France or *Gymnasien* in Western Germany give a reasonably accurate idea of the flavour and content of the secondary schools in pre-war Eastern Europe.

(*c*) They were marked by a strong *class orientation.* Good as they were, the secondary schools scarcely affected the mass of the population; they were substantially urban middle-class preserves. Fees were charged, and although there were some scholarships, these were scarce. Inevitably, working- and peasant-class children were rarities in these schools—under 5 per cent in some countries, not much higher anywhere.[1] Not surprisingly, the assumption was that secondary-school pupils would go on to universities and professional or at least white-collar occupations. Not surprisingly, too, the curricula of these schools reflected this assumption.

(*d*) *Technical and vocational education was neglected.* Schools for this type of training were few in number;[2] more significantly, they were narrow in range and content, designed for a type of education fundamentally different from that of the secondary schools. . . .

2 Changes in educational objectives in the immediate post-war period

The coming to power of communist regimes (by various means and of various complexions) led, naturally, to a drive for reconstruction and expansion in education. Any regime, however, would have had to do that, whether left, right or centre politically. More fundamentally, however, there was a change of objectives, an emphasis on ideology, a switch of orientation from *selective* to *mass* systems of education.

This meant, among other things, the 'democratisation' of the school systems, 'bringing the schools closer to life', and changing the ideological bent of the educational process, as numerous statements, then and since, have made abundantly clear. For instance, a statement of the Czechoslovak Ministry of Education in 1949 put it like this : 'All instruction and education, both in and out of school, have but one purpose : to train the rising generation for life in a socialist society. ... The guiding principle of the courses is ... to make culture, training and education democratic. ...'[15]

'Democratisation' meant, in the first instance, opening up the school systems by providing more places. It also meant moving towards some kind of comprehensive reorganization, partly as an obvious way of 'breaking the educational monopoly of the exploiting classes' (to cite an East German source),[18] and also to bring the systems closer to current practice in the USSR. This was particularly apparent in East Germany, where the earliest enactments were made by the Soviet occupation authorities.

'Bringing the schools closer to life', one way and another, was in the air from the beginning. Basically (and most obviously) the needs of industrialising economies called for much greater attention to vocational and technical training at all levels, with consequent shifts of emphasis throughout the educational systems. This would have been necessary in any event—no regime in Hungary, for instance, could have continued long to put up with a university system in which 40 per cent of the students were training as lawyers[19] ...

3 Structural changes in the educational systems

However much they may have wanted to make a break with the past, the post-war communist regimes were in no position to reconstruct the school systems from scratch. Even in the most severely war-damaged and poorly-provided countries, a start had to be made with the buildings, the teachers and, to an unrecognized extent, the values that were there already. A clean break being out of the question, the obvious thing to do was to take the systems as they were, expand them and restructure them as far as possible. Just as the old systems varied, so, necessarily, did the changes. Once again, however, a general pattern can be made out.

(a) Comprehensive reorganization. The East European systems (like others nearer home) were unable to go over to 'custom-built' comprehensive schools on a major scale; they had to adapt what they had to some kind of comprehensive system by stages. This was done in a number of ways. Sometimes, as in Czechoslovakia, the middle or lower secondary school was extended to take in the entire age-range, and amalgamated at a later stage with the elementary school to form a basic comprehensive school. More often, however, the elementary school was simply extended upwards. In either event, the basic elementary schools eventually absorbed the terminal classes, the lower secondary schools, if any, *and* the lower forms of the academic secondary schools as well. These new basic compre-hensives were usually 7-year schools at first, later extended to 8 years; in the case of Czechoslovakia and East Germany, they emerged as 8-year schools, later extended to 9 and 10 years respec-tively. Rumania, incidentally, has recently passed legislation to ex-tend the 8-year school (age 7–15) to 10 years (6–16), but has not fully implemented it as yet.

(b) The remaining classes of the existing secondary schools were retained as upper secondary schools, usually with three- or four-years courses; these can be entered by pupils who have completed the basic comprehensive schools. As a rule, some kind of selection was retained at this stage, and in most cases still is. Alongside these were developed technical or professional secondary schools, provid-ing both professional training *and* complete general secondary edu-cation to leaving certificate level, but on a somewhat narrower basis than in the general secondary schools....

(c) These new types of secondary school not only met a need for professional training combined with a higher standard of general education than before; by the same token, they opened up an alter-native route to further and higher education. This development was taken even further by elaborating an adult education network in a great variety of forms—people's universities, workers' faculties, factory classes, and a system of *general* schools for people who had taken only trade courses after basic school, or for adults who had missed opportunities to finish (or even attend) school in childhood. This provision of an ever-present second chance has been of enor-mous importance in keeping open the doors all the way up to university level, in systems where the final decisions were once made before pupils had entered their teens.

These changes took time, and proceeded at an uneven rate from

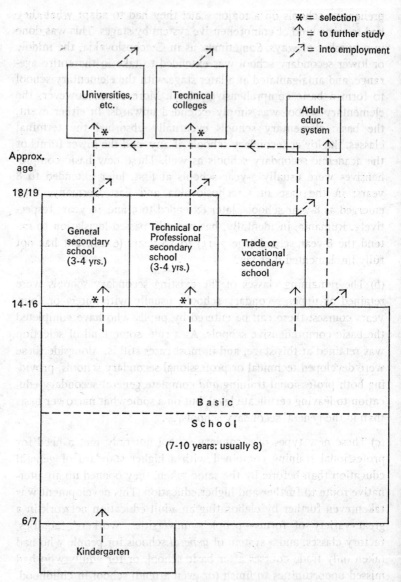

Fig. 2 The basic pattern of schooling in post-war Eastern Europe

country to country; the process, indeed, is still going on. The general pattern of the post-war systems is summarised in Fig. 2, and holds good over most of the area.

4 Changes in the content of education

(a) The development of basic comprehensive schools did not lead to any large-scale restructuring of the curriculum. In what was now the lower stage of the basic school, the emphasis remained on the mastery of fundamentals—the mother tongue, mathematics, music and art, with a newcomer, work training. As can be seen from a glance at any of the curricula, this is still the general pattern, with an overwhelming stress on mother tongue and mathematics (particularly arithmetic) in the first three or four years. The principal change was in the range of pupils rather than in the range of content, in the upper stages of the basic school. This now took into one type of school all those who had formerly gone to terminal elementary classes, lower secondary schools and academic secondary schools alike; but in this new unified school the curriculum was substantially that of the lower forms of the academic secondary school—the same subjects (modern languages, mathematics, history, geography, sciences), but now offered to the entire age-range.

There were some changes, of course. The classics suffered a decline (though nothing like their near-obliteration in the USSR); by contrast, science courses were given a new emphasis. Generally, the first foreign language taken by the great majority of pupils was Russian; this is still the case, except in Yugoslavia and Rumania, where a choice is offered from Russian, English, French or German. (In Rumania, French is the usual first choice, in Yugoslavia, English. In the other countries, a foreign language other than Russian has to wait until the pupils enter the upper secondary school.) There were also, as we shall see presently, attempts to introduce a significant element of polytechnical and work training.

On the whole, however, the most obvious result of 'going comprehensive' (in marked contrast to the earlier and much more gradual analogous process in the USA) was the development of a substantially uniform curriculum right across the age-range. The traditional curriculum, with the usual hallmarks of 'real' secondary education—sciences, foreign languages, etc.—originally designed for a selected minority, was now the curriculum for every child at the same stage, regardless of social background, vocational intention, or scholastic aptitude.

This development was probably due in large measure to the egalitarian philosophy behind the reforms, partly to the common Marxist reluctance to give more weight than can be helped to innate differences of ability (though not, as is often alleged, denying the existence of these differences),[29] and partly to the attempt to encourage the growth of a unified, classless common culture....

(b) The 1958 'Khrushchev reforms' in the USSR were followed in short order by similar enactments in Eastern Europe, with similar emphasis on polytechnical education and labour training in the schools coupled with production practice in factories and on farms. In spite of subsequent re-examinations of the practical applications of this policy, in Eastern Europe as in the USSR, it remains an important feature of the educational systems. The most recent school law in East Germany, for instance, states: 'Polytechnical upbringing and education is a basic feature and integral part of instruction in all school classes. In accordance with the pupils' age, lessons are to be combined with socially useful or productive work. In the junior grades, crafts are the nucleus of polytechnical education, and from class 7 onwards instruction in social production.'[31] ...

(c) *Ideology*. The changes in the content of education arising from directly ideological considerations took two forms. In the first place, the secondary schools and higher educational institutions introduced required courses in political theory, along much the same lines as the USSR. In the immediate post-war period, at least, variations were slight—this was the time, after all, of full-blown Stalinist orthodoxy, and the content of such courses was generally both dogmatic and strongly Soviet-oriented; Czechoslovak schools, for instance, taught courses on the constitution of the USSR as well as of Czechoslovakia. There were some exceptions; in Yugoslavia, the break with the Cominform was followed by attempts to restate Marxist principles in indigenous rather than Soviet terms, courses in civics were made much less rigid and more concerned with the social organization of Yugoslav society, while the complusory courses in political theory disappeared from the universities and colleges. In Poland, the national flavour of political courses, never entirely absent, increased in the mid-1950s; until recently, in fact, the specifically political content of the secondary school courses took two forms—'Introduction to Philosophy', and 'Knowledge of Poland and the Modern World'. The flavour of political teaching varied too, of course; even before the relative loosening-up of 1956, there were differences of approach in Poland as compared with, say, East Germany, and these differences became more noticeable as time went on. Once again, however, the fact remains that, whatever differences there may have been, the underlying objectives were shared by all the régimes in the late 1950s and the 1960s no less than during the days of the Cominform monolith—namely, to acquaint young people with the basic ideas of communist theory, convince them of their correctness, and to secure their commitment to their translation into practice.

5 Practice and reassessment

These, then, are the main areas in which the changes of direction of the educational systems have been brought into effect since the war. Many of these changes were quite fundamental, 'breaking the mould' of the pre-war systems. But the post-war changes can obviously not be viewed in any sense as a final act, but as the first stage in a process of continual change and reassessment of practice. Nothing, therefore, stands still for very long, in the curriculum as in other things. Once again, the establishment of mass comprehensive systems, the working out of the polytechnical principle, and the ideological element in the curriculum, have been the main areas where need has arisen and been recognised for re-examination (of means, if not of ends) and for further change up to the present time.

(a) *Unity and diversity in the comprehensive system.* Ironically (and perhaps inevitably) the spread of mass comprehensive education has brought further pressures to bear on the viability of the uniform curriculum. During the period of transformation of selective to mass systems, any marked degree of curricular differentiation would have been suspect as a means of fobbing off the majority with an inferior product. As has been noted already, the very fact that the new mass schools were so like the traditional academic ones in content was in itself one of the attractions to parents who had themselves missed the chance in their own day. But, as the numbers grew in the basic schools, as these schools lengthened their courses, as more and more pupils stayed on beyond compulsory schooling, and as the novelty began to wear off, the strains (never absent) began to make themselves felt. Gradually, the idea of choice and specialisation became more acceptable, helped on by evidence that in some subjects an early start appeared desirable, and, more mundanely, by evidence of overloading of pupils in the schools.

Not that this required, in itself, any fundamental reappraisal; the existence of individual differences in ability and talent, and the need to make some allowance for them, have never been denied in communist educational thinking. The idea of specialisation was not repugnant as such. But the amount of differentiation, and the age at which it can reasonably begin, have been constant bones of contention. Emphasis is still, therefore, on the common core of the curriculum, and concessions to specialisation have been slight. They have been on the increase, however, and the ways of allowing for this differ (of course) from country to country.

It would be tedious to catalogue in detail all the devices used in attempts to provide greater variety within the common framework.... It is in the upper secondary schools that differentiation is most obvious, every system attempting something at this stage. One device is the provision of some time in the programme for optional and elective courses, as extras to the uniform curricula. This is done in Poland and Bulgaria (as in the USSR); but the differences are vast. Bulgaria makes such courses available from class VIII, Poland only in the final year (though in both countries there are a few exceptions to this). In either case, the time for options is modest, two hours a week in Bulgaria and four in Poland, out of a week of about 30 hours. The other favoured device is the alternative course, where most of the time is still devoted to the common core, where practically all subjects are studied by all pupils, whether on the arts or science side, but where the amount of time varies according to the choice of course. Usually, there are two types, namely arts or science, as in Czechoslovakia, Yugoslavia or Rumania. Even here, though, the bias is slight by British standards; in Rumania, for example, science specialists spend 42 per cent of their time on science, 39 per cent on arts subjects, and 19 per cent on art, music, physical education and work training. Arts specialists, on the other hand, spend 47 per cent of the time on arts, 35 per cent on science, 18 per cent on other subjects. In Hungary, there are no less than *nine* different curricula. Again, the common core predominates; but one variant devotes 5 hours a week to work training, another only two, spreading the rest over the other subjects, while courses with more specialised emphases (foreign languages, mathematics, maths and physics, physics and chemistry, chemistry and biology, art, music) devote this time to the special disciplines, trimming a little off the other subjects as well.[36] To anyone accustomed to the pattern of specialisation of the Scottish Higher Grade (to say nothing of the 'A' levels) the amount of specialisation is slight indeed.

Slight though it is, however, it is likely to increase; statements that the authorities intend to 'expand the principle of differentiation of the curriculum contents according to pupils' abilities and interests' become more common every year.

(b) *Polytechnical education.* Polytechnical education and work training have been conspicuously subject to re-examination in recent years, principally because of practical difficulties. It was all very well to increase the time for practical work in factory and workshop, but all to often it has been found that suitable industrial establishments were lacking, or that those that did exist had no adequate training facilities, or even room—many factory managers, it is said, were at a loss what to do with the youngsters sent from the school, or even where to put them. Frequently all that could be done was to put pupils to routine and repetitive tasks, an ineffective procedure both industrially and educationally. The expected social effect—the development of more 'positive attitudes' towards manual work—has also been disappointing in many cases, especially where the work practice seemed more of a waste of time than anything else. Nor have attempts (as in East Germany) to include trade training in general secondary programmes been a conspicuous success; the narrowness of the training often defeated the purposes of *poly*-technical education, and proved to be vocationally pointless too, since the pupils rarely had any intention of following these occupations, having their eyes on higher education rather than skilled trades. Most fundamentally of all, the idea of linking the theoretical sciences with production training—physics and chemistry with industry, biology with agriculture—was frequently left to chance. Merely having them in the same curricula did not, naturally, clarify the links between them; this requires detailed planning of courses, and this was seldom done. Not surprisingly, complaints became commonplace at official and unofficial levels. . . .

(c) *Ideology.* Courses in political theory have also undergone considerable change, but rarely of a fundamental kind. In Poland, for example, the two courses 'Poland and the modern world' and 'Introduction to philosophy' have been replaced by a single course of 'Social Science'. The syllabus, as it happens, covers much the same ground, but makes a more serious attempt to integrate the fundamental theory with the current affairs element.[46] In Hungary, where until recently the secondary school had no *specifically* political courses, a syllabus on 'The basis of our world view' was prepared in 1964 and introduced in 1966.[47] There has been even less change elsewhere; Bulgaria has 'Fundamentals of communism', Rumania 'Scientific socialism', East Germany 'Citizenship'. Yugoslavia spreads this task over sociology, philosophy, social study and civics. In Czechoslovakia, there were indications earlier this year that civics courses were to be given a greater directness and flexibility; it is, of course, too early to estimate further developments in this field in that much-tried country. There have always been differences of approach, and these remain; at present, the nationalist flavour is most apparent in Rumania and Poland, the dogmatist in East Germany and Bulgaria. More than anything else in the curriculum, differences of approach in this sphere tend to reflect changes in the broader political scene, though there is often a delay. Beyond noting that all the countries still continue with political teaching, generalisation about the way of doing it is difficult in the extreme....

6 Conclusion

Changes, then, continue, but so far they have been changes in detail for the most part; the dilemmas remain, and, as we have seen, they arise in the three main areas of policy change since the war. The problems of striking the right balance between common general education and specialist interest; the problem of making the world of work relevant to general education through *meaningful* polytechnical teaching; the problem of effective politico-social education which is not deadened by sloganising yet reaches the required conviction in the end—these are still, fundamentally, unsolved. In the form they have taken they are, of course, peculiar to communist-run systems; yet, *mutatis mutandis*, they pose questions not unlike those facing us, which we too have not yet solved.

Perhaps the basic problem is really that nobody has yet thought out the relevance of 'general culture' in a mass technological society. In the East, as in the West, present-day educational systems have grown out of systems that were essentially designed for the needs of a leisured or professional élite. The ambiguities of traditional general education were not so pressing when only a minority was affected, but the growth of mass systems has thrown them into sharp relief. The outcome in Eastern Europe has often been considerable muddle and ill thought out policy switches, an odd mixture of political radicalism and educational conservatism, and considerable reliance on sentimentality and wishful thinking.

In this situation, it is interesting to note that the temptations of fragmentation and narrow vocationalism have, on the whole, been avoided. The educational systems at least try to work on the assumption that an awareness of science and familiarity with the elements of the humane studies *do* have something vital to offer to the ordinary citizen—that the man of the future should not only be a worker and a citizen, but someone aware of the working of nature and sensitive to the heritage and aspirations of man. In short, through all the hesitations and the problems remains the constant impression that general culture, in the broadest sense—is taken seriously—and that, especially in these troubled times, must surely be a hopeful sign for the generations to come.

Notes and References

1 The figure was higher in Poland (13·7 per cent in all types of secondary school), Zygmunt Parnowski. *Education in Poland* (Polonia, Warsaw, 1958). In Hungary it was 4 per cent, Márton Horváth, 'Public and higher education', in János Veres (ed.) *The experience of building a new society* (Pannonia, Budapest, 1964).

2 E.g. 10,000 students in such schools in Yugoslavia in 1938 (cf. 76,000 in 1960s). 75,500 in Czechoslovakia (cf. 250,000). 207,000 in Poland (cf. over 1 million, 1964). East Germany, with compulsory *Berufsschulen* since 1919, was exceptional. *Statistički kalendar Jugoslavie 1965*. Belgrade 1965; *Polska w Liczbach*, Warsaw 1964; Stanslav Vodinský, *Czechoslovakia: Education*, Prague, 1963.

15 *International yearbook of education 1949*, p. 101.

18 *Vocational training in the German Democratic Republic*, pp. 16–17. (Berlin, n.d.)

19 Erno Bajor Nagy, *A country at school*, p. 55 (Pannonia, Budapest, 1962).

29 *E.g.*, G. S. Prozorov, *Heredity and upbringing*, p. 3 (Uchpedgiz, Moscow, 1960).

31 *Geset* 3 IV, 1, para. 16(2).

36 Muvelodesugi Miniszterium: *Tanterv és Utasitas a gimnáziumok szamara —Ortatervek* (Tankonyvkiado, Budapest, 1965).

46 Ministerstwo Oświaty, *Program nauczania liceum ogolnoksztalcacego*, pp. 158–174 (Warsaw, 1965).

47 József Gert Farkas, Ungarn: Gymnasiallehrplan 'Grundlagen unserer Weltanschauung'. *Informationsdienst zum Bildungswesen in Osteuropa*, 10/11, pp. 50–52 (Osteuropa-Institut an der Freien Universität Berlin, 1965).

John Gardner

I:8 Education as a sorting-out process

Education acts as a selection mechanism for society. The question 'Who should go to college?' translates itself into the more compelling question 'Who is going to manage the society?' John Gardner, one of the leading liberal educationists in the United States, describes the painfulness of the sorting-out process for a society with democratic ideals.

Educational systems have always had a great deal to do with the eventual status of the individuals who pass through them. It was said of German university students at the end of the nineteenth century that one-third broke down, one-third went to the devil, and the remaining third went on to govern Europe.

Americans believe that ability should be recognized at whatever level in society it occurs. They like to think that those future presidents dashing off to school may come from any walk of life.

But as education becomes increasingly effective in pulling the bright youngster to the top, it becomes an increasingly rugged sorting-out process for everyone concerned. This is true today and it will be very much more so in the future. The schools are the golden avenue of opportunity for able youngsters; but by the same token they are the arena in which less able youngsters discover their limitations. This thought rarely occurred to the generations of Americans who dreamed of universal education. They saw the beauty of a system in which every young person could go as far as his ability and ambition would take him, without obstacles of money, social standing, religion or race. They didn't reflect on the pain involved for those who lacked the necessary ability. Yet pain there is and must be.

Although the American people have never explicitly faced up to the realities of the sorting-out process, they have demonstrated in many ways that they sense the painfulness of it. It will be worth our

From pp. 65–69, 70–71 in *Excellence: Can we be equal and excellent too?* by John W. Gardner. Copyright © 1961 by John W. Gardner. Reprinted by permission of Harper & Row, Publishers, Inc.

while to consider some examples of American practice on this point.

Even the most casual glance at our educational system will reveal our great reluctance to put labels on individual differences in general capacity. Consider the broad interpretation we give to the phrase 'college education'. When young people are graduated from high school we discuss those going on to college as though they were a homogeneous lot, all headed for a similar experience. But the truth is that they are quietly but fairly effectively sorted into different paths.

Anyone who has enjoyed a behind-the-scenes view of how a good high school deals with its graduating seniors is familiar with the process. Consider the work of Miss L., assistant principal in an Eastern high school. One of her tasks is to advise the girls who want to go on to college. Miss L. has a clear impression of every girl in the senior class. She has known most of them since they entered high school. She knows what subjects they like and what subjects they find easy. She knows how hard they work and what their hopes are for college. And she knows a great deal about colleges—what the entrance requirements are, and what kind of girl is apt to be happy in what college.

The students need not listen to Miss L.'s advice but usually do. She sends her college-bound girls out along widely diverging pathways —to colleges of the highest possible standards, to colleges of moderate difficulty and so on down to colleges which may actually be lower academically than the best high schools. But though she must appraise accurately the relative standings of colleges and the relative capacities of students, Miss L. will usually not make these appraisals explicit. She will not say bluntly that the student is of limited intelligence and therefore should go to a second-class college. She will tell the parents that their youngster is not 'a natural student' or 'not one of those with a tremendous drive to get grades' and therefore should probably go to one of the colleges 'where the entrance requirements are not quite so exacting.'

Dr and Mrs Roger Barker, American psychologists, recently made an intensive study of the daily lives of children in the small town of Leyburn, England. One of the many striking differences they found between Leyburn and a comparable American town was the degree of candor about differences in ability. In England when a school child gave a foolish answer the teacher was likely to respond with a candid appraisal of his performance and even of his native capacity.

It was not at all unthinkable for the teacher to make some remark such as, 'Johnny, sit down—you're not up to this.'

Such candor is outside the experience of most American observers. The American teacher might say that Johnny had not studied his lesson, or that Johnny was lazy, or that Johnny was inattentive. She might impugn his cooperativeness, or his ambition, or his knowledge. But she would rarely indicate that his ability was limited. We much prefer not to discuss such matters at all. Indeed we are capable of devising rather elaborate institutional arrangements to get around the necessity of telling Johnny that he is at the low end of the distribution of ability.

One point of view to take toward this national peculiarity is that it is nonsensical and that we have developed a ridiculous squeamishness about such matters. Critics trace it to our desire to make children 'happy', to our concern for psychological adjustment. But such critics are barking up the wrong tree. The reason we do not like to label differences in capacity is that individual capacity holds a uniquely important place in our scheme of things.

It must never be forgotten that ours is one of the few societies in the history of the world in which performance is a primary determinant of status. What the individual can 'deliver' in the way of performance is a major factor in how far he can rise in the world. In a stratified society, performance is not an important factor in establishing the individual's status, so he can afford to be less deeply concerned about his capacity. For every step that a society takes away from a stratified system and toward a system in which performance is the chief determinant of status, the individual will be increasingly concerned about his capacity. In our society the individual's future depends to an unprecedented degree on his own gifts.

There are all kinds of individual capacity. . . . But for complex reasons. Americans see appraisals of 'intelligence', however defined, as total judgments on the individual and as central to his self-esteem. Some critics note that we discriminate nicely between excellence and mediocrity in athletics, but refuse to be similarly precise about differences in intelligence; and they attribute this to the fact that we are more seriously concerned with athletic ability than we are with intelligence. Nothing could be farther from the truth. We can afford, emotionally speaking, to be coldly objective in judgments of athletic ability precisely because we do not take these as total judgments on the individual or as central to his self-esteem.

Another feature of our dealing with levels of ability is what I shall call our principle of multiple chances. The European system separates youngsters at ten or eleven years of age on the basis of ability, and begins preparing some for university education, others for less demanding levels of education. This is in many respects an efficient procedure; and some critics of our schools, such as Admiral Rickover, think it would solve most of our problems. It does avoid some of the problems which plague our comprehensive high schools. But in the American view, it presents a host of difficulties, only one of which need be noted here: early separation of the very gifted and the less gifted violates our principle of multiple chances.

We believe that the youngster should have many successive opportunities to discover himself. We postpone as long as possible any final closing of the door on the individual's chances. It is a unique feature of our system that the 'late bloomer' may dawdle or occupy himself with other than educational objectives until as late as eighteen or nineteen years of age (roughly first or second year of college) and still (provided that he is able) not only obtain a college education but go on to become a professional man....

It is not only the late bloomer who benefits by the principle of multiple chances. We now know beyond any doubt that the social and cultural influences of the home have a good deal to do with both motivation and performance in school. The child growing up in a home barren of educational or cultural influences may require a longer exposure to school before he wakes up.

The practice followed by many of our public universities of accepting all high school graduates who apply and then weeding them out in large numbers during freshman year is partly a response to political pressures. But it is also warmly defended by many in terms of our principle of multiple chances. It can be argued that it is better to let a student try and fail—and in failing discover his own inadequacy—than to tell him he is not good enough to try. Of course, the answer to this would be that the youngster has already had many chances to prove himself before he reaches college. True, says the defender of the system, but the extraordinary symbolic importance which college education is gaining in our society may require that the youngster be given one further try. It can be argued that allowing young people to discover their own inadequacies is a pretty sensible social strategy.

The powerful impulses on the part of the American people to temper the wind to the less able youngsters make the critics of

American education grind their teeth in despair. And their despair is not wholly unjustified. But no one has a right to join the critics until he has thought long and hard about the authentic difficulty of the social problem which the American system must solve. The sorting out of individuals according to ability is very nearly the most delicate and difficult process our society has to face.

Those who receive the most education are going to move into virtually all the key jobs. Thus the question 'Who should go to college?' translates itself into the more compelling question 'Who is going to manage the society?' That is not the kind of question one can treat lightly or cavalierly. It is the kind of question that wars have been fought over.

R. K. Harker

I:9 Social class factors in a New Zealand comprehensive

*Despite the ideology of classlessness, and of equal
opportunity for all which exists in New Zealand, this
research indicates that the relationship between socio-
economic origin and the child's level of school attainment
is significant, and of similar magnitude to that reported
by Douglas, Floud, Halsey in the United Kingdom. The
streaming process which exists in nearly all New Zealand
secondary schools (which are exclusively comprehensive)
has much the same effect on the further educational
opportunities of children from particular socio-economic
groups as the selective school system in Britain.*

It is part of the mythology of New Zealand society and of the New
Zealand educational system that it is classless, and opportunity is
open to anyone regardless of social or ethnic origin. The existence of
the 'welfare state', minimum wage differentials, and the universal
non-selective secondary school system have all been held to mitigate
against the development of class inequalities in educational and
vocational opportunities. However, if the basis of class differentials
in education is, among other things, linguistic in origin as described
by Bernstein,[1] then differentials between the educational opportunities of the children of white collar workers and those of manual
workers appear to be likely to continue to operate in a country such
as New Zealand, despite economic equality.

Briefly, Bernstein states that two languages exist simultaneously
in a society. Firstly, a 'public' language (restricted code), known to
all, of a direct, concrete nature, and of the simplest grammatical
structure. Secondly, a 'formal' (elaborated code) of greater complexity and flexibility, and of a more complex grammatical structure, enabling an individual who possesses such a language to
elaborate his experience and build up more complex and differential

Reprinted by permission from *Educational Research*, vol. 13, no. 22, 1971, pp.
155–158, published by the National Foundation for Educational Research.

conceptual hierarchies. It is Bernstein's thesis that a middle class child learns both these linguistic patterns and also learns the situations for which each pattern is appropriate, while the working class child is restricted to the 'public' mode of expression and applies it to *all* situations. Such a view can be used to explain the social class differences in verbal IQ test performance, and later achievement where such a test is used to separate children into different schools or streams.

Bearing in mind the factors set out above, it is the intention of this report to show that the streaming of pupils in a New Zealand comprehensive school performs the same function as the tri-partite selection carried out by many English education authorities. This is to say, pupils from a 'working class' background are at an educational disadvantage just as much in New Zealand as in England.

Method

One large comprehensive school, typical of suburban, co-educational schools throughout New Zealand, was used in the survey. A total of 298 third formers (the first year of entry) from the 1968 intake were used as the sample, and they were divided into four groups on the basis of their father's occupation.[2] Such a grouping does not imply that the author sees New Zealand society as consisting of four social classes: it is simply a device used to try to determine the influence of socio-economic circumstances upon some aspects of educational achievement. The four groups are as follows:

1 *Professional* (P). The children of doctors, solicitors, professors, architects, engineers, accountants, directors of large companies, and high level civil servants (N = 42).

2 *Upper White Collar* (UWC). The children of middle grade civil servants, university lecturers, training college lecturers and secondary school teachers (N = 97).

3 *Lower White Collar* (LWC). The children of small businessmen, foremen, technicians, contractors, salesmen and clerks (N = 84).

4 *Manual* (M). The children of painters, taxi-drivers, railway workers, drivers, factory hands, scaffolders, mechanics, carpenters and fitters (N = 75).

On the basis of these four groups, the scores of the children on a verbal IQ test (Otis) were analysed, together with scores on a reading test (ACER) and an arithmetic test (VG 7). It is on the basis of these scores that the children were streamed. The social class content of the streams was then examined, as were the option choices made by the children. (Apart from a 'core' course, pupils can opt for one of Latin, French, Book-keeping or Modern (woodwork-metalworks for boys, commercial–home science for girls).)

Results

Group	Boys	(SD)	Girls	(SD)	Total	(SD)
P	114·125	14·73	119·6	9·71	115·43	13·9
UWC	107·4	14·48	112·4	12·5	109·7	13·81
LWC	103·77	13·7	106·61	16·0	105·0	13·65
M	99·05	12·75	97·32	15·12	98·27	13·9
All Children	105·66	12·445	107·21	15·1	106·31	14·9

Table 1 : Mean Otis test scores for each socio-economic group

Group	Boys	Girls	Total
P	36·41	42·7	37·9
UWC	32·8	38·53	35·45
LWC	31·6	34·25	32·74
M	29·125	30·75	29·48
All Children	32·09	35·52	33·53

Table 2: Mean score on the ACER reading test for each socio-economic group

Group	Boys	Girls	Total
P	22·47	24·1	22·85
UWC	21·37	22·25	21·77
LWC	18·92	22·06	20·26
M	17·5	18·09	17·53
All Children	19·87	21·21	20·43

Table 3: Mean score on the VG 7 arithmetic test, by socio-economic group

As can be seen from Tables 1, 2 and 3, the relationship between socio-economic group and achievement is consistent and significant and of a similar order to that found in England.[3] With such a pattern emerging in the tests, then it is to be expected that the professional group would get proportionally more places in the upper streams and be more likely to choose the academic options (bearing in mind parental influence in this latter case).

Table 4 shows that the Professional group has 60 per cent of its members in the top three streams, while the Manual group has only 1·3 per cent. Conversely, the bottom three streams contain half the Manual group, but only five per cent of the Professional group. Bearing in mind that the majority of the future university students in the total group can be expected to come from the top streams,

Group	Top Streams (Latin, 1 and 2)			Bottom Streams (6, 7 and 8)		
	Boys	Girls	Total	Boys	Girls	Total
P	56	70	60	6	0	5
UWC	46	53	50	21	11	16
LWC	35	31	32	33	36	35
M	12	15	13	49	50	49

Table 4 : Percentage of each socio-economic group in the top and bottom streams

then already, in the first year of secondary schooling, the proportion of Manual group children in the most favoured group for further education is greatly reduced. This characteristic of the Manual group is reinforced by Table 5, Option choice.

Group	Latin			French			Book-keeping			Modern		
	Boys	Girls	Total	Boys	Girls	Total	Boys	Girls	Total	Boys	Girls	Total
P	47	50	48	31	30	31	16	10	14	3	10	5
UWC	19	22	21	42	51	46	29	13	22	10	13	12
LWC	12	11	12	15	14	14	29	22	26	46	53	49
M	0	6	3	5	12	8	34	15	25	61	68	64

Table 5 : Option choice by socio-economic group (percentages)

This table indicates a marked preference for the more academic subjects on the part of higher socio-economic groups (79 per cent for P group against 11 per cent for the M group—Latin and French combined). The clustering of the lower socio-economic groups in the 'Modern' option (woodwork, metalwork) could be seen as indicating a preference for 'concrete' learning as opposed to the more abstract nature of a foreign language. It could be hypothesized that it is the nature of verbal learning in the lower class home which restricts their children to this option choice, but more detailed research would be needed to establish this. The influence of socio-economic background can be highlighted in this respect by examining option choice, holding IQ score constant at a low-average level (95–105).

Table 6 shows that despite the fact that the Manual group children in such a range will be inherently more able than the Professional group (due to the verbal loading factor in favour of the pro-

Group	Latin	French	Book-keeping	Modern
P	—	3	2	1
UWC	1	7	7	3
LWC	—	6	8	12
M	—	2	5	19

Table 6 : Option choice by fathers' occupation (Otis scores constant).
No. of children

fessional group), the Manual pupils are clustered at the vocational, non-academic end of the scale, while the higher groups move progressively into the academic options.

Discussion

The school does not select children on the basis of socio-economic background directly, but selects on the basis of verbal ability, which indirectly achieves the same purpose. The linguistic differential, as outlined by Bernstein, can be seen to have a marked effect upon educational achievement and the possibilities of further education. This is not to say, of course, that the school should change its criteria of internal selection, for without adequate and confident verbal ability it is not likely that a student will succeed in higher education. Rather does this evidence suggest that the primary schools have failed to cater for the linguistic impoverishment of lower socio-economic group children. The abolition of streaming (or of the 11-plus in the English context) merely seeks to cure a symptom rather than to attack the real cause—the *linguistic* impoverishment of the home and neighbourhood of the *economically* impoverished.

This problem is even more serious in New Zealand since Maori children come very largely from the lower socio-economic group and are therefore doubly handicapped at school. On the one hand they suffer all the disabilities of the European child from the lower socio-economic group, and on the other, the school makes few concessions to their culture, its value or its language. The same situation exists in England with regard to the children of immigrants and the situation in both countries demands action:

1. in terms of linguistic enrichment programmes at pre-school and primary school;
2. the adaptation of the school to the children it is trying to teach.

The alternative to such action in multi-racial societies is the increasing solidification of classes along ethnic lines and the creation of an explosive social situation.

Notes and References

1 Bernstein. B. 'Some sociological determinants of perception'. *Brit. J. Sociol.*, 9 June 1958. 159–174. But see Jensen, A. R., 'How much can we boost IQ and scholastic achievement?', *Harvard Educ. Rev.*, vol. 39. no. 1. Winter 1969, 1–123, for the likely limits of such environmetal factors.
2 The grouping is my own, as the standard New Zealand classification of occupations (that of Congalton, A. A. and Havighurst, in the *Austral. J. Psychol.*, vol. 6, 1954) is in need of revision.
3 See, for example, Douglas J. W. B., *The home and the school.* London, Mac-Gibbon and Kee, 1964, or Floud, J. and Halsey, A. H., 'Social class intelligence tests, and selection for secondary schools, in Halsey, A. H., Floud, J. and Anderson, C. A., *Education, economy and society*, 209–215. New York, Free Press, 1961.

Marten Shipman

I:10 Curriculum for inequality

*While comprehensive reorganization in the United
Kingdom is beginning to bring together the education of
the academic élite and the education of the non-academic
majority, there are signs that the various innovations in
curriculum development are actually strengthening the
old divisions. Both in content and teaching method the
new Schools Council curricula for the average child
differ markedly from the traditional 'O'- and 'A'-level
work. Academic, discipline-centred, formal, exam-oriented
work for the few and integrated, interdisciplinary,
contemporary work for the many, may divide education
into two systems in the 1970s as effectively as selection
has done in the past.*

The consequences of reforms in education have often disappointed
the reformers and distorted their intentions. As the rate of social
change increases and the schools come under greater pressure to
accept innovations, the importance of trying to anticipate these
unintended consequences increases. Sociologists particularly have
been active, not only in showing that the emerging school system
favoured children from middle class homes, but in pressing for de-
streaming and comprehensive education as steps to remedy the
inequality. Yet it is difficult to view new forms of school organisation with optimism. Furthermore, it may be that this drive for a
fairer school system is being counteracted by contemporary curriculum developments. Both movements are being promoted by reformers anxious to improve the quality of education for all, but
they may be cancelling each other out, or even producing a greater
divide than ever between the education of the elite and the majority.

These unintended consequences of curriculum development are
coming less from actual content than from the introduction of new
courses into a school system that is still clearly divided into two
sections, one geared to a system of external examinations, the other

Revised and shortened version of a paper read to the British Sociological Association Annual Meeting, 1969. Reprinted by permission.

less constrained. The former is closely tied to the universities and is within established academic traditions. The latter has a short history and is still in its formative stage. It is the consequences of innovation into these two separate sections rather than the curriculum themselves which may be producing a new means of sustaining old divisions.

The struggle to revise the curriculum to make it more relevant to the contemporary world has had most success in the primary schools which are furthest removed from the universities and employment. But even here, the moves to involve children in active learning and to give a lower priority to the memorisation of facts have not come evenly. While there may now be less constriction of primary school curriculum due to selection procedures, the persistence of streaming as the most common way of organising junior schools means that there is usually a difference in both the content and the methods of teaching the higher and lower streams once the children get older. The top stream is prepared for the curriculum of the grammar school or stream, while the lower forms anticipate the developments in the secondary schools for those who will not go on to higher education.

The constraints on the secondary school curriculum for those who are assumed to be heading for higher education are strong. They come mainly from the universities through their O and A level entry requirements. The G.C.E. examinations act to support a concentration in the schools on a narrow range of subjects and on formal teaching within these. Employers too reinforce these constraints by asking for formal qualifications that present any teacher wanting to experiment with the dilemma that he may be jeopardising the future of his pupils if he diverges from the traditional academic pattern. Consequently there has been a resistance to innovation for those taking external examinations and those that have been accepted have been within traditional subject boundaries, do not involve the loss of possible examination passes through any merging of previously separate subjects and rarely involve a break from formal teaching methods.

However, while the universities have acted to inhibit innovation in the education of their potential intake, they have been sharing in promoting new curriculum for those who will go into employment or further education straight from school. It is the anomaly of the universities acting on the one hand to limit innovation for those they want and on the other to stimulate change in the education of those they will never teach that is crucial in the new divisions that are emerging.

The Newsom Report acted to accelerate the re-thinking of the education of the average and below average child to whom it gave its name. Yet foreign observers looking at this report have noted, not only its built-in assumption that there should be a different sort of education for the above and below average child; but that the British public accepted this division as normal. Even more important, this report recommended that courses should be made relevant to the life that this majority would live. Whether called 'outgoing' or 'life adjustment' courses, they are now being introduced and welcomed into the schools. At a time when the climate is favourable for innovation and the problems of teaching poorly motivated children are great, the new curriculum have found ready access, particularly where they can offer teaching materials or kits.

There was an obvious need for a reform of the teaching of the average and below average children. The diluted academic education based on the traditional grammar school curriculum was often a source of frustration for both staff and pupils in secondary modern schools. Relevance to the life of the children was an obvious criterion for use in designing new courses. However, the concentration of resources on developing relevant courses within new subject boundaries has contrasted too sharply with the parallel developments for the above average pupils, where the priority has left the traditional subject framework intact. It is this difference in priorities rather than the actual content of each development that is the source of concern.

Behind many of these developments, particularly in the humanities, lies the Schools Council, whose terms of reference are to review curriculum, teaching methods and examinations and assist the schools to meet the needs of their pupils and those of the community as a whole. The Nuffield Foundation has backed many projects financially and the universities have supplied many of the staff for the projects. Innovation is now fully institutionalised.

The new curriculum, involving topic centred approaches, interdisciplinary enquiry, projects taking the children outside the school and experience of social service and working conditions, will probably increase the motivation of the pupils and give them an insight into the working of the world around them. They are often lacking in real academic discipline and at worst can be a pot-pourri of trivia chosen because they are believed to be of interest to the young. But regardless of their worth, they could separate the education of the Newsom child from that of the future elite as effectively as when these groups were educated in different schools or systems. The content of these courses is diverging from that found in O and A level syllabuses and there has been a simultaneous separation in the teaching methods employed. The Newsom report continued a tradition of separate kinds of schooling, and these developments, however praiseworthy in themselves may prove a way of maintaining this divide. At the top of the secondary school, the contrasting content and methods effectively separate those whose full time education will continue and those who will go into employment direct. The further down the school the new integrated courses spread, the more difficult it will be for anyone to be promoted successfully into formal academic work in traditional subjects.

The best way of confirming this trend is to compare the Working Papers of the Schools Council with the syllabuses of the various G.C.E. and even C.S.E. examination boards. These give a glimpse of two different and diverging worlds of education. One is firmly planted in revered academic traditions, is adapted to teaching from a pool of factual knowledge and has clearly defined, if often irrelevant subject boundaries. The other is experimental, looking to America rather than our own past for inspiration, focusses on contemporary problems, groups subjects together and rejects formal teaching methods. One emphasises a schooling within a framework of external examinations, the other attempts to align school work to the environment of the children. The projects in O and A level courses in Mathematics, Sciences and Languages financed by the Nuffield Foundation have produced teaching material for traditional subjects after considering the key elements in each discipline. The parallel developments in the Humanities under the Schools Council have started instead by considering relevance as a basis for choosing new content, materials and teaching methods, regardless of the usual subject categories.

As a consequence, most grammar schools or grammar school streams in comprehensive schools have changed little and are clear about their objectives and responsibilities within a narrow curriculum. In contrast, schools or streams catering for the majority have not only had little time to establish aims, content and methods, but are under continual pressure to accept new ideas. Secondary modern and comprehensive school headteachers are exposed, not only to requests to introduce new courses, new subjects, teachers qualified in new subjects, counsellors and teacher-social workers, but are being pressed to welcome these developments by local advisers, in-service courses, and official publications such as the Schools Council working papers, the D.E.S. Reports on Education, Dialogue and Trends. But new developments are only welcomed if they do not disturb the examination streams or reduce the number of subjects that can be taken by these pupils.

The consequent changes may divide education into two systems in the 1970s as effectively as selection has done in the past. It may be that in a technological society a minority educated to administer and a majority educated to enjoy leisure and reconciled to a super-fluous role will be appropriate. But an elite schooled in academic disciplines and the rest knowledgeable about clothes, pop culture, the local environment and family life around the world will not be a just division of culture and was not the objective of those who have been pressing home the changes that are creating this separation.

This warning is not an attack on either parts of the evolving system. Any remedy will need action at both ends. The search for a relevant and interesting education for the 'Newsom' sector is worthwhile, but it should not make the mistakes the Americans are now trying to remedy. Relevance and interest should not exclude academic discipline and more resources should be allocated to improving the teaching of the traditional subjects. Conversely, the curriculum of those going on to higher education could probably benefit from some erosion of subject boundaries, the introduction of more active methods of learning and the use of relevance as one criterion for selecting content. The overlapping of criterion would not only halt the drift apart of the education of these two groups, but might improve the quality of the innovations for both.

Secondly there is a need for more informed scepticism at this time when innovation is respectable. The evaluation of new schemes should be given a high priority at an early stage of their development. Once backed by kits and text books they will become the new orthodoxy. At the same time action is needed to speed up change in the education of the future elite, even if this means overcoming the resistance of the universities and the examination boards. Only if change occurs in all parts will contact be maintained between the two wings of schooling.

Finally there is a need to shift the focus of research into education by the social sciences from the processes of selection to the curriculum as an agency of discrimination. Social scientists can take much of the credit for illuminating the relation between education and social background. But the unanticipated result of their recommendations may have been to alter only the way in which this relation is maintained rather than to reduce the unfairness which it produces. It may even be that the maintenance of inequality through the curriculum is not only more subtle, but also more effective than depending on more obvious selection procedures.

Paul Goodman

I:11 Freedom and learning: the need for choice

One of the most outspoken radicals in contemporary American education, Paul Goodman, here argues for a dismantling of the present curriculum. Drawing on a number of progressive ideas, he calls for the end of compulsory schooling and in its place suggests a system of multiple options where each individual learner could find an interesting path, with plenty of opportunity for backtrack and change.

The belief that a highly industrialized society requires twelve to twenty years of prior processing of the young is an illusion or a hoax. The evidence is strong that there is no correlation between school performance and life achievement in any of the professions, whether medicine, law, engineering, journalism, or business. Moreover, recent research shows that for more modest clerical, technological, or semi-skilled factory jobs there is no advantage in years of schooling or the possession of diplomas. We were not exactly savages in 1900 when only 6 per cent of adolescents graduated from high school.

Whatever the deliberate intention, schooling today serves mainly for policing and for taking up the slack in youth unemployment. It is not surprising that the young are finally rebelling against it, especially since they cannot identify with the goals of so much social engineering—for instance, that 86 per cent of the federal budget for research and development is for military purposes.

We can, I believe, educate the young entirely in terms of their free choice, with no processing whatever. Nothing can be efficiently learned, or, indeed, learned at all—other than through parroting or brute training, when acquired knowledge is promptly forgotten after the examination—unless it meets need, desire, curiosity, or fantasy. Unless there is a reaching from within, the learning cannot become 'second nature', as Aristotle called true learning. It seems stupid to decide *a priori* what the young ought to know and then to

Saturday Review, May 1968, pp. 73–75. Copyright 1968 Saturday Review Inc. Reprinted by permission.

try to motivate them, instead of letting the initiative come from them and putting information and relevant equipment at their service. It is false to assert that this kind of freedom will not serve society's needs—at least those needs that should humanly be served; freedom is the only way toward authentic citizenship and real, rather than verbal, philosophy. Free choice is not random but responsive to real situations; both youth and adults live in a nature of things, a polity, an ongoing society, and it is these, in fact, that attract interest and channel need. If the young, as they mature, can follow their bent and choose their topics, times, and teachers, and if teachers teach what they themselves consider important—which is all they can skillfully teach anyway—the needs of society will be adequately met; there will be more lively, independent, and inventive people; and in the fairly short run there will be a more sensible and efficient society.

It is not necessary to argue for free choice as a metaphysical proposition; it is what is indicated by present conditions. Increasingly, the best young people resolutely resist authority, and we will let them have a say or lose them. And more important, since the conditions of modern social and technological organization are so pervasively and rigidly conforming, it is necessary, in order to maintain human initiative, to put our emphasis on protecting the young from top-down direction. The monkish and academic methods which were civilizing for wild shepherds create robots in a period of high technology. The public schools which did a good job of socializing immigrants in an open society now regiment individuals and rigidify class stratification.

Up to age twelve, there is no point to formal subjects or a prearranged curriculum. With guidance, whatever a child experiences is educational. Dewey's idea is a good one : It makes no difference *what* is learned at this age, so long as the child goes on wanting to learn something further. Teachers for this age are those who like children, pay attention to them, answer their questions, enjoy taking them around the city and helping them explore, imitate, try out, and who sing songs with them and teach them games. Any benevolent grownup—literate or illiterate—has plenty to teach an eight-year-old; the only profitable training for teachers is a group therapy and, perhaps, a course in child development.

We see that infants learn to speak in their own way in an environment where there is speaking and where they are addressed and take part. If we tried to teach children to speak according to our own theories and methods and schedules, as we try to teach reading, there would be as many stammerers as there are bad readers. Besides, it has been shown that whatever is useful in the present eight-year elementary curriculum can be learned in four months by a normal child of twelve. If let alone, in fact, he will have learned most of it by himself.

Since we have communities where people do not attend to the children as a matter of course, and since children must be rescued from their homes, for most of these children there should be some kind of school. In a proposal for mini-schools in New York City, I suggested an elementary group of twenty-eight children with four grownups: a licensed teacher, a housewife who can cook, a college senior, and a teen-age school dropout. Such a group can meet in any store front, church basement, settlement house, or housing project; more important, it can often go about the city, as is possible when the student–teacher ratio is 7 to 1. Experience at the First Street School in New York has shown that the cost for such a little school is less than for the public school with a student–teacher ratio of 30 to 1. (In the public system, most of the money goes for administration and for specialists to remedy the lack of contact in the classroom.) As A. S. Neill has shown, attendance need not be compulsory. The school should be located near home so the children can escape from it to home, and from home to it. The school should be supported by public money but administered entirely by its own children, teachers, and parents.

In the adolescent and college years, the present mania is to keep students at their lessons for another four to ten years as the only way of their growing up in the world. The correct policy would be to open as many diverse paths as possible, with plenty of opportunity to backtrack and change. It is said by James Conant that about 15 per cent learn well by books and study in an academic setting, and these can opt for high school. Most, including most of the bright students, do better either on their own or as apprentices in activities that are for keeps, rather than through lessons. If their previous eight years had been spent in exploring their own bents and interests, rather than being continually interrupted to do others' assignments on others' schedules, most adolescents would have a clearer notion of what they are after, and many would have found their vocations.

For the 15 per cent of adolescents who learn well in schools and are interested in subjects that are essentially academic, the present catch-all high schools are wasteful. We would do better to return to the small preparatory academy, with perhaps sixty students and three teachers—one in physical sciences, one in social sciences, one in humanities—to prepare for college board examinations. An academy could be located in, and administered by, a university and staffed by graduate students who like to teach and in this way might earn stipends while they write their theses. In such a setting, without dilution by nonacademic subjects and a mass of uninterested fellow students, an academic adolescent can, by spending three hours a day in the classroom, easily be prepared in three or four years for college.

Forcing the nonacademic to attend school breaks the spirit of most and foments alienation in the best. Kept in tutelage, young people, who are necessarily economically dependent, cannot pursue the sexual, adventurous, and political activities congenial to them. Since lively youngsters insist on these anyway, the effect of what we do is to create a gap between them and the oppressive adult world, with a youth sub-culture and an arrested development.

School methods are simply not competent to teach all the arts, sciences, professions, and skills the school establishment pretends to teach. For some professions—e.g., social work, architecture, pedagogy—trying to earn academic credits is probably harmful because it is an irrelevant and discouraging obstacle course. Most technological know-how has to be learned in actual practice in offices and factories, and this often involves unlearning what has been laboriously crammed for exams. The technical competence required by skilled and semiskilled workmen and average technicians can be acquired in three weeks to a year on the job, with no previous schooling. The importance of even 'functional literacy' is much exaggerated; it is the attitude, and not the reading ability, that counts. Those who are creative in the arts and sciences almost invariably go their own course and are usually hampered by schools. Modern languages are best learned by travel. It is pointless to teach social sciences, literary criticism, and philosophy to youngsters who have had no responsible experience in life and society.

Most of the money now spent for high schools and colleges should be devoted to the support of apprenticeships; travel; subsidized browsing in libraries and self-directed study and research; programs such as VISTA, the Peace Corps, Students for a Democratic Society, or the Student Nonviolent Coordinating Committee; rural reconstruction; and work camps for projects in conservation and urban renewal. It is a vast sum of money—but it costs almost $1,500 a year to keep a youth in a blackboard jungle in New York; the schools have become one of our major industries. Consider one kind of opportunity. Since it is important for the very existence of the republic to countervail the now overwhelming national corporate style of information, entertainment, and research, we need scores of thousands of small independent television stations, community radio stations, local newspapers that are more than gossip notes and ads, community theaters, high-brow or dissenting magazines, small design offices for neighborhood renewal that is not bureaucratized, small laboratories for science and invention that are not centrally directed. Such enterprises could present admirable opportunities for bright but unacademic young people to serve as apprentices.

Ideally, the polis itself is the educational environment; a good community consists of worthwhile, attractive, and fulfilling callings and things to do, to grow up into. The policy I am proposing tends in this direction rather than away from it. By multiplying options, it should be possible to find an interesting course for each individual youth, as we now do for only some of the emotionally disturbed and the troublemakers. Voluntary adolescent choices are often random and foolish and usually transitory; but they are the likeliest ways of growing up reasonably. What is most essential is for the youth to see that he is taken seriously as a person, rather than fitted into an institutional system. I don't know if this tailor-made approach would be harder or easier to administer than standardization that in fact fits nobody and results in an increasing number of recalcitrants. On the other hand, as the Civilian Conservation Corps showed in the Thirties, the products of willing youth labor can be valuable even economically, whereas accumulating Regents bluebooks is worth nothing except to the school itself.

(By and large, it is not in the adolescent years but in later years that, in all walks of life, there is need for academic withdrawal, periods of study and reflection, synoptic review of the texts. The Greeks understood this and regarded most of our present college curricula as appropriate for only those over the age of thirty or thirty-five. To some extent, the churches used to provide a studious environment. We do these things miserably in hurried conferences.)

We have similar problems in the universities. We cram the young with what they do not want at the time and what most of them will never use; but by requiring graded diplomas we make it hard for

older people to get what they want and can use. Now, paradoxically, when so many are going to school. the training of authentic
learned professionals is proving to be a failure, with dire effects on
our ecology, urbanism, polity, communications, and even the direction of science. Doing others' lessons under compulsion for twenty
years does not tend to produce professionals who are autonomous,
principled, and ethically responsible to client and community.
Broken by processing, professionals degenerate to mere professional-
personnel. Professional peer groups have become economic lobbies.
The licensing and maintenance of standards have been increasingly
relinquished to the state, which has no competence.

In licensing professionals, we have to look more realistically at
functions, drop mandarin requirements of academic diplomas that
are irrelevant, and rid ourselves of the ridiculous fad of awarding
diplomas for every skill and trade whatever. In most professions and
arts there are important abstract parts that can best be learned
academically. The natural procedure is for those actually engaged in
a professional activity to go to school to learn what they now know
they need; re-entry into the academic track, therefore, should be
made easy for those with a strong motive.

Universities are primarily schools of learned professions, and the
faculty should be composed primarily not of academics but of
working professionals who feel duty-bound and attracted to pass on
their tradition to apprentices of a new generation. Being combined
in a community of scholars, such professionals teach a noble apprenticeship, humane and with vision toward a more ideal future. It is
humane because the disciplines communicate with one another; it is
ideal because the young are free and questioning. A good professional school can be tiny. In *The community of scholars* I suggest
that 150 students and ten professionals—the size of the usual medieval university—are enough. At current faculty salaries, the cost per
student would be a fourth of that of our huge administrative
machines. And, of course, on such a small scale contact between
faculty and students is sought for and easy.

Today, because of the proved incompetence of our adult institutions and the hypocrisy of most professionals, university students
have a right to a large say in what goes on. (But this, too, is medieval.) Professors will, of course, teach what they please. My advice
to students is that given by Prince Kropotkin, in 'A Letter to the
Young': 'Ask what kind of world do you want to live in? What are
you good at and want to work at to build that world? What do you

need to know? Demand that your teachers teach you that.' Serious teachers would be delighted by this approach.

The idea of the liberal arts college is a beautiful one : to teach the common culture and refine character and citizenship. But it does not happen; the evidence is that the college curriculum has little effect on underlying attitudes, and most cultivated folk do not become so by this route. School friendships and the community of youth do have lasting effects, but these do not require ivied clubhouses. Young men learn more about the theory and practice of government by resisting the draft than they ever learned in Political Science 412.

Much of the present university expansion, needless to say, consists in federal- and corporation-contracted research and other research and has nothing to do with teaching. Surely such expansion can be better carried on in the Government's and corporations' own institutes, which would be unencumbered by the young, except those who are hired or attach themselves as apprentices.

Every part of education can be open to need, desire, choice, and trying out. Nothing needs to be compelled or extrinsically motivated by prizes and threats. I do not know if the procedure here outlined would cost more than our present system—though it is hard to conceive of a need for more money than the school establishment now spends. What would be saved is the pitiful waste of youthful years—caged, daydreaming, sabotaging, and cheating—and the degrading and insulting misuse of teachers.

It has been estimated by James Coleman that the average youth in high school is really 'there' about ten minutes a day. Since the growing-up of the young into society to be useful to themselves and others, and to do God's work, is one of the three or four most important functions of any society, no doubt we ought to spend even more on the education of the young than we do; but I would not give a penny to the present administrators, and I would largely dismantle the present school machinery.

Part II

Design of the curriculum

Introduction

The way we set about designing curriculum follows logically from what we think curriculum is. A narrow definition of curriculum—to mean just subject matter or content—still is found in the academic reaches of the educational system. The teacher in the grammar school, for example, talks of doing justice above all to the subject matter. The university teacher is intent on covering all the main points of a particular topic. In both cases the statement of content is the statement of teaching objectives. As a result the learner is often expected to do little more than memorize the content to which he is exposed and recall it for the sake of examinations. If curriculum is defined only in terms of content then '...the objectives of education [are] pared down, the methods used are undesirably restricted as well' (Paul Hirst, II:8).

A more complex view of the curriculum is needed if the teacher is to do justice to the content *and* to the learner. Teachers should teach subjects *and* they should teach children. John Kerr (II:5) puts forward a model of the curriculum which contains four elements: objectives; content; methods; evaluation. This is broadly similar to models put forward by Hilda Taba (II:3), Philip Taylor (II:4), John Merritt (II:6) and Paul Hirst (II:8). 'The value of this simple model of the curriculum is that it suggests four basic questions for use in the construction of a new curriculum. What is its purpose? What subject matter is to be used? What learning experiences and school organization are to be provided? How are the results to be assessed?' (Kerr, II:5).

These four basic elements of the curriculum—objectives, content, methods, evaluation—do not constitute neat, discrete categories. They are closely interrelated and each element is influenced by, and influences, the others. The curriculum constitutes a 'system' and curriculum development is in one sense a form of 'systems analysis'. Education, and the curriculum within it, '...has a set of *inputs*, which are subject to a *process*, in order to attain certain outputs. which are intended to satisfy the system's *objectives*. These form a dynamic, organic whole. And if one is to assess the health of an educational system in order to improve its performance and to plan its future intelligently, the *relationship* between its critical components must be examined in a unified vision' (Philip Coombs, II : 2).

A model of curriculum showing its constituent elements does not by itself give any guidance as to which objectives to select, what content, what methods, which types of evaluation. Yet an effective curriculum design must make clear '... what the bases of the selection ... are, as well as the sources from which these criteria are derived' (Taba, II : 3).

This is where the disagreements and controversies begin, because selection involves values and opinions. The basic model of curriculum is straightforward and generally agreed on, but the actual *use* of the model to generate a curriculum is far from straightforward. While it may be difficult to state a particular objective for, say, a mathematics course, it is even more difficult to justify why this objective was chosen in preference to another. 'Curriculum planning is not just a question of whether what is learnt is worthwhile, it is a question of whether or not it is the *most* worthwhile ...' (Paul Hirst, II : 8).

Taking each of the four curriculum elements in turn—objectives, content, methods, evaluation—what are the curriculum designer's criteria of selection, and what are the sources from which these criteria may be derived.

Objectives

Objectives are dependent on such factors as the type of teacher, the level of financial resources, the characteristics of the learner. Belief in the absolute purity of objectives, as if they exist and can be formulated independently of the more mundane facts of life, has led to unrealistic goals that are seldom reached.

Much of the pressure on educationalists to specify their objectives has come from psychologists anxious to evaluate what goes on in classrooms. Behavioural psychologists led by B. F. Skinner claim that most educational objectives are so general as to be unmeasurable. While the overall, long-term aim of a literature course might be 'to develop the child's appreciation and love of great literature', short-term objectives are required which specify visible changes in the learner's behaviour that can be measured. There is a real danger of course of short-term measurable objectives being stressed to the neglect of the necessarily vague, longer term aims. Over-precision in the statement of objectives, defined in narrow behavioural terms, may drive out the richness and diversity of education. Nevertheless, as a result of the behaviourists, a primary criterion for selecting objectives is that they be '... statements of ways in which the knowledge, cognitive abilities, skills, interests, values, and attitudes of students should change if the curriculum is effective' (Musgrove, II:7).

John Kerr (II:5) identifies three main sources from which objectives may be derived: (i) information about the level of development of the pupils, their needs and interests (ii) the social conditions and problems which the children are likely to encounter; (iii) the nature of the subject matter and types of learning which can arise from study of the subject matter. In each of these three areas—the needs of the learner, the state of society, the nature of knowledge—there is considerable disagreement. Bantock (II:9), White (II:11) and Hirst (II:8) disagree, for example, fundamentally about the needs of the 'average' pupil in the secondary modern and comprehensive school, and the nature of knowledge suitable for that pupil.

There is, however, some agreement about objectives derived from each area. Merritt's emphasis (II:6) on the importance of developing the pupil's personal autonomy would generally not be disputed: 'What we must do is to help children to understand their own immediate and long term needs and to appreciate the legitimate needs of others. That is what the syllabus is about. We must help children to learn to satisfy those needs, while respecting the reasonable needs of others. That is what the curriculum is about. We must help children to determine their own life course with due regard for others. That is what education is about.' It is doubtful, however, whether many teachers and curriculum designers would take this as far as John Holt in *How children fail* (Penguin Books, 1964): 'We cannot have real learning in school if we think it is our duty and our right to tell children what they must learn. We cannot know, at any moment, what particular bit of knowledge or understanding a child needs most, will most strengthen and best fits his model of reality. Only he can do this. He may not do it very well, but he can do it a hundred times better than we can.'

Objectives derived from the second source—the social conditions and problems which the children are likely to encounter—will be agreed on to the extent that a view of the 'good' society is agreed on. Musgrove's diagnosis of modern education in this area would be generally approved: 'Our curricula are still geared to a society in which the majority would be engaged in manual work, knowledge once acquired had a permanent value, the age of puberty was 17, life was over at 40, and father never bathed the baby' (II:7). But Musgrove's prognosis, or anyone else's, is unlikely to be generally approved.

There is agreement in the third area—the nature of the subject matter—about the need to move beyond objectives which are just statements of the content to be covered. '... one needs to determine what is learned in two different dimensions: what content is mastered and what mental processes are acquired...'. 'This is noticeable in the curricula for mathematics proposed recently. There is a definite emphasis on content, but its development is related, even though not always consciously, to such objectives as understanding mathematical principles and developing a method of thinking, creativity, and discovery. This is a far cry from the older "content" emphasis which was characterized by sheer mastery of content and manipulative skills with practically no attention to the principles of learning intellectual processes' (Taba, II:3). These objectives, which emphasize the processes a scientist or a historian uses, are often called 'process' objectives to differentiate them from 'content' objectives. A recent science curriculum for the primary school, developed in the United States by the American Association for the Advancement of Science, has analysed the complex set of skills a scientist uses in conducting a scientific investigation. These skills are broken down into a number of processes which the child must master—observing; using space/time relationships; inferring; formulating hypotheses; interpreting data, etc. Within the process of, for exaple, *observing*, a hierarchy of sequentially ordered process objectives is identified. The child starts by being taught to 'identify and name the primary and secondary colours' and this leads through other objectives to the child being able to 'identify and name changes in such characteristics as temperature, size, shape and colour observed in solid–liquid changes'.

The move towards the use of process objectives is traced by Philip Taylor (II:4) to the influence of educational psychologists on curriculum thinking over the last thirty years. Educational philosophers have given the movement further impetus, for example Paul Hirst's organization of knowledge into 'seven or eight distinguishable cog-

nitive structures' (II : 8). Process objectives became fully institutionalized with the publication in 1956 and 1964 of Bloom's famous
handbooks on *The taxonomy of educational objectives*—the first
book dealing with cognitive objectives (II : 12), the second with
affective objectives (II : 13).

Content

Decisions about the second element of the curriculum—content or
subject matter—derive from an analysis of the characteristics of the
knowledge represented by school knowledge and of the characteristics of the learning process. 'When this rationale is not clear, distortions occur in the manner in which content is organized, or else
the content is organized in a manner which makes it "unlearnable" '
(Taba, II : 3). There is an overlap here with the analysis required to
formulate objectives. While it is necessary to separate out the
elements of the curriculum, the separation can be arbitrary. The line
dividing decisions about objectives from decisions about content is
far from clear.

The organization of content stems from the structure of the disciplines and the ways of thinking these disciplines embody. Hirst's
theory of knowledge—embodied in 'seven or eight distinguishable
cognitive structures' (II : 8)—would tend to justify a curriculum
which emphasized the individual disciplines. Both Pring (II : 10) and
Kerr (II : 5) examine theories of knowledge which justify the integration of disciplines within the curriculum. The argument about
discipline-centred versus interdisciplinary curricula is as unresolved
as the argument about the aims and content of secondary education
mentioned above.

Decisions about content also stem from a more practical necessity. 'A method of curriculum development which devotes a long
time to the analysis of objectives and philosophy, and which then
omits the organizing of teaching units, usually results in guides on
paper which do not function in classrooms' (Taba, II : 3). Taba suggests that content must be organized with a view to getting adequate scope, sequence and integration. Scope means identifying
what is to be covered and learned—and this is again two-dimensional in the sense of content and process objectives. Sequence concerns the order in which content and processes are presented to the
learner. 'Much of the confusion and difficulty in developing cumulative and continuous learning comes from the fact that in setting

up sequences in curriculum designs, only the sequence of content is considered, while the sequence of the powers and competencies is largely overlooked' (Taba, II:3). Integration of content concerns the relationship between the learnings in various areas of the curriculum which take place at the same time.

Methods

In selecting and organizing the methods of achieving curriculum objectives, the primary consideration is how the pupil learns. '. . . learning theory as it exists today is a highly inelegant and unfinished entity. Nevertheless, there do appear to be some fairly fundamental and stable principles which serve to tell us what learning is *not*, and to suggest the outlines of what it *is* like' (Gagné, II:14). What bedevils the question of how people learn is the existence of marked individual differences among learners. These differences—in pace, learning strategy, attention span, interest in given subject matter, preference for learning by one medium rather than another —are to a large extent disregarded in the conventional school curriculum where groups of learners move through forty-five minutes and uniform chunks of subject matter. But, Gagné stresses, 'Learning is an individual matter. In a fundamental sense, it is determined by what the learner does, and not by what the material does or what the teacher does. One can even go a step farther, in drawing implications for education. If one is concerned about how to make learning efficient, the focus of emphasis must be the student. The design of efficient conditions for learning demands that learning be conceived as an individual matter.'

Any move towards the creation of an individualized system of learning is influenced at the outset by considerations of resources. Provision must be made—at the curriculum planning stage—for instructional materials, using as wide a range of media as possible. Choice of methods—whether for individual or group instruction—is also influenced by the quantity and quality of teachers available, and often the actual architecture of the educational institution (Glaser, II:17). Methods, like objectives, are constrained by a large number of factors. They do not exist independently of the context in which they are employed.

Evaluation

The fourth element of the curriculum—evaluation—depends on the first element—objectives. Without a definition of objectives, evaluation is impossible. Unfortunately, for education, the reverse is not true. The definition of objectives does not depend on evaluation. The sort of evaluation of objectives done by McNicol (Musgrove, II : 7) reveals only too clearly the discrepancy between claims made for the curriculum and the actual results.

In developing evaluation systems within the curriculum a number of different criteria must be met. They are summarized by Wilhelms (II : 15) as follows : evaluation must '. . . facilitate self-evaluation . . . encompass every objective valued by the school . . . facilitate learning and teaching . . . .produce records appropriate to the purposes for which records are essential . . . provide continuing feedback into the larger questions of curriculum development and educational policy'.

The concept of evaluation as feedback stems from the technology of cybernation and is central to the management process in any field of activity (I : 1). Feedback introduces the dynamic element into curriculum development. Evaluation leads to a recycling of the process of curriculum development, incorporating changes suggested by results achieved and changes in educational thought (Miel, II : 18).

Conclusion

A model of curriculum—containing the four elements of objectives, content, methods and evaluation—enables us to construct a model for designing the curriculum. Designing the curriculum requires us to answer the four questions outlined by Kerr (II : 5)—what is the purpose of the curriculum? What subject matter is to be used? What learning experiences and school organization are to be provided? How are the results to be assessed? The criteria used for answering the questions should be made explicit.

The important thing is that the four key curriculum questions cannot be answered sequentially as is so often assumed in speeches about the curriculum when the teacher is requested *first* to state his or her objectives, *then* to choose the best methods of meeting those objectives. Effective curriculum design requires an iterative process, where each question is constantly being reprocessed in the light of answers to subsequent questions. This can be illustrated most vividly in the relationship between ends and means. Much curriculum discussion is infertile because discussion of objectives is not permitted to be contaminated by discussion of means. Yet the two interact constantly. Form and content are fundamentally inseparable even though we must attempt to separate them out for purposes of analysis.

'Content cannot be divorced from pedagogy. For it is the pedagogy that leads the child to treat content in critical ways that develop and express his skills and values... For a curriculum is a thing in balance that cannot be developed first for content, then for teaching method, then for visual aids, then for some other particular feature.' Jerome Bruner. *Toward a theory of instruction*, The Belknap Press of Harvard University, 1966, p. 164.

One of the continuing problems with operating the 'objectives' model of curriculum planning—which has become something of a sacred cow among curriculum designers—is how to differentiate objectives from content (subject matter). The more precisely the objectives are specified, the more completely is content selected— as a result it can be argued that the demarcation between the two is basically spurious. The objectives model of curriculum planning can lead to a degradation of content—with the 'process' objectives— driving out the more traditional 'content' objectives. 'How the learner thinks' becomes the aim of education—not *what* he thinks. In an article published in *Paedagogica Europaea* (1971, Vol. 7) Lawrence Stenhouse* argues that the play *Hamlet*, for example, cannot just be reduced to a listing of Bloom-type student behaviours: 'To use the play as a vehicle for teaching skills is to imply—and students rather readily pick up the implication—that the skills and vocabulary and so forth are the important matter rather than the play ... the result ... is the use of methods to distort content in order to meet objectives' (p. 62). 'The objectives model of curriculum design and planning', he claims. 'is no doubt a useful one, but it has severe limitations. Accordingly, it is wrong that it should be taken for granted, or advanced as universally applicable' (p. 60).

---

* In II:16 Stenhouse describes the Schools Council Humanities Project of which he is the director. The project is at the centre of the controversy about secondary curricula: see Shipman (I:10), White (II:11), and Lawton (III:6).

II:1 The management process cycle

This is an excerpt from a guide to the use of network analysis in the management of US government departments. It identifies five basic steps that must be taken in any successful management process: (1) definition of objectives; (2) development of plan to reach those objectives; (3) the conversion of the plan into schedules for implementation; (4) regular evaluation of progress against scheduled plans; (5) recycle of process to change plan in the light of evaluation and need for improvement.

The function of management entails the continuous, intelligent direction of others by determining and communicating the prime and supporting objectives of an organization. This function necessarily includes the development and utilization of an integrated time-phased plan of action, demanding reasonable requirements in the way of resources and the subsequent balancing of resources as they are made available and used.

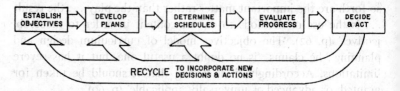

This document emphasizes the distinct form of the cycle of applied effort. The basic steps of this process follow:

the determination and effective communication of the prime and supporting objectives;

the development of a coordinated plan of action for the accomplishment of the objectives;

the conversion of the plan into integrated schedules within allocable resources;

PERT guide for management use, US Government Printing Office, 1963, pp. 1–2.

the regular reporting and concurrent evaluation of progress against the scheduled plan and cost estimates;

the recycling of the above process to achieve the incorporation of a desired new action into a new cohesive scheduled plan.

Establish objectives

The determination and definition of objectives is the initial and most important step in the management process, largely because the objectives of an organization are its sole reasons for existence. All organized activity must have as its motivating and guiding force the attainment of some predetermined objective or objectives. The current purpose or purposes of the organization must be the yardstick against which all requirements and accomplishments are measured and evaluated. The progressive passing down of specific coordinated objectives from higher to lower levels of management sets the target for and the authorization of detailed planning effort on the part of the receiving organization.

The importance of the effective communication of concise planning objectives from level to level of responsible management cannot be over-emphasized.

Develop plans

Given the determination or assignment of an objective, the next step is the development of a plan. The planning function sets forth the nature, sequence, and interrelationships of the supporting objectives which must be accomplished to achieve the prime objective. Planning is primarily concerned with the structuring and relationships of units of required effort. It considers and answers questions of capability by determining in-house versus subcontracting effort. It establishes the feasibility of meeting the directed due date for the successful attainment of the objective. There must be a broad operating plan in existence at the highest level of management to serve as a guide for selection of specific supporting objectives.

This plan must be realistic in its requirements and consistent with the available resources and time. The planning function at each level sets forth the important objectives of the kind, quality, and quantity for the work to be performed. If this planning is not accomplished, there can be no assurance of a coordinated, balanced use of resources. Initial planning considers the required resources, including elapsed time, but does not consider the competition for these resources.

Determine schedules

Scheduling is the bridge from the planning stage to coordinated, effective implementation. It is the translation of the plan, with its elapsed time estimates, into calendar time. The scheduling function considers the competition for available resources both within and between programs. If the earliest attainable scheduled completion date of the current plan is later than the desired date, the manager will pass the plan to the planners for readjustment. If the planners cannot achieve this, they must determine a new completion date with the next higher level of management.

The goal of the scheduling function is to produce a calendar time-phased plan consistent with desired completion dates for the assigned objectives. This schedule is the vehicle for authorizing effort and resources to be expended. It serves as a basis for the continuous evaluation of progress.

Progress evaluation

Once the scheduled plan has been activated a formal procedure for the regular reporting of progress against scheduled plan is necessary. A process for the early detection and specific description of a potentially significant problem area while there is still time for management to seek solutions to that problem is required. The management process described in this Guide emphasizes, therefore :

regular, continuous, evaluation of actual performance against current scheduled plans;

detection and isolation of significant deviations from the scheduled plan as a forecast of time and cost overrun.

The principle of 'significant reporting' effects a great reduction in the volume of statistical reports. By considering only the significant deviations from the scheduled plan, the manager need only obtain a detailed analysis of the specific problem covering :

what remedial action is being taken and by whom?

what results may be expected and when?

Management decisions and actions

The magnitude and relationships of all desired changes must first be examined in the light of their effect on the scheduled plan. Changes may result from alteration in prime objectives or isolation of the problems at any level of effort. The point of origin of the changes is not so important as the orderly method of authoritative approval and implementation.

Deviations from the scheduled plan may require only a change in schedule. Deviation could however require a change in plans, or even a change in objectives. By concentrating on the most important current or forecasted problems, management can expend its efforts to achieve the maximum potential returns relative to the assigned objectives.

A clear distinction must be made as to new action that is within the authority of the operating organization and action which calls for lateral or higher authority. The first can be handled by direction; the second calls for a careful presentation of the facts and a request for the action desired.

Recycle

The incorporation of change is achieved by a recycling of the management process to provide a revised scheduled plan. Dynamic recycling is the method of achieving and maintaining management control of objective-oriented effort. The formal progress, reviews, and evaluation meetings held by management with their supporting managers provide an opportunity to accomplish the mechanics of the recycling process.

Philip H. Coombs

II:2 Systems analysis: a framework for diagnosis and strategy

Philip Coombs, director of UNESCO's International Institute for Educational Planning, takes the technique of systems analysis which has been extensively used in business and government and applies it directly to education. Education is a system in that it has a set of inputs (money, children, etc.) which are subject to a process, in order to attain certain objectives, which appear as outputs (educated children, etc.).

A 'systems analysis' of education resembles, in some respects, what a doctor does when he examines the most complicated and awe-inspiring 'system' of all—a human being. It is never possible, nor is it necessary, for the doctor to have complete knowledge of every detail of a human being's system and its functional processes. The strategy of the diagnosis is to concentrate upon selected critical indicators and relationships within the system and between the system and its environment. The doctor, for example, is concerned especially with correlations between such critical indications as heartbeat, blood pressure, weight. height, age, diet, sleeping habits, urinary sugar content, white and red corpuscles. From these he appraises the way the total system is functioning, and prescribes what may be needed to make it function better.

What the doctor does in his analysis of the human body, modern management does in its 'systems analysis' approach to the operations and plans of everything from department stores to military establishments. The 'indicators' differ from context to context, but the strategy remains much the same. By extension, this is also true of a systems analysis applied to an educational system.

There is no incompatibility between looking at an educational system in this way and the time-honored view that education,

Coombs, Philip H., *The world educational crisis: a systems analysis*, Oxford University Press, New York, London, Toronto, 1968, pp. 8–13. Reprinted by permission.

though a means to many ends, is first and foremost an end in itself. This is not at issue here. What is at issue is the organized *process* by which a society pursues education, and whether that process and its results can be made more relevant, efficient, and effective within the context of the particular society.

In our use of the phrase 'educational system' we mean not merely the several levels and types of formal education (primary, secondary, post-secondary, general, and specialized) but also all those systematic programs and processes of education and training that lie outside 'formal' education. These, called nonformal education, include, for example, worker and farmer training, functional literacy training, on-the-job and in-service training, university extension (extramural), professional refresher courses, and special youth programs. The formal and nonformal educational activities collectively comprise the nation's total organized educational efforts, irrespective of how such activities may be financed or administered.

Even beyond these wide limits, of course, there are a myriad of other matters which, in any broad view of learning, are educative in nature, often profoundly so. They include things that are often taken as much for granted as the air we breathe—books, newspapers, and magazines; movies, radio, and television broadcasts; and above all the learning that goes on daily in every home. For the present, however, we must confine our view to those activities which are consciously organized for the express purpose of achieving certain prescribed educational and training objectives.

An educational system, *as* a system, obviously differs greatly from the human body—or from a department store—in what it does, how it does it, and the reasons why. Yet in common with all other productive undertakings, it has a set of *inputs*, which are subject to a *process*, designed to attain certain *outputs*, which are intended to satisfy the system's *objectives*. These form a dynamic, organic whole. And if one is to assess the health of an educational system in order to improve its performance and to plan its future intelligently, the relationship between its critical components must be examined in a unified vision.

This, however, is not the way we customarily view an educational system. We call it a system but we do not treat it as one. The school board meets to deal item by item with a laundry list of things. Each item is taken up and examined seriatim on its own terms. The daily calendar of the overworked school administrator is typically a similar mélange of 'items to handle'. He moves as expeditiously as he can from one to the next, having little time to reflect on how they impinge on each other, or on yesterday's and tomorrow's calendar of things.

Chart I—to deal with it briefly—presents a simplified diagram showing some of the more important internal components of an educational system. How they interact on each other can be illustrated by the following two examples:

Let us assume that a decision is made to alter the system's aims or priorities in some fashion—for example, a decision to diversify secondary education, to include a new 'technical' track to higher education and new 'terminal' programs with a vocational bias. To implement this decision may require far-reaching changes in the system's academic structure, in the curriculum and teaching methods, in facilities and equipment, and in the distribution of teachers and the flow of students within the structure. In short, virtually every component is substantially affected by such a change.

Similarly, without any change of basic aims or priorities, a significant innovation in the curriculum, such as the adoption of 'new mathematics' in place of traditional mathematics, may entail substantial alterations in teaching and learning methods, which in turn may require changes in the deployment of time, in physical facilities and equipment, and in the number and kind of teachers required. This chain reaction may thus have considerable consequences for the system's input requirements and for the quantity and quality of its final outputs.

Chart I, however, does not show the whole of what must be looked at in a systems analysis. The chart is confined to the internal components of the system, detached from the environment. Yet since it is society which supplies the educational system with the means of functioning—just as the educational system in turn is expected to make vital contributions to society—something more must be added to the picture of systems analysis. Education's inputs and outputs must be examined in their external relationships with society, for these reveal both the resource constraints that limit the system and the facts that ultimately determine its productivity to society. Hence Chart II shows the multiple components of the inputs from society into the educational system, followed by the multiple outputs from that system which flow back into society, upon which they ultimately have many diverse impacts.

EDUCATIONAL PROCESS

1. Aims and priorities
  to guide the system's activities

2. Students
  whose learning is the main aim of the system

3. Management
  to co-ordinate, direct, evaluate the system

4. Structure and time schedule
  to deploy time and student flows among different purposes

5. Content
  the essence of what students are intended to acquire

Resource INPUTS → **6. Teachers**
  to help provide the essence and orchestrate the learning process ← **Educational OUTPUTS**

7. Learning aids
  books, blackboard, maps, films, laboratories, etc.

8. Facilities
  to house the process

9. Technology
  all the techniques used in doing the system's work

10. Quality controls
  admission rules, marks, examinations, 'standards'

11. Research
  to improve knowledge and the system's performance

12. Costs
  indicators of efficiency of the system

Chart I. The major components of an educational system

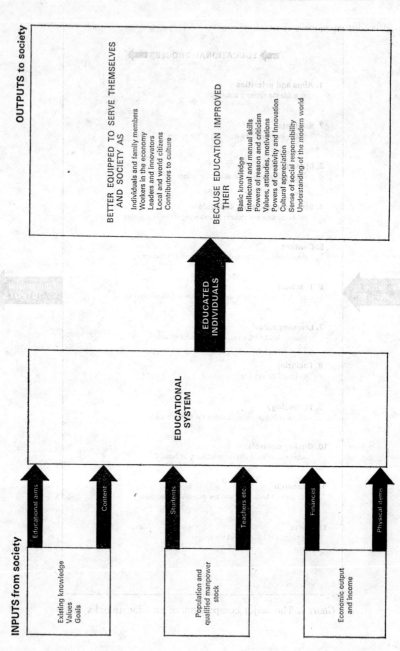

INPUTS from society

Existing knowledge
Values
Goals

Population and
qualified manpower
stock

Economic output
and income

Educational aims

Content

Students

Teachers etc

Finances

Physical items

EDUCATIONAL SYSTEM

EDUCATED
INDIVIDUALS

OUTPUTS to society

BETTER EQUIPPED TO SERVE THEMSELVES
AND SOCIETY AS

Individuals and family members
Workers in the economy
Leaders and innovators
Local and world citizens
Contributors to culture

BECAUSE EDUCATION IMPROVED
THEIR

Basic knowledge
Intellectual and manual skills
Powers of reason and criticism
Values, attitudes, motivations
Powers of creativity and innovation
Cultural appreciation
Sense of social responsibility
Understanding of the modern world

Chart II. Interactions between an educational system and its environment

To illustrate how things interact, suppose that an educational system is called upon to produce more scientists and technologists. For this it needs more specialized teachers, but they are in scarce supply because they are being underproduced by the system, relative to market demand. To raise its production, education must get back from its own limited output of such people enough of them to serve as inputs. But to this end its offers to such qualified personnel must be able to meet the market competition from other users. This may require a considerable change in its teacher-salary policies and structure.

. . . it is in point here to establish a clearer relationship between the two charts—the first dealing with the internal aspects of an educational system, and the second with its external linkages. The relationship can be put in a capsule by postulating the following. First, if external conditions lead to changes in the inputs available to the system—as when a national manpower shortage and an unfavorable salary structure result in a shortage of teachers—the effect within the system may be a decline in the size and quality of its outputs. On the other hand, the input stringency may conceivably provoke a change in 'technology' and in the use of resources calculated to avert a decline in the size and quality of the outputs. The systems analysis thus shows that *there need be no rigid pattern of internal responses* to which an educational system must adhere in meeting external stringencies. Aided by such an analysis, the system is in a position to choose its own response, and the choice it actually makes can have a considerable influence on the quantity and quality of its output, and on its internal efficiency and external productivity.

Hilda Taba

II:3 The functions of a conceptual framework for curriculum design

*The curriculum contains certain key elements—aims and
objectives, content and learning experiences, and
evaluation—which in many curriculum designs are either
missing or not sufficiently interrelated. An effective design
makes clear the criteria for selecting aims and content,
but also goes beyond that to the problems of curriculum
organization. Organization involves moving from a
general analysis of aims to a highly specific statement of
scope (what content is to be mastered and what mental
processes acquired), sequence (the ordering of content and
the ordering of the learner's competencies and skills),
and integration (relationship between the learnings in
various areas of the curriculum which take place at the
same time). Taba recommends organizing the curriculum
around ideas and learner skills, rather than by subjects and
content topics. With ideas as the centres of curriculum
organization, teachers can be free to select and adapt
their own content rather than submit to the tyranny of
uniform, fixed and static content.*

In order to develop a design for a curriculum it is necessary to
identify its basic elements. Tyler, for example, points out that 'it is
important as a part of a comprehensive theory of organization to
indicate just what kinds of elements will serve satisfactorily as
organizing elements. And in a given curriculum it is important to
identify the particular elements that shall be used' (Herrick and
Tyler, 1950, p. 64).

But even among the meager statements about these elements,
there is no consensus as to how to categorize them.... Perhaps one
way of identifying these elements is to consider the major points
about which decisions need to be made in the process of curriculum
development, including such considerations as the principles of
learning and ideas about the nature of learners and of knowledge.
The points of these decisions—the aims and objectives, the content

and learning experiences, and evaluation—then become macro-scopic elements of the curriculum.

Most curriculum designs contain these elements, but many have them in defective balance, mostly because these elements are poorly identified or have an inadequate theoretical rationale. For example, the subject design usually pays relatively little attention to objectives, or defines them in too narrow a scope. The core curricula stress learning experiences but are often defective in describing their content, or else the scope of the content is defective. Many curriculum designs eventuate in a program which is inappropriate to the students for whom it is intended, either because it is based on an inadequate concept of the learning process or because a greater uniformity of learning is assumed than is warranted. Few curriculum designs postulate and provide for the upper and lower limits in achieving objectives according to student backgrounds or for different qualities of depth according to differences in ability. Such defects in design usually pose difficulties in implementation.

An analysis of the curriculum designs described either in books on curriculum or in curriculum guides also reveals that, while each involves something of all elements, these elements are inadequately related to the stated central emphasis. For example, an integrated curriculum will usually contain some provisions for specialized knowledge. An experience curriculum usually includes organized subject-matter content, and a subject curriculum will employ first-hand experiences. Either these 'extras' are bootlegged, or else what are supposed to be black and white differences in the central emphasis are nothing more than an accentuation of one element over others. The main difference among these designs lies more in how the various elements are balanced than in the complete absence of attention to any one element.

With a greater clarity about the structure of curriculum and about its elements, these black and white differences among the various designs should increasingly disappear. This is noticeable in the curricula for mathematics proposed recently. There is a definite emphasis on content, but its development is related, even though not always consciously, to such objectives as understanding mathematical principles and developing a method of thinking, creativity, and discovery. This is a far cry from the older 'content' emphasis which was characterized by sheer mastery of content and manipulative skills with practically no attention to the principles of learning intellectual processes.

An effective design also makes clear what the bases of the selection and the emphases on the various elements are, as well as the sources from which these criteria are derived. It should, furthermore, distinguish which criteria apply to which element. For example, a design should make clear whether its objectives are derived from consideration of the social needs as revealed in the analysis of society, the needs of individual development as revealed by the analysis of the nature of learners and their needs as individuals, or both. In a similar manner, both the choice of content and its organization need to be accounted for by an analysis of the unique characteristics of the knowledge represented by school subjects and of the characteristics of the learning process. When this rationale is not clear, distortions occur in the manner in which content is organized, or else the content is organized in a manner which makes it 'unlearnable'. Some current designs pay too little attention to the needs of society, or the perspective on these needs is derived from an inadequate analysis of the data on culture and society. This results in objectives of narrowed scope, or objectives which are removed from social realities. Still other designs are based on analysis or the content of the disciplines only, with little or no attention to the characteristics of learners or of the learning process. Many curriculum guides involve all these bases implicitly but fail to state them explicitly. This makes it difficult to establish priorities in applying criteria and principles or their combinations.

Designs with no rationale, or a confusing one, result in a curriculum framework with a high overtone of prescription because the requirements regarding content or the nature of learning experiences are difficult to explain and seem to demand a docile acceptance of directives by those who implement the curriculum in the classroom. As a matter of fact, much of the distance between theory and practice may be caused by just such lack of rationale. Such a curriculum also tends to remain inflexible. An implied rationale is not easily subject to examination and revision according to changes in any of the bases on which it was founded. New data which become available on learning or on changes in the cultural needs, in the nature of student population, or of the content are not easily translated into the curriculum. Such a curriculum can be changed only by what could be called an earthquake method of curriculum revision: a periodic reshuffling of the entire scheme instead of a continuous readaption.

Relationships among the elements

It is especially important for a curriculum design to make clear how the various elements and the criteria or considerations connected with them are related to each other. A decision made about any one element out of relationship to others is bound to be faulty, because each element of curriculum acquires meaning and substance in reference to other elements and by its place in the pattern that encompasses all others. For example, the specific objectives derive their meaning from the larger aims of the school. If the main aim of the school is to develop intelligent citizenship, then the development of the ability to think critically becomes important. The fact that critical thinking is an important objective imposes certain requirements on the selection and organization of learning experiences, and this, in turn, makes it necessary to include the evaluation of thinking in the program of evaluation. The type of content organization adopted sets limits on the learning experiences which are possible. The consideration of the nature of the students and their backgrounds determines what approaches to the content and to establishing the sequences of learning experiences are effective. The way in which the content of a subject is organized for curriculum purposes is, in a similar manner, controlled by the structure of the discipline which the subject represents.

If the essence of learning mathematics is the capacity to handle abstract symbols and a system of ideas, then the learning experiences in mathematics need to be designed to develop this capacity. If the essence of literature is to develop empathy and capacity to identify with human values, problems, and dilemmas, then the experiences in learning literature must include activities designed to develop this empathy and not be limited to intellectual analysis of forms of literature, the quality of expression, or information about characters. Often inadequate decisions are made at points involving such relationships partly because of lack of clarity about the nature of the elements, or a failure to see the relationship between the criteria which apply to each of them. We tend to apply first one and then another criterion individually instead of thinking of these criteria as a constellation, in which each has a bearing on the others.

Herrick illustrates the necessity for examining the relationships among the elements of the curriculum by analyzing schematic models for curriculum designs (Herrick and Tyler, 1950, p. 41). One of these is a diagram of the elements of a curriculum and their relationships as seen by the curriculum consultants in the Eight Year Study (Giles, McCutcheon, and Zechiel, 1942, p. i).

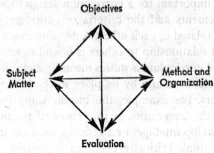

This design describes four elements: objectives, subject matter, method and organization, and evaluation. In essence, it suggests for the curriculum maker four questions: What is to be done? What subject matter is to be used? What methods and what organization are to be employed? How are the results to be appraised? The design also indicates that each of these elements is related to the others and that, therefore, decisions regarding any of them are dependent on decisions made on others.

However, this design fails to indicate the bases on which the decisions regarding these elements are to be made: the sources from which objectives are derived, which criteria, in addition to objectives, govern the selection and organization of content, and what relationships exist among these criteria.

A design also needs to make explicit its relationship to the factors in school organization and the instructional resources which are necessary to implement it. B. O. Smith, Stanley, and Shores include these considerations in their discussion of the various types of curriculum patterns. They point out, for example, that the subject curriculum requires teachers with intensive training in one subject field, that the best training for teachers for the activity curriculum is one which combines broad general training in counter fields with 'specialized training in child and adolescent development, guidance and project methods of teaching'. Flexibility of scheduling and in grouping of students is a special requirement of the core curriculum (Smith, Stanley, and Shores, 1957, pp. 239, 324).

While the organization of the school and its institutional facilities should be shaped to implement the curriculum, the reverse is usually the case. The functioning curriculum is fitted into the existing arrangements and shaped by the limitations in these conditions.

When the conditions necessary for implementing a curriculum design are not fulfilled, a discrepancy between the intended and the actual curriculum is naturally created. It has already been pointed out that a fully integrated curriculum remains an impossibility as long as evaluation and accounting of the program for college entrance is in terms of separate subject areas, as long as teachers are trained along specific subject-matter lines, and as long as the patterns of team teaching are ineffectively developed. When teaching materials are limited to texts, a curriculum design centered on problem solving and calling for sophistication in handling a variety of resources is somewhat unrealistic. The failure to assess realistically the effect of existing conditions has often led to the discrediting of a given curriculum design when the difficulty may not have been in the design but in the discrepancy between the requirements of the design and the conditions for implementing it.

Further, a good design describes the elements and the relationships among them and their supporting principles in such a fashion as to indicate priorities among the factors and principles to be considered. Not all criteria and principles have equal significance in developing an adequate design, or even as norms for a good curriculum. At present there is little analysis of the priorities of these considerations, with the result that often criteria of least significance have a priority over those of greatest consequence. For example, the criterion of efficiency and economy seems to be the major consideration in such proposals regarding curriculum change as team teaching and the use of television. One wonders also whether the advantage to the development of talent in the few gifted is worth the disadvantage accruing from the ability grouping in the form of social and psychological consequences of such a grouping.

Some curriculum analysts consider the decisions about the centers around which to organize curriculum central to the whole business of curriculum development. Herrick, for example, proposes that a curriculum design becomes more usable in improving educational programs if its major focus is on problems of selecting and organizing the teaching-learning experiences of children and youth (Herrick and Tyler, 1950, p. 44).There are many reasons for allocating a central role to decisions regarding the selection and organization of the curriculum. Certainly, in practice, this is the central task around which decisions regarding selection of objectives revolve. All other decisions, and the criteria and considerations pertaining to them, come into focus in relation to this central decision.

The problems and principles of organization

The problems of organization are central to a design of curriculum. A design should, and usually does, convey an idea of how it deals with the major issues of organization: what centers are used for organizing curriculum experiences, what the concept of scope is and how to determine an adequate scope, what provisions are made for sequence of content and of learning experiences, and how to handle integration of knowledge.

The centers for organizing the curriculum

In curriculum development, decisions about what centers to use for organizing curriculum experiences are rather crucial.... For example, it is around the task of formulating a unit that it is possible to perceive and to examine the relationships among objectives, content, learning experiences, and evaluation. The development of organized teaching units also brings home the extent to which all curriculum decisions need to be made in the light of consciously understood criteria and relationships. It is impossible to make good decisions about the method of learning and teaching apart from considering the objectives that students should attain, or apart from concepts regarding the nature of the learners and the principles of learning. The decisions faced regarding organization of content bring into play the necessity of analyzing the functions of the various levels of content as well as the nature of learners and thus demonstrate a way of applying multiple considerations in making curriculum decisions which curriculum makers cannot learn abstractly.

How the nature of organizing centers influences the selection of the content and learning experiences and vice versa becomes clear also. For example, if the basic ideas are the centers for organizing the unit, these ideas then determine which specific details of information are relevant and which particular learning experiences are useful to develop these concepts and ideas and to achieve other non-content-related objectives.

The organizing focuses are also crucial to the manner of dealing with the problems of scope, sequence, and integration. For example, the kind of centers used in organizing each unit of social studies determines the kind of sequence which can be built into the entire social-science curriculum as well as the relationships which can exist between social sciences and other subjects. such as literature.

In reverse, once the scope and sequence are established they determine to a certain extent how the specific areas of curriculum can be organized, such as which centers of organization can be employed or which sequence of learning experiences can be used. It becomes clear that decisions regarding the focusing centers of specific units and those pertaining to scope and sequence as indicated in the framework of the curriculum are interdependent. The decisions about focusing of specific units cannot be made out of context of the total design without the danger of discontinuity and inconsistency.

This means, of course, that the two types of activities, analysis of the various elements of the curriculum and organization, represent two separate but interrelated steps, and this interrelationship needs to be maintained on both the specific and the general level of curriculum organization. The description of ways for dealing with the elements of the curriculum may outline the objectives and set criteria for selection of content and of learning activities in general. These essential aspects of curriculum planning and thinking are faced only at the point of putting these elements together into a functioning unit. A method of curriculum development which devotes a long time to the analysis of objectives and philosophy, and which then omits the organizing of teaching units, usually results in guides on paper which do not function in classrooms.

The general analysis only furnishes the bricks from which to compound a functioning curriculum. But the general analysis is insufficient without the subsequent step of translating general objectives into specific ones and without a methodology of translating into a functioning curriculum the criteria which apply to these decisions severally and collectively. One qualification for the focus or center of curriculum organization, then, is that the organization which it produces lives up to such criteria as adaptability to the ability levels of students, the varied conditions in schools, the resources of the teachers, and the interests of children.

Scope, sequence, and integration

A design should indicate clearly the bases and provisions for the scope and continuity of learning. Scope is a way of describing what is covered, or what is learned. As was pointed out earlier, one needs to determine what is learned in two different dimensions: what content is mastered and what mental processes are acquired (or what non-content objectives are achieved). The failure to see scope as a two-dimensional problem has created the dilemma of breadth and depth. When scope is seen solely as the breadths of content covered, the demands of coverage are in conflict with demands aris- ing out of requirements of depth. The wider the coverage, the less time there is to develop depth of understanding and a high level of conceptualization, to incorporate ideas into a personal system of thinking, and so on. Often these two dimensions are confused and a more extensive coverage of the subject is identified with depth. The continuity of learning has two aspects : that of a vertical progress from one level to another, and that of a relationship between the learnings in various areas of the curriculum which take place at the same time. The first of these is associated with the term *sequence*, the other with the term *integration*. The problem of providing con- tinuity of learning also presents itself on two different levels : the level of organizing specific units of teaching and learning, and the level of the design for the entire curriculum.

Much of the confusion and difficulty in developing cumulative and continuous learning comes from the fact that in setting up sequences in curriculum designs, only the sequence of content is considered, while the sequence of the powers and competencies is largely overlooked. The result is that the curriculum sequence re- flects growth in the mental powers only to the extent that the level of content requires it, and not because of a clear plan for the de- velopmental sequence of these powers, competencies, and skills. Out of this confusion grow all sorts of difficulties : poor articulation between the levels of schooling, the perennial complaints by each level of lack of preparation on the preceding level, misplaced expectations, and a lowered amount of growth. The attempts to 'cure' these difficulties by changing the content and setting standards of excellence in the light of content achievement alone are bound to be less successful than addressing the standards of excellence to the formulation of developmental sequences in either intellectual or other types of performance.

When the problems of both scope and sequence are seen in two dimensions—one which sketches out the pattern of the content to be covered, and the other which indicates the kinds of powers or capacities to be developed and a sequence of developing them—the dilemma of scope and depth can be put into a more balanced per- spective. This perspective would aid in deciding when the extension of the scope of content interferes with the development of the scope of mental powers and how the sequence of content could assure a sequence in levels of mental powers, or vice versa.

This double pattern of scope and sequence makes certain requirements on the centers of organization. Centers of organization need to combine most advantageously the requirements for advancing both the level of content and the level of mental operations. Using the basic ideas as focusing centers has several advantages in this respect. First, if the basic ideas are clearly outlined, it is also easier to see which intellectual powers and operations are necessary to deal with them. If units are organized around ideas, it is, for example, easier to determine what levels of abstraction may be required and what type of relationships between various ideas are possible and necessary than it is when only the topics and their dimensions are available for analysis.

This organization also makes it possible to examine more precisely both the sequence of content that is being employed and the sequence in the powers and capacities that are developed in the successive levels of curriculum. The units on different grade levels can be examined to see what ideas have been added and which are extended, and whether the contexts in which these additions are being made add up to sufficient scope of understanding. It will also be possible to determine whether there is an increment in such powers as the capacity to analyze data, to organize ideas, to respond to feelings and values, to appreciate aesthetic qualities, or to express feelings and ideas.

On p. 144 is an attempt to analyze for the elementary social studies the sequence in content and the cumulative maturation of the concept of difference, which is a recurring concept from one grade level to another.

Content organized around large central ideas is also amenable to analysis of the ideas drawn from various disciplines in order to check validity and significance. For example, the units in the areas described above were analyzed to see what ideas they contained that might be classified as history, sociology, geography, economics, and anthropology. An example of the sociological ideas in social studies from Grades 1–3 is given in the chart that follows.

A sequence of mental operations

A chart of learning activities makes possible a similar analysis of the mental operations represented by the learning experiences. If the learning activities in the various units are clearly stated, they can be examined to determine the scope and range they represent and the

SEQUENCE OF THE CONCEPT OF DIFFERENCE

Grade level	Areas in which the concept is developed	Sequence of the concept of 'differences'
I	Home, family, school	Differences in families in: 1. Family composition 2. Occupation 3. Income
II	Work in community: farm, transportation, and super-market	People do different things to meet life's needs.
III	Comparative communities	People do things in different ways today than long ago, and differently in different cultures.
IV	California—now and before	Differences in reasons for people coming to California, for different kinds of occupations here, etc. Differences in ways of life according to geographic and historical conditions.
V	Life in the United States	Extension of IV. Different feelings about coming to or moving about the U.S. Different patterns of life. Effects of different environments.
VI	The Western Hemisphere—how the various functions of life are carried on, such as economy, education, government	The functions of life are met in different ways as determined by climate, topography, history, type of people.
VII	World trade	Different ways the various countries process, use, or distribute the natural resources of the earth.
VIII	United Nations	Different ways in which the various cultures can be helped to meet life's needs.*

* From the minutes of a curriculum planning session, Contra Costa County Schools, Pleasant Hill, California.

cumulative growth they provide in powers other than the understanding of content—thinking, academic and group skills, attitudes,
values, and sensitivities. A sequence in developing sensitivity to
differences starts in the first grade by reading about a new child in
the school and then discussing what it feels like to be one and what
the ways are of making a new child feel at home. The second-grade
unit on the farm inducts the students into feelings about farm life
and ends with writing a story, 'The Farmer Who Would Not Move
Away'. In the third grade the children have the task of projecting
themselves into the life in many cultures, and they begin to explore
how the various kinds of people—the primitives in the rain forest,
the Hong Kong boat dwellers, the Sahara nomads—feel about their
culture. They are asked to write on themes such as, 'If I were a
primitive child I would like to ...'.

Such an analysis permits a projection upwards. What other
aspects of cultural sensitivity can be built on this particular one, and
how can an increasing capacity to put oneself in other people's
shoes be cumulatively developed? What additional dimensions are
necessary to develop the degree of cosmopolitan cultural sensitivity
needed and which particular contexts are especially appropriate?

A cumulative sequence is observable also in logical and critical
thinking. After observing and analyzing what the teacher, principal,
custodian, and cafeteria workers do, the first graders develop chart
stories on the theme, 'We have many helpers at school.' They begin
to differentiate such things as what must be done for the baby, what
is fun to do and what is troublesome, what people might like and
dislike about different types of houses, or what responsibilities are
carried by different family members. The burden of differentiation
and abstraction increases in the second grade, where the children are
asked to differentiate the services needed and provided in different
types of communities and the ways in which these services are paid
for. They now write on topics such as, 'This is the day when the
electricity failed.' In the third grade, the students are asked to
analyze a film on the idea of what is primitive by developing a list
of qualities and activities which are evidences of a primitive way of
life. Subsequently they read a story about life in the rain forest and
are then asked to determine which statements in the list are true of
the family described in the story and in which way that family
shows evidence of being primitive. This requires a degree of abstraction, of logical inference, of contrasting and comparing.

What should be the expectation on the next level of children who

A SAMPLE FROM A CONTENT ANALYSIS

*Sociological Ideas in Units, Grades 1–3** *

Central Ideas	Grade 1	Grade 2	Grade 3
Groups, Society, and Communication	As students at school we expect to learn certain things and we expect to behave in a particular way. Children feel differently about what schools expect of them. A family group may differ in structure, i.e., one-parent home, foster home, etc. A child has two sets of relatives—his mother's relatives and father's relatives. Families have different rules for their children. The teacher is also a member of a family	The clerk in the supermarket is also a member of a family and a consumer. The farmer is an employer, a consumer, and a member of a family. A supermarket needs the newspaper for advertising.	A Zulu child and a nomadic Arab child are members of a tribe as well as of a family. A Chinese child has an extended family. A Swiss child has a family structure more nearly like ours. People who have no written language pass along their knowledge and tradition by word of mouth. Our form of writing was first evolved among the Arab people. The Chinese have a pictograph form of writing. Music, dance, and ceremonies can be used to communicate with others. The primitive of Africa, the Arab, the Chinese, and our communities have each developed a certain kind of music. Among the Chinese celebrations are held for the entire family.
Human Ecology	Homes in cities may differ from homes in small towns or on a farm. Schools in the country may be different from schools in town or city. Some 'grandparents' receive checks from 'the county'.	People live in different kinds of communities. When a community grows larger more services, such as schools, churches, libraries, etc., are needed. A commuting community needs many roads and filling stations. A small community may have a volun-	Primitive people (Zulu or rain-forest primitives) use the plants and animals of their environment to provide food, clothing, and shelter. Modern communities (Swiss people or our community) are less dependent on their environment for food, clothing, and shelter.

* Contra Costa County Schools, June 1961

Where there is water in the hot, dry lands we find farms. The farmers live in permanent homes.

The nomad of the hot, dry land and the people who live on boats in Hong Kong harbor must trade to meet their basic needs.

The people of Switzerland are concerned with the tourist trade as a result of their natural scenery.

The family and tribe of the primitive community provide religion, recreation, teaching of the young, and enforcement of tribal rules. Our community has schools, churches, and government to do this.

Each community celebrates occasions in a traditional manner.

Modern transportation helps the Swiss people secure chocolate beans from another country and deliver the Swiss chocolate to far-away markets.

Zulu children are taught to accept the ways of their people. Arab, Chinese, and Swiss children are each taught a particular way of behaving.

Each of the four cultures teaches girls to behave a special way and boys to behave in a special way.

Among the Zulu the oldest son of the chief will inherit the position of chief.

Among the Arabs the male has a special position.

In the Chinese culture age is given great respect.

---

teer fire service; larger communities have full-time firemen.

A community may not meet all the needs of the people who live there—employment, hospitalization, etc.

Some services (school, fire, etc.) are provided by taxes, some are provided by individuals (TV repairs, barber), and some by companies (banking, electricity).

Irrigation canals are built by the government to bring water to farms.

The farmer needs schools, recreation, etc., just as people in large communities do.

Personality and Socialization Processes

At school where there are many children we have rules for the sake of safety.

Family living demands that we share space, parents' time, etc., with other members.

Families teach their children to behave a certain way. They may punish them for not obeying the rules.

In some families the role of the 'breadwinner' is carried by someone other than or in addition to the father.

Father's work is very important to the family.

A SAMPLE FROM A CONTENT ANALYSIS—continued

Central Ideas	Grade 1	Grade 2	Grade 3
	Some jobs, such as shopping, fixing things, etc., may be done by different family members.		
Social Processes	Families carry on many work and play activities together.	We have laws related to keeping milk clean and cows free from disease.	
	Parents who commute to work have little time to spend with children in the evening.	We have laws related to keeping food markets clean and free from disease.	
	Fathers who travel have time with their families only on certain days.	All businesses need fire and police protection.	
Social Relations and Culture			Traders and missionaries have brought changes to primitive people.
			The United Nations and WHO are bringing many changes among primitives and underdeveloped peoples.
			People do not always like the changes that are brought to them.
Social Control			The Zulu have certain rules the members must follow, such as obedience to the chief on a hunt.
			Brave behavior is rewarded by the chief.
			In our communities there are laws related to trade—a limit on how much a tourist may bring back into this country.

have mastered these intellectual processes? In other words, what is the sequence in the processes of thinking? If students in one unit have learned to classify simple ideas, is the next attempt at classification more demanding? If they have learned to derive simple generalizations from fairly simple facts, are they challenged in the next unit to move on to a higher and a more complex level? Do students who have learned to compare and contrast a simple set of conditions have an opportunity next to do the same on a more abstract or complex level? Do those who have learned to state simple sequences of events next learn to state and to discover sequences in argumentation?

As the students return to the same central idea or concept, it is possible to determine whether they only add to its content and meaning or whether these additions also increasingly demand higher levels of mental operations, such as an increasingly higher level of abstraction and an increasingly wider radius of application. In other words, it is necessary to plot a developmental sequence of cumulative growth both in power and in content in order to determine whether the subsequent contexts merely yield new information while requiring the same powers of comprehension and the same level of thinking, or whether there is an increment in both.

Advantages of a double sequence

Such a double scheme of composing scope and sequence by ideas and concepts treated and by the behaviors expected has several advantages. Both the behavior reactions and the content are accessible to an objective analysis of their cumulative effect. The scheme of scope and sequence is not jeopardized by a varied type of organization, and, in reverse, no one single type of organization needs to be imposed for the sake of a coherent scope and sequence. It is equally possible to apply such a scheme to a curriculum organized by subjects, by topics which cut across disciplines, or by problems. And it would also be possible to vary the schemes of organization from area to area, such as using problems as the main approach in one and a topical organization in the next. If ideas serve as centers of organization, variety in approaches does not destroy the comparability of the threads.

Such a scheme would also open up the possibility of developing a single consistent pattern of scope and sequence from the elementary through the high school, and across all subjects, which the current curriculum designs do not provide. None of them encompasses all grade levels or everything that the curriculum contains.

The same would be true of establishing and examining the integration or the horizontal relationship among disciplines or subjects. If ideas are used as the basic threads for establishing these relationships, integration can be achieved on several levels and in several ways, and not limited to the combining of particular subjects. For some ideas a crossing of historical, sociological, and anthropological material may be necessary to give proper dimension. Integration of scientific and social facts may be most relevant for others. Still others may require a combination of practical life situations with theoretical principles. In other words, it would not seem necessary to apply a single pattern of integration in all subjects or at every step in their study.

Another advantage of structuring the scope, sequence, and integration by ideas and behaviors rather than by subjects and content topics is that such a scheme has a flexibility which permits adjustments to the nature of student population and to the local conditions in particular schools. As was pointed out, units structured around ideas and developed by dimensions of topics and sampling of content permit a variety of adjustments. Each dimension can be extended or contracted according to the limits in students' perception and their level of understanding. These extensions and contractions can be made at any point: in the depth required, by developing an idea only on a certain level; in the extent of comparisons required, by limiting comparison only to certain aspects of culture or carrying it only to a certain level of exactitude; in the number of the concrete samples used, by using a larger number of concrete examples with the less able. One can require more or less exacting types of analysis, abstracting, and generalizing. Alternatives can be substituted either in specific ideas to be pursued or in specific samples of content, provided these alternatives are equally relevant to the main ideas. Coverage and level of expectation are thus brought into a rational control, and changes in each can be effected without revising the entire scheme.

This makes it possible to have a *common* curriculum pattern without necessitating a uniform curriculum. Teachers can be free to give adequate attention to content without having to submit to the tyranny of uniform, fixed, and static content. While the same threads go through all grade levels and all areas, these threads may be developed with different student groups in different ways.

This type of sequence and scope requires careful experimentation

A MODEL FOR CURRICULUM DESIGN

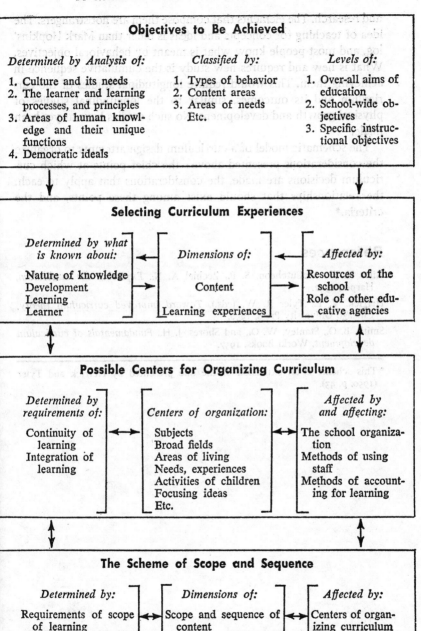

Objectives to Be Achieved

Determined by Analysis of:
1. Culture and its needs
2. The learner and learning processes, and principles
3. Areas of human knowledge and their unique functions
4. Democratic ideals

Classified by:
1. Types of behavior
2. Content areas
3. Areas of needs
Etc.

Levels of:
1. Over-all aims of education
2. School-wide objectives
3. Specific instructional objectives

Selecting Curriculum Experiences

Determined by what is known about:
Nature of knowledge
Development
Learning
Learner

Dimensions of:
Content
Learning experiences

Affected by:
Resources of the school
Role of other educative agencies

Possible Centers for Organizing Curriculum

Determined by requirements of:
Continuity of learning
Integration of learning

Centers of organization:
Subjects
Broad fields
Areas of living
Needs, experiences
Activities of children
Focusing ideas
Etc.

Affected by and affecting:
The school organization
Methods of using staff
Methods of accounting for learning

The Scheme of Scope and Sequence

Determined by:
Requirements of scope of learning
Requirements of continuity of learning

Dimensions of:
Scope and sequence of content
Scope and sequence of mental operations

Affected by:
Centers of organizing curriculum

and research. The elements that compose them are not strangers. The idea of teaching for concepts and ideas is older than Mark Hopkins' log, and most people know what is meant by behavioral objectives. What is new and requires new study is the cumulative sequence in achieving them. This would require longitudinal studies of the curriculum and its outcomes, similar to the longitudinal studies of physical growth and development. No such studies have as yet been made.

The schematic model of a curriculum design attempts to organize the considerations presented above: the chief points at which curriculum decisions are made, the considerations that apply to each, the relationships that should exist among these points, and the criteria.*

References

Giles H. H., McCutcheon, S. P., Zechiel A. N.. *Exploring the curriculum*, Harper, 1942.

Herrick, V. E., Tyler R. W. (eds.), *Toward improved curriculum theory*, Chicago University Press, 1950.

Smith, B. O., Stanley, W. O., and Shores, J. H., *Fundamentals of curriculum development*, World Books, 1957.

---

* This scheme is an extension of the one presented by Herrick and Tyler (1950, p. 43).

Philip H. Taylor

II:4 Purpose and structure in the curriculum

*Taylor begins by describing a model for thinking about
the curriculum which has permeated curriculum design
for thirty years. Called the learning experiences model,
it emphasizes the modes of thinking used by pupils in
different subject areas, drawing heavily on evidence from
educational psychology and learning theory. Another
model is proposed which is likely to be more acceptable
to the teacher in that it relates knowledge, teaching
methods and objectives more specifically. This model is
related to curriculum event theory—which Taylor
describes as no more than speculation about a planned
series of encounters between a pupil and a selection of
subjects or aspects of culture. For the teacher to weld the
curriculum into a dynamic and effective unit of knowledge,
teaching methods and objectives, teacher education will
need to be of increasing complexity.*

1 Introduction

In this paper I shall attempt to do four things: I shall attempt to
explore where our thinking about the curriculum of the school has
got to, propose a model for it, illustrate how this and other models
can be used, and discuss the nature and determinants of curriculum
objectives. I shall also touch on some issues which are currently of
general interest.

First, then, where has our thinking about the curriculum got to?
Not very far I'm afraid. Educational thinkers in this country have
been caught napping over much that has been taken for granted
about the curriculum. In the last decade only one book, and that by
a Scot (Nisbet, 1957), has appeared which has attempted in any
formal way to analyse the meaning we give to the term curriculum
and to relate this to the way in which the curriculum functions in
the school. Similarly, there have been few articles of note. The most
important have been by a psychologist with a keen interest in both
the theory of knowledge and education (Meredith, 1946). This is not

Educational Review, (University of Birmingham), vol. 19, no. 3, vol. 20, no. 1,
1967, pp. 159–172, pp. 19–29. Reprinted by permission.

to say there hasn't been a welter of books about the curriculum. There has. But they have invariably had their starting-point in purely practical considerations. Formal analysis and theory have not raised their heads in them nor has research been called into service. They are like much other literature in education, statements of good intentions and gospels of personal practice.

Given this state of affairs, I feel I must start at the beginning, sketching out as I go along what has been latent in our thinking about the curriculum of the school and ending up by suggesting ways in which our thinking about the curriculum may become of increasing value in planning the changes that lie ahead as well as informing them by research.

2 The learning experiences model

The curriculum is usually thought of as a subject or a grouping of subjects for study which are to be treated in a way that will promote learning in pupils. In order for learning to take place certain things must follow. Pupils need to have their attention drawn to relevant subject matter and teachers have to create experiences for them out of which their learning can arise. The kind of learning which it is hoped to promote in the classroom is preferred to other possible learning and it is, therefore, valued. It is that learning, the elements of which as they build up over time have a 'structure', a structure which belongs to one or other body of knowledge: to history, science, mathematics and so on. It is this structured nature which distinguishes it from the learning arising from everyday experiences, and for which among other reasons, it is valued.

Learning, as psychologists have made us aware, brings about a change in behaviour. This being so it would seem that the purpose of the curriculum is to seek to bring about valued changes in pupil behaviour. These changes can be specified as the intended outcomes or the objectives of the pupil's curricular experiences.

Moreover, as Bruner (1963) has pointed out, in order to achieve these objectives the pupil must submit to a number of rather peculiar demands. 'He must regulate his learning and his attention by reference to external requirements. He must eschew what is vividly right under his nose for what is dimly in the future and is often incomprehensible to him, and he must do so in a strange setting where words and diagrams and abstractions suddenly become very important.... And often it puts the learner in a spot where he does not know whether he knows, sometimes for minutes, sometimes for hours on end. He has no indication as to whether he is on the right track or the wrong track.' And, one might add that many pupils never know whether or not they have been on the right track or what their curricular experience has been about. Studies of school leavers have been sharply salutory in this respect. For some pupils their learning experiences seem to have had little or no point, except as Musgrove has suggested, in writing themselves off (1966).

It is possible to know this because considerable attention has been given to the part learning plays in curricular experiences. This attention has given rise to a model for our thinking about the curriculum. Schematically it looks like this:

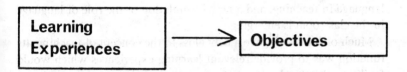

The larger part of the model is learning experiences. It is these experiences, the events associated with them, which give rise to desired learning which are the objectives, the intended ends of the activities associated with the curriculum.

It is such a model as this which has been latent in much of other thinking about the curriculum over the past thirty years or more. Attention was drawn away from considerations of subject matter, and the aims of education which dominated educational thinking until then, to the domain of child psychology, to the how and why of intellectual, social and moral development, and to the problems of human learning; to questions of motivation and stimulus and response. Insight, concept formation, reinforcement and readiness as well as intelligence operationally defined in terms of IQ became familiar in the education of teachers. Masters of Method departed from the training colleges to be replaced by lecturers in educational psychology and child development. A knowledge of statistics and the design of psychological experiments became for an increasing number of students the means to a higher degree in education. Teachers in the classroom acting as stimuli concentrated on arousing interest. Their attention was focused to a greater extent than before on their pupils. We teach children not subjects, gained currency as a rallying cry for action. Action which resulted in the recasting of the methods of teaching for many subjects and in a new ordering of criteria against which to assess teaching capabilities. Robertson (1957), for example, in a research conducted about a decade ago, found that 'attitude and insight in dealing with others ...represented the most important aspects of teaching ability as judged by supervisors of student teachers'.

More centrally, the *learning experiences* model for the curriculum drew attention to the modes of thinking used by pupils in particular subject areas: to their reasoning in mathematics, science and history, and to their thinking strategies. Recent work of this kind in the area of children's thinking about religious concepts promises a quite new approach to religious education in the schools (Goldman, 1964). Moreover, this work has impinged strikingly on the function of language in teaching, and a new formulation of the role of language in the classroom is emerging.

Much of this work gave a new gloss to the concept of teaching. Its function was to provide relevant learning experiences which would facilitate the development of concepts and the emergence of productive thinking. Teaching methods came as a consequence to be described in terms of understanding, problem solving and discovery, and much current curriculum development work is well salted with these terms.

The effect on the way in which many teachers now behave in the classroom is witness to the potency of these terms. Engaged in discovery or problem solving with their pupils, they are not so often to be found formally addressing the class. More frequently they are to be found in an intimate give and take with the individual pupil or with small groups. New relationships between teacher and taught have also arisen under the impress of the *learning experiences* model for the curriculum. The child psychologists' assertion that children need 'love' has not gone unnoticed by teachers nor has the idea of personality as self-directing and purposive. The development in the pupil of a realistic and stable self-concept cast the teacher to some extent in the role of a therapist and some studies have suggested that the important part played by the pupil's self-concept in curricular achievement depends on how he is treated by the teacher (Staines, 1958). Other studies have explored the relationship between certain personality dispositions, extroversion and introversion, for example, and academic attainment (Lynn, Gordon, 1961). The introvert may have an anxious time but does well.

Teaching methods have also been studied in terms of the kind of learning which they promote and it is fairly clear from many of these studies that the method of teaching used and the learning promoted are intimately related, though not in any simple and direct way. Both the teacher's and the pupil's personality are also important factors as is the extent to which the subject matter is structured for learning.

A considerable step forward in our understanding of the problems to be faced in elaborating teaching methods has been made possible by developments in the field of programmed learning, particularly in analysing the 'task' to be presented to the pupil and in determining the most effective sequencing of subject matter. This work has been greatly influenced by the 'behaviourist' school of psychology, especially by J. B. Skinner, one of its most inventive practitioners.

The *learning experiences* model for the curriculum is grounded in psychology, one of the social sciences. As a science psychology has developed an appropriate form of measurement and in so doing has given to many ostensive definitions an operational meaning. A good example, and a fine hare to chase, is the measurement of intelligence : a human quality which teachers want to use and to expand. From the psychological interest in, and development of techniques for measurement, there has sprung an educational counterpart. Thus, measures of educational achievement have been developed and used in the evaluation of different methods of teaching the same material, in the allocation of pupils to different kinds of curricular treatment and in assessing the relative contribution to curricular attainments of home and school.

It is a rule of educational measurement that the operational definition to be employed has to have meaning in terms of specified pupil behaviour. The definition has to say what the pupil will be doing when measurement is taking place : whether he will be recalling something taught, solving a problem in a familiar or unfamiliar setting, comprehending a prose passage, a graph or diagram, or recording an interest, an attitude or a value. Moreover, the pupil behaviour has to be judged as to its educational worthwhileness, i.e. it has to be a valid educational or curriculum objective : the intended end point of valued learning.

Work in the field of educational measurement has made it possible to assess the outcome of the *learning experiences* model for the curriculum provided these outcomes or objectives are stated in operational terms, i.e. in terms which make the intended pupil behaviour clear. The objectives of curricular learning experiences are to encourage pupils to acquire knowledge, understanding and skills, to develop values, interests and beliefs. History, for example, is taught, it is claimed by teachers of history, so that pupils will acquire historical knowledge, understand historical concepts, develop insight into the nature of historical judgment and so that they will become interested in and curious about things historical as well as develop practical skills in using source materials. All these objectives can be given an operational definition in terms of how the pupil will behave when he has achieved them.

Of course history is also taught for reasons less easily defined in operational terms: to exercise a general influence on character, to develop freedom from prejudice and to encourage a sense of our national heritage. In fact most subjects of the curriculum carry a burden of objectives which go well beyond the subject matter and over into the realms of character and social conscience. These, in many cases, are the subject's 'ring of confidence' and make it an acceptable member of the club. Teachers themselves no longer take such claims as these as seriously as they once did. Empirical studies of the 'transfer of training', of the extent to which learning in one subject carries over to a much more generalised area, have cast very considerable doubts in this direction. It can no longer be claimed as strongly as once it was that mathematics for instance gives rise to a sense of beauty through the experience of order and symmetry which it affords or that the study of literature makes pupils sensitive to the suffering of others. The claims made by a Newman or a Whitehead for the curricula which they advocated now seem extravagant and unlikely to be substantiated.

Such broad claims apart, educational objectives operationally defined in terms of pupil behaviour cover the whole range of human achievements. Some attempts have been made to classify them. These attempts, all American, had their origins in the construction of objective-type achievement tests. The most noteworthy is the *Taxonomy of educational objectives*. In the two handbooks of objectives which have so far been published Bloom and his co-workers (1956) have made a systematic attempt to classify them accordingly to distinct logical types. They have so far used two main headings for their work: the Cognitive Domain and the Affective Domain. The first might very generally be thought of as intellectual objectives: knowledge of facts and principles, of theories and structures and the ability to interpret various types of data; and the second, as objectives related to attitudes, interests, value and beliefs.

This scientific, tough-minded approach of Bloom's, which incidentally owes much to the pioneering work of Tyler in the late 30's, to insist on the precise formulation of curriculum objectives is beginning to have a marked effect on our thinking about the extent to which the curricula we use are successful. Successful, that is, in terms of their own intentions. Thus, like any other respectable field of study, that of the curriculum may in time come to elaborate for itself its own criteria and its own tests. But Bloom's work has too strong a psychological bias for many educationists. It takes, they say, too little account of the 'unique educational yield' of particular fields of study. Nevertheless, it represents the best disciplined approach to the formulation of objectives so far undertaken and may well force educationists to develop their own thinking more rapidly.

Psychology then would seem to have provided a very fruitful model for thinking about the curriculum and for practice in relation to it. . . . It is a model which remains fruitful, in that through the researches and enquiries which it continues to generate we come to a more comprehensive understanding of what makes an effective method of teaching, what sequencing of material is necessary for learning to take place and what contribution to learning, the interests, personality and general ability of the pupil makes.

But for all that psychology has been and remains a powerful stimulus to educational thinking and practice there has remained the constant concern with why we teach what we teach: the role of subject matter and its purpose in the curriculum. No-one has been more concerned about this than the teacher in the classroom. This concern is reflected in the 'trade press' which finds its way into every staff room, in the constant stream of books on the teaching of this or that subject, and in the pages of national reports. The Newsom Report, for example, devotes some 70 per cent of its discussion of the curriculum to subject matter.

Much of this writing is aimed to provide reassurance, to give a new basis for beliefs in the worthwhileness of this or that subject for teaching, and to pass on ways of teaching which have proved, at least for some teachers, effective. It is, of course, not surprising that teachers should be interested in this kind of writing. Knowledge in subject form is what they daily traffic in with their pupils. It is more their bread and butter than is psychology. They can and do, get along without a formal knowledge of instrumental conditioning, motivation and personality structure. They know what works if not why it works and are certainly greatly expert in much that they do.

Related to the teacher's concern about knowledge, and their role and function in transmitting it, is a much wider issue: that of our cultural heritage. 'The funded capital of social experience' (Brubacher, 1956), as it has been described; those 'realms of meaning' (Phenix, 1964) which we have come to know as subject discipline and which include the systems of moral beliefs which men have elaborated for their own good. Studies in the role of the teacher suggest that most teachers place first in importance moral training with instruction in subjects a close second. This tends to be true whether they are teachers of sixth formers or of infants.

Now the teacher of infants knows, as anyone who visits an infant class can see, that the beginnings of knowing both about morals and about subject is 'artless' (Ryle, 1949). This 'artless' experience is given form and shape by the ways in which the teacher progressively directs the attention of her pupils by the methods and matter which she uses toward more formal modes of meaning. No less than the teacher of sixth formers, the teacher of infants is opening windows on domains of knowledge and understanding. In the sixth form the structure of the subject matter is more clearly discernible as history, mathematics, or science. But in both situations subject knowledge, its meaning and teaching methods have to be brought together for a purpose. It is out of this bringing together that pupils learn though not in many cases without encouragement.

3 A proposed model

This description of the curriculum as a bringing together of knowledge, methods and objectives may be much more acceptable to the teacher than the *learning experiences* model. It is perhaps a better representation of the interplay of forces associated with the curriculum in action. It is a better analogue and it is easier to locate the pupil as someone undergoing a purposeful experience created for him in terms of matter and method as a consequence of which he is encouraged to know those things which the adult community considers worthwhile. Perhaps this diagram illustrates more clearly what the curriculum seems to be.

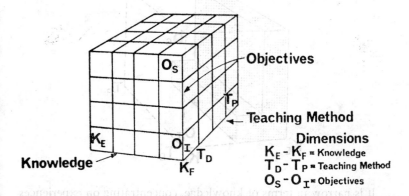

The three axes of the cube are knowledge (K), teaching methods (T) and objectives (O). It is described as the *total intended curriculum* because at no one moment is the pupil experiencing more than part of it though during his educational career he may experience much of it.

The knowledge axis (K) ranging from K_E to K_F embraces knowledge arising from simple elements of experience to formal knowledge or knowledge of the disciplines including those of aesthetics and morals. The teaching methods axis (T) ranges from direct teaching (T_D) or the didactic method to (T_P), the point at which the pupil is his own teacher. It is somewhere toward this point on the teaching method axis that the pupil is when he is engaged on a project or thesis of his own choice.

Where curricular materials—books, maps, charts, diagrams, learning programmes, and the like—replace the teacher in immediacy of contact with the pupil you still have the range of teaching methods. Books can be used as directed by the teacher or as directed by the pupil. Similarly where the teacher employs a 'discovery' method there is more for the pupil to do for himself than where the didactic method is employed.

The objectives dimension, O_I to O_S, ranges from intellectual objectives such as the knowledge of some specific facts, the names of things, from simple intellectual skills such as reading, to self-knowledge including knowing what one knows and how it is known both about oneself and about the world around one.

In terms of the diagram the curriculum of the infant school would look like this:

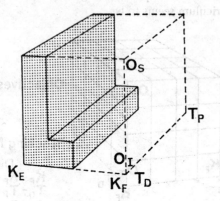

It is narrow in terms of knowledge, concentrating on experiences and some pre-formal knowledge in number and reading. It is so because the pupils have reached only an early stage in their development. On the other hand it is broad in terms of objectives because the pupils need both to begin to make meaning out of their experiences and to begin to develop self-awareness in relation to it. And it is broad in terms of teaching methods because the teaching has to be adapted to the needs of the pupils.

Similar abstractions from the diagram can be made to demonstrate other curricula or, for that matter, curricula which we know to be in operation and about which we want to say something.

Frequently we want to say that a curriculum is too *narrow* or is *lacking in depth* or is too *specialised* and we want to *broaden* it. To what are we referring? To which dimension—knowledge, teaching methods or objectives or to all three? Each dimension can be broad or narrow and it might be of great help in discourse about the curriculum to be clearer about what it is to which we refer. Similarly, the term *balance* used about the curriculum can refer to knowledge, teaching methods or to objectives. Thus an elementary model of this kind may be of use in helping us to talk about the curriculum.

There is also another way in which this model of the curriculum can be used. It can be used to distinguish between the motivation of pupils which is extrinsic to the curriculum, outside the cube, and that which is intrinsic, inside the cube. In this way we can see, for example, more clearly what a philosopher of education means when he writes:

'The aim of the educator is to get others on the *inside* of worth-while activities and forms of awareness so that they will explore them for ends which are intrinsic to them. But in the early stages he may have to use extrinsic motivation both to get children started on them and to sustain their interest when the stage of precision begins to exert an irksome discipline' (Peters, 1966).

4 Models for planning

It has been possible to present the curriculum as that interacting complex of knowledge, teaching methods and objectives which provides the learning experience for pupils largely, though not solely, because of the impact of psychology on educational think-ing. This I trust, has made more explicit what has been to a degree implicit in practice in the schools and in our thinking about the curriculum. There are, of course, other models of the curriculum. Models which illuminate aspects of general curricular problems in other ways. Lamm (1966) in discussing curriculum planning uses three intersecting circles, the commonly shared area in the centre being the curriculum.

The purpose of curriculum planning, he argues, is to indicate the means whereby the pupils, the teacher and an aspect of culture, the three dynamic elements of the curriculum, can be brought together so that in the end the pupil himself may inhabit a territory of culture. If the planning is to be effective there is a need, Lamm suggests, to translate an aspect of culture into a subject for teaching, and once translated, determine the didactic layers or sequences which will facilitate the progress of the pupil. Bruner (1963) is say-ing much the same thing when he writes, 'The structure of any domain of knowledge may be characterised (for teaching) in three ways, each affecting the ability of any learner to master it: the *mode of representation* in which it is put, the *economy* and its effec-tive *power*. Mode, economy and power vary in relation to different ages, to different "styles" among learners, and to different subject matters.'

That a subject for teaching is different from, though related to a subject of culture is by no means a novel idea. It has just not been explored very thoroughly. It is well established folk-lore at many levels in education that the essence of good teaching is a knowledge of one's subject. Given that the teacher knows his subject the folk-lore has it, all that is required further are some techniques for

presenting it. Nothing could be more of a half-truth than this and
nothing more calculated to stand in the way of effective teaching or
of effectively educating teachers. Viewed from the standpoint of
folk-lore what results is teaching from conclusions, whereas what is
needed by the pupil is teaching which leads him *toward* conclusions.
The first concentrates the pupil's attention on knowing what, and
the second on knowing how. It is the latter which enables the pupil
to stand on our shoulders and see more clearly the distant prospects
of emerging knowledge and culture. The former keeps him at our
feet.

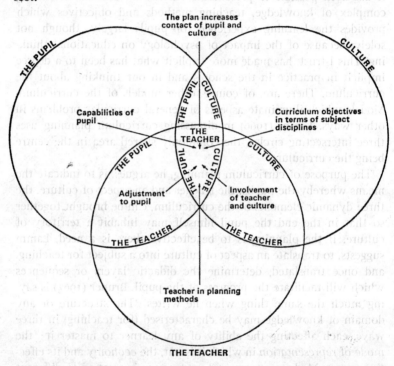

However, the purpose of both models of the curriculum is to
bring into view things which have gone to a degree unnoticed and
by so doing make it possible to elaborate better curriculum theory
and make tractable important curricular problems. The planning of
curricula is one such area of problems which is of considerable contemporary importance. Agencies such as the Nuffield Foundation
and the Schools Council have both embarked on the planning of
new curricula on the grand scale. They have both undertaken to

plan and to pilot through the schools major new curricula in the sciences, in mathematics, in English, in modern languages, and in the humanities, not to mention a whole range of feasibility studies.

Both the Nuffield Foundation and the Schools Council place the planning of these new curricula very largely in the hands of teachers. These teachers, who are themselves subject specialists, have the advice of subject experts and of H.M. Inspectors. But none of these educationists as yet has much use for principles for curriculum planning. This is not to say there are no principles. It is that educationists cannot at present see the need for them. In fact the discussion of such principles as are available give rise in them to fears, anxieties and antipathies which can be quite violent in their expression. This is an interesting aspect of curriculum reform not only in this country but also in the U.S.A. and elsewhere. Such fears are understandable and relate to the teaching profession's history. Teachers see in the principles of curriculum planning the ghost of 'payment by results'.

Now a cardinal principle of planning any complex series of events such as the planning of a curriculum, requires that at all stages in the execution of the plan there will be feed back of the extent to which the plan is being effectively implemented. Judgments based on feed back evidence are made so that the 'plan-in-action' can, if necessary, be modified with some chance that the final product will be either much like the planners intended or the planners' intentions as stated in the plan will be modified in known and specified ways. In both cases a rational base for action emerges. This is not for action against teachers but action for better intelligence about the effectiveness of planned curricula.

But the notion of curriculum planning in the minds of many educationists, 'payment by results' apart, is depressed by three factors. One I have already touched on. The proposition that to know one's subject is largely to know how to teach it. The second is bound up in the word 'syllabus'. When one looks at most syllabuses and listens to the talk about them one is immediately struck by how much ends and means are inextricably compounded. As Lamm says, 'The syllabus is a translation of aims into a language of subjects, a translation which does not explain at all the aims . . . just the opposite it adds non-clarity by the use of symbols of many meanings' (Lamm, 1966). A syllabus is a statement not only about the subject matter or content of teaching for a particular group but also about the objectives for that group stated in subject terms. This we should begin to recognise in the way we use the term.

The third factor is in the meaning of the word plan. Many people use the word to convey hopes, dreams, expectations and wishes rather than to convey the reality of an object having special characteristics which can be constructed to serve a purpose, and which calls for the employment of a range of techniques. This implies technology *in* an educational process which all too readily leads to the conclusion that the claim being made is that education *is* a technology.

No such claim is being made. All that is being suggested is that the intuitive judgments made about the curricula should be given as far as is possible an objective and verifiable form. What we seek to know in this respect is whether the plan works, how well and why. This is its technology. The worthwhileness of the plan is not a question of technology. It is a matter of values.

Such factors as these make one doubt whether the curriculum development work being sponsored at the moment in this country will leave us at the end of the day with any more worthwhile knowledge than we now have of the effectiveness of the new curricula or with any better techniques than we now have for planning curriculum changes. Certainly many pupils will be familiar with more up to date knowledge of science, mathematics, history and language than they are to-day, but will they make either better scientists, mathematicians and English scholars or understand better what science and mathematics is about than the pupil of today? Much will accrue in terms of motivation both of teachers and pupils from these changes and in that they are founded on a syllabus approach to curriculum planning, some old objectives for teaching will give way to newer ones. More teaching may be directed away from knowing what and towards knowing how. But what will account for whatever desirable changes in the pupil do occur? Will it be in the new content, the new objectives, the new teaching methods which may arise or the motivation of the pupil and teacher? If the last, will the drive arising from it have a long or short 'cooling-out' period? After all the much celebrated Hawthorne effect on industrial productivity disappeared when the psychologists packed their bags and left for factories new. In the long run, questions such as these will have to be tackled if curriculum development is to get away from the stop–go policies of the past. As in the economic field, curriculum changes arising from market forces alone may have to be subject to planning if they are to be cumulatively beneficial.

But my strictures are too severe. Apart from the fact that the Schools Council is as yet a young organisation which has shown remarkable energy in its first two years of life despite its complex representative committee structure, it has already shown itself willing to tackle this problem by setting up a Working Party to produce recommendations about methods for evaluating curricula. Nevertheless it remains the case that if we in this country are to initiate worthwhile curriculum changes we may need to recognise not only the value of techniques for planning and evaluation but also the value of a theory for planning. More than this we must begin to rely on evidence of effective implementation. In short we may need to learn about, and not be frightened by *praxiology* which is the science of efficient action.

There is also much in the fields of operational research and systems analysis which may prove useful. I am, myself, struck by how much 'path analysis' may have to offer the curriculum planners. After all it is about 'the right order of things' and this is what is called for in planning curricula.

5 Curriculum evaluation

One of the salient issues which arises again and again where curriculum change is planned and initiated comes in the form of a general question: 'Is curriculum A better than curriculum B?' Now this question can refer to any one of the three dimensions of curriculum or to all three at once. Much depends on who is asking it. Furthermore, there are quite distinct criteria for evaluating each of the dimensions separately and for judging them as a functioning whole. If the questioner is concerned with curriculum objectives, evaluation is a matter of judging the worthwhileness of desired pupil behaviour. Up to a point this is an empirical question though in the end it is not. If the concern is with teaching method, this is an empirical question though whether it is a *scientific* one is a matter of contention. If the concern is with knowledge or subject matter, this is a question about what is, for example, science, mathematics, history and so on *for teaching*, with all this implies in the selection of content from a larger body of knowledge. Moreover this last question cannot be answered adequately unless it is placed in the context of the wider question. What is science, history, mathematics? Unfortunately most educationists are not able to answer such questions. Their training has not fitted them to do so nor does what they read encourage them to think such questions important. However, in science and mathematics scholars are coming forward with help and there is some evidence that this is having a considerable effect on the quality of thinking which is going into the reform of mathematics and science curricula. But it is not happening to any thing like the same degree in the humanities. If it does not, then questions about the relative merits of humanities curricula may be answered on a totally wrong basis.

Now none of the foregoing questions about the comparative merits of different curricula is a small one but each, I suspect, can be answered. The trouble is that most of the questions about the curriculum have, up to now, been lacking in clarity of direction. It has not been made plain to what they refer. But if it is clear that the question refers to the functioning complex of all three dimensions together and to whether curriculum A is better than curriculum B then the answer will be, of necessity, a complex one. It will be a matter of curriculum evaluation, of something which has only very recently been invented and is, as yet, little understood. It will certainly be necessary to write in extremely clearly the clause *other things being equal* and just as necessary to specify whether the evaluation relates to long or short term effects. Even then it will be as well to advise people as a general rule that even where the evaluation suggests that curriculum A is better than curriculum B, or B than A, neither may be as good as another curriculum which could be invented from what has been discovered in studying the comparative merits of A and B.

In a period of radical curriculum change new curricula are likely to be different in more than one major respect from old curricula, in which case things are likely to be very unequal indeed and there is not much to be gained from comparisons. This is the situation that exists at the present and resources would, it seems to me, be better employed in the efficient planning of new curricula rather than in attempting to demonstrate the irrelevant. But there may come a time when comparative studies are worth while and could provide a base for the continued inventing of improved curricula.

6 Curriculum theories

Up to this point, I have tried to demonstrate that a model for the curriculum can be shown to match, at least up to a point, the reality we refer to when we talk about curriculum, that the model has a structure, that the parts of the structure—the dimensions of knowledge, teaching methods and objectives—correspond to a reality which is familiar to many of you, and that the interaction of the dimensions symbolised by K, T and O represented the curriculum in action. I have also tried to show how this model has emerged from a psychological model for the curriculum and in a general way I have indicated how this and other models may have value for discussing problems of curriculum planning and evaluation, of distinguishing between a subject and a subject for teaching, and in seeing what is embedded in the term syllabus. What I have not yet done which I will now try to do is indicate how the model relates to curriculum theory in general and how such a theory relates to a family of theories.

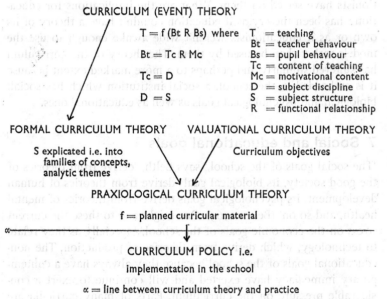

CURRICULUM (EVENT) THEORY

$T = f (Bt \ R \ Bs)$ where
$Bt = Tc \ R \ Mc$
$Tc = D$
$D = S$

T = teaching
Bt = teacher behaviour
Bs = pupil behaviour
Tc = content of teaching
Mc = motivational content
D = subject discipline
S = subject structure
R = functional relationship

FORMAL CURRICULUM THEORY

S explicated i.e. into families of concepts, analytic themes

VALUATIONAL CURRICULUM THEORY

Curriculum objectives

PRAXIOLOGICAL CURRICULUM THEORY

$f =$ planned curricular material

CURRICULUM POLICY i.e.

implementation in the school

$\alpha =$ line between curriculum theory and practice

After E. S. Maccia, Schema: Kinds of curriculum theory and policy, 1965.

A model is a special type of theory, a framework for improving one's guessing about a perceptual complex, about something which can be talked about and is known to exist. It is a metaphor. It is *as if* thinking. It is not the theory itself but a means to the understanding of that theory. In this instance, a means to the understanding of the content of teaching: the curriculum. It is a certain kind of picture which attempts to show to what some of the events in the classroom relate. The model, as I have used it, is related to *curriculum event theory* which, as you will see from the diagram, Maccia shows related to other theories and to policy. Curriculum event theory is no more than speculation about a planned series of encounters between a pupil and a selection of subjects or aspects of culture. It is not only what we choose to teach him but also why. The model I have used tries to indicate this.

'The price of the employment of models,' says Braithwaite, 'is eternal vigilance' and in this case the need is to be vigilant about which curriculum theory one has in mind when using the model. But educationists use models habitually and just as habitually they are not vigilant about them. Educational theory, so called, is full of models used *as if* they were theory. Philosophers from Plato and Aquinas to Rousseau and Dewey have developed models and educationists have seized on them. What are the implications for education? has been the cry as if education couldn't have a theory of its own or as if educationists weren't wide awake enough to use the models rather than be used by them. The theory of the curriculum has suffered similarly and perhaps to a more marked extent because it is embedded in the school, a social institution which has social, biological and psychological goals as well as educational ones.

7 Social and educational goals

'The social goals of the school,' says Belth, 'derive from theories of the good society, its biological goals derive from theories of human development, its psychological goals derive from theories of mental health, and so on' (Belth, 1965). One might add to these the current stress on the economic goals of the school, especially as they relate to technology, which derive from theories of production. The non-educational goals of the school because they always have a contemporary immediacy have exerted and will continue to exert a considerable pressure on the curriculum. Parts of many curricula are deliberately designed to serve the physical, psychological and social needs of the child. Physical education, religious education, home economics and wood and metalwork are examples, as is art and drama when their psycho-therapeutic role is stressed. They are designed to help the pupil grow, to become well adjusted, to find an occupational role in society and to become a law abiding member of it. Much current curriculum reform has as its objectives the production of more scientists, mathematicians and technologists, the inculcation of certain concepts of social justice, the amelioration of a sense of personal alienation which besets so many of our young people, the arming of them against the images of the mass-media and the inoculation of them against its potential for mass ignorance.

A great deal that is of current social concern is directed onto the curriculum. What are the curricular implications of a rising tide of crime, road accidents, of racial prejudice, of interest in and capacity for sex, of social problems both personal and general? And in response to such questions the curriculum changes either in terms of new objectives for old subjects or of new subjects altogether. Few subjects of the curriculum are eliminated. More are pressed into service. Of course the pressure is exerted unequally. High status subjects have less need to change their objectives or content than have low status subjects. Similarly the curricula of high status schools are less exposed than those of low status schools, and so it is with the curricula of pupil groups within schools. A comparison of the Crowther Report with the Newsom Report will bear witness to the truth of these assertions. The first stresses literacy and numeracy, the second 'relevance'. Relevance to the contemporary conditions and needs of the average child of to-day. The Crowther Report, though by no means a great document, is in the main an educational document. The Newsom Report is in the main a social one. But it is the Newsom Report which gives the game away. The telling phrase is in the Minister's foreword. 'The essential point is,' he says, 'that all children should have an equal opportunity of acquiring intelligence...' (Newsom Report, H.M.S.O., 1963).

It is this acquired intelligence and its nurture which is a major goal of education and therefore, its nurture is a major role for the curriculum. It is against criteria elaborated from our concept of intelligence and from such allied concepts as intellectual and academic that we can judge whether or not curriculum objectives are educational. But this concept of intelligence is not to be confused with that which is general in psychology. It is that intelligence which is susceptible of improvement by teaching. It manifests itself in the deliberate and methodical acts of thinking, of describing, explaining, exploring, and inventing in particular fields of knowledge. This intelligence cannot be caught from the passing events of life nor inherited except through language, symbol and ikon. Furthermore, the acts of describing, explaining, and exploring and inventing differ within themselves in relation to a context or framework. Explanations, to take an example, in history are different from scientific explanations which in turn are different from mathematical explanations and from explanations in literature and religion. It is the cultivation of the aptitude for these acts in the young in a range of fields that not only secure for them access to powers of thinking but also secure for them powers which may enable them to conceive not only new worlds of the mind to inhabit but also new, and it is to be hoped, better worlds in which to live.

These, put very generally, are the educational objectives of the curriculum at *all* levels. They are not subject to a consensus of opinion, or to any other form of social agreement. They are a matter of logical deduction, and are likely, because of the complexity of the tests which verify them as 'educational' to be difficult to perceive and to use in an unadulterated form in the classroom. Furthermore, because they involve thinking, reflective discourse and the like, and because this may lead to thoughts which have unknown consequences, they are likely to be feared and guarded against even in the way curricula are structured.

Of thinking, Arendt says, 'No other human capacity is so vulnerable and it is in fact easier to act under conditions of tyranny than it is to think' (Arendt, 1958). Under the press of social need, the educational objectives of the curriculum are the most likely to suffer erosion. Even more than this may well be at stake. When pupils have been taught to describe, explain, explore and invent within frameworks of history, science and mathematics, literature, language, morals, religion and art—or only in some of these—they may be able to think for themselves and, with courage, about themselves and others. They may be able to construct for themselves out of a discourse with others a model for living which is governed by rules, is realistic and has an evolutionary potential, and they may wish to test it out in action. In doing this they may well be challenging established social forces.

It would be unrealistic, even dangerous, to assert that the sole purpose of the curriculum of the school is to achieve educational objectives. Like many other practical human agencies the curriculum has to serve two masters. In fact, if it does not serve society it may not be in a position to serve education. The curriculum serves society through a range of objectives—biological, psychological, economic and moral—which have a special flavour. They represent the aspirations, the best hopes of society at a particular point in time. They embrace such things as the concept of the English gentleman: literate, cultured, philanthropic, amateur and open minded. Of course such ideologies become, in time, *disfunctional*, as the social scientists say. It is at such time that the curricular counterpart of the ideology comes under attack, and when the baby is in danger of going down with the bathwater. It is at such times that the watch over the educational objectives of the curriculum needs to be at its sharpest.

8 Need for experiment

But this is not to advocate a stern, unbending sacred cowness. Rather the opposite. There are more than the conventional ways to nurture in pupils the powers of thinking scientifically, mathematically, historically, in literary, artistic and moral modes. In fact there is mounting evidence to show that the conventional ways of nurturing these powers may be costly in human terms. Hostility to oneself, to others and to one's environment are some of these costs. It may be that they must be borne. But the price is being asked in a monopoly market: few if any alternatives are being offered. Educationists need to be more inventive in their attitude and to take as their model the scientific approach to the solution of curricular problems while at the same time remembering that educational problems are very different from scientific ones. Whether an educational problem has or has not been solved is a matter of educational tests not scientific ones. But curriculum theory and practice could benefit from the scientist's mode of operating particularly that of setting up hypotheses which the scientist gets from an *as if* model and then, with this model as the framework for exploration, sets up experimental situations out of which to establish verification. Sometimes this will require creating an *enclave* of schools freed from demands of conventional examinations and given assurance that their pupils' prospects both vocational and educational will not suffer. Nuffield have shown that this can be done within a subject curriculum. The Schools Council shows a willingness to throw its not inconsiderable weight on that side of the scales which will open up the situation for exploration and it might do well to do this at a level of status in the curriculum which will have a salutary effect on the whole of secondary education: at the sixth form level.

The current proposals of the Schools Council about the sixth form curriculum are posited on the grounds that its educational objectives can be secured by an arithmetic of periods of study: eight periods for a major course and four periods for a minor course and so on. There can obviously be no doubt that more time needs to be spent on a major than on a minor course, but should it be more time for teaching, more time for reflection or more time for the pupil to come back at the teacher? It may after all be the way in which the time is spent which will secure for the pupil one or more educational objectives rather than the time put in. It may be that no more time need be spent on being taught in a major course than on being taught in a minor course but that more time should be spent by the pupil in exploring for himself the dimensions of his major courses and in testing his explorations against the understanding his teacher has of the subject. There are no ready made answers to these issues. But there are plenty of hypotheses which could be set up from what we already know about the effectiveness of different teaching methods and about higher level intellectual abilities and it should not be too difficult to clarify the objectives of major and minor courses sufficiently to mount a scientific study provided that schools can be freed to engage in it.

Another of the objectives of the Schools Council's proposals is to secure for pupils a *general education*. Indeed this has been a major objective of the sixth form for many years. But can a general education be secured merely by ensuring that pupils have no choice but to take a diverse range of courses? Yes, it can and it must be done this way if what is meant by a 'general education' is that pupils ought to have at least a minimum knowledge of the significant conclusions arrived at in important fields of knowledge. If we echo with C. P. Snow that an educated person ought to know the second law of thermodynamics, then this is the way to achieve it. The corollary of this is that if the pupil is forced to spend more time at a range of subjects, he cannot acquire so many significant conclusions as he otherwise would in any particular field of knowledge and he becomes, therefore, less specialised. On the other hand if what is called a 'general education' is a familiarity with the modes of thinking, of describing, explaining, discovering and inventing which characterise science, history, religion, morals and other realms of intellectual endeavour then these may well be acquired within a few broad domains of study. But for it to be successful it must concentrate on the models for thinking characteristic of particular disciplines and not simply on the conclusions arising from their employment. Put briefly and as an example, science has a history, a morality, that is, it has rules governing the conduct of people desiring to call themselves scientists, and science has an ideology and an accretion of myths which if not exactly a religion of science might provide an introduction to religious thinking. Of course this kind of general education would bring the history teacher and the teacher of religious education into the territory of science teaching and take the science teacher into the territory of history teaching and religious education, but each might discover they have more in common in the education of the young than they have in sustaining their own territorial independence. There might also be an outcome for pupils from such a form of general education in increasing insight into the function of models and metaphors in the winning of new realms of meaning. If the teaching is sound, pupils may come as adults to be able to use models and not be used by them. 'To be,' as Turbayne puts it, '...aware that there are no proper sorts into which facts must be allocated, but only better pictures or better metaphors; and also aware that even to adopt a metaphor as a metaphor is to alter one's attitude to the facts.'

It is in model making that the road to intellectual inventiveness lies. 'The explosion of knowledge' which has created much anxiety among teachers and has set so many on the road to curriculum reform did not happen solely because of the advent of computers or of any other technical aid. It happened also because of the invention of new models and metaphors for sorting old facts, and in the sort-crossing which comes in applying the models of one discipline in the grounds of another. It is in the nurturing of just such intellectual inventiveness that one finds the highest educational purpose of the curriculum. But as yet we do not know how best to support its nurture for *all* pupils in the schools. It is certain, however, that we will not if we deny any one of them an intellectual component in the curriculum, for intellectual inventiveness has its roots in thinking within a disciplined study. This is the challenge of to-morrow's curriculum so far as education is concerned. A challenge which, I believe, can only be met by controlled experiment and research.

But this challenge will not be met if the agent which welds the curriculum into a dynamic and effective unit of knowledge, teaching methods and objectives is neglected. The teacher is this agent, and a free agent at that. His education must be of increasing complexity as his role changes from that of a transmitter of knowledge to that of a catalyst of future intellectual innovations because it will become less a matter of knowing what knowledge to transmit and more a matter of knowing how and why new knowledge is created and this last is a more demanding study. Moreover, he will be called on not only to nurture intellectual inventiveness but also to nurture a morality which teaches the inventors under what conditions it is right to act on their inventions. This teaching of morality may need to be done more directly than before because we can no longer be confident that it will 'transfer' from such subjects as history and literature in which it features or even from religious education. But as yet we do not know how best to do this. Nor will we if we do not undertake research. Furthermore, the challenge of to-morrow's curriculum will not be met if society's demands of the curriculum are ignored or arbitrarily set down. There is no scope for and only danger in, writing and talking about education with a capital E. What we are, therefore, faced with in the curriculum, as has been pointed out elsewhere, is a 'strategy of choices' (Morell, 1966) and in our kind of society this must arise out of a continuing discourse about the worthwhileness of those structured and purposeful activities which are the curriculum of the school. In the last analysis this discourse has both an educational and a moral intent and its outcome is a prescription about the kind of people we want pupils to become. The curriculum is, after all is said and done, a complex tool not only for emphasising desirable changes in pupils but also for bringing such changes about.

I have leaned rather heavily on the need to be clear about the components of the discourse about the curriculum and have suggested the usefulness of models in this; even elementary ones. I have also tried to say which curriculum objectives are educational ones as well as to advocate a scientific approach to curricular problems. But I have not featured the pupil either in the here and now or as he represents man in the society of to-morrow. The purpose of the curriculum is for him so that his thinking and living will be more potent for good than ours has been. But it will not be so if we do not take greater pains than we have so far to explain to him the objectives of his curricular experiences, nor will it be so if in doing this we show little regard for the kind of person he is and the kind of beliefs he holds. The curriculum will not have achieved its purpose unless at the end of the day the pupil is 'master of his own learning through his own motives' (Bruner, 1963, p. 284). Only a curriculum designed to this end will shape men and women to be intellectually free. That such is a central aim of education in our kind of society needs little or no justification. What we have to set about is understanding how curricula can be planned to achieve this aim. The curriculum is the tactical side of the educational enterprise. As much if not more than other sides, it needs a theory and technology so that it can operate efficiently in the school and the classroom. As this is forged it may become increasingly possible to translate intentions into achievement and to measure our progress toward a central purpose in the curriculum, an intellectual education for all pupils.

References

Arendt, H., 1958. *The human condition*. University of Chicago Press.

Belth, M., 1965. *Education as a discipline*. Allyn & Bacon Inc., Boston.

Bloom, B. S., *Taxonomy of educational objectives*. David McKay & Co., New York.

Brubacher, M., 1956. *Modern philosophies of education*. World Books, New York.

Bruner, J. S., 1963. *Motives for learning*, in Jenning Scholar Lectures, 1963. Educational Research Council of Greater Cleveland, Cleveland, U.S.A.

Bruner, J. S., 1963. *The process of education*. Harvard U.P., Cambridge, Mass.

Goldman, R., 1964. *Religious thinking from childhood to adolescence*. Routledge & Kegan Paul, London.

Lamm, Z., 1966. *Curriculum planning models* (unpublished).

Lynn, R. and Gordon, J. E., 1961. 'The relation of neuroticism and extraversion to intelligence and educational attainment', *Brit. J. Educ. Psychol.*, vol 31, pt. II.

Meredith, G. P., 1946. *The method of topic analysis*. Educ. Devel. Assn.

Morell, D. H., 1966. *Education and change*, Joseph Payne Memorial Lectures 1965–1966. College of Preceptors, London.

Musgrove, F., 1966. *Faith and scepticism in English education*, Inaugural Lecture, Univ. of Bradford.

Newsom Report, 1963. *Half our future*. H.M.S.O., London.

Nisbet, S. D., 1957. *Purpose in the curriculum*. Univ. of London Press.

Peters, R. S., 1966. *Ethics and education*. George Allen & Unwin, London.

Phenix, P., 1964. *Realms of meaning*. McGraw-Hill, London.

Ryle, G., 1949. *The concept of mind*. Hutchinson, London.

Robertson, J. D. C., 1957. 'An analysis of the views of supervisors on the attitudes of successful graduate student teachers', *Brit. J. Educ. Psychol.*, vol. 27, pt. II.

Staines, J. W., 1958. 'The self-picture as a factor in the classroom', *Brit. J. Educ. Psychol.*, vol. 28, pt. II.

John F. Kerr

II:5 The problem of curriculum reform

*Theory has not played an important part in any of the
recent curriculum changes sponsored by the Schools
Council and the Nuffield Foundation because a coherent
theoretical framework for guiding curriculum design is
lacking. A simple model of curriculum includes four
components—objectives, knowledge, learning experiences
and evaluation. The model does not give guidance as to
choice of objectives, content, etc. To achieve this, some
sort of curriculum theory is required. Two approaches to
the building of curriculum theory are discussed—one
deductive, one inductive. In the absence of an acceptable
model of a curriculum theory, Kerr goes on to apply a
model for the curriculum to the immediate problems of
the school. This operational model analyses the four
components—objectives, knowledge, learning experiences
and evaluation—in more detail. Kerr ends by looking at
the implications of this curriculum theory model for the
pre- and in-service training of teachers.*

It is not only in education that new ideas and new procedures move
in an apparently random manner from one emphasis to another
without any obvious signs that the progression has been planned or
even anticipated. The turning-points in science, in history, in social
development are so often the results of social crises or hunches or
the chance emergence of an outstanding mind or personality. It is
much the same in education. Why should real progress in education
not be subject to more efficient planning and development? Perhaps
we have not been sufficiently concerned with the basic determinants
of effective learning. I am not even sure that we know what they
are.

When public education was first provided in this country, the
teachers were not well enough trained to decide what and how they
should teach. The educational process was controlled centrally by
the allocation to year-groups, which we called 'standards', of precise
instructional units designed to give training in basic skills. School

Kerr, J. F., *Changing the curriculum*, University of London Press, 1968, pp. 13–
38. Reprinted by permission.

boards, inspectors, and even 'payment by results' for a short time, ensured conformity. The teachers worked hard to achieve some degree of professional autonomy and by the 1950s it was generally accepted they were free to decide what and how they should teach. Although by now local education authorities had statutory responsibility for secular instruction, they had willingly delegated this responsibility to individual teachers and schools. The general liberalizing effect on the education provided was perhaps most evident in the increase of understanding and attention given to individual children—that is, towards a child-centred curriculum. In the meantime, the central government, having set aside much of its responsibility for what went on in the classroom, continued to exercise its authority through control of building programmes and school organization, including examinations. The curriculum received scant attention until about five years ago when, largely through the initiative of groups of teachers brought together as members of professional associations,[1] a curriculum renewal movement began. It is of interest to ask ourselves why the knowledge taught in schools had grown so outmoded and inflexible; why the national demand for change was delayed for so long. Had we misused our freedom to decide what should be taught? Had we been too much concerned with the child-centred philosophy? Certainly the rapid social changes resulting from advances in technology and automation and the alarming growth of knowledge are forces which should have influenced the schools—and indeed the universities—long before the present decade.

Through the support of grant-giving bodies, particularly the Nuffield Foundation, projects for curriculum reform started, for obvious social reasons, in mathematics and the sciences. Since the beginning of the Nuffield Science Teaching Project in December 1961 over £1 million has been spent. The Nuffield model for curriculum construction is becoming a standard pattern. Teams of school teachers, college lecturers and university consultants backed by advisory committees draft new programmes which are tried out in selected schools. As a result of feedback from the pupils and teachers, the courses are modified and put to more extensive trial before publication. A wide range of course material is produced, including guides for teachers, texts for pupils, reference books, laboratory notes and background readers; newly designed apparatus and equipment; films, charts and models; and test instruments designed to measure specific outcomes of the course. When the Department of Education and Science established the Schools Council for the Curriculum and Examinations in October 1964, it was official acknowledgment of the need to plan the curriculum and examinations with a view to the achievement of carefully defined ends. National projects in many areas of the school curriculum are now in hand, including a 'resources for learning' project, sponsored by the Nuffield Foundation, in which a study will be carried out of the ways of organizing work in schools so as to make the best use of teachers' skills, and of new developments in method and equipment. Further evidence of growing attention to a formerly neglected area of education has been the recent appointment by several universities to chairs of education of people whose main interest lies within the field of curriculum research and development.

At the practical and organizational levels, the new curricula promise to revolutionize English education. Better decisions should be made by teams about the selection and organization of the content of courses, and about the relative merits of different teaching methods. But these decisions, or most of them, result from persuasive discourse in which each member of the team draws on his experience and personal judgment to arrive at a consensus of opinion. Theory has not played an important part in bringing about curriculum change simply because a coherent theoretical framework capable of guiding curriculum design is lacking. To build order into the process, a greater infusion of theory, research and evaluation is essential.[2] The pattern and interrelationships among the various disciplines might be clarified by a theory of the curriculum. The field trials of the new programmes might be designed to conform most closely to the requirements of rigorous operational research. Evaluation might be used not just for the terminal assessment of pupil changes but also to produce independent evidence about the effectiveness of each stage of the course as it is developed. At present curriculum workers lack adequate frames of reference for the assessment of progress and for the correlation of research efforts. They need these theoretical tools but, because of the impetus with which the movement for curriculum renewal is forging ahead, they are unable to wait for the curriculum theorist to work out effective models on which the new curricula might be based. This is the subject of my paper—the problem of curriculum reform. How far is it possible to develop a curriculum theory? What are the most appropriate models to start with? How can we arrive at a consensus of view about educational objectives? How should we take account of individual differences in children? What are the contributions of philosophy, psychology, sociology and history to curriculum development? These are some of the matters which are being referred to collectively as 'curriculum studies'—a new field for educators in this country in spite of thirty years' pioneer work by the Americans.

Before an attempt can be made to examine the problem of curriculum improvement more closely, it is necessary to make clear the sense in which the term 'curriculum' is being used. The range of meanings given to the concept of curriculum has been one of the sources of confusion in curriculum study. Many writers use the term loosely as being synonymous with 'syllabus', 'courses of study', 'subjects' or even 'timetable'. In many Colleges of Education the word, by tradition, is associated with narrowly conceived short courses which deal mainly with the methods of teaching a particular subject. The definition of curriculum used by Elizabeth Maccia, whose work at Ohio State University will be referred to later, is 'presented instructional content', instruction being conceived very specifically as a function of the relation between teacher behaviour and pupil behaviour.[3] Beauchamp's working definition is 'a design of a social group for the educational experiences of their children in school',[4] an example of many interpretations based on the notion of 'experience' offered by Dewey. The more comprehensive meaning used in this paper is *all the learning which is planned and guided by the school, whether it is carried on in groups or individually, inside or outside the school.*[5]

Consideration of this broad inclusive definition suggests that the curriculum may be divided into four interrelated components—curriculum objectives, knowledge, learning experiences and curriculum evaluation. The interrelatedness of the four components may be represented by a regular tetrahedron with a component at each vertex (Fig. 1). The value of this simple model of the curriculum is that it suggests four basic questions for use in the construction of a new curriculum. What is its purpose? What subject matter is to be used? What learning experiences and school organization are to be provided? How are the results to be assessed? The model itself gives no guidance about choice of objectives, content, or methods of teaching. It does suggest facets of the curriculum which might be appropriate sources for the formulation of a theory of the curriculum.

During recent years, the importance of theory as the basis for curriculum building has been stressed by many American writers. It is apparent from the literature that there is confusion as to what theory is in this connection and how it can be applied to curriculum. The term 'theory' should not be used in the scientific sense. We might legitimately use the term in the empirical sense, which includes speculation, especially when it relates to a number of hypotheses or a general conceptual background.

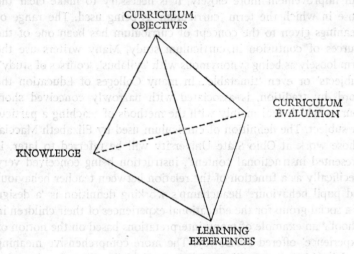

Fig. 1 A simple model of the curriculum

Two broad approaches to the building of curriculum theory, both in their infant stages, can be distinguished. The first is mainly deductive in that it involves taking theoretical formulations from other disciplines, substituting concepts, deducing hypotheses and laws, and testing the results against observable data. The work of Elizabeth Maccia and others since 1962 at the Ohio Educational Theory Centre is an example of the deductive approach. Maccia[6] states the meaning of theory in logical terms and identifies four kinds of theory : form theory, event (or reality) theory, valuational theory and, what she calls, praxiological theory or theory about practices. Each kind of theory is in turn used as a theory model from which a sub-theory of the curriculum is derived. So, formal curriculum theory gives meaning to the form of the main themes of a particular discipline, to its structure; curriculum reality (event) theory sets forth a group of propositions about content of instruction, how the component parts are interrelated and how they change; valuational curriculum theory is speculation as to curriculum objectives; and praxiological curriculum theory is speculation as to the appropriate means by which curriculum objectives can be achieved. From these four curriculum sub theories, a curriculum theory model (Fig. 2) is constructed.[7] This particular theoretical

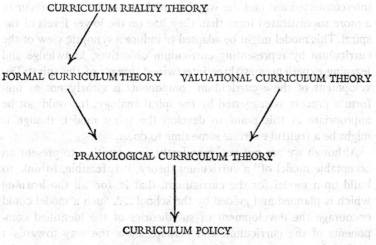

CURRICULUM REALITY THEORY

FORMAL CURRICULUM THEORY   VALUATIONAL CURRICULUM THEORY

PRAXIOLOGICAL CURRICULUM THEORY

CURRICULUM POLICY

Fig. 2 Maccia's curriculum theory model

framework has been criticized on the grounds that the methods of logic are not applicable to those human activities which are value-directed; and also that it does not provide for the evaluation of the curriculum. Educational theories do not as a rule have the logical bases which Maccia seems to be looking for.

In the second approach to the building of curriculum theory, referred to as the inductive approach, a synthetic method is adopted to build up a synoptic view of the curriculum from observable data. Assumptions and postulates are made which are basic to curriculum development, leading to prescriptions for curriculum design and evaluation. The stages or elements of this design guide curriculum choices. A criticism of this inductive approach is that one cannot approach data without theory—without some conceptual background to make selection from observed data possible : what Medawar referred to as the 'myth of the inductive method'.[8] Another drawback to this approach is that it results in a curriculum model which resembles a completed jig-saw puzzle. This is an unsatisfactory concept of curriculum. It ought to be a dynamic and continuously-evolving system.

Professor Miel of Columbia University used a dynamic model based on a spiral to represent the path of change in educational thought.[9] The spiral was designed to enlarge as it ascended and represented a time line on which the major trends of thought were placed. It pictured not only the progression of events but also their interconnectedness and the way in which particular trends recur in a more sophisticated form than they had on the lower levels of the spiral. This model might be adapted to induce a synoptic view of the curriculum by representing curriculum objectives, knowledge and learning experiences as three intertwined threads of the spiral. Development of these curriculum components is clearly not as uniform a process as suggested by the spiral analogy. It would not be appropriate at this point to develop the spiral model, though it might be a fruitful exercise some time to do so.

Although we are not yet, manifestly, in a position to present an acceptable model *of*[10] a curriculum theory, it is feasible, I think, to build up a model *for* the curriculum, that is, for 'all the learning which is planned and guided by the school . . .'. Such a model could encourage the development of sub-theories of the identified components of the curriculum and perhaps show the way towards a unified theory. It is proposed to attempt a synthesis of such a model in brief outline, dealing with objectives, evaluation, knowledge and learning experiences in turn, and then to consider the implications of the model, especially for curriculum renewal and the in-service education of teachers. As far as possible, I shall develop the model in specific operational terms rather than in conceptual terms. The infinitely complex nature of the curriculum, with its many interdependent facets, makes it impossible to produce more than a blurred image of the reality, especially in the time available (see Fig. 3).

Commonly, curriculum discussion in schools, colleges and universities is about the content of syllabuses and methods of teaching. The really important questions are about objectives and this component of the curriculum is the logical starting point, although one could break into the cycle of interrelated parts at any point. For the purposes of curriculum design and planning, it is imperative that the objectives should be identified first, as we cannot, or should not, decide 'what' or 'how' to teach in any situation until we know 'why' we are doing it. The task of identifying objectives calls for precise thinking and is a difficult exercise. Thus, few would disagree with Richard Peters's view that 'education is initiation into worth-while activities', but before such a generalized statement can be useful to the curriculum builder, we must decide what is 'worth-while'. In his inaugural lecture in 1965, Professor Bantock[11] was more specific, and therefore helpful to the curriculum builder, when he said that the ultimate purpose of education is 'clarification of the world of nature, of the world of man, and of the internal world of sensation and reflection, of emotion and cognition'. For curriculum purposes, the term 'objectives' is being used in a sense which was first

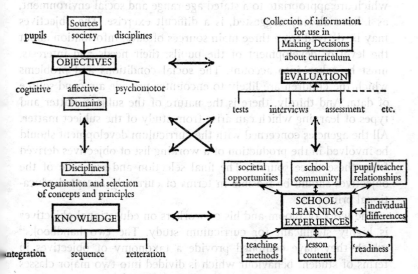

Fig. 3 A model for curriculum theory

formulated by R. W. Tyler[12] in 1933; that is, as changes in pupil behaviour which it is intended to bring about by learning. Teachers have in mind certain cognitive skills, attitudes and interests which they encourage pupils to acquire by the provision of appropriate learning experiences. It is in this sense that we speak of curriculum objectives as the intended outcomes of learning. So, a curriculum objective is a more conditional specification than an educational aim. An aim is no more than a target, but there are operational criteria associated with an objective; that is, the pupil must have been or will be involved in a particular kind of behaviour if the objective has been achieved.

In the construction or reconstruction of any part of the curriculum, decisions are made at each stage of the development which are based on the extent to which it is thought the stated objectives, if they have been made explicit, are being achieved. These decisions are too often reached on the basis of personal impression or, at best, consensus of opinion. We need to collect and use more valid and reliable data for this purpose. This is the object of curriculum evaluation. Since without evaluation we cannot be sure that the proposed objectives are attainable, the evaluation component of the curriculum is inseparable from the objectives component.

The formulation of specific and detailed curriculum objectives which are appropriate to a stated age range and social environment, as I have already suggested, is a difficult exercise. The objectives may be derived from three main sources of data. Information about the level of development of the pupils, their needs and interests, must be taken into account. The social conditions and problems which the children are likely to encounter provide a second source of data. And thirdly, there is the nature of the subject matter and types of learning which can arise from study of the subject matter. All the agencies concerned with the curriculum development should be involved in the production of a working list of objectives derived from these three sources. The final selection and sequence of the objectives should be feasible in terms of currently accepted educational principles.

The work of Bloom and his co-workers on educational objectives is highly significant for curriculum study. The two handbooks[13] which they have compiled provide a taxonomy of objectives in terms of student behaviour which is divided into two major classes or domains: the cognitive and the affective. A third group is recognized but has not been developed. This is the psychomotor domain which covers the manipulative or motor skill area. Behaviours are arranged from the simplest to the most complex, primarily from the curriculum viewpoint. Thus, in the cognitive domain ways of remembering, reasoning, problem solving and forming concepts are used to construct a detailed taxonomy based on levels of understanding. The classification ranges from the simplest knowledge of specific facts to the understanding and judgment of abstract theories and evidence (see Fig. 4). These are the distinctions which we claim to make when we teach. They are also the goals which should be tested. The affective domain is concerned with objectives related to interests, attitudes, values, appreciations and emotional sets. They range from simple attention to selected phenomena to complex relationships. In this case, the taxonomy is based on a complex and multi-dimensional concept known as 'internalization' through which, as defined by Bloom, 'there is at first an incomplete and tentative adoption of only the overt manifestations of the desired behaviour and later a more complete adoption'.[14] 'Willingness to attend' is at the lowest level of the affective scale.

1.0 KNOWLEDGE
    1.1 Knowledge of specifics
    1.2 Knowledge of ways and means of dealing with specifics
    1.3 Knowledge of universals and abstractions in a field
2.0 COMPREHENSION
    2.1 Translation
    2.2 Interpretation
    2.3 Extrapolation
3.0 APPLICATION
4.0 ANALYSIS
    4.1 Analysis of elements
    4.2 Analysis of relationships
    4.3 Analysis of organizational principles
5.0 SYNTHESIS
    5.1 Production of unique communication
    5.2 Production of a plan or a proposed set of operations
    5.3 Derivation of a set of abstract relations
6.0 EVALUATION
    6.1 Judgment in terms of internal evidence
    6.2 Judgment in terms of external criteria

Fig. 4 Summary of the cognitive domain

This scale extends to those objectives which characterize the individual almost completely—his philosophy of life and view of the universe (see Fig. 5). The separation of educational objectives into cognitive and affective classes is an artificial division, but it is sometimes convenient for the purposes of curriculum construction and evaluation to consider them separately.

It has been argued that the evaluation component of the curriculum—the second area of the operational model which is being described—and the objectives component are inter-dependent since without knowing what we are supposed to be assessing, we can hardly make assessments. Through evaluation, more rational decisions might be made about the extent to which precisely-defined

1.0 RECEIVING (attending)
    1.1 Awareness
    1.2 Willingness to receive
    1.3 Controlled or selected attention
2.0 RESPONDING
    2.1 Acquiescence in responding
    2.2 Willingness to respond
    2.3 Satisfaction in response
3.0 VALUING
    3.1 Acceptance of a value
    3.2 Preference for a value
    3.3 Commitment
4.0 ORGANIZATION
    4.1 Conceptualization of a value
    4.2 Organization of a value system
5.0 CHARACTERIZATION BY A VALUE OR VALUE COMPLEX
    5.1 Generalized set
    5.2 Characterization

Fig. 5 Summary of the affective domain

objectives have been, or can be, attained. But we have not behaved in this way. Indeed, it seems to be a characteristic of Man that he evaluates, judges or appraises almost everything which comes his way, but the criteria which he uses for his evaluations, judgments and appraisals are often highly egocentric.[15] It is easier to form opinions than to make judgments. Curriculum developers have not been exceptional in this respect. We are not clear yet about what we can do, or should try to do, with the potentially powerful techniques of evaluation.

If the objectives of a course have been identified and described in concise operational terms, it is logically a simple exercise to identify those aspects of a course which it is desirable to evaluate and then to choose an appropriate instrument or technique for each job. It is likely that information would be sought about the feasibility of the objectives; about the suitability of the content and the methods by which it is taught; about the pupils' needs and their achievements; and about the effectiveness of teacher preparation, before and during service.

A number of standard evaluation instruments are already available which might be modified to enable this information to be collected. Apart from traditional objective-type and essay-type tests, there are attitude scales, interest inventories, interviews, multiple assessments, survey techniques, and group observation methods. It will be more usual, however, for the teacher or evaluation unit to find that it is necessary to devise a special instrument for the assessment of a particular aspect of the new curriculum. Few teachers have the necessary skill to construct appropriate instruments of measurement, and training courses are urgently needed. Otherwise, the application of measurement techniques to curriculum development in this country will continue to be confined largely to the conventional examination of individual gains in terms of simple cognitive end-products. We are not concerned in curriculum evaluation with selecting or ranking individuals but with overall changes in group performance. For this purpose, the evaluation instruments do not need to be as refined as tests for discriminating between individuals, although account still needs to be taken of the principles of test construction such as the validity of the instrument, its reliability and sensitivity. Curriculum evaluation is an integral component of the curriculum which we have not utilized adequately. If the techniques were developed, it would enable us to make a more scientific attack on the problem of curriculum renewal.

Turning now to the knowledge component of the curriculum, the prime question posed by the model is: how can the curriculum content be selected and organized so that the objectives of the school are most likely to be attained? We are agreed that the school's responsibility extends beyond the teaching of artificially circumscribed packages of information. The knowledge component is synthesized from the disciplines. The disciplines are the raw material by means of which we expect to achieve our stated objectives. They are the resource from which appropriate experiences arise for the education of children and adults. One of the most significant contemporary developments in curriculum study at school level has been the re-examination of the disciplines as sources for learning. More attention is being given in curriculum building to the basic concepts and methods of enquiry which are used by scientists, by mathematicians, by historians and so on. Our understanding of knowledge depends on the concepts we invent, such as force in physics, the bond in chemistry, scarcity in economics and style in literature; and the broader organizing principles that we find, for example, in the early years of the Nuffield Foundation chemistry course

—mass relationship among reacting substances, energy in chemical reactions, and the importance of structure. In this new chemistry course, two alternative schemes are proposed through which an understanding of the same broad principles might be gained. The factual information in the two schemes differs significantly. By drawing attention to the fundamental structures of the disciplines in school work—not, of course, by direct teaching but through deliberately contrived learning experiences—the possibility of transfer is increased; that is, application to other situations of the principles and concepts which characterize a discipline is more likely. Another reason for a greater emphasis on structure is that it could bring elementary and advanced knowledge into a closer relationship since the sequence and relevance of fundamental ideas would be more carefully worked out. The selection of characteristic principles and concepts in any particular discipline and the arrangement of them in sequential and logical order is too big a job for one person. It is a task for a team which should include university specialists and other consultants as well as teachers. If school work is to become more relevant and remain relevant to the rapidly growing bodies of knowledge and to the increasingly complex society in which we live, we should no longer expect individuals to write syllabuses and text books. It is a foolish builder who does not take advice before he lays the foundations for his building. Teachers are builders and they cannot be expected to keep in touch with what is going on at the rock face of knowledge. Having designed a new course, the team of teachers and specialists should keep it under review to ensure that it continues to reflect the changing nature of the discipline. In the curriculum projects developed in this country during recent years, groups of people have been responsible in each case for the knowledge components of the courses. There has been some uneasiness on the part of a few teachers about the apparent loss of freedom to teach what they want to teach. Perhaps the professional autonomy of teachers should rest more on the freedom to decide how to teach rather than what to teach.

An unfortunate result of contemporary curriculum developments, even in the junior schools, has been to focus attention on individual disciplines without concern for their relationships to other fields and to neglect the overall structure of the whole school programme. We need to consider the types of relationships that should obtain both *within* and *between* the main areas of knowledge. Essentially, problems of relationships are problems of classification (on which there is a growing literature). The theory of knowledge raises many questions about the relationship of the various disciplines to the development of mind and to the nature of knowledge. For the purposes of understanding relationships between disciplines in curriculum study, two views of the nature of knowledge are helpful.

First, it is generally recognized that the natural sciences, mathematics, the humanities and the social sciences are four distinct groupings of organized disciplines, each of which uses key concepts and methods to view the environment in a different way. But, with the possible exception of mathematics, curriculum workers are giving little attention to these recognized broad groups. As already stated, attention tends to be directed to individual disciplines. In the Nuffield Foundation Science Teaching O-level Project, physicists, chemists and biologists have gone their way largely independent of each other. If we are to organize curriculum content for the purpose of attaining well-defined objectives and, in particular, to give experience of the unique concepts and methods used in each area of learning, the isolation of separate disciplines at school level should, it is suggested, be questioned. A gradual shift to broader groupings of knowledge seems desirable. Perhaps the four groupings of disciplines could furnish a framework for a planned programme of general education which would give the child adequate experience of all the ways of knowing and doing, and which would avoid inefficient repetition of a limited range of kinds of experience. Our treatment in schools during the 1940s and 1950s of general science and social studies has taught us to be cautious about grouping disciplines together. Certainly, during the general science movement we were more concerned with the informational content of courses than with underlying concepts and methods of enquiry. Teachers were not adequately prepared for the change through in-service courses and continued to think and teach in terms of biological, chemical and physical topics. The textbooks and the examination papers continued to reflect sharply the separate disciplines. The lesson is that unified courses must evolve slowly out of those principles and methods from the separate disciplines which are interrelated and fundamental. A willingness on the part of subject specialists to search for new patterns of knowledge for use in the curriculum might provide a greater measure of coherence and relatedness for the curriculum as a whole.

Consideration of the kind of integration which should be aimed at in curriculum-building *between* the broad areas of knowledge, rather than *within* each area, is helped by a second view of the nature of knowledge which relates the disciplines to specific modes of thinking or kinds of cognitive operation. Peterson[16] urges us to stop thinking of general education in secondary schools in terms of general knowledge, but rather in terms of the development of four main modes of thought : the analytic, the empirical, the moral, and the aesthetic. Phenix[17] proposes six realms of meaning in his generic classification of knowledge : symbolics, empirics, aesthetics, ethics, synoptics, and synnoetics (a term used by Phenix to represent personal or relational knowledge as in certain aspects of philosophy) (See Fig. 6.). Disciplines are rarely assignable to a single mode

REALMS OF MEANING	DISCIPLINES
Symbolics	Ordinary language, mathematics
Empirics	Physical sciences, social sciences
Aesthetics	Music, visual arts, literature
Ethics	Moral philosophy
Synoptics	History, religion
Synnoetics	Philosophy, psychology

Fig. 6 Classification of knowledge

of thought or realm of meaning : for example, literature contributes to the development of both moral and aesthetic judgments. This view of the heterogeneous character of knowledge needs to be taken into account when building the curriculum if the child is to experience all the ways of thinking appropriate to his level of attainment and to his environment. There is little evidence that there is one universal method to deal with problems in all fields, as Dewey's problem-solving approach seemed to suggest; or that there is a recognizable unity in knowledge which when found will close Snow's gap. Indeed, as we have seen, the trend today is towards a multitude of methods and conceptual schemes. The view of the nature of knowledge which relates different disciplines to specific modes of thought or meaning seems to suggest that an appropriate relationship in the curriculum between the broad areas of knowledge would be that which resulted in the exercise of *all* modes of thought at a level appropriate to the learner.

Apart from integration within and between areas of knowledge, there are two further criteria which the teacher uses for the effective construction of the knowledge component of a curriculum. These are reiteration, and sequence of elements of the courses.

'Reiteration' refers to the repetition of major curriculum elements. For example, the fundamental concept of energy in science must recur again and again at many points in a course. 'Sequence' is related to reiteration, but sequence, as a criterion for curriculum building, emphasizes that each successive experience—relating to energy, for example—should build upon the preceding one. Reiteration, sequence and integration are guiding principles for the teacher in the detailed organization of an effective course.

Paul Hirst[18] has warned us that 'decisions about the content of courses cannot be taken without careful regard to the abilities and interests of the students for whom they are designed'. What learning experiences can be provided *through* the organized content of the curriculum that are likely to result in the attainment of the teacher's objectives? This is the last major curriculum component, 'Learning Experiences'.

The term 'learning experiences' is intended to refer to the interaction between the learner and the external factors in the environment to which he is exposed and can react. When we are referring to the curriculum model, learning experiences must be restricted, by definition, to those which are 'planned and guided by the school', including societal opportunities arranged by the school, the nature of the school community, the relationships between pupils and teachers, variations arising from individual differences and levels of readiness, the actual content of each lesson and the methods by which it is presented to the child. This is the area of curriculum to which most attention is given in the day-by-day work of the school and during courses for student teachers and teachers. The other curriculum areas tend to be set aside. The general principle that a pupil learns through what he does or experiences is emphasized and, if these experiences are appropriate and within the capacity of the pupil, the objectives may be attained. In teacher-training we are concerned with the process of planning the learning experiences to achieve particular aims. To guide us in this planning, ideas have been freely borrowed from other disciplines, particularly from psychology and sociology. Although these disciplines do not pretend to speak with one voice about any aspect of human learning or behaviour, educators have tended to use selected findings for prescriptive purposes. Professor Simon[19] dealt with this problem in his inaugural lecture (November 1966) when he reminded us that 'some of the worst mistakes [in education] have followed from transferring techniques and concepts uncritically from one province to another'. Two American curriculum theorists[20] wrote recently that the application of psychology, sociology and anthropology to practical considerations of schooling 'magnifies their normal limitations and clouds the dialogue on curriculum'. There has been a tendency to pick out findings which seem to support one's own opinions with the result that extreme positions acquire apparent support. The study of curriculum, along the lines which are being proposed, holds out some hope for the 'fruitful co-operation' with other disciplines about which Professor Simon spoke.

The curriculum model steers the selection of learning experiences towards precisely defined ends so that the curriculum builder is in a position to consult the psychologist or the sociologist about quite specific questions. For example, recent work suggests that a child's experience is at least as important as maturation in determining his readiness for certain kinds of learning. If this is so, it would be feasible to plan the experiences that children have through the curriculum to achieve, say, a faster rate of development. In a particular area of the curriculum, such as scientific activities with junior school children, psychologists might look at the question of the optimum age at which children are capable of carrying out certain kinds of problem-solving activities. Empirical classroom-based curriculum studies offer the possibility of more fruitful co-operation with allied disciplines.

Another example of possible co-operation at the operational level relates to the new technology of learning—team teaching, television, language laboratories, programmed learning and other innovations. Many specific problems[21] face teachers who are beginning to use these instructional media. Which combination of resources is appropriate for teaching a particular topic to achieve a named purpose with a given group of children? In view of the changing theories about individual differences, how can we reconcile the development of mass instruction through television with the technology associated with individualized instruction, such as teaching machines? How does one medium interact with other media? How do these media interact with different types of pupils and teachers?

It must be acknowledged again that the completed model which has been presented inevitably results in a Procrustean view of the curriculum. But the model makes some theoretical formulation and empirical study of curriculum matters possible and limits the occasions when a crude pragmatic approach has to be used. It also promotes

an interactive relationship between educational theory and classroom practice, and checks the false separation of theory from practice about which teachers and student teachers, with justification,
complain. Assuming this model for the curriculum has some validity, what are its implications, particularly for the education of
teachers both before service and during service? The remainder of
this paper is concerned with the implications of the curriculum
theory model which has been outlined.

There seems to be an overriding need for a drastic change of
policy towards many curriculum matters. If the trial-and-error
methods, which individual teachers at present practise within a
framework of control from outside the classroom, are to be replaced
by a system based on co-operative effort and objective evaluation,
then there must be a willingness on the part of everyone concerned
to participate actively in the curriculum building process and to try
out the programmes which by co-operative effort have been produced. Many teachers are discouraged by their efforts to influence
the direction of curriculum change. They feel thwarted by a policy
which in their view leaves insufficient authority in their hands. Does
the professional relationship between teachers, headteachers, administrators and central authority inhibit curriculum development
in any way? Enquiry suggests that teacher involvement in curriculum projects might be encouraged and made more efficient by some
shifts in the power structure, in the distribution of economic and
human resources, and in the management of policy.

A second change is implied, particularly for the secondary school
and higher education, by what has been said about the autonomy
and diversity of the various disciplines of knowledge. This view of
knowledge exposes vast areas of many syllabuses of work which are
useless and outdated and which overlap in educational purpose. For
reasons given earlier, a more central position for knowledge in curriculum planning is claimed. There are no signs in curriculum
studies, either in England or elsewhere, as far as I know, of detailed
attention being given to the integration of the curriculum as a
whole. Curriculum projects deal usually with single subjects. The
implication of the view expressed about the nature of knowledge is
that we should be moving cautiously from patterns of single subject
study to grouped disciplines. Professor Neustadt[22] and Professor
Grodecki[23] each referred in their inaugural lectures to the same
integrative problem in relation to the teaching in universities of
sociology and law.

But the message arising from the proposed rationale for curriculum construction which rings louder and clearer than any other is that the reform of the curriculum will not come about without the total involvement of teachers. How can this be achieved? How are conditions to be created for the necessary involvement? We have started to develop a new concept of in-service education for teachers in the School of Education at Leicester, but, before I refer to it, let us first look at the national picture.

It is becoming manifest that the projects for curriculum renewal which have been introduced during the past five years by the Nuffield Foundation and the Schools Council are not passing phenomena but indicate what will become the accepted pattern for building new curricula. During the trial stages of a project, the pre-training of those teachers who are participating in the trials can be centrally organized. But when the new materials become generally available—as happened last summer with the Nuffield O-level science books, specially designed apparatus and audio-visual materials—the demand from teachers for re-training courses cannot be met from existing resources, either centrally or locally. The Department of Education and Science spent only £18,000 on short courses during 1963–64. During 1966–67, it was proposed to spend £100,000.[24] Although this is a notable increase, it is only 6s. 8d. per teacher per annum, or £14 over the whole of his working life. Services provided locally by the universities, local education authorities and professional associations have also been stepped up, but the re-training of all the teachers who wish to use each newly completed curriculum project is already beyond our existing means. At the present time, the potential market for courses in primary mathematics and also in primary science exceeds 100,000 teachers, and tens of thousands of secondary school science teachers are eager for the opportunity to discuss the interpretation and use of the new Nuffield courses. Furthermore, in many cases a single short course is not likely to bring about the degree of modification in teaching methods which is desired. Radical changes based on a new set of objectives are often proposed. Unless the teacher is given support over a period of time, he may just move towards a superficial appearance of change. In the C. D. Butler Memorial Lecture at Exeter in October 1966, Robert Morris[25] warned us about the danger in the changeover to comprehensive education of being 'lulled into a state of damaging complacency about the rectitude of the system without being concerned about its purposes'. It is so with each new curriculum programme. Real reform can only be achieved, in my view, through a full measure of teacher involvement.

The road to this kind of involvement seems to be, first, to interest the teachers in a particular line of development—not usually difficult; then to bring teachers together in circumstances which will create a willingness to enter with confidence into a commitment to work as a member of a curriculum group; and finally to arrange for the provision of all the resources and specialist help for which the group asks. The conventional method of in-service provision through conferences and short courses of lectures rarely provides all three conditions for total involvement—interest, commitment and resources. There is no doubt that the short series of lectures is an effective way of keeping the teaching profession informed and interested about changes in educational theory and practice, but there is evidence that it is not an effective method of bringing about desirable changes in the classroom. For this purpose, teachers' centres are proving to be effective instruments of change. The concept of a teachers' centre, such as we are trying to develop at Leicester, is a deliberate attempt to involve teachers in their own curriculum problems and development. At the present time, twelve different groups of teachers are provided with some of the resources they need, including specialist guidance largely from my colleagues on the staff of the School of Education. Most of these study groups are using the curriculum model which I have outlined as a design for solving the curriculum task each group has set itself. The creative consequences are, I think, most encouraging. The local education authorities in the area are beginning to make provisions for their own teachers' centres and, if this trend develops, the School of Education might appropriately assume the rôle of consultant and co-ordinator in the area. We might also help to train the leaders of curriculum groups in the principles and techniques of curriculum construction and evaluation. Not the least of our rôles must be to continue with operational research, particularly in the area of curriculum evaluation which we have made our special concern. Curriculum development and research work along the lines indicated cannot proceed without the full co-operation of teachers and local education authorities.

Two further implications of the curriculum theory model should be mentioned briefly—its significance for the pre-service training of teachers and for the dynamics of curriculum change.

Although we are aware that it is not desirable to separate theory from practice in the initial training of teachers, we fall too often into the trap of dealing with a part of curriculum study, which we call 'method' work, as though it was a separate entity from selected aspects of educational psychology, philosophy, sociology and history, which we call 'theory'. A model for the curriculum could have a co-ordinating function. If the educational objectives of College of Education or University teacher-training courses were set out in operational terms—and the difficulties of this exercise have been stressed—it would become feasible to ask more precise questions about the knowledge component of the education course and about relevant learning experiences. These questions could well act as new foci for the selection of the most relevant concepts, principles and theories from the appropriate disciplines. Perhaps the material dealt with would not differ greatly from the content of education as we know it, but the emphases would certainly be different and much material would be discarded. Educationists would then be in a position to consult specialists in the disciplines allied to education for advice about particular problems in the same way as the medical profession calls upon physiologists, biochemists, bacteriologists and so on.

And, finally, the last implication of this approach to the study of curriculum relates to the need for consideration of the implementation of the changes suggested. The manner in which dominant forces of the day have shaped the curriculum of the past is challenged. Although the influence of historical tradition, political expediency, economic priorities and social prejudice cannot wholly be eliminated—and it is not suggested that they should be—the theoretical model for the curriculum which has been put forward suggests the possibility that change can be effectively planned and predetermined on educational grounds. There is need to explore the nature of this planned collaborative process which involves relationships between teachers and curriculum specialists as well as between teachers and pupils. There is need for more adequate agencies for change, such as teachers' centres and a national evaluation service along the lines of the Educational Testing Service at Princeton, New Jersey. There is urgent need for research work into these matters if the dynamics of change in the curriculum development process are to be understood and, to some extent, controlled. There is *no* need to polarize the argument between planners and non-planners. A compromise is envisaged between planned decision-making and free choice as a result of more and better theory, and more and better research.

Some of the changes proposed will require a revolution in attitudes and methods related to curriculum development. That the revolution has started, there is no doubt. The goal is to plan and guide more of the child's experiences—not all—on the basis of a conceptual framework which is at least partly susceptible to theoretical study.

References

1 For example, the *Reports of the Science and Education Committee of the Science Masters' Association*, John Murray, 1961.

2 *Review of Educational Research*, vol. 36, no. 3, June 1966, p. 341.

3 E. S. Maccia, 'Curriculum theory and policy', *Occasional Paper 65-176*, Educational Theory Center, Ohio State University.

4 G. A. Beauchamp, *Curriculum theory*, Kegg Press, Wilmette, Illinois, 1961, p. 34.

5 Modified from V. E. Herrick and R. W. Tyler (editors), *Toward improved curriculum theory*, Chicago University Press, 1950, p. 59.

6 E. S. Maccia, *Methodological considerations in curriculum theory building*, presented to A.S.C.D. Commission on Curriculum Theory, Chicago, 1965. In the brief statement about Maccia's work, I have used her form of words in places to retain the precision of her writing, but much of the carefully reasoned analysis is omitted. The original papers should be consulted to ensure a full understanding of the work.

7 E. S. Maccia, *Occasional Paper 65-176*, *op. cit.*, p. 11.

8 P. B. Medawar, 'Is the scientific paper fraudulent?' *Saturday Review*, 1 August 1964, pp. 42-3.

9 A. Miel, 'Reassessment of the curriculum—Why?' in *A reassessment of the curriculum*, edited by D. Huebner, Bureau of Publications, Columbia University, New York, 1964, p. 20.

10 E. S. Maccia, *Methodological considerations in curriculum theory building*, *op. cit.*, p. 7. It is suggested that 'model of' and 'they' could be synonymous terms, but 'model for' cannot be more than theory models to develop theory.

11 G. H. Bantock, *The implications of literacy*, Leicester University Press, 1966, p. 16.

12 *Educational Research Bulletin XIII*, no. 8, 1933, pp. 196-206.

13 B. S. Bloom, *et al.* (editors), *Taxonomy of educational objectives: Handbook I, The cognitive domain*, Longmans Green, 1956; and D. R. Krathwohl, B. S. Bloom, and B. B. Masia. *Taxonomy of educational objectives: Handbook II, The affective domain*, Longmans Green, 1964.

14 *Ibid.*, II, p. 29.

15 *Ibid.*, I, p. 185.

16 A. D. C. Peterson, *Arts and science sides in the sixth form*, Oxford University Department of Education, 1960.

17 P. H. Phenix, *Realms of meaning*, McGraw-Hill, New York, 1964, p. 28.

18 P. H. Hirst, 'Liberal education and the nature of knowledge', in *Philosophical analysis and education*, edited by R. D. Archambault, Routledge and Kegan Paul, 1965, p. 135.

19 B. Simon, *Education: the new perspective*, Leicester University Press, 1967.

20 A. R. King and J. A. Brownell, *The curriculum and the disciplines of knowledge*, John Wiley, New York, 1966, p. 109.

21 *Review of Educational Research*, vol. 36, no. 3, June 1966, ch. 4.

22 I. Neustadt, *Teaching sociology*, Leicester University Press, 1965, pp. 15–18.

23 J. K. Grodecki, *Legal education: dilemmas and opportunities*, Leicester University Press, 1967.

24 R. Morris, *The in-service education of teachers*, Exeter University Institute of Education, 1966, p. 6.

25 *Ibid.*, p. 9.

John E. Merritt

II:6 Reading and the curriculum

In this paper John Merritt describes a way of designing curriculum, based on four main stages—Motivation, Plan, Implementation and Review. At a second level of greater specificity, each stage is divided into two components: Motivation—Aims and Objectives; Plan—Strategies and Tactics; Implementation—Methods and Technique; Review —Evaluation and Consolidation. Examples are taken from the area of the teaching of reading to illustrate the procedure in operation.

What we must do is to help children to understand their own immediate and long term needs and to appreciate the legitimate needs of others. That is what the syllabus is about. We must help children to learn to satisfy those needs, whilst respecting the reasonable needs of others. That is what the curriculum is about. We must help children to determine their own life course with due regard for others. That is what education is about.

And this is the point at which we singularly fail. We are content to be teachers of subjects, or teachers of tool skills such as mathematics or reading. We are not prepared to be educators and consider whether the knowledge we purvey is adequate in range and relevance. We are not prepared to tie tool skills sufficiently closely to their applications. We are not prepared to do either within a context which ensures that children develop all those abilities necessary to self-determination and humanitarian consideration. We train them instead as manual or intellectual labourers.

Education in self-determination

... In order to do what is required well enough you must analyze what you do and do it consciously and deliberately at all times—not fittingly as the mood takes you, and sometimes not at all.

But what is this 'it' that I am talking about, which is so commonly practised, yet so neglected? 'It' is simply that logical

Reprinted by permission from John Merritt's article 'Reading and in the curriculum' in *Reading and the curriculum*, Ward Lock Educational, London, 1971.

sequence of events which is essential to the efficient making of decisions and the taking of effective actions. I propose to describe this sequence so that you can see how essential it is to self-determination. I shall then use this same sequence in tackling the problem of the relationship between reading and the curriculum.

Let us first look at the simple sequence which may be observed in any complete action. Motivation Plan Implementation Review. We may remember the initials: MPIR. There is no action without motivation, no satisfaction without a plan that is then implemented, no satisfactory profit from experience without review.

But this is a simple descriptive account of what naturally happens. Our job is to be prescriptive. It is our job to analyze this process and see whether we can help children to control their own actions in accordance with an adequate appraisal of their own needs and the dictates of humanity and responsibility. Let us therefore take each stage separately and consider the implications for the teacher.

Motivation
It is not enough that a child should have knowledge of his needs, he must be able to weigh one need against another and determine his priorities. To do this, he must first distinguish between his aims and his objectives. His aims are those states of body or mind which he wishes to attain. His objectives are the environmental correlates of those aims. Thus, the satisfaction of hunger may be an aim. A plate of steak might be the correlated objective.

An academic distinction you may say. But Alexander was frustrated because he ran out of objectives. There were no countries left to conquer. He had failed to recognize life's essential paradox—that is the material objectives which prove ephemeral to the mind and the intangibles, i.e. the aims, that alone have substance. How many millionaires—and headmasters—are frustrated because they have reached the pinnacle of their ambitions. Having achieved their objectives they are left without the aims that would make them worthy custodians of their fortunes.

I must ask you, is this the first consideration in each segment of your teaching? Do you really help the child to survey all his needs, define his aims and set his own objectives? Or do you cunningly limit his choice, if you give him any, to that which is convenient to you? Or again, do you hasten through this process quickly so that you can get down to 'brass tacks', mistaking the shadow—reading age perhaps, or examination marks—for the substance of educational progress?

Plan
This subdivides into strategies and tactics. Strategies are the theoretically possible ways of achieving an objective; tactics are the ways in which actual resources are to be deployed. An academic distinction? But how often do we narrow a child's horizon by imposing aims, objectives and strategies, then praise him to our colleagues for his ingenuity in seeing how to carry out the task we set. We might as well praise a lemming for its ingenuity in overcoming obstacles on its route to self-destruction in the sea. Surely, if a child has so much ingenuity he can be educated to operate at the higher levels and not merely at the lower, for this calls on no greater powers of intellect.

Implementation
This subdivides into method and technique and I will not elaborate on these distinctions at this point. This is the area on which the vast bulk of what passes for education is concentrated. We spend millions of man hours teaching children what and how to do. All we forget is to spend sufficient time helping them to discover why they need to do it in the first place. Of course we can tell them it is for their own good, but a method is only as good as the results it produces, and telling children things is not the most effective of our methods.

Review
This resolves into evaluation and consolidation. Evaluation is the assessment of each phase of an action in terms of the extent to which it helped in the achievement of aims. How can we expect children to develop the habit of evaluating aims if in the first place they knew little of them and cared less?

Again, how much useless activity do we ourselves continue to indulge in simply because we do not take the trouble to evaluate what we are doing in terms of aims? Like Alexander, we are too 'hooked' on objectives. If our children show progress on a word recognition test or get the 'right' number of O levels we are quite content that we are doing our job. But if we do not look beyond these objectives and evaluate in terms of aims we are neglecting our professional responsibility. If we do not systematically ensure that children evaluate each action they carry out in terms of aims we are neglecting our educational responsibility.

Consolidation is the final stage. Here, we allow children to labour for years then consign the products of their endeavours to the waste-paper basket. Little wonder that so many children have as much contempt for school work as we have—and see little point in providing fodder for our litter bins. If work is worth doing it is surely worth storing for future reference. If it is to be discarded it should only be because it is replaced by something better. The child needs to consolidate his educational endeavours by storing the products of his labours so that he can refer back to them at any time. He must learn to select what is of lasting value, to edit and to update. If he spends the bulk of his time discarding the products of his endeavours then we, and he, must question the validity of the original exercise.

You will see from this analysis that educating children towards responsible autonomy is not some high flown aim towards which we may merely pay lip-service, nor is it something that can be achieved by well-meaning but woolly minded 'progressives'. Neither can it be achieved by limiting a child's educational diet to subject teaching and skill training. Instead, it is a curriculum component which requires the most meticulous analysis and assiduous effort on the part of the teacher. The aim of personal autonomy must be converted into precise educational objectives, and the above analysis is the first stage in that process.

This cannot be left to any single teacher but must be developed at all times and in every curriculum activity by every member of a school staff acting as a member of a team. This team must devise strategies and tactics to achieve these objectives and devise new methods, or adapt existing methods, in order to implement these plans and evaluate and consolidate each gain. Now the question is how may we marry the teaching of reading to this curriculum requirement?

Aims in teaching reading

The aim of reading is to profit from the experiences of others in seeking to satisfy our own needs.

Different needs call for us to think in different ways. We do not think in precisely the same way about food as we think about personal relationships. We do not think in the same way about science as we do about art. But reading is thinking in the context of print, therefore reading in relation to one need is often very different from reading in relation to another need. If, then, we wish to develop an overall competence in reading we must develop reading in the context of those needs which are immediately significant to the child and which will be significant to him as an adult. We must, as our American colleagues say, teach reading in the content areas—but this must be a need-content and not merely a subject-content....

Still within the context of aims we must consider the nature of the media which must be read in order to gain information to satisfy our various needs—newspapers and magazines, private and official letters, forms and instructions, and so on. Anyone who has made any serious study of reading skills knows that the skills required in reading vary according to the medium. An income tax form is very different from a love letter and must be read for somewhat different kinds of implication! Again, a publicity brochure or advertisement calls for skills rather different from those required when reading an authoritative textbook on a well established subject.

Finally, in considering our aims in teaching reading we must consider the mode of approach in reading. From what I have said earlier it should be quite clear what this should be. Reading entails a motive, requires a plan, must be implemented and must be followed by review—again MPIR or motivation, plan, implementation, review. Let us spell this out in a little more detail.

Motivation

The reader's aims. These must be defined following an analysis of needs, the kinds of resource materials to which he may have recourse, and priorities to be observed in selection of material.

The reader's objectives. These must be specified in terms of the particular questions to which answers are required, and the specific materials to be accessed for each question, bearing in mind the suitability and availability of each unit of material.

Plan

The reader's strategies. These must be designed to ensure that the reader selects materials which are suitable in terms of his criteria and which are feasible from the point of convenience of access.

The reader's tactics. These must satisfy the criteria of economy of time and his own capabilities in selecting each specific source or section of material within each source.

Implementation

The reader's methods. This is the process of identifying sequences and perceiving main ideas. It includes gambits such as locating key words and noting factual detail, gaining impressions and scrutinizing assumptions, identifying arguments and evaluating conclusions.

The reader's techniques. These are the hierarchies of learning sets relating to linguistic competence which I have referred to elsewhere (Merritt, 1970) as the intermediate skills, and those more elementary recognition skills which we may call the primary skills. They are manifested in the flexible use of scanning, skimming and processing habits which are deployed according to the objectives to be achieved in successive units of material.

Critical as these skills are, note how low down they come in our list. This is because they are not what reading is about. Like the data tape or the filmstrip, they are merely the medium through which we get the message.

Review

The reader's evaluation. This entails checking the answers against the questions in a systematic fashion and checking back on any discrepancies. It includes evaluation of performance in each phase of the reading sequence as well as evaluation of the results.

The reader's consolidation. This entails committing to memory the key concepts, relating each item to every relevant area of personal knowledge, storing useful material in the resource unit with appropriate cross references, and communicating significant information to those who want it and will make good use of it. This is the critical phase of the action and it is clear that we are as inadequate in this as we are in the preparatory stages. This is the point at which the reader's subjective schema must be modified and his horizons enlarged.

These then are the aims of the teacher: to develop reading in the context of the child's needs, to develop the ability to read the particular kinds of material which must be processed if those needs are to be understood, and to develop the child's autonomy as a reader. Our aims for the reader are simply a facet of our curriculum aims.

Objectives in teaching reading

Our objectives in teaching reading must be defined in terms of the competence which we think our children should attain and they must be limited to those we need to teach. In this day and age, when presidents, business executives and academics are taking courses in efficient reading it is alarming that so many teachers think that learning to read is something that happens in the infant school and determine their objectives accordingly. They equate reading with that essential but minute area which I briefly mentioned under the title of primary skills.

No doubt many of those present today would reject such a view, but how many have worked through the analysis made above and gone on to define the whole range of objectives which are essential if their pupils are to make satisfactory progress? Alas, not many!

This, of course, is an exacting demand. But no one entering the profession was ever given a certificate stating that the job was easy. Only those who have failed to work through the implications of the foregoing analysis systematically can jog along complacently, assuring themselves that they do 'that sort of thing'.

Strategies in teaching reading

There are four principal strategies which we may adopt in teaching reading and these, not surprisingly, are the four principal curriculum strategies:

1 the provision of reality situations
2 simulations
3 practical investigations
4 theoretical studies

1 Reality situations

When I speak of a reality situation I refer to a situation in which whatever actions occur are directly related to someone's immediate needs. Thus, if children from a primary school run errands for an infirm adult or relieve the loneliness of a senior citizen, that is a reality situation. If pupils in a secondary school relieve the anxiety of an overanxious parent by looking after her children for periods in the school flat, that is a reality situation. If they research the holiday resorts in Britain and abroad so that parents can use the school as a resource unit, that is a reality situation. If they research the leisure facilities available in their own neighbourhood, that is a reality situation. One could go on for ever giving examples, but I would suggest to you that it is convenient to consider reality situations under five headings: Home and Family; The Community; The Consumer; Employment; Leisure.

Through the exploitation of reality situations in each of these areas, children can learn about their own needs as well as the needs of others, and how both may best be satisfied.

Such activities provide excellent opportunities for children to define their own aims, establish objectives, devise strategies, and so on. In other words, putting children in reality situations provides the teacher automatically with opportunities to help children to develop personal autonomy—provided, that is, that the teacher has taken the trouble to master the routines I have described above. If not, the product will simply be a lot of busy-looking children, working like ants to create a display of work that looks marvellous to the visitor but is fully understood only by the teacher—not the children.

The reality situation, like any other, only works for the children if the teacher is concerned to see that they do their thing, not his. How many exhibitions are simply products of the teacher's professional ego rather than the children's understanding? This occurs when the teacher has set the wrong objectives. The only antidote to self-deception of this kind is for the teacher to undertake the somewhat tortuous task of working through his own personal autonomy routine using the model exemplified in the structure of this lecture.

Given the reality situation and full pupil participation, the reading routines fit in as one of the many varieties of the autonomy routine that children may adopt. You should, at this point, go back and check through the MPIR sequence which I spelled out in terms of reading, and think of this in relation to a variety of realistic situations.

Returning however to our own strategies in teaching reading, our next consideration is that of media. The reality situation demands realistic media. In the case of the resource unit on leisure facilities, for example, one might well consult brochures, guide books and newspaper articles. However these often provide a somewhat biased picture, or fail to give information which is of direct concern to child or parent.

The people who may be in the best position to fill in the picture are children in the areas concerned. They can readily provide information about, for example, what is really a 'stone's throw' from the beach, oil on the foreshore, exorbitant prices, tatty amusement arcades, and so on.

Information obtained from other children provides an extra dimension to a child's understanding. On the one hand, such information provides a check on his other sources and makes him appreciate how careful he must be about what to rely upon as evidence. On the other hand, it provides him with a viewpoint that is more likely to coincide with his own, and which is therefore more significant to him.

2 Simulations

This is the world of make believe. Children love make believe and can learn a great deal from simulation. One example is the commercial department in the comprehensive school which sets up a number of 'firms', each 'doing business' with each other. Experiences that would take months or years in reality can thus be telescoped into weeks or days. This approach can be infinitely more satisfying and meaningful than the dreary routine of book keeping exercises.

There are, of course, many kinds of simulation exercise, varying from the games children play in the nursery school—doctors, schools, mummies and daddies to the harsher economic games of the business school or the war games of the Pentagon. It is not in my brief to examine and evaluate all the possible applications here. For a useful introduction Tansey and Unwin (1969) and Walford (1969) might be consulted.

In simulations, as in reality situations, there are numerous opportunities for children to work systematically through the personal autonomy routine—defining aims, specifying objectives, defining strategies, devising tactics, etc. Indeed, these situations have minimal value if they do not. In addition, there will be many occasions when this routine will automatically convert to a reading routine. If simulations are conducted with more than one school taking part, then once again we have opportunities for developing communication skills with children using material prepared by other children to add an extra dimension to their understanding.

3 Practical investigations

These are the present favourite for the 'progressive' teacher, and the investigations carried out are often monumental in their pointlessness. Their greatest value lies in their use for developing personal autonomy and the ability to perceive relevance. Too often they become exercises for converting children into mines of useless information. If there is some real point in a practical investigation, and if it is clearly perceived as relevant by the child, then it is most likely that children will benefit by sharing their experiences. Thus, once again, communication between schools may be seen as an important educational strategy and one which provides suitable materials for reading.

4 Theoretical studies

As this form of education is the norm rather than the exception, I do not propose to dwell upon this theme. It is unfortunate that theoretical studies are associated, in the minds of many teachers, with formal teaching. I would affirm, on the contrary, that in helping a child to undertake formal studies our aim should be help him towards independence, not teacher dependence. The teacher must be only one of many sources which the child can use. This means that every subject teacher should be concerned, first and foremost, to develop the child's ability to go through the routines referred to throughout this paper.

Children pursuing theoretical studies may work independently or in small or larger groups. Like investigators at college or university they should be capable of communicating with others pursuing studies in the same field. Thus the exchange of experiences between children is as vital in theoretical studies as in those which have a severely practical basis. I do not intend now to proceed to an examination of the teacher's tactics. methods and techniques; I will, however, conclude by commenting on the review phase.

Evaluation in teaching reading

This stage, like each other stage, has its own discipline, and I am very conscious of the fact that hitherto I have given you the main headings but not the subheadings which guided my exposition. For this stage it is essential that I should spell them out. In fact, they follow obviously from what I have already said.

First, one must look back at the aims and reappraise them in the light of experience. Next one must compare the aims with the objectives achieved and consider the discrepancies. One must review the strategies and consider how effective they were as procedures for achieving objectives. One must also check that they were entirely consistent with the aims. For example, the strategy of stealing money might be excellent in terms of some financial objective but it is hardly consistent with what I hope would be included in our aims. Similarly, one must check tactics against strategies and against aims, methods against tactics and against aims, and techniques against methods and against aims. The formula for this may be set down as follows: A–AO; OS–AS; ST–AT; TM–AM; MT–AT.

The evaluation may be subjective or objective. That is, you may rely on personal judgment, or on some sort of measures, or on tests. Either way, the evaluation must be systematic and lead to a clear recognition of what still needs to be done.

Consolidation in teaching reading

Just as the pupils need to store what is of value, so must the teacher. Much of our failure in our work, our inability to make sufficient progress, springs from the fact that we do not organize ourselves so that we can profit adequately from experience. How many exciting things have you done in the past that are not now included in your repertoire? How many of you can readily put your hands on that article that so stimulated your imagination and which would now serve to fire the imagination of a colleague? How many of you can now find that pamphlet which is just what this child now needs? How many of you can lay your hands on the essential details of that project which you must now plan again from scratch? Or if you can find all these things, how long will it take you? Are they all stored neatly and indexed for convenient retrieval? Or are they piled up amongst a heap of miscellaneous items whose only relationship is that achieved by the frantic random search you made last time you wanted to look something up?

I'm afraid that most of our consolidation falls in the latter category. Worse, like the farmyard hog wallowing smugly in its sty, we tend to be proud of it. This sentimental, self-indulgent, self-protective attachment to inefficiency from which we all suffer may be good enough for managing our private affairs—although I personally do not believe this. It is certainly not good enough for the work we have to do.

Again, we are stuck in the implementation rut. We spend so much time being busy we don't stop to think what it is we are being busy about. In order to do thinking of this kind, and to make steady progress in developing our teaching skill, we need to be able to draw readily upon our previous experience, and those of our colleagues. Our need for a resource unit is just the same as that of the child. We can use his resource unit to help him to evaluate his progress. We can use our resource unit to evaluate our own and to use previous experiences as a springboard for further action.

Perhaps I should reverse the argument. Once we have learned how valuable it is to practise efficient consolidation in our own work, we may realize how important this is for the child. As we develop consolidation skills ourselves—collating, analyzing, summarizing, editing, storing, referencing and retrieving—we realize how invaluable this process is in the development of critical and evaluative reading skills in children.

Now, let me review experience exchange in relation to the total process of reading. As I have shown, the manner in which children's material can be handled provides opportunities for development in each aspect:

1 The children can establish their own aims, determining their own needs and specifying their own objectives.
2 The children can devise their own strategies and their own tactics.
3 The children can assume complete responsibility for the operation and this creates, in them, an understanding of the need to develop their methods and techniques, their word-attack skills, and scanning, skimming and processing skills.
4 After any exchange of material the children are highly motivated to evaluate what has been achieved. They are highly critical of their own work and that of others. They are ready to indulge in surprisingly perceptive analyses of what is and is not worth doing, and how things should be done. They have opportunities when consolidating to relate each aspect to each previous experience and to previous knowledge. In so doing, the aim is not to blur important distinctions but to note important relationships and so develop their understanding of the world and of themselves.

For an account of how this approach works with less able children at the secondary stage, the reader should refer to Laybourn (1970).

Conclusion

I have taken you through a rigorously analyzed and rigorously argued examination of the relationship between reading and the curriculum. I have also presented you with a framework within which to examine your own role in relation to both. If you ask yourselves now how much you can remember, the answer, I'm afraid, will be 'not very much'. You will be tempted, as I said at the outset, to agree with what I have said, assume you already do it, and forget it. Only if you have had the experience of debating at length the implications of each separate point and working through to actual implementation and review, would you begin to appreciate the full significance of what I have been saying.

Reading to some purpose: schedule for the development of effective reading routines

Motivation

Deciding what information is needed and where it may be found

Aims

Modules: What are the major units within which the information obtained is to be organized for the particular purpose for which it is required?

Media: What classes of printed material may be accessed in order to obtain this information?

Mode: Will the material be subjected to overview, reference or systematic study?

Formulate aims, in terms of priorities, indicating mode to be adopted in relation to each class of medium.

Objectives

Modules: What are the specific units of information that can be obtained from each kind of medium?

Media: In the case of each unit of information, what class of source will provide answers?

Mode: What questions may be posed in the case of each specific kind of source material?

Specify objectives in terms of the questions to be answered by reference to each kind of source material taking into account utility of the sources for the purpose and their availability.

Plan

Deciding how to find and how to select the most likely sources of information

Strategies

Modules :   What are the resources which might be accessed for each class of source materials? (e.g. libraries, firms, associations)

Media :   What or who are the media which may be utilized in order to locate and obtain these sources? (e.g. information services, tutor librarians, personal contacts etc)

Mode :   In each case, how may these media best be utilized in order to obtain appropriate sources?

Design feasible strategies for obtaining access to the most suitable sources.

Tactics

Modules :   What are the best sources among those located? (e.g. which book, index, pamphlet, newspaper, journal etc.)

Media :   What are the parts of each source which provide information which can be used in evaluation?

Mode :   What criteria may be adopted for the purpose of arriving at an evaluation?

Devise tactics for making an efficient selection of sources which are within your capability.

Implementation

Methods

Modules :   What kinds of item must I identify in respect of each question?

Media :   How are these items dispersed throughout the medium?

Mode :   How may I locate each item?

Apply economical and convenient routines and gambits in locating each item.

Technique

Modules :   What relevant facts or ideas are to be found in this passage?

Media :   How are these facts or ideas expressed?

Mode: How can I ensure that I have read this passage sufficiently accurately for my purpose?

Deploy those habits and skills which require least effort but which are most effective in decoding.

Review

Getting maximum benefit from reading

Evaluation
Modules: What must be evaluated?
Media: What materials may be used in evaluation?
Mode: What kinds of procedure may be adopted in evaluation?

Evaluate achievements systematically in terms of aims.

Consolidation
Modules: What are the categories to be used in consolidating?
Media: What resources may be used in consolidating?
Mode: What are the essential considerations?

Consolidate achievements comprehensively and constructively, storing material required for future reference in appropriate sections of personal resource unit, cross-referencing where necessary and communicating information to others when this is necessary or desirable.

References

Laybourn, M., 1970. 'An experiment in experience exchange' in ACE *Forum 4: Teaching reading in junior and secondary schools*, London: Ginn.

Merritt, J. E., 1970. 'Reading skills examined' in *Readings in educational psychology*, Stone, E. (ed.), London: Methuen.

Ruddell, R. B., 1965. 'The effect of oral and written patterns of language structure on reading comprehension', *The reading teacher* no. 18.

Tansey, P. J. and Unwin, D., 1969. *Simulation and gaming in education*, London: Methuen.

Walford, R., 1969. *Games in geography*, London: Longman.

F. Musgrove

II:7 Curriculum objectives

*The methodology which has often been employed to
validate the claims of different curricula is highly suspect.
Recent developments in curriculum evaluation are,
however, beginning to bring a new rigour to the scrutiny
of ends and means in education. The claims that teachers
make for their teaching are being empirically investigated
and often found wanting. The problem with curriculum
evaluation is that it may narrow down too much the
functions of the curriculum and thus miss the point. The
main need in today's world, according to Musgrove, is
for broad and flexible curricula in which pupils are given
lots of room to move. Curricula must be constructed in the
light of major trends within society—decline in demand
for unskilled labour; greater expectation of life; rapid
obsolescence of knowledge; earlier maturing of the young.*

This paper is not a sermon. There is already a voluminous collection
of pious works on curriculum objectives. Perhaps that is why there
is a curious unreality about the subject. But there are also deeper
reasons. Statements about objectives seem often to be little more
than a rationalization of activities which are conducted for other,
forgotten, or only half-suspected purposes. They often have the
air—in official reports, the writings of educationists, and Speech
Day orations—of a marginal commentary, an irrelevant accom-
paniment to an activity with its own determinism and private goals.
The curriculum has a function which avowed objectives may or
may not faithfully reflect.

The claims which are made for various curricula were never so
rich and varied. Subjects which began modestly as drill, cookery,
woodwork, or reading have relegated the acquisition of skills to a
minor position and aim at more elaborate and sophisticated objectives in the realm of personality development and social awareness.
'Instructors' have disappeared and 'training' is a term of abuse. Subjects are pressed into service for which they were never intended.
This is not necessarily an improper development. There is no reason
why curricula devised for one purpose should not serve others. But

Journal of curriculum studies. vol. 1, no. 1, 1968, pp. 5–18. (Published twice-
yearly by Wm. Collins Sons & Co. Ltd.). Reprinted by permission.

we are now beginning to ask whether they are in fact capable of rendering the manifold services we demand of them.

The methodology which has often sufficed to validate different curricula is highly suspect. It has usually taken the form of a rough-and-ready social accountancy which relates achievement in various walks of life to educational background. We have seen the rise in recent years of a sort of 'directory research': *Who's Who* and similar enumerations of men of some distinction provide educational data which enable us to classify the eminent according to their educational experiences. A brief survey of Vice-Chancellors and Public School headmasters leads us to ascribe remarkable properties to 'Greats,' and even Modern History, at least as taught at Oxford. A rapid survey of Professors of Education leads us to ascribe perhaps more dubious qualities to Eng. Lit.—at least as taught at Cambridge.

The shortcomings of arguments based on such evidence are too obvious to need detailed refutation. We are given no information about the less distinguished and incompetent who experienced the same curricula; and we have little knowledge of all those other circumstances of family background and connections which may have been related to recruitment to particular fields of education. The curriculum must be validated in the last resort by its end products, their quality and performance in life both present and future but we need more sophisticated and elaborate methods of studying the products of educational institutions than we have yet devised. Follow-up studies are expensive and complicated. They are beginning—for instance with teachers. They are not always re-assuring; but little of the work in curriculum evaluation is, whether it is concerned with long-term or short-term effects.

Curriculum evaluation

During the past ten years or so curriculum evaluators have introduced a new and welcome, if often discouraging, note into the perennial discussion of educational ends and means. In America Bloom, Cronbach and others have examined the curriculum with a new rigour. Similar developments are occurring in Britain. While this work is sometimes crude and naïve, it is likely to have a salutory effect on the curriculum in the future. Curriculum evaluators are insisting on appropriate evidence for discussions of the curriculum, and are devising the tools to obtain it. And they are insisting on clear, precise, and unambiguous language in which the discussion shall be conducted. This work is of great importance and is likely to produce radical changes in curriculum content and teaching methods—so much so that our teachers must constantly re-think their position and re-learn their craft. It is not my intention to belittle the significance of this work. It is a necessary, but not therefore a sufficient, approach to the study of the curriculum and its objectives.

Curriculum evaluation starts from a particular view of the nature and purpose of the curriculum: it is an instrument for changing student behaviour; its objectives are statements of ways in which the knowledge, cognitive abilities, skills, interests, values, and attitudes of students should change if the curriculum is effective. Of course young people are changing anyway as they grow toward maturity. The curriculum is an artificial contrivance designed to accelerate change, promote change which would not have occurred, and control the direction of change. It is the contrived activity and experience—organized, focused, systematic—that life, unaided, would not provide.

The school curriculum is not the only instrument in use for changing people. The techniques of the psychotherapist also have this objective. These techniques differ from those of the teacher in a variety of ways, not least in their derivation from a body of theory which plausibly indicates the probable consequences of different practices. Education has no such coherent theory of human development, at least for the later stages of school life and the university years, which can generate hypotheses about the relationship between educational means and ends. We lack the psychological theory which would enable us to make reasonable predictions about individual change; and we lack the social-psychological theory which would enable us to make reasonable predictions about long term behaviour and performance after school. Follow-up studies are likely to leave us constantly surprised.

But the educational sciences are beginning to provide information which points the way to goals which are attainable, at least in the short term. The nature of children, of subjects, and of learning processes are explored and throw light on what can, and what cannot, be achieved. We need no longer make do with Whitehead's theory of rhythmic intellectual development, which did sterling service in the inter-war years. Curricular changes were recommended—for instance in the 'Spens' Report on Secondary Education (1938)—on the basis of Romance, Utility, and Generalization. There is no longer any excuse for such speculative psychology in curriculum design. Goldman's recently published work on religious education[1] is an excellent example of the way in which empirical studies of children, learning processes, and the nature of a school subject can raise doubts about accepted curriculum objectives and suggest new and more realistic alternatives.

Precision of statement is dangerous in education. Precise statements of aims are hypotheses which can be checked. The notion of 'transfer of training' was sufficiently precise to be subjected to empirical verification. This chastening experience seems to have led to a retreat into wide-sweeping generalities. This is perhaps particularly the case when the curriculum in the humanities is under discussion. It is given the credit for a remarkable, if ill-defined, potency in the sphere of personality development.

Of course such ambitious claims are not new. Even a careful thinker like Newman would have been the despair of Bloom: Newman's objectives for a liberal curriculum would have defeated Bloom's tidy taxonomy.[2] At first sight Newman's claim that the objective of his curriculum 'is simply the cultivation of the intellect as such, and its object is nothing more or less than intellectual excellence', appears to fit neatly into Bloom's 'cognitive domain'. But the 'large knowledge' acquired in the course of a liberal education has 'connatival qualities': it produces 'a delicate taste, a candid, equitable, dispassionate mind, a noble and courteous bearing in the conduct of life'. Our confident categorization was clearly incorrect: 'intellectual excellence' has now slipped over into the 'affective domain'. I think it is doubtful whether Bloom's taxonomy can accommodate this characteristic product of our curriculum—the English gentleman.[3]

Claims for the humanities

There are some indications that the extravagant claims traditionally made for the humanities are beginning to collapse under their own weight, without benefit of empirical research. In a recent book, *Crisis in the humanities*,[4] two Cambridge dons examine the objectives commonly ascribed to literary and Classical studies respectively, and from their own experience and observation reach a position of extreme scepticism.

Hough and Finley doubt whether the changes in values, attitudes and behaviour which literary studies are commonly supposed to promote in fact occur on any significant scale—at least among their students at Cambridge. Similar doubts have been expressed still more forcefully elsewhere, and on better evidence. Ten years ago the academic world in America was shaken by the famous 'Jacob Report',[5] which collated the work which had been done on students' changing values and attitudes in relation to particular curricular experiences. Jacob was forced to the conclusion that the curriculum in the social sciences and the humanities has little of the potency which is usually claimed; that little change occurs in the values of university students; and the changes that do occur cannot be related to the content of the curriculum.

More recent work does not vindicate the extreme pessimism of the Jacob Report. In particular, liberal attitudes seem in general to be promoted by educational experiences at least in America.[6] But while more change undoubtedly occurs than Jacob would allow, it has not been shown to result from particular courses of study. This, indeed, was the broad conclusion to emerge from Newcomb's famous investigations at Bennington more than twenty years ago. Value changes were the product of community-wide relationships rather than the outcome of a particular field of academic specialization.[7]

Rather curiously, one of the most devastating evaluations of the school curriculum is to be found embedded in the study of 'Prairie City', the midwestern town subjected to prolonged and elaborate scrutiny in the forties by Robert Havighurst and his colleagues. In their book, *The psychology of character development*,[8] Peck and Havighurst explore the nature and origins of the socio-moral values of Prairie City's adolescents. Their investigations had enabled them to establish with some plausibility the relative influence of parents, friends, institutions, figures vicariously experienced, and other adults. 'Institutions' included the school, church, and community organizations; 'figures vicariously experienced' included the personalities encountered in historical and literary studies.

Out of 34 sixteen-year-olds who were intensively studied, only three appeared to owe anything whatsoever to the impact of 'figures vicariously experienced'; only 12 appeared to have derived socio-moral values from institutions other than the home. (Friends were not a major influence, either; the major source of socio-moral values was the parents, particularly the mother.) The study of history and great literature appeared to have made a negligible impact on the socio-moral values of Prairie City's youth.

It is possible, of course, that these subjects are more effectively

taught in the United Kingdom. Certainly there is no dearth of ambitious objectives for the history teacher, at any level. History is expected to promote tolerance, racial harmony, and international
peace. As an article in *The Times Educational Supplement* put it a
few years ago: 'the purpose of history is salvation'.[9]

Even more modest objectives have not been vindicated by the
little empirical investigation we have managed to conduct. When
McNicol decided to investigate the claims that history teachers were
making in the mid-nineteen-forties, the result was complete loss of
faith. He turned in despair to Social Studies.

The work of McNicol is not remarkable for its technical sophistication; but it is not without interest as a pioneering effort in curriculum evaluation. An important objective of history teaching propounded in the thirties—notably by Jeffreys—was the development
of an 'historical sense'. 'It is the developmental perspective that
makes the study 'historical' and not the particular subject-matter,'
Jeffreys maintained.[10] McNicol set himself the task of finding out
how widespread were historical attitudes in this sense among people
who had engaged in the study of history during their ten years at
school. He devised tests which, he claimed, would reveal 'the habit
of regarding the present in terms of its antecedents'.

McNicol carried out his programme of testing with schoolchildren and with samples of adults in the Armed Forces. His subjects
appeared to have 'either the vaguest idea or no idea at all of the past
as a sequence'. The historical knowledge of children and adults was
in general 'chaotic'. 'I have reached the conclusion,' said McNicol,
'that history is not a fit subject for schoolchildren; that, like many
other subjects, it is failing to make good the contribution to education which specialist teachers commonly claim for it.'[11]

The attainment of objectives

The objectives which specialist teachers set themselves are unlikely
to be attained unless they have been formulated in the light of an
adequate psychology of personal development. Of course objectives
are seldom set nowadays with complete disregard for the nature of
the pupils who will pursue them. The psychology of individual
differences has at least taught us not to expect the same results with
all children from the same curriculum—results which were con-
fidently expected by the heirs of Helvétius. Indeed, alleged differences between categories of children form the basis of the famous

recommendations of the Norwood Report. And it is precisely this Report which warns us not that such psychological considerations are irrelevant, but that they can be dangerously inexpert. They might have been far more expert than they were, even a quarter of a century ago.

Unrealistic expectations of the curriculum will continue to be held unless we study the interaction between curriculum and personality. The nature of the recruitment to different subject fields will profoundly affect the educational outcome. We continue to make naïve assumptions about the automatic effects of different curricula—given, perhaps, a certain minimum level of measured intelligence—particularly in the field of higher education. Such assumptions underlie compulsory foundation years in our universities; they underlie compulsory liberal studies for students of science and technology. These studies are assumed to have a variety of consequences for students' personality development regardless of the manner of student recruitment. One has profound doubts whether these alleged humane studies have the effect on, say, engineers and biologists, that are tacitly assumed or openly claimed. The remarkable thing is that such curricula can persist from year to year—at great expense—without any attempt to discover whether they really do what they are supposed to do.

The method of recruitment of a particular subject field, though on the face of it appropriate and relevant, may in fact make the attainment of a variety of ostensible and quite plausible objectives extremely difficult. The poise and equanimity that Newman claimed as the outcome of humane studies at the university may not be achieved if students have arrived by a particular route which has given little reward for equanimity. Recent research at Oxford shows a disproportionte number of students of literature and philosophy among cases of psychiatric breakdown over the ten years after 1950.[12] There are similar findings in American research.[13] But it seems unlikely that severe personality problems are a *direct* consequence of a literary education.

This work raises more questions than it answers; and clearly underlines the need for research into the relationship between curriculum and personality which must inform our decisions about educational objectives. Such research would be complicated. We need to compare the development of pupils with similar personality profiles who are following different curricula with pupils with different profiles engaged in the same curricula. We need to look at the effect of the same field of study on people who have entered it for different reasons. Whatever objectives educationists ascribe to a curriculum, different pupils will in fact get different things out of it; it is time we knew what they were.

The function of the curriculum

The hard-headed work on curriculum evaluation which is now being conducted at some levels and in some areas of education will help to show us what is being achieved, what is possible, and what is not. It can lead to an economy of effort and a realistic pursuit of attainable goals. And yet I am left with an obstinate sense of unreality, a persistent feeling that we are somehow missing the point.

This feeling is intensified by even the most cursory examination of the extensive literature which has been produced on the curriculum over the past century. At different times—or even at the same time—diverse claims are made for the same curriculum. Objectives attributed to subjects appear to mirror only currently fashionable philosophical, psychological, or sociological theories. A curriculum may perform important and vital functions even if the currently fashionable objectives are not being attained.

The functions of the curriculum have varied greatly over time with changing social needs. Often the same curriculum has been able to meet quite fundamentally different needs at different times. This is particularly the case with the Classical curriculum, which provided a training for the professions and even for scientific pursuits in the Middle Ages. The scientist was the man who knew the writings of the Classical authors on the sciences; he was perforce a student of Latin, and particularly of Greek.

In later centuries the same curriculum met quite different needs. Instead of certifying a man as vocationally equipped, it testifies to his vocational ineptitude. As Veblen argued—and I believe correctly—a Classical education becomes valued because it indicated a man's unfitness for any gainful occupation. It testified to his status as a gentleman, who had no need to earn his living but might engage in activities which carried little or no remuneration like politics or war. Yet the same curriculum (Fred Clarke maintained) was ingeniously used by Jowett to equip men for proconsular service and the burdens of Empire. It has not been without value subsequently as a rather protracted, laborious, and uneconomic intelligence test.

The curriculum in the past has served a variety of social purposes. Of course it has often been directly vocational; and it has been used to maintain the social divisions of a stratified society. The curriculum was used in the nineteenth century, by no means unsuccessfully, to promote morality in a barbarous juvenile population. But I suggest that since the later nineteenth century the advanced industrial nations have made two major and unprecedented demands on the schools for normal children : the first is to provide activity for an economically redundant juvenile population; the second is to provide more protracted opportunities for young people to explore themselves. In meeting the first demand the schools have often been plunged into a sense of futility; from which they can be effectively rescued if they set themselves to meet the second.

If compulsory education was a response to urgently felt needs for an educated population, it is curious that the elementary and secondary modern schools have so often appeared to lack any sense of purpose. Over the past half-century they seem to have spent much of their time wondering what to do. It is ironical that after almost a century of compulsory education the recent Newsom Report, *Half our future*, should need to devote a chapter to 'An education that makes sense'. Sense, apparently, would at last be made if the education of the average child were 'practical, realistic, and vocational.' I submit that there is a profound sense in which compulsory education over the past century has been essentially senseless. The curriculum to which educationists have ascribed a variety of subtle objectives has been a structure of activity designed to fill the time. Pupils have often been only too aware that they were digging holes in order to fill them up again.

In the closing decades of the nineteenth century, the advanced industrial nations no longer needed a vast supply of juvenile labour. The physical skills and agility of the young were no longer in demand. I have examined these developments elsewhere.[14] The rise of the American high school at this time has been similarly interpreted by Hollingshead as 'a response to the loss of economic functions of adolescents in American culture'.[15] This development occurred, as Hollingshead says, 'under the guise of the need for more training for adult life'.

The economic superfluity of young people is, I believe, one of the most important social facts of our time. It becomes necessary that the young shall not grow up too soon. Even the demand for the labour of young adults may diminish rapidly in a developing industrial society. And indeed, Nevitt Sanford sees the current explosion of the university population in America largely in these terms. Of course, society needs very highly educated manpower on an ever growing scale; but it has a reduced demand for the young and relatively immature. Sanford interprets the increasing demand for college as a concomitant of increasing affluence. 'Since there is little need for young people in the world of production,' he says, 'a practical choice is to keep them in school for as long as possible, and college is the next step after high school.' [16]

In these circumstances the curriculum becomes in some degree a contrivance for occupying time. There are few ready-made objectives available, as in purely vocational training. And I think it is significant that the growing points in the school curriculum over the past century have not been in subjects with a clear social and economic urgency. In the main the curriculum has expanded by incorporating activities which had previously occupied the leisure side of life. History, literature, art, games, drama, even modern languages, were a leisure-time affair, strictly extra-curricular. As they have been taken into the curriculum, more suitably serious objectives have been ascribed to them.

Of course, if time has to be occupied, it may as well be occupied in an edifying way. These developments which I am describing in fact provide the opportunity to meet the second major need of 20th-century society: the need for a protracted period in which young people can explore not only their world but themselves. If we think of the school curriculum in these terms, we see it, quite properly, as an extension of the play of the young child in which the manifold possibilities of the world and of the self are tried out and put to some experimental test, but without dire consequences if the experiment goes all awry. The Oxford Union is a good example of the highly serious anticipatory play that I have in mind.

The society of the future is likely to require this extended period of 'play' for a variety of reasons. In the first place, the sheer speed of social change, the frequent changes of role which will be required of adults, will call for versatility and flexibility of a high order. The growing child must not be set too early in too rigid a mould. In the second place, social justice requires that youth of the future shall not be committed at too early an age to the life-style into which they happen to have been born.

The rapid obsolescence of knowledge and probably of various kinds of employment, as well as the longer life-span that people can

now reasonably expect, have brought about a radical change in the
social circumstances against which the school curriculum must be
seen. A modern curriculum can provide the opportunities for extensive self-exploration and for accurate self-evaluation. The boy who
started work at seven, or the young man committed early to a particular course of vocational training, could never know the other
selves he might have been.

And if our school curricula are too narrow, or if specialization
begins too early, they will have the same limiting effect. Every
curriculum has a 'cost'; and the cost of a curriculum is the other
curriculum that might have been. The curriculum teaches a pupil
the kind of person he is, it shapes his conception of himself. It must
not confine his exploration to a narrow front. We must devise curricula and means of assessment which make accurate self-knowledge possible. The proper need for self-evaluation must be met in a
competent manner.

There is little doubt that our present curricula often give pupils a
quite erroneous notion of the kinds of people they are. (There are
probably far more mathematicians and engineers among them than
they know.) And a curriculum which is, as I suggested, based largely
on traditional upper-class leisure pursuits, is not necessarily the most
appropriate instrument for self-exploration for most of our children.
Too many have 'written themselves off' because of their failure in
activities which are culturally parochial; others have written themselves off because their talents and performance have been measured
by means which are suspect or simply incompetent. And a few have
narrowed their conception of themselves because they have been
certified, too early, by no less suspect means, as 'successful' in a
particular specialism.

There is no doubt that children—like all of us—demand and need
evaluation. We do them no service by refusing it. They demand
evidence with which to make a valid self-appraisal. I suspect that
the remarkable rise in the popularity of psychology as a university
study owes something to this need. The same need exists in the
schools, and can be met, in part, by teaching psychology, there. But
the main need is for broad and flexible curricula, highly provisional
verdicts on abilities and talents—but verdicts nonetheless—and
abundant opportuntities to make fresh starts in new areas of activity. The Puritan morality of steady persistence on a set course is no
longer appropriate to a shifting and unpredictable social order.

Future possibilities

So far the philosophical question : What ought the objectives of our curricula to be? has been avoided. This does not seem to be a very sensible question unless we know more thoroughly what they *can* be. But even realistic possibilities offer a range of alternatives, and we must consider the grounds on which to choose between them.

There are some curricula which have strictly de-limited, built-in objectives. The curriculum of a school for handicapped children takes its objectives from our notions of normality. It is true that these may be somewhat arbitrary; but in a given cultural context the curriculum required for subnormal and handicapped children is reasonably self-evident. Its purpose is to move them nearer to generally accepted and recognized norms.

It is the general education of the vast majority of 'normal' children at the secondary stage which raises problems. When this education is no longer tied to vocational aims, the possibilities of allocating objectives are endless. Anyone can offer his particular brand—and usually does.

In the immediate post-war period sociology seemed to be offering—particularly in the works written or inspired by Fred Clarke—not only an explanation of what is, but a valid prescription for what should be. This was essentially the morality of inevitability. 'Social facts', in Durkheim's sense (like the culture into which we are born), were external to the individual but inescapable and obligatory. And they appeared to have the essential characteristics of Rousseau's 'General Will' : we had a moral duty to conform to them. 'It is the first business of education,' maintained Clarke, 'to induce conformity in terms of the culture in which the child will grow up.'[17]

The functional analysis of society in the hands of contemporary sociologists often seems to have a similar implication. What is 'functional' must be : there seems little point in discussing its morality.

Fred Clarke was a more overt moralist. A society's culture was a fact; and the curriculum was in fact and in morals obliged to reflect it. Wales must be forever Wales, and the curriculum of Welsh schools must ensure this. It must be 'based on as many as possible of the elements in the cultural background of a child'.[18] At least Clarke appeared to have got hold of a hard and tangible criterion for assessing the legitimacy of curriculum objectives; and he was not so bound by the needs of logical consistency that he failed to provide a loophole for deviation and innovation in the light of individual conscience.

Both psychological and sociological studies can give us guidance about the possible. But the problem of the legitimacy of different curriculum objectives remains. Facts, whether psychological or sociological, are like force—they cannot constitute a right or an obligation.

We have come to regard it as legitimate to assign different objectives for children of different age and 'ability' as rather narrowly conceived and measured. It is no longer legitimate to do as the Taunton Commission did a hundred years ago—assign different curricula to children of different social classes. We may say that children from underprivileged homes require special treatment: but most of us dare not say that they should pursue different educational aims. The legitimacy of assigning different curriculum objectives for boys and girls is still a matter of dispute.

My prescription from the commonsense standpoint is that education is essentially preparatory for the life ahead. (Of course even this view was strongly contested in the inter-war years on the mighty authority of Whitehead's dictum that 'the present is holy ground'.)[19] Education is not *only* preparatory; but in all cultures its purpose is to prepare the young to cope effectively with the circumstances of the life which they are likely to encounter.

I shall hazard a few predictions. But as I try to look into the future, I am not proposing to invent new subjects for the schools. Nor would I expect any radical re-grouping or re-alignment of subjects. While established subjects may develop in various ways (in response to curriculum evaluation and other pressures), they seem likely to insist on their separate existence. A subject is a social institution with its sense of identity and loyalty exacted from its members. In conflict with other subjects it defines its boundaries and its sphere of influence. Subjects are highly organized, hierarchic, bureaucratic. They are busy discovering reasons for their existence and importance. They develop their own defensive systems against encroachment. We saw this particularly in the Historical Association's vigorous response to the threat of Social Studies after the War.[20]

I doubt whether the elaborate organization we call 'subjects' will give much ground to new arrivals. Even subjects which are now well established in the university, like Engineering and Sociology, have difficulty in finding a foothold in the schools. Various proposals to modify subject boundaries have met with scant success over the past 30 or 40 years, at least at the secondary stage of education. I would attribute this more to the properties of subjects as social, rather than intellectual, systems. I suspect that curriculum changes, at least in the schools, will occur within traditional subject boundaries rather than across them. The Newsom Report realistically accepted this probability.

I shall speculate briefly about the curriculum which seems reasonable in view of the possible shape of the future. I suggest that five tendencies in modern society can be extrapolated into the future to guide our reflections on curriculum reform: they are the declining demand for unskilled labour; the greater expectation of life; the rapid obsolescence of knowledge; the earlier physical (and perhaps emotional and intellectual) maturing of the young; and even less distinction between the social roles of men and women.

Our curricula are still geared to a society in which the majority would be engaged in manual work, knowledge once acquired had a permanent value, the age of puberty was 17, life was over at 40, and father never bathed the baby.

The reduced demand for manual labour and the opportunities for more sophisticated skills and personal qualities mean that we have to discover how more academic curricula can be made to work with less naturally gifted people, at least at some stage in their lives. I think there is little doubt that many children in our secondary modern schools are working well below their true capacities. C.S.E. may help to remedy this. The problem is to teach academic courses not only to those who, for a variety of reasons, already possess the qualities of memory, verbal ability, and motivation, which teachers have been able with comparative ease to exploit.

The rapid obsolescence of knowledge means that the style and content of the curriculum must change, too—as, indeed, they are doing, particularly at more advanced levels of university work. Above all the child must learn how to learn: he must be inducted into subjects which are essentially a way of inquiry rather than a collection of factual information.

The blurring of the distinction between the sex roles is a trend which we may or may not approve; but it is likely to continue. In their recent investigations in Nottingham the Newsons found that there had been 'a massive change in the masculine role' within the home over the past 30 years.[21] Margaret Mead has reached similar conclusions, with regret, from her observations of the American social scene.[22] These trends suggest not simply that more girls do engineering, but that more boys engage in a new version of domestic science.

We have not yet come to terms in our educational and social arrangements with the longer expectation of life and the earlier maturing of the young. The ages at which we customarily do a great many things—receive our education, marry, settle to a career, retire—are appropriate to social and psychological circumstances which no longer obtain.

We probably need to re-phase the life-cycle of man in contemporary society. We are doing too many things at the wrong time— including a good deal of our educational effort. We impose a uniformity on the life-cycle which is no longer either appropriate or necessary. We have gradually assimilated the entire population to the life-cycle of the medieval knight.

While there are reasons, which I suggested earlier, for keeping the young at school and off the labour-market, there is no immutable reason why 'redundancy' should not be spread, or at least staggered, over the life-span; why retirement ages should not be variable, according to inclination and rates of declining competence; and men and women in their middle years return to educational institutions both for personal renewal and re-equipment for the changing character of their employment.

With ample provision for later educational opportunities I think we could devise more realistic curricula for the various episodes of education. For some a straight run through until their middle twenties would still be appropriate. Many others would return, after a briefer education, in accordance with their changing interests and aspirations. The late thirties would probably be the time for the higher education of most women. It seems to me ludicrous to expect young women who first menstruate at 11 to pay close attention to academic studies until their early twenties; and we need no longer assume that by 40 all life will have deserted them. And there are probably many men of talent but early physical maturity who might follow a similar pattern : returning to formal education when their families were off their hands.

I suggest, then, that we should think of curricula appropriate to a far more flexible social and educational order; that we should consider the possibilities of a more episodic type of education; that we should think of curricula which are relevant to the real (and changing) nature of knowledge, man, and society.

References

1 R. Goldman, *Religious thinking from childhood to adolescence* (Routledge, London, 1964).

2 Benjamin S. Bloom, *Taxonomy of educational objectives* (David McKay & Co, New York, 1956).

3 J. H. Newman, *The idea of a university* (Longmans, Green & Co, London, 1929). Discourse V. 'Knowledge. Its Own End.'

4 J. H. Plumb (ed.), *Crisis in the humanities* (Pelican Books, Harmondsworth, 1964).

5 P. E. Jacob, *Changing values in colleges* (Harper Bros., New York, 1957).

6 E.g. W. Plant, 'Changes in ethnocentricism during college years', *Journal of Educational Psychology* (1958), vol. 49, and Bruno Bettelheim and Morris Janowitz, *Social change and prejudice* (Free Press of Glencoe, 1964).

7 T. M. Newcomb, *Personality and social change* (Dryden, New York, 1943).

8 R. F. Peck and R. J. Havighurst, *The psychology of character development* (John Wiley, New York, 1960).

9 'Prospect for History', *The Times Educational Supplement*, 29 November, 1957.

10 M. V. C. Jeffreys, *History in schools: the study of development* (1938).

11 Harry McNicol, *History, heritage and environment* (1946).

12 M. A. Davidson and C. Hutt, 'A study of 500 Oxford student psychiatric cases', *British Journal of Social and Clinical Psychology* (1964), vol. 3.

13 C. Bereiter and M. B. Freedman, 'Fields of study and the people in them' in N. Sanford (ed.), *The American college* (John Wiley, New York, 1962).

14 F. Musgrove, 'Population changes and the status of the young in England since the eighteenth century', *Sociological Review* (1963), vol. 11.

15 A. B. Hollingshead, *Elmtown's youth* (John Wiley, New York, 1949), pp. 149–50.

16 Nevitt Sanford (ed.), *The American college* (John Wiley, New York, 1962), p. 13.

17 Fred Clarke, *Freedom in the educative society* (University of London Press, 1948).

18 *The curriculum and the community in Wales* (Welsh Department Ministry of Education Pamphlet No. 6, 1952).

19 A. N. Whitehead, *Aims of Education* (1932).

20 See W. H. Burston, *Social studies and the history teacher* (Historical Association Teaching of History Leaflet No. 15, 1954).

21 John and Elizabeth Newson, *Infant care in an urban community* (Allen and Unwin, London, 1963).

22 Margaret Mead, *Male and female* (Pelican Books, 1962).

Paul H. Hirst

II:8 The logic of the curriculum

In the United Kingdom there are two major curriculum problems which raise a number of philosophical issues—what sort of curriculum are we to have in secondary schools in an age of universal secondary school provision? What can be done about persistent deficiencies in the grammar school curriculum, particularly the effects of specialization? Hirst argues that the development of mind has been marked by the progressive differentiation in human consciousness of some seven or eight distinguishable cognitive structures. Thus the acquisition of these different forms of knowledge, different ways of thinking about the world, must be universal objectives for the curriculum. If these forms of knowledge are denied to certain categories of child, for example the 'average' child, then they are being denied certain basic ways of rational development. Secondary curricula must therefore be devised which initiate all children into these distinct cognitive structures. In the grammar school curriculum Hirst's 'map of knowledge' can be used to avoid the dangers of over-specialization on the one side and over-generalization on the other.

It is abundantly clear nowadays that the ultimately important questions of the curriculum are complex practical questions which no philosopher of education has a right to answer. Anyone who today advocates curriculum changes on pure philosophical grounds without considering the psychological and sociological factors that are relevant, is simply irresponsible. For rational curriculum planning, we must, for instance, have sound empirical evidence on how children learn, we must know the demand in our society for people with specialist knowledge. On these technicalities, no mere philosopher is competent to pronounce. But if a philosopher cannot hope to give any definitive answers this does not mean that he has nothing to say on these matters, or that what he has to say is of merely peripheral importance. Indeed, I hope to show that some of the most basic doubts and questionings about the curriculum from

Journal of Curriculum Studies, vol. 1. no. 2, 1969, pp. 142–158. (Published twice-yearly by William Collins Sons & Co. Ltd.) Reprinted by permission.

which we now suffer, are in part philosophical in character, and that philosophers have at least some centrally important things to say on them.

It may be thought that the title of this paper is ambiguous and vague, but as little as thirty years ago a philosopher would probably have preferred an even vaguer and more pretentious title, probably simply 'A Philosophy of the Curriculum'. His paper would have been likely to contain a comprehensive sketch of the writer's views on the place of man in the scheme of things, and then a series of statements about the curriculum needed if men are to be educated to live satisfactorily in the light of this. The title, however, bears witness to the more modest ambitions of philosophers these days, and at the same time gives at least some indication of the kind of questions they are specialists in. These are above all logical questions, questions whose answers turn not on an examination of empirical facts or on legislation or speculation about the ultimate nature of things, but on an examination of the structure of the concepts and principles which we use in understanding our experience. Logical questions are not about, say, particular facts or moral judgments, but about what we mean by facts, what we mean by moral judgments, how these fundamental elements in our understanding relate to each other, and so on.

Philosophers therefore, come into their own not when people begin to question about particular facts or about particular moral judgments, but when they come to ask questions about these fundamental units in our understanding. They come into their own not when people begin to ask for particular facts about our present secondary school curriculum, about its effectiveness in providing the general knowledge people need in our society, or how best to interest pupils in what we wish to teach; they come into their own when we turn from questions of empirical investigation to ask what is the nature of the things we wish pupils to achieve, what we mean by the acquisition of knowledge and what we mean by capturing pupils' interests. It is when people recognise that in planning the curriculum we are working with unclear and confused notions that logical issues come to the fore. Just as in a time of moral upheaval, when a reformulation of the moral code is necessary, people may well begin to ask what is meant by right and wrong and how any justification of moral principles is possible, so today when well-established curricular practices are being re-assessed, it may be necessary for us to get a better logical grip on some of the fundamental concepts we are using. That, in the questionings that are now going on, there are signs of serious philosophical confusion in our ideas about the curriculum, I do not doubt, and it is with these alone that I am concerned in this paper. Let me repeat, however, philosophical clarification will not of itself answer our practical problems, even if it cannot but help in promoting more rational solutions of them.

Before going any further I must say something about the confusions that can arise from uncertainties about the meaning of the term curriculum itself. It will, I suggest, help if we distinguish three closely inter-related elements in curriculum planning. First there are the objectives we are after as a result of our teaching: the qualities of mind, the knowledge, skills, values that we wish pupils to acquire. Secondly, there is the programme of activities and work, the plan of what we as teachers and our pupils as learners do to achieve these objectives. This will consist of an outline of the instruction, the discussions, the visits, the exercises, the laboratory work, and so on, that are used. Thirdly, there is the content or subject matter of these activities, what ground is being covered in them in the effort to reach our objectives. Adequate planning of a curriculum as I understand it then, demands first a set of clear objectives that constitute the point of the whole enterprise, and then a programme of activities with an appropriate content as the means to the desired ends. The term curriculum would seem, from its derivation, to apply most appropriately to the programme of activities, to the course to be run by pupils in being educated. Not infrequently however, the term is used as a label merely for the content or subject-matter used in this programme. Indeed more often than not the total statement of a school's curriculum consists of a bald list of subjects, topics or items of knowledge to be covered as a content to lessons, without any reference to the objectives that should govern the use of this content or the best methods that might be employed.

This crude mapping of the enterprise of education simply in terms of the content does, I fear, often lead to serious distortions of educational practice. With no clear statement of educational objectives set out to guide them, teachers only too easily take the statement of the mere content of the curriculum or syllabus as a statement of the objectives to be pursued. In this way the teacher pares down what is to be achieved to the acquisition of a body of information and the ability to perform a number of stated operations. Of course the content stated is intended to be gone through and much to be learnt in the process. But if Boyle's Law, Pythagoras's Theorem and *King Lear* are taken as labels of objectives, the result will often be the mere mastery of propositions. Taken as labels for a content to be used, they will be employed as the means of developing understanding, judgment, imagination and many other complex qualities which education worthy of the name seeks to achieve. In a stable context or tradition, where the objectives of education can be assumed to be fully understood by all teachers, then everything may be well if teachers are given no more than a suggested content for their courses. But under the present circumstances of education, no such accepted tradition exists any more. We are all too frequently guilty of allowing the established content of syllabuses and curricula to set our objectives for us. We can then evade the difficult matter of deciding what precisely our aims ought to be, we can reduce the task of education to its most manageable elements and easily appear to be pretty efficient at the job. Of course what is learnt by pupils in courses of this sort is not only unobjectionable, it may be very valuable in many ways. But that is no adequate justification for education in these terms. Curriculum planning is not just a question of whether what is learnt is worthwhile, it is a question of whether or not it is the *most* worthwhile, and how these most worthwhile things can best be attained.

If the traditional school curriculum and syllabuses assume an established background of objectives they equally assume an established background of appropriate teaching methods, for these are similarly unspecified. Maybe many of the teaching methods used are excellent, but if the statement of content is taken as setting out what is to be learnt, there is a strong temptation to assume that traditional chalk and talk are pretty well all that is needed. If strings of propositions are to be mastered, and a number of formal skills acquired, what better way is there than the clear precise formal presentation of them and plenty of disciplined practice? In this way not only are the objectives of education pared down, the methods used are undesirably restricted as well.

But the old style curriculum or syllabus does at least have this value, that in stating the content of a course, it gives at least a strong hint of some of the worthwhile objectives the teacher is to pursue. If the curriculum is set out in terms of projects and activities however, even this degree of specification may well be lacking. It matters vitally what is done in a project on the neighbourhood for instance as to whether or not its objectives are worthwhile at all. The objectives themselves are not stated, and certainly their worthwhileness in a general sense is not sufficient to justify these activities as having a place in the curriculum. Perhaps this approach, setting out the curriculum or syllabus in terms of projects, prevents teachers being misled by traditional curricular formulations as far as methods are concerned, but it seems to me that it may all too readily lead to little significant learning of the kind it is the school's function assiduously to pursue. In a time of upheaval and radical change in education, it seems to me too much freedom for the teacher is not necessarily a good thing.

From this discussion, I suggest it is clear that in responsible curriculum planning we must not evade the fundamental task of formulating clearly and precisely what the aims and objectives are. We must set about finding practical and efficient means for achieving the full range of these objectives and we must in every way seek to assess the value of the means we use, being prepared to change both content and methods where these are patently not the best for achieving the objectives.

There are two major curriculum problems that are forcing on us in the U.K. fundamental questionings of a philosophical character. First, there is the question of the curriculum we are to have in secondary schools now that we have universal secondary education. Sctdonly, there is the persistent problem of the deficiencies of the education provided by our traditional grammar school curriculum,[1] particularly the effects of specialisation. Granted universal secondary education, we have yet to get really to grips with the question of what the objectives are of an education that is so widely spread. Can there in fact be genuinely universal objectives? Irrespective of the kind of institutions that we have, does it make sense to set about trying to achieve the same ends with pupils whose I.Q.'s are about 120, and those whose I.Q.'s are, say, well below 100? Is it that we need different means for different pupils, or must we formulate different, but equally justifiable, ends? In fact, what is equality of educational opportunity if you stick to strictly *educational* opportunity? Is it the equal chance to go toward the same goals, so that we need to discover how best to help the less able pupil along the line, or do we recognise quite different goals for the less able and seek to provide them with every facility to pursue these? In fact, how far does it really make sense to talk of educational objectives as alternatives? To begin to get clear on this matter there is, I think, no escaping an examination of the nature of educational objectives and the significance of pursuing different goals.

What is more, we need to know how these objectives are related to each other. Are they simply isolable items of knowledge or skill that can be acquired as one might collect individual pebbles from a beach? Can the objectives we want be quite freely classified and arranged by teachers into any convenient units, so that there is an endless variety of organisations of curricular means to these ends? Or are many of the objectives so closely interrelated to each other that one must necessarily pursue them in logically cohesive groupings? What in other words are the structural or logical features of the objectives we are interested in, features we cannot ignore if our curricula are to be coherent? I suggest then that uncertainties about the secondary school curriculum go deep, and that to help sort matters out we need philosophical aid in two particular respects. We need to understand what is implied in choosing different educational objectives and we need to know what kind of demands educational objectives put on the curriculum plan itself.

Just the same two forms of philosophical aid are needed to help us with the problems of our traditional grammar school curriculum. The principle of specialisation has been the schools' answer to the vast increase in knowledge and its progressive fragmentation into ever narrower and more technical domains. We have allowed, or rather have insisted on, the dropping of subjects from an early age, trusting to the forces of interest, ability, and vocational intention to do a responsible selection job for us. But unfortunately the narrow-minded boffin reared on a restricted diet of science and mathematics from fourteen or fifteen, is now all too common a phenomenon, as also is the arts man, blank in his incomprehension of the scientific outlook. In our worst moments we argue either that this situation doesn't matter, or that it is inevitable, there being some pseudo-justification of a psychological kind for our current practices. You will recall the Crowther Report's fantastic contention that our most able children, and only those who are most able, just do by nature undergo a period of specialist subject-mindedness in their later teens.[2] In our wiser moments we begin to think twice about our selection of educational objectives and our ways of achieving them. What if narrow mindedness is a necessary consequence of our failure to educate a person in certain respects? In that case the remedy is in our own hands. To be clear on this point, an examination of the nature of educational objectives is precisely what we need.

We must also ask, if, with the vast increase in knowledge, the only satisfactory way to limit what is pursued is in fact by selecting some limited areas for specialist treatment. It is at least possible that within the structure of knowledge itself there are other more suitable bases of selection. There is also the problem that at a time when we are so specialist minded in our grammar schools, the old traditional demarcations between the subjects or disciplines from which our young specialists must choose, are themselves being called in question. New subjects are being freely developed in the universities, and they are creeping into even the most conservative schools. As a result the whole domain of knowledge seems to be disintegrating into a strange chaos, so that no one person can begin to have any significant map of knowledge as a whole, only a limited grasp of certain particular areas. Certainly, we are failing to communicate an over-all view of the range of the intellectual achievements of man, even in that section of our secondary education where we are surest of the positive value of the curriculum. The result is that many of our pupils are not only ignorant of major forms of human understanding, they are intolerant of them, unable to appreciate that they have their appropriate place and value in the life of man. We must then ask the philosophical question whether or not there are within the domain of knowledge demarcatory features in terms of which the domain is intelligible as a whole, and whether or not there are possibilities of significant selection other than that of ruthless specialisation.

Let me then turn to these two important philosophical problems. First, what kind of objectives does education have, and secondly, how are these objectives related to each other—what formal structure have they got? The objectives of education are surely certain developments of the pupil which are achieved in learning, and I suggest that these are all basically connected with the development of a rational mind. This is not to say that education is concerned only with intellectual development, as if, for example emotional development was to be ignored, and knowledge and belief taken to be the only manifestations of mind. Nor is it even to say that education is concerned only with mental development in its widest sense. Rather it is to say that all those forms of development with which education is concerned are related to the pupil's progress in rational understanding. This means that physical education, for instance, is pursued in accordance with a rational appraisal of the place and value of physical activities in human life which we wish the pupil to acquire, that the activities themselves are viewed as those of a developing rational being, not merely an animal, and that they therefore constitute part of the life of a rational person. But to characterise the objectives of education in relation to the development of rationality, is certainly to put at the very centre of what is pursued those forms of knowledge and belief in which we make sense of our experience. It is necessarily by means of knowledge, if not by knowledge alone, that fancy gives place to a recognition of fact, that irrational wishes give place to reasonable wants, and that emotional reactions give place to justifiable actions. Thus, although all the possible or justifiable objectives of education are not themselves explicitly developments of mind, it is, I suggest, by their connection with such specific developments that other objectives have their place and their justification in education at all. As I cannot here begin to consider the nature and interrelationship of educational objectives of very different kinds, I shall therefore confine myself to considering what is involved in the achievement of those most central objectives of all, the acquisition of knowledge and rational beliefs, without which the development of rationality in any wider sense is logically impossible.

What then is involved in the acquisition of knowledge? Certainly it involves learning many different concepts, using these in a growing awareness of facts, truths and forms of many kinds, mastering many logical operations and principles, applying the criteria of different types of judgment, and so on. What an exhaustive list of the elements would be, I would not like to say, but what matters for my purpose at the moment is not a complete classification of them in independent categories, so much as a recognition of the kind of achievements that these are. They are, in fact, neither more nor less than the very achievement of mind itself.

Unfortunately our concept of mind is so persistently bedevilled by myths, largely of an empiricist nature, that we all too easily misconceive entirely what is going on in learning to understand and in acquiring knowledge. We have an almost ineradicable conviction that the mind is to be thought of as a room or box into which, via the senses, ideas or images come as ready-made copies of objects or events or facts in the external world. Further, these ideas come into the mind as quite distinct elements of awareness, rather as furniture might be put into a room. The ideas are there in the room, but they are in no sense essentially part of the room. In addition we tend to regard the mind as a kind of machine, designed to carry out certain processes of rational thought on the ideas which the senses convey, thereby building new ideas from what is given, by processes of abstraction, deduction and the like. Thus there is produced new furniture to be housed and stored, within the mind, ready for use when required. Some of us have less effective machinery than others when it comes to reasoning, and practice and exercise are needed to get the best out of what each of us is given. But essentially the processes of rational thought are regarded as natural activities of the mind. On this kind of picture, the acquiring of knowledge and understanding as the objective of education, involves two major tasks: furnishing the mind with the right ideas, and getting the machine working properly.

Now there are many reasons why this kind of account of mind must be totally rejected, three of which are particularly relevant here. First the account does not begin to do justice to what we know about the development of understanding, even at the level of sense-perception. What we see or understand about any situation is not a simple given. It is dependent on those concepts and categories, those basic units of intelligibility, which the mind brings to the situation. The possibility of discriminating elements in our experience at all, necessitates having concepts. To see things is not just to register things for what they are, it is for them to be picked out or articulated in our consciousness. Only by the use of certain concepts is the mind able to discriminate. What the development of understanding involves is, in fact, a progressive differentiation of our experience through the acquisition of new concepts under which it is intelligible. The mind is therefore not a passive recipient of ideas which bring understanding from the external world. It is rather that we achieve understanding through the use of categorical and conceptual apparatus. Having such an apparatus of concepts is a necessary part of what it means to have a mind. Thus the development of a mind involves the achievement of an array of concepts and on this all intelligibility depends. The provision of experience in itself is quite inadequate for developing even the simplest body of concepts, and without these nothing more complex can possibly be achieved.[3]

In the second place, the view I am criticising regards knowledge as something which the mind may or may not possess. Knowledge is not in any sense constitutive of mind. To acquire new knowledge is simply as it were to acquire different furniture or new furniture for a room. To have scientific knowledge as distinct from historical knowledge, is for the furniture to be of one kind rather than another. For the mind itself, nothing turns on this, the room itself remains unchanged; it simply lacks the other type of furniture. In essence minds do not differ in any way by having different knowledge. The real differences between minds are simply in what is naturally given. To acquire one form of knowledge rather than another in no way affects the fundamental characteristics of the mind. Yet surely this will not do. To be without any knowledge at all is to be without mind in any significant sense. Nor is it just that the mind needs some content to work on, as if otherwise its characteristics could not be expressed. The acquisition of knowledge is itself a development of mind and new knowledge means a new development of mind in some sense. Knowledge is not a free-floating possession. It is a characteristic of minds themselves. Thus to fail to acquire knowledge of a certain fundamental kind, is to fail to achieve rational mind in that significant respect. Not all knowledge is of equal importance in the development of rationality of course, yet the fundamental relationship between knowledge and the development of mind is of central educational significance. Nor must we regard knowledge as unrelated to the development of other aspects of mind, an outlook encouraged by the view I am opposing. It is in large measure by acquiring new knowledge that we begin to reconceive our activities and that we come to feel differently about them.

In the third place we must, I suggest, reject the notion that the mind naturally carries out certain mental activities according to the canons of valid reasoning, as if logical principles were laws of psychological functioning. The question of the development of the rational mind is surely not a question of the strengthening or habitualising of certain patterns of mental functioning. It is rather a question of developing a recognition that one's beliefs and one's arguments, the outcomes of thought, must satisfy important public tests. Tests of rationality are tests to be applied to the *achievements* of one's thought as formulated in propositions, not tests for thought *processes* themselves. To say one has reasoned something out is not to describe a particular sequence of mental occurrences, it is to say that one has achieved in the end a relationship between propositions which satisfies the public criteria necessary for giving reasons. What is more, these standards that define the achievements of reason, are certainly not natural possessions of minds. They have to be learnt, usually by dint of considerable hard work. The development of rationality is, therefore, not dependent on the exercising of particular mental processes, but it is dependent on one's coming to recognise that there are tests of validity for one's arguments and tests of truth for one's beliefs.

But I must turn to the other philosophical question. If the fundamental objectives of education are developments of the rational mind, what formal relationships are there between the various objectives, the concepts, facts, norms, principles, and so on? In spite of an immediate tendency to think of these items of knowledge as detached and isolated from each other, a little reflection quickly suggests this is not the case. It is because the concepts are used in a particular way that any proposition is meaningful. The concepts on which our knowledge is built form distinctive networks of relationships. If we transgress the rules of the relationships which the concepts meaningfully permit, we necessarily produce nonsense. If we talk about magnetic fields being angry, actions being coloured, beauty having weight, or stones being right or wrong we have simply produced conceptual confusions. But not only do we convey meaning by the use of networks of interrelated concepts, meaningful propositions are judged true or false, valid or invalid, by criteria appropriate to the types of propositions. A moral judgment is not validated in the same way as a mathematical theorem, nor a historical explanation in the same way as a theological proposition. There are thus within knowledge a number of distinct types of rational judgment. From considerations of this kind it can be seen that the acquisition of knowledge in any area involves the mastery of an inter-related group of concepts, of operations with these, of particular criteria of truth or validity associated with these concepts, as well as more general criteria of a reasoning common to all areas of knowledge. Indeed, the objectives of education we have been considering are closely related together as elements of distinguishable cognitive structures, each unique in crucial respects.

Looked at this way, the development of mind has been marked by the progressive differentiation in human consciousness of some seven or eight distinguishable cognitive structures, each of which involves the making of a distinctive form of reasoned judgment and is, therefore, a unique expression of man's rationality. This is to say that all knowledge and understanding is logically locatable within a number of domains, within, I suggest, mathematics, the physical sciences, the human sciences and history, literature and the fine arts, morals, religion and philosophy. These would seem to me to be the logically distinct areas, though this division might well be disputed. It is not, of course, that these forms of knowledge are totally separate from each other. That is not what I am saying. Manifestly there are overlaps in the concepts used in the different forms, and there are overlaps in the patterns of valid reasoning. But in respect of the distinctive rational judgments concerned, each structure involves elements which are irreducible to any of the others, singly or in combination. Moral judgments and scientific judgments are different in logical character, needing distinct forms of justification, and that in spite of the fact that these may at times use some of the same concepts and some of the same criteria for reasoning. The objectives with which education is most centrally concerned are thus not isolated ends, but elements within integrated developing structures of understanding. Certainly all the concepts, truths, norms, principles, criteria, all the developments of mind we are interested in, have their appropriate place in relation to these structures, and even those elements which are common to different areas have significance only within these structures.[4]

If what I have said is valid, then the domain of knowledge can be seen to have important structural features, and nothing could be further from the truth than to suggest that that domain is an unintelligible chaos. Knowledge has not disintegrated, it has become more clearly differentiated. It is not even that the traditional medieval map of knowledge has become totally unacceptable, for many of the logical distinctions there made are perfectly valid.[5] It is simply that the development of knowledge necessitates some new lines in the picture, and we are not yet sure of the precise details as to where to put them. We may no longer have a hierarchy of knowledge based on realist metaphysics, but we are not without the important logical distinctions that make it possible for us to see some intelligible pattern in knowledge. We may no longer have a clear grasp of the unity of knowledge, as if it all formed, in the end, one coherent network of harmonious elements. Yet unifying theories are part of the pursuit of the sub-divisions within the areas I have mentioned and there is every reason to hope that we can become much clearer on the relationships between the logically distinct forms that I have distinguished.

Yet what then of the modern transgressions of the old frontiers? Is it not the case that besides the progressive differentiation of say the sciences or historical studies, there are new disciplines or forms of knowledge emerging? Maybe this is so. I see no a priori reason whatever why new forms of knowledge should not arise. But there is, I think, little positive reason to think that this is in fact what is happening. What there are in abundance now, are new interdisciplinary areas of study in which different forms of knowledge are focused on some particular interest, and because of the relations between the forms, what is understood in each discipline is thereby deepened. Such new areas of study do not constitute new areas on a map of knowledge based on the logical distinctions I have mentioned. They are essentially composite, second order constructions, not to be confused with the primary forms of knowledge which I have distinguished on logical grounds. In terms of these primary forms of knowledge, the new areas seem to be exhaustively analysable.

As a final comment on the structure of knowledge, it must be said that the internal logical characteristics of the distinct forms and their relationships to each other, are likely to contain important principles that should govern the teaching of these areas. In some forms certain concepts logically pre-suppose others. That is to say, certain concepts are unintelligible unless other concepts pre-supposed are already understood. Equally, certain areas of knowledge pre-suppose others, parts of the physical sciences, for instance, are plainly unintelligible without a good deal of mathematical knowledge. In general terms the necessary elements of order in learning have been recognised for a long time, but there is a great deal of detailed logical work needed here, which is only now beginning to be done, and it might well transform much of our teaching in due course.[6]

But let me now return to the curriculum problems which led me into these philosophical considerations. What is the bearing of these remarks on the issue of the curricula for universal secondary education? One crucial implication is, I think, plain. If the acquisition of certain fundamental elements of knowledge is necessary to the achievement of the rational mind in some particular respect, then these at any rate cannot but be universal objectives for the curriculum. If the objectives of our education differ for sections of our society so as to ignore any of these elements for some of our pupils, either because they are considered too difficult, or for some reason they are thought less important for these pupils, then we are denying to them certain basic ways of rational development and we have indeed got inequality of educational opportunity of the most far-reaching kind. Our schools may set themselves, and often do, objectives which I have not considered. They may concern themselves with the pursuit of interesting and worthwhile activities of an endless variety, with vocational skills, with many forms of general socialisation and so on. But it is education which I take to be the prime function of the school, and it is only because of the connection these other objectives have with rational development that they have a place in education at all. If once the central objectives of rationality are submerged, or are given up so that these other pursuits take over, then I suggest the school has betrayed its educational trust, no matter how successful it may be in these other respects, and no matter how laudable these other ends may be in themselves. Whatever other principles may govern the curriculum I am arguing that we can have no adequate grounds for forsaking a child's progressive initiation into all the distinctive forms of rationality, until we have done everything in our power to achieve just this. As noted earlier, we are all too ready on psychological grounds to rationalise our present practice. In this case we most often escape our responsibility by a rigid view of human abilities, saying that children just cannot understand these things, by a curious notion of the needs of the pupil in which other needs are of higher priority than the development of rationality, and by a perverted doctrine of the importance of a pupil's present interests.

But if the universality of these objectives is granted, what further can be said about the curriculum? How, for instance, are we to choose the particular elements from the forms of knowledge in order best to obtain our objectives of rationality? One thing must, I am sure, be made plain here. The purpose of the curriculum I am concerned with, is not the production of even embryonic specialists in the different forms of knowledge. Manifestly one can study any subject in different ways, with the emphases on very different parts of the interrelated whole. We do not in this case want pupils to amass a great deal of, say, scientific information, nor do we want a mastery of techniques of investigation. Nor is it a matter of teaching what has everyday usefulness. The point is that the pupil shall begin to think in a distinctive way, and that means acquiring such a hold of those features which most distinctively characterise this form of knowledge, that one's thought is developed into autonomous functioning using the relevant concepts and criteria. This will mean selecting, and then concentrating one's teaching on, the most central and fruitful concepts, forms of explanation, criteria and methods of justification in the area. The idea is that pupils themselves will master the use of the concepts in the right way, and, by formulating and considering truths in the domain, that they will appreciate the features of knowledge of this particular kind, and know the reasons or kinds of evidence on which its truths turn. Manifestly we have not yet begun to discover in any systematic sense what is involved in producing courses of this nature. Our eyes have been far too fixed on the specialist training of the young physicist to find out what is needed in courses in physics that will develop a sympathetic grasp of the cognitive structure of science, an appreciation of what it involves and thereby a recognition of its significance in the rational life. This is not to ask for courses *about*, say, science rather than courses *in* science. It is to ask for courses in science which direct their attention away from the mastery of detail that a specialist requires and towards the mastery of the general and basic elements of the mode of thought.

But can such courses be taken by every pupil? The answer, from what I have argued already, must surely be that it is imperative that we find courses involving these central elements that all pupils can take successfully. I see no adequate grounds for saying this is impossible when we have in fact spent so little of our effort trying to achieve this. Such courses need not be identical for all pupils in spite of their common objectives and a likely high degree of common content. There are many different ways that teachers can use in approaching a particular concept, a particular scientific law or a particular historical explanation. Granted even that one is going to teach precisely the same course to groups of differing ability, there are ways of easing the difficulty. But there are good ways of doing this and bad ways, and we need to distinguish between them. It is all too easy, with the best intentions in the world, to cease to teach the subject to the less able pupil in any significant sense at all. By not really bothering whether or not they have got hold of the concepts and can use them, by being content with memorised statements, by allowing pure repetition of operations, by omitting anything which demands even the briefest unrehearsed argument or justification, we simply evade all the problems and totally fail to develop any significant understanding. However we accommodate ourselves to the less able, it must not be by losing essential concepts, by losing genuine operations with them, by being uncritical of invalid reasoning, and so on.

The necessary elements of knowledge are necessary elements and we cannot evade the implications of that simple tautology, try as we may. Yet there are things we can do. We can reduce the complexities by seeing that the conceptual relations we include are those absolutely essential for our purpose. Every unnecessary element that might befog an explanation can be omitted. We can cut down the extent of sustained argument by carefully analysing the stages that are demanded. We can use every opportunity to emphasise the central core of what is being done, rather than go in for extension and exploration of the ideas and their more complex applications. At least this is how we can set about things in the first place, and in our best teaching we do this already.

But what about the general structure of the secondary curriculum? The logical distinctness of the different forms of knowledge and the close inter-relation of the various elements within a form of a sub-division of it, would seem to suggest that the most rational way in which to develop the distinct modes of understanding, would be by direct organisation of the curriculum in units corresponding to the forms. There is good historical precedent for this as it is precisely what we do to a large extent in the traditional subject curriculum of the grammar school. Such an approach has many obvious merits from a logical point of view, as it is less likely than any other to cause confusion between the concepts and criteria which belong to the different areas, and it enables a thoroughly systematic approach to be made to the development of the form of thought in terms of the concepts to be acquired, the operations involved, and so on. But it has the disadvantages that go with its advantages, for it emphasises the differences between forms of knowledge, and the many important interconnections between them can be forgotten to the impoverishment of them all. Unfortunately too, the subject approach of the grammar school is still associated with very formal teaching methods, though these are not necessarily connected with it, and such an organisation of the curriculum has as a result largely been taken to be unsuitable for less able pupils. It seems to me there is place here for a careful reassessment of the benefits of such a curriculum and for experiment in its wider application with more enlightened teaching methods.

The alternative, of topics approached from different points of view, is necessarily less systematic in the development of understanding it involves, and it does not permit the choice of content to be aimed so directly at central concepts, operations, criteria and other logically distinct features of the various forms of knowledge.

Indeed, from the point of view of the general development of rationality, such a curriculum by topics is difficult to handle efficiently and effectively, and, I suggest, hard to justify. Indeed, its central justification is not to be found in the contribution it makes to the development of rationality, but elsewhere, in that a suitable choice of topics can overcome many motivational problems with less able pupils, and much practical and useful information and many useful skills can be acquired easily and efficiently when approached this way. There is here, in fact, a most genuine tension between different principles which must be taken into account when deciding the best curriculum in any one particular case. What must be remembered however, is that whatever curriculum pattern or syllabus pattern is adopted, the elements of learning which pupils are to acquire must find their place in the coherent yet logically distinct cognitive structures which the pupils are slowly mastering. Significant learning cannot be a random business. The more we are aware of the logical relations involved, the more we promote our pupils' mastery of these, the more genuinely effective our teaching will be.

On the traditional grammar school curriculum I need to say little, as indeed all I have just said of the secondary curriculum in general, has particular application here. But I must give direct answers to the specific questions I raised earlier. From what I have said of the significance of knowledge for the development of the rational mind, the narrow-mindedness of so many of our grammar school products is, I think, an inevitable outcome, and a vicious indictment, of the curriculum we use. It is also, I think, a witness to the fact that the courses which pupils drop at 'O' level, however satisfactory they may be for future specialists in these subjects, are not in themselves adequate in achieving any long-standing development of rational thought in these areas, for many pupils. This, I am sure, is primarily a matter of the intention of the courses and the particular content used. We have yet to seriously face the truth that 'doing physics' can mean many different things, each of which has its distinctive values. When we get hold of the fact that any area of knowledge has many distinct elements to it, and that courses can therefore be directed to highlighting quite different features, we might set about producing courses that have greater general educational value in developing rational understanding than those we have at present. It seems to me not only unnecessary, but fundamentally miseducative, both to allow our present specialisation in the curriculum, and to teach many subjects from the start as if all pupils were eventually to become specialists in them. The remedies for our ills in these cases are surely in our hands, and I am afraid at the moment we simply lack the will to effect the cure.

As to the problem of the selection of knowledge that is to be made for inclusion in the curriculum, it seems to me there are clear indications of how this can be done on logical grounds rather than by the ruthless butchery of specialisation. The logically distinct forms of knowledge are comparatively few and not all of them need to be taught all the time; yet serious and sustained attention must be given to all these, and surely none of them should be dismissed for good from the enterprise of education earlier than is absolutely necessary, certainly not at the stage at which we permit this in our schools today. Within any one form of knowledge, the content can be chosen according to the importance of the elements for the development of the form of thought, if this is indeed accepted as a fundamental aim. The aim of specialisation certainly makes the domains of knowledge seem vast and overwhelming, so that one hardly knows what to choose. Yet set oneself rather different objectives, in this case the pursuit of rational understanding in these areas, and I suggest that the enterprise is by no means so unmanageable.

In this paper I have argued that there is, at least to some extent, a map of knowledge, and if so, the logical demarcations it shows cannot but be helpful in providing our pupils with an idea of the range of human understanding, and therefore some perspective on human pursuits. But this does demand that pupils develop to a significant degree the various forms of thought, that they appreciate their distinctive functions and their relationships to each other. We cannot expect pupils to acquire a rational perspective on the lives and affairs of men unless we equip them to achieve this by developing the forms of thought that define that perspective.

Finally, what of the organisation of the curriculum into the traditional subjects? Though I am very concerned about the specialist type of content to these subjects as we now have them, the principle of division between the subjects seems to me to be supremely justified in the education of able pupils. It has the strongest justification in those logical distinctions within knowledge which I have outlined. The sustained discipline, according to the necessary features of the subjects, that this approach demands, is obviously of immense value. More modern organisations of study that are being

250iG

THE CURRICULUM

developed in the universities and are now coming into schools, may
have their good points. But achieving the basic modes of thought is
a difficult business, and if the newer approaches result in any evasion
of the discipline necessary to the development of those forms of
thought, then it seems to me they will do us a great disservice in the
end.

I have tried in this paper to make one or two general philosophical points and to show their bearing on certain curriculum questions. All I have said must be taken together with considerations of
other kinds that I have ignored. I hope I have vindicated my claim
that on curriculum matters philosophers have things to say that
cannot go unheeded or unexamined in responsible curriculum planning. As I said at the beginning, the practical problems of education
must never be left to philosophers to solve, but to ignore what they
can contribute to their solution is a sure way to ill-considered
judgments. In this area as in so many others, philosophers may not
be kings, but I trust I have shown that they cannot with impunity
be totally excluded from the conduct of the affairs of state.

Notes and References

1 I use this term to denote a kind of curriculum, whether it happens to be
   implemented in a grammar school, a comprehensive, or a public school.

2 *15 to 18*, report of the Central Advisory Council for Education (H.M.S.O.
   1959, vol. I, ch. 25). See also A. D. C. Peterson, 'The Myth of "Subject-
   mindedness"' (*Universities Quarterly*, June 1960).

3 R. S. Peters, *Ethics and education* (Allen & Unwin, 1966, ch. 2); also
   W. Kneale, *On having a mind* (Cambridge University Press, 1962).

4 For a further discussion of the distinctions between different forms of
   knowledge see P. H. Hirst, *Liberal education and the nature of knowledge*
   in R. D. Archambault (ed.), *Philosophical analysis and education* (Routledge
   and Kegan Paul, 1965). See also S. Elam (ed.), *Education and the structure
   of knowledge* (Rand McNally, Chicago, 1964).

5 J. Maritain, *The degrees of knowledge* (G. Bles, 1959, Pt. 1).

6 See papers by D. W. Hamlyn and P. H. Hirst in R. S. Peters (ed.), *The concept of education* (Routledge & Kegan Paul, 1967).

G. H. Bantock

II:9 Towards a theory of popular education

G. H. Bantock puts forward specific curriculum proposals to provide a satisfactory education for the mass of children for whom the present watered down academic education is failing. Bantock dissents from the view of Professor Hirst that there is no need for a radically new pattern of the curriculum. Bantock argues also against Hirst's view that all curricula for all children should have as its central objective the development of mind. Instead of a cognitively based curriculum with emphasis on linguistic and abstract forms of thought, Bantock argues that the basis of the curriculum should be more concrete, more practical and 'affective-artistic' in orientation.

Two fundamental and highly intractable educational problems have arisen out of the scientific and technological revolution of the last 200 years, and the industrialization which has accompanied it.

In the education of the meritocracy, which has replaced the old landed aristocracy as the ruling elite, we are faced with the need to find a substitute for the old classical curriculum as the central humanistic and civilizing discipline which in the past penetrated into so many aspects of our social and cultural life.

Only Dr F. R. Leavis has suggested a solution to this problem in pointing to English literature as the civilizing agency, a solution, however, which is necessarily partial and in any case not likely to achieve universal acceptance.

The second problem relates to the need to provide a satisfying education for those children who have entered the schools as a result of the universal provision of education following the 1870 Act, but for whom the watered down academic education we still provide as the core of the curriculum would seem to have failed.

What is common to both is a concern for the content of education, in contrast to controversies which currently distract us and which centre on organization and methodology and thus avoid the fundamental issues about what to teach—and to whom.

Times Educational Supplement, 12 and 19 March 1971. Reprinted by permission.

Before I proceed I had better explain my title. A theory of education implies the bringing to bear of the various disciplines relevant to education in an attempt to clarify aims and purposes. History, sociology, psychology and philosophy provide us with information or clarification in a variety of ways which can help us in coming to practical decisions about how to educate people. As Professor Hirst has indicated, an educational theory is perhaps best classified as a form of moral knowledge.

By popular, in this context, I intend in the first place a general reference to those children with whom our present schooling would appear to have failed. As a group, they are perhaps most clearly defined in the pages of the Schools Council inquiry *Young School Leavers* (1968). I quote from the introduction:

'The intended raising of the school leaving age to 16 ... means retaining in school for a fifth year of secondary education some 60 per cent more of the age group than now stay on voluntarily. The majority of those affected have an ability for scholastic work which is average or below average. Some will come from homes which will attach small value to extended schooling. For many, vocational motivation will be weak; it will be difficut to gain their interest and sense of relevance; some will actively resent having to study longer in school.'

I would be happy if, in the first place, my suggestions could be applied to approximately the bottom 50 per cent of this group and throughout their secondary school careers, from 11. They will be children of low achievement, probably though not invariably of low I.Q., come from culturally deprived homes, wish to leave school as soon as possible and find themselves employed on leaving in unskilled or semi-skilled jobs. To be more specific still, I am thinking of the bottom stream in small secondary modern schools, in the bottom two or three streams in larger modern and comprehensive schools.

Let me begin by attempting to place what will inevitably be the majority of these children in their historico-sociological setting. This historical dimension is often lacking in our thinking about them. In pre-industrial times there were two broad cultures—that based on literacy for the sophisticated and that based on an oral tradition for the folk. Most of the children I have picked out above will, in terms of cultural background, come from the traditional folk group—dull children from the traditionally sophisticated group are likely to find themselves in the private education sector.

As a help to diagnosing their level of understanding it may be helpful if we seek some clues concerning the traditional nature of folk consciousness. In Professor Owst's *Literature and pulpit in mediaeval England* he quotes with approval Miss Evelyn Underhill's statement that 'It is characteristic of the primitive mind that it finds a difficulty about universals and is most at home with particulars' : and Professor Owst adds that the characteristic features of English medieval preaching 'exhibit this same desire to escape as far as possible from the abstract and universal in religion and to be at home in particulars'.

If we then turn to a nineteenth century comment on the peasant consciousness in George Bourne's *Change in the village*, we read :

'... We may say that a modern man's thought goes on habitually at two main levels. On the surface are the subjects of the moment—that endless procession of things seen or heard—which make up the outer world; and here is where intercourse with the old type of villager was easy and agreeable. But below the surface, the modern mind has a habit of interpreting these phenomena by general ideas of abstract principles ... and into this region of thought the peasant's attention hardly penetrated at all.'

D. H. Lawrence, the one twentieth-century working-class imaginative writer of genius, spoke of his father's generation in these terms :

'The colliers were deeply alive instinctively. But ... they avoided, really, the rational aspect of life. They preferred to take life instinctively and intuitively.'

Lawrence's whole analysis of the working-class consciousness implicit throughout much of his work is, of course, of the deepest significance for my theme. But these evocations drawn partly from the past and partly from an imaginative writer would cut little ice with many were they not uncannily picked up by the findings of a modern empirical sociologist.

In a paper on 'Social class, language and socialization', Professor Bernstein has analysed what he terms 'the two codes employed by English people' and which he refers to respectively as elaborated and restricted. He argues that 'elaborated codes orient their users towards universalistic meaning, whereas restricted codes orient and sensitize their users to particularistic meanings'.

The implication of universalistic he explains is that 'the meanings are less tied to a given context'; where the orders of meaning are particularistic they are 'more context bound'—that is, 'tied to a local relationship and to a local social structure'. Finally, '... restricted codes draw upon metaphor whereas elaborated codes draw upon rationality'.

If I am right to place the group of children in whom I am interested among those whose language code is significantly restricted, then both the historical and contemporary evidence points to features of their language usage which can be empirically demonstrated and which must be taken into account in considering the viability of any system of education, such as ours, which conventionally is deeply linguistically oriented.

Our present system of education, indeed, is language oriented not only in the demands that it makes on conceptual development needed for an understanding of the relevant school subjects, but in the very nature of the consciousness which is fundamental to its whole meaning and significance. Fundamental to the culture of the school is the book; and it is astonishing how little we have asked the apparently simple question: 'When we teach people to read, what do we do to them?'

I have attempted to explore this problem in my inaugural lecture at Leicester University, *The implications of literacy*. Briefly, the effect is to introduce a child at an early age into a quite different level of consciousness than that implicit in the early folk tradition. Reading implies a concentrated attempt to translate inanimate shapes on a printed page into significant meaning. Whereas, in face-to-face contact, our voice, gestures, facial expressions, vocal emphases, add meaning, none of these aids are present where the printed word is concerned; our need then is to evoke meaning from something that is essentially inanimate and dead.

As R. G. Collingwood put it in his *Principles of art*: 'The written or printed book is only a series of hints from which the reader then works out for himself the speech gestures which alone have the gift of expression.' Anyone who has had any experience of attempting to teach reading to backward children does not need to be told how fantastically difficult a task some of them find this to be.

Yet it is upon this subtle understanding of printed language that the culture of the school continually makes demands. The school curriculum, it is true, constitutes a watered-down and simplified high culture; but in general its meaning structures become progressively more universalistic as its material becomes increasingly more complex. By nature it is primarily cognitive and even when it involves some degree of affectivity, as in literature, it still necessitates a capacity for highly subtle translation of written symbol into meaning—a meaning both cognitive and affective.

Furthermore, the culture of the school as at present constituted involves delayed satisfaction and a whole set of cultural expectations and requirements which make it not surprising that it is the middle classes rather than the working classes that benefit most easily from it. The working class ethos as, for example, it is defined impressionistically by writers such as Richard Hoggart, contains elements of emotional warmth and a stress on the immediacies of social contact which belie the isolation and intellectualization of the school curriculum. The social conditions of the working classes do not encourage the detachment from immediate contacts which the nature of school subjects imposes.

Since most of the children I have in mind are likely to come from those descendants of the traditional folk, the working classes—if only because such classes contain more members than any other section of the community—and, furthermore, the theory of embourgeoisement has recently become less acceptable and we are less sure than we used to be that gradually working class people are becoming assimilated to middle class habits, the precise nature of working class gregariousness is of paramount importance for my theme—as is the nature of working class expectations and satisfactions.

Clues concerning these will be noted in the predominating nature of mass media communications. The popular culture of television, radio and mass circulation newspaper evokes immediate satisfaction and reveals the vital role of affectivity in its appeal. Advertisements do not stress rationality, but use images evocatively to persuade and cajole.

A typical popular manifestation on the media implies an interest in personality and transmits its meaning as often as not visually (even when the medium is print—our most popular newspapers make excessive use of visual aids for what is primarily a print medium) in ways which imply that visual symbols rather than language is a potent way into the consciousness of the folk. Identification with people and life styles rather than critical assessment is what is invited. It is not surprising when the nature of much of our popular culture is assessed that D. H. Lawrence should have indicated that knowledge for the people must be 'mythical, symbolical, dynamic'.

I believe that this general picture of the level at which the people of whom I am speaking operate, is supported by such psychological insight as we have acquired in recent years into the nature of children's learning. It is first of all reasonable to expect that not all children can be brought to the same level of achievement. It is true that recently the fashionable doctrine has tended to be that even allowing for the observed deficiencies of many children, these are explicable in terms of inhibitory environmental factors which can be compensated for; thus there has been a stress on compensatory education in order to aid deficiencies in conceptualization. Implied has been a near equality of endowment which only inequalities of background have inhibited from full fruition.

Latterly, the claims of heredity have again been put forward and the work of Burt, Eysenck and Jensen has stressed the element of hereditary endowment. Difficult and complicated though the nature–nurture controversy is, the notion of the almost infinite plasticity of human intellectual endowment has suffered a number of blows from which it is not likely to recover. Compensatory education in America especially has been directed to filling in the gaps in achievement in order to equalize opportunity to take advantage of the current curriculum. The current curriculum, however, with its cognitive emphasis seems to remain obstinately beyond the grasp, in any meaningful sense, of the children about whom we are talking; results of American compensatory programmes have not on the whole been propitious.

Professor Arthur Jensen, indeed, has made the interesting suggestion on empirical grounds that two different levels of mental functioning exist—one at the conceptual level and one at what he has termed 'the level of associative learning'. This seems to tally uncannily with the impressionistic diagnoses of mental functioning on which I have drawn earlier in this article from my historical sources.

Some evidence for the possibility that many children may remain roughly at Piaget's level of concrete operations at a time when their more sophisticated fellows are moving into the abstractions of formal operations may supply further supportive evidence to this picture. Thus, Mr Roger Hallam has conducted some investigations into children's capacities to grasp historical concepts used in history teaching ('Paiget and the teaching of history', *Educational Research*, vol. 12, no. 1, November 1969). Using Piaget's work on logical thinking as a basis, he has come to the conclusion that:

'Whatever stage might have been reached by a particular pupil, the majority of secondary school pupils up to the mental age of 16 years seem to be at the concrete operational level of thought. The syllabuses should therefore be organized to take account of the limitations in pupils' reasoning.'

Hence he points to the need to concentrate, for many pupils, on what he terms concrete history. The need for care in the use of specialist terms is further illustrated in Mr Douglas Barnes's admirable Penguin paper on education, *Language, the learner and the school* where in his analysis of the language of instruction he also draws attention to the use of language forms which, while not specific to any one subject, is nevertheless of a kind a pupil would be unlikely to encounter in everyday informal speech.

It is true that Dr Hallam's own work on the use of specialist terms peculiar to history is limited in scope and needs to be followed up by further investigations. It is even more true that we need many more of the sorts of investigations he has mounted into the precise capacity of children to grasp the abstractions peculiar to particular subject areas of the school curriculum; and further, that we need to know a great deal more about what Mr Barnes refers to as 'the language of secondary education'—school language of a non-specialist kind but peculiar to the classroom. What can be said is that much is misunderstood by children of lesser intelligence. The ability to understand abstractions at different levels and in different conceptual fields is fundamental to the implementation of our present purposes in education and a major reason for thinking some extensive reorientation of our present practices desirable.

I can perhaps illustrate this point and at the same time begin to move towards a more positive statement of the implications of this analysis by considering a statement made by Professor P. H. Hirst in *Working Paper no.* 12, published by the Schools Council, on 'The educational implications of social and economic change'.

There, Professor Hirst explicitly asserts that there is no need for a 'radically new pattern of the curriculum'. He continues:

'As I see it, the central objectives of education are developments of mind.... No matter what the ability of the child may be, the heart of all his development as a rational being is, I am saying, intellectual. Maybe we shall need very special methods to achieve this development in some cases. Maybe we have still to find the best methods for the majority of people. But let us never lose sight of the intellectual aim upon which so much else, nearly everything else, depends. Secondly, it seems to me that we must get away completely from the idea that linguistic and abstract forms of thought are not for some people.'

This view represents a powerful body of opinion in the educational world and, unlike some such opinions, is backed by some of the best minds working in education. At the same time, it is a view from which I must in many respects dissent. The grounds of dissent will already have been implicit in a good deal of what I have

said . . .; but a brief analysis of Professor Hirst's statements may
perhaps help in further clarifying my objections to his position.
He deprecates the idea that 'linguistic and abstract forms of thought
are not for some people'.

Now, it is perfectly true that linguistic forms of thought must be
for everyone above the level of the seriously brain damaged. Language is the characteristic feature of human communication and is,
indeed, one of the features in terms of which one can define what it
is to be human. Insofar therefore as people are capable of thinking
at any level at all in a rational way, language is likely to be the
mode through which their thought processes are made manifest. In
this trivial sense, then, we may well admit that linguistic forms of
thought are for all.

It is the inclusion of the word 'abstract' that causes the difficulty.
Abstraction, according to the dictionary, denotes 'the act of considering something as a general quality or characteristic apart from
any concrete realities, specific object, or actual instance'. All normal people make use of some abstractions. No one, for instance, is
likely to have any difficulty in understanding the sentence 'All
chairs are meant to sit upon', where one is considering the general
characteristic of chairs apart from any specific instance.

There are, too, certain abstract terms which are sufficiently
context-bound to indicate clearly their significance. No one, again, is
likely to have much difficulty with the word 'free' in the sentence
'You are free to leave the room'. But what is at issue is not the ability
of people to understand and employ abstractions of this sort, but to
comprehend complicated abstract arguments on the use of abstractions in contexts which make their precise significance much more
difficult to decide upon.

Many school subjects, after all, develop complex patterns of
abstractions as an essential part of their logical framework. When
terms are used, as in areas like social studies (often thought highly
relevant to the 'needs' of less able children) which are also in general
usage—terms like 'freedom', 'authority,' 'responsibility', 'representative'—it is not surprising that the often highly abstract nature of the
discourse is beyond the grasp of many. If, for instance, one utters
the sentence 'Freedom is an essential human right', notions of
'freedom' and 'rights' are much more difficult to determine with any
degree of precision and the appearance of such sentences in the
course of a developing argument is likely to bewilder many.

Clearly one has to go carefully here. I have already ... pointed to the absence of detailed empirical studies which would guide us in understanding the precise levels of abstraction which in different subject areas children at different ages are likely to be able to encompass.

At the same time, my initial evidence drawn over a long historical period and the particular analysis which Professor Bernstein has given us, make it reasonable to assert that many levels of abstraction are likely to be beyond the capacity of numbers of people and that among those numbers are likely to be included the particular group of children with whom I am specifically concerned in this article.

It is no good persisting in our current ways on the grounds that we just do not know whether some different approach might not enable people to encompass the necessary abstractions determined by the school curriculum. After all, we have tried a watered down 'high culture' for nearly a hundred years—and still not found the way. It is entirely reasonable to make extrapolations from what we already do know and can observe, and to act responsibly on a basis of this.

It would be the more justified if it were possible to provide an alternative curriculum which would avoid the trivialities implicit in much of the vocational and life adjustment work done as a sop to the less able.

The question that faces us is indeed: 'Can we find a syllabus which will be at once demanding but which, based on different principles from the current one, will afford greater opportunities to those who at present show little aptitude for the cognitively based curriculum?' I believe it is, and that its basis should be affective-artistic rather than cognitive-intellectual.

It is interesting in this respect to note that Professor Hirst asserts in the working paper mentioned that 'we must get away from what can be called a retreat into the Arts and practical activities, as being more suitable for the less intellectually able'. His use of the word 'retreat' seems to me highly significant. I will, for the moment, avoid his reference to 'practical activities' and concentrate specifically on his reference to the arts.

I am particularly interested in his view that work in the arts should seem to betoken a 'retreat', as if somehow they constituted an inferior way of looking at the world than that implicit in the more rational subjects. Admittedly, and to be fair to him, Professor Hirst does indicate that 'there is a central place in education for the Arts'; but he proceeds: 'the significance of the Arts is limited and any retreat from the demands of other forms of development in language is to set barriers to the developments open to many children'. Of course, the significance of the arts is limited as, for that matter, is the significance of the sciences; either forms only a segment of the totality of human awareness and understanding. But the use of the word 'retreat' would seem to indicate that Professor Hirst would have serious reservations about regarding the arts as the key to the education of any children.

Put it another way, his persistent emphasis is on the linguistic as the tool of thought rather than on expressive action as the key to emotional discipline. And here I would disagree with him.

Before, however, I proceed to clarify my meaning, it is desirable to summarize what has emerged implicitly from my analysis as relevant to the formulation of a curriculum for these children.

The level to be aimed at must, it would seem, as far as possible, be that of practical common life. This is implicit in the need to be concrete and specific. But it must be practical life without any of the more dismal overtones which the word 'practical' too often conveys. 'Practicality', indeed, does not necessarily imply undertakings of limited vision and imaginative poverty. Practical life at the domestic and work levels is important for these children, but so is the 'practical' life of entertainment and human relationships.

Television, film and the popular press are part of their culture and these, in however poverty stricken a way, make demands on their imagination—as spectators of course, not as participants. Part, too, of the practical world is that of marriage and human relationships and these test at the profoundest and subtlest levels.

It will be necessary then to appeal to 'practicality' not only in the mundane terms of adding up the change, but at levels which can make the most intense demands at the appropriate levels on the individual's personality and imaginative capacities.

Furthermore, the emphasis on the affective which has been implicit in much of the preceding analysis, points to the need for an education of the emotions in ways which our cognitive curriculum sorely neglects. Freud has shown the extent to which our emotional life is fundamental and the arts provide traditional means by which we may seek to come to terms with these emotions.

Finally, the new leisure that may characterize later twentieth century living as a result of the development of automation, means that an element of liberal education is central to any genuine education for these children. Traditionally, a liberal education has implied a leisure class. It is highly possible that we are moving into an era when all will participate in some degree of leisure which it is vitally important that education should help to fill.

The fundamental discipline of the old education, whether elementary or advanced, was the act of reading, the gateway to the inner consciousness, social detachedness and the opportunity to develop rationality. The fundamental discipline of a revised educational system for those who have found the culture of the book almost totally unacceptable is the art of movement with its emphasis on motor skills, communal participation and the opportunity to develop perception and empathy. I refer in the first instance to the particular type of movement education which Rudolph Laban has done so much to develop. Bodily movement is a fundamental characteristic of all human beings, a means through which their affectivity can be expressed: and the development of a kinetic sense is a means to entry into various of the ordered activities of the arts and of the qualities of mind which the practice of the arts demands. (The important role of mind and intellect in art has been persuasively argued by Professor Edgar Wind in *Art and Anarchy*.)

Movement in the disciplined sense intended involves the exploration of space in ways which can afford expression involving inner feelings and the images of human behaviour they evoke. At the same time, as Laban indicated, 'Dance is not to relieve feelings, it is not self-expression. Dance is no longer spontaneous gestures, but deliberate acts.' (All arts involve, at bottom, a making, not simply an outlet; it is this which makes them educative.) Thus, movement, as it merges into dance as a socialized participatory form based on rhythmic repetitions and patterned bodily behaviour becomes an art form, an articulation of gestures.

Music here is clearly relevant, both to respond to and to create in its own right. It is noteworthy that T. R. Fyvel found that music was the one expressive form to which even the most apathetic and bored of his 'insecure offenders' would respond to.

Another route from movement is in mime and drama. Here Dr V. R. Bruce's *Dance and dance drama in education* provides an admirable introduction to rationale and possibilities. Drama implies the spoken word as well as the written text and these children certainly need practice in ordered and imaginative speech as well as in working from the printed word.

It must be clear that reading and writing must still inevitably form an important part of the work they are to do, though the approach I am suggesting will be a different one; they will arise out of other activities rather than form the central core of their schools' culture. The ability to read and write is a fundamental necessity in the twentieth century, but it needs to be done in terms which are affectively rather than cognitively oriented. Fortunately, Mr David Holbrook has pointed the way here in his *English for the rejected*, a way where the links with movement, drama and other arts so far mentioned are clearly possible.

Other aspects of movement in a more limited sense merge into design and craft work and art in two or three dimensions. The Schools Council project under the direction of Professor S. J. Eggleston has shown the way forward into new areas of significance where traditional craftwork is linked with a profounder awareness of design. Art has long been part of our normal school syllabus and Herbert Read's *Education through art* which is highly relevant to this curriculum is now nearly 20 years old.

What, however, also need exploiting are possibilities specifically within the characteristic twentieth-century art forms like film, television and radio. Film making and film editing, photography in general, are means through which children can develop iconographic awareness, which are already part of today's cultural consciousness. The use of microphones and tape recorders in the classroom offer opportunities for verbalized projects which again exploit important modern media. The aim where these and the study of television are concerned should be critical as well as creative. What is needed is not only some attempt to induce critical awareness where print is involved (e.g., the study of newspapers) but some awareness of the possibilities of the media which form the background leisure-time activities of the bulk of the population of this . country.

Whether this constitutes a 'radically new pattern of the curriculum' is a moot point. It certainly lays the stress in quite different ways than does the current curriculum. At the same time some elements among my suggestions—like art—are to be found extensively taught in schools, others, like film education, are to be found in a few at least. Anything too radically new would fail to attract possible support because of its totally untried nature. There is in nearly all cases I have mentioned, then, a limited body of expertise to be drawn upon. At the same time the fundamental role assigned to movement education supplies the reorientation of attitude necessary.

The approach to consciousness and mind (still the ultimate aim, for it is a fundamental error not to see that, as the arts develop, they inevitably come to involve knowledge and understanding) is through body awareness. This awareness is projected into a variety of kinetic disciplines which combine 'practicality' with imagination, affective expression and discipline and which exploit characteristic twentieth-century cultural forms.

All this at the appropriate levels, together with some emphasis on the physical life, games, outward bound projects, the opportunities which form part of the new physical education, should take up approximately three-fifths of the children's time. The rest of the time would be concerned partly with the domestic life (home management, preparation for marriage which so many parents tend to neglect, some knowledge of human relationships and sex education). This is something which boys and girls should share, though perhaps there should be a greater emphasis for girls. The other area of concern would be the technical, which would exploit especially the boys' interest in some of the mechanical inventions by which they are surrounded.

I am, of course, fully aware of the fact that if able children come to tackle this curriculum, they would accomplish it much better— academically bright children, as is well known, tend to be able all round, and indeed, Miss Marion North has recently shown that there is good reason to believe that intelligent children have a wider and subtler range of movement than children with a lower I.Q.

Nevertheless, I remain convinced that the specific and concrete nature of the crafts and those arts which arose historically out of the crafts, provides a better route for children whose minds find existence easier to grasp in terms of the concrete and the particular—and who need help in coping with the cultural media which are the prime influences in their lives to an extent which the book is not.

This is not an education for helots, an inferior sop handed out to the inadequate, because it provides an entry into many of the greatest riches of our civilization; the point is, however, that it exists positively on many levels (as the groundling at the Shakespeare play discovered) to an extent that logical and rational thought does not.

Half-baked 'ideas', indeed, the off-shoot of an attempted rationality by those ill-equipped to do the necessary thinking constitute one of the gravest menaces to the future of our civilization.

I hold in fact what might seem to be two somewhat contradictory views. One is that children differ ineluctably in capacity for both intellectual and affective experience—heredity alone sees to that. At the same time, I am equally convinced that many children in our schools (like many people in our society) are grossly and palpably underfunctioning. The crucial question is indeed that of content—of the way to exploit such talents as they have. It is distressing to think, when the problem so clearly lies here, that we have wasted so much time and effort on the futilities of organization, as if justice was not a matter of appropriateness rather than sameness.

Richard Pring

II:10 Curriculum integration

Curriculum integration is fashionable—integrated day, interdisciplinary enquiry are 'in' words. Pring argues that any recommendation for curriculum integration implies some underlying theory of knowledge and that too many educationists are using the word as though the value of integration was self-evident. The value is not self-evident and integrated programmes require critical examination. The integrationalist must be ready to defend himself against those who wish to retain the subject-centred curriculum on the basis of the theory of knowledge put forward by Hirst. Pring puts forward a number of theoretical positions which could justify curriculum integration and concludes by noting that curriculum integration is a much more complex notion than is often realized.

There is no doubt that integration is an 'in' word. Plowden and Newsom recommend it; junior schools have their 'integrated day'; 'interdisciplinary enquiry' features in many secondary schools; colleges prepare junior/secondary students for interdisciplinary learning situations; the Schools Council publishes examples of good 'integrated approaches'; and there is talk of the 'seamless cloak of knowledge', the 'unity of learning', or 'a single view of the world and of life', all of which, so we are told, can be reflected adequately only in an integrated curriculum.

Integration is also a 'pro'-word. It is contrasted with the *fragmentation* of the curriculum which typifies the *traditional* school, with subject *barriers*, the *compartmentalization* or *pigeon-holing* of knowledge, with specialization and *irrelevance* to life as a whole. Rather is it connected with the *natural* enquiry of children which does not respect subject divisions.

To be both an 'in' word and a 'pro' word has its dangers. Educational theory is rife with such words : 'growth', 'needs of the child', 'creativity', and so on. They play a significant part in much educational argument, are often accepted uncritically, and have an emo-

London Institute of Education Bulletin. Spring 1970, pp. 4–8. Reprinted by permission.

tive meaning that dares anyone to challenge the educational aims
which they embody. (Who for example would be against children
growing, developing their personalities, fulfilling their needs, or even
creating?) 'Integration' is quickly becoming such a word. Who
would object to knowledge or personality or life being 'integrated'?
Unity, integration, wholeness seem to have a fascination and value
of their own. But what do they mean? 'Integration' as such is an
empty word. There must be integration of something and one
cannot really understand or appreciate what is meant by curriculum
integration until one has clarified what it is that is being integrated.
Yet to clarify this is by no means easy. It raises important questions
in epistemology and ethics. Failure to see these questions, let alone
to attempt an answer to them, renders a lot of writing on curriculum integration superficial in its argument and confusing in its
practical recommendations. What I would wish to argue at much
greater length is that any particular recommendation for curriculum integration implies some underlying theory of knowledge or of
value or of learning, and that to explain what one means by
integration necessarily involves one in such theoretical considerations. Because of the failure of so many educationists to understand
this, the word integration is bandied about as though its meaning
were clear, and recommendations for curriculum integration are
made as though its value were self-evident. Here however I can only
indicate why its meaning is not clear, why its value is not self-
evident, and why therefore there is a need for a much closer analytic
and critical examination of 'integrated' programmes if education is
not to be sacrificed to yet more conceptual muddle and practical
confusion.

Curriculum integration is frequently contrasted with the 'compartmentalization' of knowledge which, apparently, is characteristic
of the 'traditional' syllabus. A subject-based curriculum is said to
limit enquiry, set up barriers, and confine study to a limited range of
information. Often these barriers are seen to be arbitrary or simply
conventional, and the integration of subjects is seen as a necessity if
there is to be a 'truer', more comprehensive picture of reality. For,
so it is argued, the division of knowledge into distinct subject division is artificial and does not reflect correctly the essential unity of
reality and of our ordinary way of understanding and judging. It is
foreign to the natural and spontaneous (words that frequently crop
up in this context) method of enquiry. What is important for the
school to do is to encourage 'enquiry' (and enquiry knows no limits)

and for this purpose to provide a 'rich' and 'stimulating' environment.

At this stage however it is necessary for the 'integrationalist' to pause awhile and to examine a little more closely the case put forward by those who wish to retain a curriculum that is largely subject based, for the 'specialists' would argue that the distinctions between subjects are not arbitrary at all and that to blur or ignore these distinctions is to debase any claim to knowledge. To pursue this argument further would raise questions in the theory of knowledge that can be dealt with, in the limits of this paper, only in the most superficial way. But some attempt must be made to pinpoint where the issues lie.

Understanding (and education would seem to be about the development of the understanding) lies in the formation of conceptual schemes that consist in the organization, discrimination, and interpretation of experience so that it can be expressed and communicated symbolically. The development of meaning is the development of this symbolic organization characterized by certain general concepts and modes of inference and by certain accepted canons of verification and enquiry. Outside these unifying principles of experience there can be no meaning. No enquiry can take place except within a particular system of thought, and this involves recognizing the implicit rules of procedure built into the acceptance of *this* system rather than another. In a way it does not make sense to talk of children simply making an enquiry. It must be an enquiry of a certain sort. As soon as one 'enquires', one is involved in the use of symbols which already dictate, as it were, what moves are correct or at least permissible. Any enquiry must involve the meanings revealed at different levels within one or other of the disciplines. This is a logical point—it follows from what one *means* by mind, rational behaviour, and hence enquiry. The subjects on the curriculum, so this argument goes, are there because among other things they initiate the pupil into the different modes of understanding that are characterized by distinct organizing concepts, principles of verification, and logical connexions. Far from being merely conventional or arbitrary, they represent in their distinct disciplines of thought what it is to think, to know and to enquire.[1]

I am not wanting to defend this thesis against the advocates of curriculum integration. I wish merely to say that it is with such a thesis they must deal if they are to suggest that subject divisions are merely conventional or arbitrary. They must argue either that such is a false theory of knowledge or that it is not a complete account of knowledge and that the recognition of autonomous disciplines needs to be supplemented by some form of integration within the curriculum.

Where the second line of argument is adopted, there can be distinguished quite different theoretical reasons for proposing curriculum integration, although in practice the reasons are rarely made clear. Firstly, integration might be argued for as follows. No proposition or argument of any enquiry is, admittedly, without a logical structure which can be identified as such and which determines to some extent the role it can play in the enquiry. One knows that a given proposition is, say, an empirical claim to truth within a certain conceptual structure and that the test of truth or falsity of this kind of proposition is such and such. One knows that a particular argument implies certain criteria of validity and one can compare this argument with the norms assumed by it. Nonetheless many problems including those of considerable personal importance cannot be raised, let alone answered, within any one cognitive structure. Different sorts of enquiry have to be brought to bear upon a particular problem. Sex education, or giving adequate answers to practical questions raised about sexual behaviour, is an obvious example. No one discipline can claim a monopoly of the sorts of consideration relevant to the determination of practical principles. In many areas of understanding, especially where practical decisions have to be made, the integration of distinct disciplines of thought is essential yet cannot logically be given within any one discipline. The putting together of the distinctive enquiries represented by the disciplines is itself an educational task that should have a place within the curriculum. In other words, one might recognize the autonomy of different bodies of knowledge while at the same time recognizing the problems inherent in their synthesis. And one might make provision in the curriculum for this synthesizing element by concentrating, for at least part of the time, on areas of thought and decision-making where such an integration is indispensable. One would, as it were, learn to integrate by integrating (just as one learns to teach by teaching).[2]

A second line of reasoning for some degree of curriculum integration might be summarized as follows. The disciplines represent the *worked out* structures of knowledge, the systematic organization of experience, the particular conceptual schemes which determine how one classifies, individuates, and proceeds with yet further enquiry.

The disciplines therefore constitute in the most complete and developed form the logical structure of knowledge. They do not however reflect the pupil's level and mode of understanding, nor do they indicate the process whereby the pupil might attain these structures of knowledge. For, on this line of argument, the finished product, tidied up into the logical neatness of distinct disciplines, does not contain within it the way in which it should be presented. All too often, we are told, the subject matter is presented in its completed and worked out form, and not in the manner through which is was worked out.[3] On the other hand, if the student were allowed to pursue his own interests and to satisfy his own curiosity, he would raise questions which would gradually be refined into the precise systematization characteristic of the different disciplines of thought. The 'natural' curiosity of the pupil, his 'spontaneous' enquiry, would lead to the gradual differentiation of a conceptual structure that typified the worked out modes of understanding. Although the end product might be the different forms of knowledge, the educational process towards this goal would be an integrated activity, focused upon or united in the current interest or enquiry of the pupil.

Of course it may be argued that there are no distinct disciplines of thought, characterized by different modes of enquiry. Rather is all enquiry a matter of solving problems—one is in a sort of forked-road situation. First, one is puzzled how one might proceed. Secondly, as much relevant data as possible is gathered. Thirdly, a principle of procedure is tentatively formulated in the light of this data. Finally, this is put to the test and applied in practice. Either one's problem is solved or the principle is rejected, or at least reformulated. In any case there is always the same pattern to any enquiry and the resulting knowledge is essentially that of tentative hypothesis constantly tested and reformulated. The differentiation of knowledge into distinct modes characterized by different processes of enquiry and verification is dismissed. Enquiry is basically of the same pattern, though the resulting structures of understanding might be distinguished by their respective organizing concepts (as physics is distinguished from chemistry). But the method is the same, and if encouraged and pursued will provide the integrating factor in all the classroom activities.

Sometimes of course the pupil does not appear to be 'spontaneously' or 'naturally' curious. In such cases the pupil needs to be 'stimulated'. Interdisciplinary enquiry sometimes begins with a key lesson in which the pupil is given a battery of 'stimuli' in order to 'spark him off'. Ideas are scattered freely, possible lines of enquiry suggested, problems presented, questions asked. Themes or topics might be provided and these, if suggestive enough, will make good 'starters'. Having started, the pupil is free to travel in whatever direction he likes provided that in travelling he is raising questions that open his enquiring mind to yet new experiences and fresh connexions of ideas. Themes or starters in this sense are not intended to control or set limits to the enquiry, only to trigger it off.

A further sort of reason underlying some proposals for curriculum integration arises more from ethical than from epistemological or learning theory. To the question 'What is the aim of education?' an answer might be given in terms of the needs of the child or those of society. Such an answer does not raise the epistemological issues that I have been considering. Whatever its nature, knowledge is said to be of value in so far as it meets the needs of the pupil or is of social utility. The 'needs' of the pupils are listed (different books give different lists) and these become the unifying factors in determining the balance of the curriculum. Themes like 'Man and his environment' are subdivided into smaller themes such as 'Family', 'Home', 'Leisure', 'Work'. To study material within the ambit of such themes will, it is claimed, enlighten the pupil in matters relevant to his immediate needs. Often such a programme of enquiry will be called social studies in which history, geography, literature, religious knowledge, and other subjects are integrated within the particular theme and are thereby directed to shed light on the needs of the pupil.[4]

It has been the purpose of this brief article not so much to justify or to criticize the different proposals for curriculum integration, but rather to indicate some of the different theoretical considerations which at different times underlie them. Curriculum integration is frequently pursued without any analysis of the nature of knowledge and therefore without any clear cognitive objectives. However, where there is such an analysis and where areas of autonomous studies are respected, integration may still remain an objective for curriculum planners for the quite different reasons that I have given and that I summarize here. Firstly, it is claimed, a mastery of the different disciplines is not all there is to knowledge; there is a further educative task of integrating the disciplines in so far as these are brought to bear upon a problem which cannot be fitted into the limits of any one discipline. Secondly, the curiosity and free enquiry of the pupil might be seen as the integrating factor and the final systematization of knowledge, manifest in the different disciplines, would be said to develop from such an enquiry. Thirdly it is held by some that the method of enquiry itself is unitary and that there is no theoretical justification for the proliferation of modes of understanding upon which the fragmentation of the syllabus is based. Fourthly, it is argued that the value of knowledge depends on the degree to which it satisfied the 'needs' of the individual or of society; 'needs' give direction and purpose, and thereby an integrating thread to the educational process. Fifthly, certain concepts such as 'power' and 'communications' are complex in meaning, are central to our thinking in the different disciplines of thought, need close scrutiny in themselves, and thereby offer fresh ways of entering into different areas of knowledge.

I have sought briefly to identify quite different reasons which might underlie proposals for curriculum integration. Not to recognize these distinctions which raise fundamental questions of epistemology and value is a source of confusion in practice. Let me in conclusion show how this can occur. It is a frequent practice in interdisciplinary enquiry to suggest (or impose) a theme which, instead of the traditional subject, will be the focus of study. But in the light of the distinctions that I have made in this article the theme might function in quite different ways. Firstly, it might in some way delineate an area in which practical decisions have to be made and which must therefore be a focal point of interdisciplinary thinking (e.g. sex, war, authority, etc.). Secondly, it might be the name for a complex of information which is thought relevant to the needs of the pupil or of society. Thirdly, it might through an association of ideas be a starting off point for enquiry. Fourthly, it might itself suggest a certain structured body of knowledge that needs to be mastered but which transcends the subject boundaries, and here one often hears talk of 'exploring a concept' (e.g. 'power'). Not to have clarified beforehand the function of the theme or concept may lead to a very confusing situation. It may be used simultaneously both to trigger off a line of enquiry and to set limits to the enquiry—and these are quite different functions, often in practice incompatible with each other.

Depending, too, on the particular conception of curriculum integration that one has, are such matters as the role of the teacher, the pattern of the school timetable, the use of resources, and so on. Current writing on the 'integrated day' suggests the need for a 'rich and stimulating environment'. Resources are rather like pep pills—

stimulating, maintaining, and extending the pupil's interest. On the other hand where the centre of integration is an area which *ought* to be explored by the pupil or which is judged relevant to his human needs and concerns, the 'bank' of resources should be developed with these quite different reasons in mind. Items are chosen because of the lead they give along a pre-conceived line of enquiry rather than for the interest they arouse.

Curriculum integration is a much more complex notion than is often realized, not only in its conception but also in its effect upon teaching roles, use of time, organization of the school and the classroom, and so on. There is no opportunity here to enter into this in detail. Suffice to give some indication of this complexity and of the need to look much more closely at the deeper issues that lie beneath it.

References

1 Reference might be made to Professor P. H. Hirst's article 'Liberal education and the nature of knowledge' (from *Philosophical analysis and education* edited by Archambault) where similar, though not identical points about what it means to know or to understand are made and developed at considerable length. Reference should be made also to Professor Hirst's contribution to *Proceedings of the Philosophy of Education Society* 1966, 'Language and thought'. A much more extensive account of the development of meaning and the structuring of experience in language is, of course, to be found in P. H. Phenix *Realms of meaning* (McGraw-Hill, 1964).

2 Pring, R. A. 'Philosophy of education and educational practice' (*Proceedings of the Philosophy of Education Society*, 1970) especially pp. 66–68, where this point is developed at much greater length, with special reference to the study of education.

3 See Dewey, J. *Democracy and education.* chap. 14.

4 See Vincent Rogers's *Social studies in education* for examples of 'broad organizing concepts' that will supposedly provide integrating links. Unfortunately the study of 'man both as an individual and as a member of a host of groups; with man both changing and adjusting to his environment' is so broad that it includes everything and gives few clues for integration.

John White

II:11 The curriculum mongers: education in reverse

*John White asserts that the radical tradition in secondary
education has been eroded. The radical's aim in education
is to see that everyone in society is acquainted with the
higher culture, that everyone should be initiated into those
forms of experience which constitute this higher culture
—arts, mathematics, etc. All secondary schools, according
to White, must provide a compulsory curriculum in the
higher forms of thought to all normal children. The
Schools Council is not doing this with its curriculum
reforms. Instead of a common curriculum for all, the
Council is perpetuating with its different curricula the
old elementary and secondary differences of the 1902–1944
era.*

There was, not so long ago, what might be called a radical tradition
in secondary education in this country. Remnants of it still exist
here and there—although, ironically, the longer Labour has been in
power the more the tradition had disintegrated. How and why this
disintegration has come about is what I wish to investigate here.

It may seem odd to talk of the decay of radicalism in this way.
Isn't it true, on the contrary, that there has scarcely been a time of
such rethinking as in the last few years? And not only by theoreti-
cians. Teachers themselves have never before been involved on such
a scale—helping to forge new curricula on the committees of the
Schools Council or in their local curriculum development groups;
introducing interdisciplinary studies; removing the impersonality
and mechanicalness of traditional education by tailoring courses
more to individual pupils' needs, and pressing for school counselling
services to strengthen pastoral care; breaking down the barriers between school and community; promoting action research in the
classroom; revolutionising teaching by team-teaching and new audio-

This article first appeared in *New Society*, the weekly review of the social
sciences, 6 March 1969, pp. 359–361. 128 Long Acre, London W.C.2. © IPC.
Reprinted by permission.

visual aids, language laboratories, teaching machines . . .

Why do I speak of the decline of radicalism at a time when our schools are being revitalised in every way? To put it as I think R. H. Tawney might have put it: radicalism in educational, as in industrial, reform is essentially about *ends*. The 'new' thought in education has avoided ends and substituted an obsessive devotion to means. All the colourful new departures I have mentioned are only machinery: like any machinery they can be put to bad ends as well as good, serving reaction as efficiently as reform. This, briefly, is why the radical tradition is disintegrating; our very fascination by machinery has made us forget what we are about.

What are the ends as the radical sees them? Very briefly, a good education system is one designed to help create a good society. A good society is one in which desire for *status*—power, wealth, prestige—is no longer the mainspring of social life, where no more reverence is paid to the bank manager than to the boilermaker; each is seen as contributing equally to the common good.

But this is not in itself sufficient. We may respect the boilermaker as a man, even though he leads a life cut off from higher culture, from art, the sciences and philosophy. This is nothing more, so far, than the Christian ethic, without its transcendental trappings. Radicalism is grounded in this Christian ethic but goes beyond it: it claims there is no necessary connexion between a professional career and access to the higher culture. This connexion exists *de facto*, but is not rationally based. If most children will later have to do jobs which are not intellectually demanding, there is no reason why they should be taught only those things which will make them efficient workers—and perhaps efficient consumers and law-abiding citizens as well.

For men are not only workers or consumers or good citizens: they are also *men*, able, if taught, to contemplate the world of a poem or a metaphysical system as well as to enjoy more easily accessible pursuits. If, as Tawney said, we think the higher culture fit for solicitors, why should we not think it fit for coalminers—those 'other inhabitants of places of gloom'?

The radical's aim in education to help produce a society in which everyone is acquainted with the higher culture entails more specific objectives in the schools. For it follows from this that every secondary school child, unless good reasons can be produced to the contrary, should be initiated into those forms of experience which together constitute this higher culture—the arts, mathematics, the human and physical sciences, philosophy ... i.e., very roughly, activities whose nature, unlike cookery, say, or cricket, is utterly incomprehensible until one begins to engage in them. It follows from this, too—and this is merely another way of making the same point—that every secondary school child should be given a compulsory curriculum in at least these forms of thought. None should be allowed to drop any of these disciplines until he is sufficiently inside it to understand why its devotees are devoted to it.

This would mean in practice that every child should carry all these disciplines to something like sixth-form level. However much some individuals may race on past this point, in the same time as it takes the average child to reach it, still no one should normally leave school without having attained this basic understanding of the disciplines. If he is 'less able' at one of them—mathematics, say— then, far from being allowed to give it up in favour of something with which he can cope, he should be given *more*, perhaps differently oriented, teaching in the discipline, so that he *becomes* able at it. Ability in this context is not a given thing, but a goal.

This, then, is what radicalism implies in practice. All secondary schools must provide a compulsory curriculum in the higher forms of thought to all normal children. If they fail to do so voluntarily, they must be made to do so. This is no more than a spelling out of what I take to be the comprehensive ideal.

Here, I imagine, many will part company with me. Surely progress is incompatible with coercion, uniformity : isn't this scheme a return to the bad old days of close state supervision of curricula? Or perhaps it is an attempt to introduce state control on the French pattern, where according to the much scorned legend, at five past twelve on a certain day, each third form history class in each lycée in the land ... Progress means not uniformity, but diversity—diversity for each school to work out its own curricula as it sees best : for how can there be progress without experiment, without thought?

At this point the objector may point to the achievements of the 'new look' in secondary education with which I began. But let us take stock. If one accepts the radical view of the good society—that is, if one agrees that all men should be equipped to follow the higher cultural activities if they so choose, then how *can* the schools be left to teach what they want? If one school insists on compulsory games or metalwork, but not on compulsory physics or poetry-appreciation, then one cannot rationally both allow it to do so and at the same time oneself desire the radical end. For this way the end will never be attained—or if it is, it will be in spite of the school's efforts, not because of them.

There is no logical escape. Given the end, there must be public control over the curriculum, a public guarantee that no child shall be deprived of access to the higher culture. But this does not necessarily mean detailed state supervision of syllabuses on the French pattern.

First, as long as there is public control over what children are expected to have learnt by the time they leave school, there is room for all sorts of new techniques and experiments in methods of getting them to this end and there are infinitely many routes to the same destination.

Secondly, there is no reason why public control of the broad framework should be in the hands of the *state*, if by this is meant the government of the day. A Teachers' General Council is clearly another possible alternative, and no doubt a more desirable one. Just as the British Medical Council controls professional standards in medicine, so a general council of teachers could do the same for teaching—provided that there is sufficient common agreement about the ends of education.

I argue that all children must be compelled to study certain disciplines—history, physics, etc. This does not imply that they must be taught these things by coercive methods—namely, by threats of punishment. Clearly there are more efficient and more benevolent ways of teaching them. There is no necessary connexion between compulsion and coercion. But this connexion is often made, at a not-too-conscious level, in a person's conceptual scheme—and constitutes a quite understandable, if not quite valid objection to the radical point of view I have propounded.

Mention of such confusion leads me back to where I began—to the paradoxical decay of radicalism at a time of Labour rule. Often the Labour government itself is blamed for this. It has no clear policy on the curriculum issue, has allowed things to drift along as they did under the Tories, etc., etc. There is some justice in these complaints, but there is something to be said on the other side, too. The plain truth is that, over the last five years, there has been such a barrage of anti-radical opinion directed at the teaching profession that the original issue—that to do with ends and the nature of a good society—has been obscured. No doubt much of it is just a continuation of more ancient anti-radical thinking. But the result, if not the intention, is a confusion in the minds of many teachers, which does not so much turn them against questioning ends as prevent them from even seeing that there are questions to be raised about them. It channels their desires to improve the system wholly into the task of remodelling its machinery.

One fashionable line now being preached from educationists' pulpits is this: the very notion of there being aims, or objectives, in education, is a hopelessly muddled one. Educational theorists have talked far too long about such woollinesses as 'self-realisation' or 'the whole man'; teachers should forget all this claptrap and direct their thinking to the actual teaching situation, making sure that what they are doing is presented in such a way that children understand and want to learn.

Now there is some truth in this: some statements about the aims of education have often been intolerably vague. But it does not follow that we should give up talking about aims altogether. It is difficult to see how we rationally could do this. It may make sense to tell a teacher to pay attention to immediate classroom problems and forget the nonsense about *pseudo*-aims. But unless he is to be as blinkered as a slave, carrying out his master's orders punctiliously and holding it no business of his to inquire what their purpose is, he cannot but connect his present actions with larger, more long-term purposes.

Not all statements of aims are so vague as to be useless as a guide to conduct. The radical's aims are clear enough. The creation of a good society entails that all be initiated into the disciplines of the higher culture. The more teachers see each other as engaged in the *same* task, under the aegis of this shared, explicit radical rationale, the more one will be justified in talking of teaching as a united profession; the more atomistic they become, the more their horizons become restricted to the here and now, the more they will become like slaves.

A large share of the responsibility for turning the teachers' attention recently from ends to means must be attributed to the Schools Council, which throughout the period of Labour rule has been enormously active in promoting new ideas about curriculum reform. It may seem paradoxical that a body set up by the government specifically to get teachers to think more about curriculum ideas—both by having a majority of teachers on the central committee of the council and by setting up local curriculum development groups among teachers—should be the object of such a complaint. But I believe the complaint is justified. For in scarcely any of the innumerable working papers, reports and bulletins which have poured out from the council since 1965 has there been any consideration of the overall rationale of the curriculum. There have been papers on specific topics—science for the young school leaver, sixth-form curricular reform, Certificate of Secondary Education exams in different subjects, French in the primary school. But very little on the larger issues.

In a way, this omission is understandable in the light of the council's own official objective of upholding and interpreting 'the principle that each school should have the fullest possible measure of responsibility for its own work, with its own curriculum and teaching methods based on the needs of its own pupils and evolved by its own staff . . .' For it is not the Schools Council's job to get teachers to think out what shall be a *common* curriculum for all schools; this would fly straight in the face of its own terms of reference. It is by its constitution committed to an anti-radical position.

There is a further paradox here. On the one hand, as I have said, the Schools Council is committed to uphold the principle that every school should have its own curriculum, evolved by its own staff. On the other hand, most of its publications—at least its earlier ones—have propagated a similar view about what curricula ought to be like. There are two quite distinct sorts of curricula which they recommend. This can be seen quite easily by looking through its earlier working papers, published between 1965 and 1967.

Of the first five, two concerned the 'young school leaver' and two the sixth-former. The next eleven were more variegated; but even here three directly, and one indirectly, concerned the young school leaver and one was on the sixth form. Of the first 16 working papers, then, at least half—and, if we discount those not about the curriculum at all but about examinations or organisational matters, the overwhelming majority of them—have been devoted to curricula for children in their last year or two at school. This is clearly only a small fraction of all schoolchildren.

Not only this: since these eight or nine papers recommend one sort of curriculum for the young school leaver and another, very different, curriculum for the sixth-former, they merely reflect traditional anti-radical thinking about the curriculum. Instead of pressing for a common curriculum for all pupils, for a common depth in the disciplines to which all pupils should be expected to have penetrated, they give us a streamlined curriculum in the grammar school tradition and a streamlined curriculum in the elementary school tradition. Thus the paradox : they claim that schools must be free to work out their own curricula; and yet these publications already presuppose a framework in which these 'autonomous' curricula must fit : the old dualist framework we have had throughout this century.

True, the old gap between the sixth-form university candidate and the young school leaver has been plastered over a little by leavers who get the Certificate of Secondary Education or GCE O level. But the Schools Council's suggested curricula for those—the great majority—at the extreme ends shows how little has really changed.

Not much need be said about the council's sixth-form proposals. Sixth-form courses are still to provide an initiation into the higher culture; 'minor' subjects and general studies are also brought in, to counteract over-specialisation and provide, if anything, a rather better initiation. The working papers on the young school leaver, on the other hand, like their inspiration, the Newsom report, *Half our future*, are depressingly and uniformly anti-intellectual.

Take, for instance, the repeated theme that subject barriers must be broken down and that the curriculum must be 'integrated.' Now, in one sense of the term, an integrated curriculum is highly desirable. But what I would like is a curriculum unified by a rational principle. The separate disciplines should be seen as fitting people to be members of the good society. This does not entail—though it does not rule out—any fusion of the disciplines. But 'integration' in the Schools Council sense has nothing to do with any such rational principle. It seems in many cases to mean the virtual disappearance of the disciplines, their swallowing-up in topic-based courses which may well keep school-leavers happily occupied, but seem to be more of a barrier than a help to their acquiring the higher culture.

Another depressing feature found in these papers, as in the Newsom report, is the emphasis on vocational education. There is everything to be said for vocational education, if this means that on leaving school everyone is intellectually equipped to understand what any vocation, 'professional' as well as non-professional, involves. But the only vocations which, in either the Newsom report or the Schools Council's papers, are to influence the curriculum of the young school leaver are those in manual or service industries. Why only these? No one can rationally prejudge that any normal child will never be able to hold down a professional career, so there is no good reason to cut him off from this. True, the economy needs non-professional workers; but there is no good reason to shape most children's education with only economic ends in view.

The main thing that differentiates the present scheme from the old secondary v. elementary pattern of the 1902–1944 era is that sixth forms are now to have a rather *better*, because more general, initiation into the higher culture; and the young school leaver is to be given a more up-to-date training in those skills and attitudes which industry and commerce require of him, both as producer and consumer....

II:12 A condensed version of the cognitive domain of the taxonomy of educational objectives

This is the summary section of Bloom's famous Taxonomy of educational objectives, one of the most influential books in curriculum development. The Taxonomy was published in two parts—the first covering educational objectives in the cognitive domain, the second covering objectives in the affective domain (see p. 289).

KNOWLEDGE

1.00 Knowledge

Knowledge, as defined here, involves the recall of specifics and universals, the recall of methods and processes, or the recall of a pattern, structure, or setting. For measurement purposes, the recall situation involves little more than bringing to mind the appropriate material. Although some alteration of the material may be required, this is a relatively minor part of the task. The knowledge objectives emphasize most the psychological processes of remembering. The process of relating is also involved in that a knowledge test situation requires the organization and reorganization of a problem such that it will furnish the appropriate signals and cues for the information and knowledge the individual possesses. To use an analogy, if one thinks of the mind as a file, the problem in a knowledge test situation is that of finding in the problem or task the appropriate signals, cues, and clues which will most effectively bring out whatever knowledge is filed or stored.

Bloom, B. S. (ed.), *Taxonomy of educational objectives: the classification of educational goals. Handbook I: Cognitive domain,* David McKay Co., 1956, pp. 201–207 (Appendix). Reprinted by permission.

1.10 Knowledge of specifics

The recall of specific and isolable bits of information. The emphasis is on symbols with concrete referents. This material, which is at a very low level of abstraction, may be thought of as the elements from which more complex and abstract forms of knowledge are built.

1.11 Knowledge of terminology
Knowledge of the referents for specific symbols (verbal and nonverbal). This may include knowledge of the most generally accepted symbol referent, knowledge of the variety of symbols which may be used for a single referent, or knowledge of the referent most appropriate to a given use of a symbol.

To define technical terms by giving their attributes, properties, or relations. Familiarity with a large number of words in their common range of meanings.*

1.12 Knowledge of specific facts
Knowledge of dates, events, persons, places, etc. This may include very precise and specific information such as the specific date or exact magnitude of a phenomenon. It may also include approximate or relative information such as an approximate time period or the general order of magnitude of a phenomenon.

The recall of major facts about particular cultures.
The possession of a minimum knowledge about the organisms studied in the laboratory.

1.20 Knowledge of ways and means of dealing with specifics

Knowledge of the ways of organizing, studying, judging, and criticizing. This includes the methods of inquiry, the chronological sequences, and the standards of judgment within a field as well as the patterns of organization through which the areas of the fields themselves are determined and internally organized. This knowledge is at an intermediate level of abstraction between specific knowledge on the one hand and knowledge of universals on the other. It does not so much demand the activity of the student in using the materials as it does a more passive awareness of their nature.

---

* Each subcategory is followed by illustrative educational objectives selected from the literature.

1.21 Knowledge of conventions

Knowledge of characteristic ways of treating and presenting ideas and phenomena. For purposes of communication and consistency, workers in a field employ usages, styles, practices, and forms which best suit their purposes and/or which appear to suit best the phenomena with which they deal. It should be recognized that although these forms and conventions are likely to be set up on arbitrary, accidental, or authoritative bases, they are retained because of the general agreement or concurrence of individuals concerned with the subject, phenomena, or problem.

Familiarity with the forms and conventions of the major types of works; e.g., verse, plays, scientific papers, etc.
To make pupils conscious of correct form and usage in speech and writing.

1.22 Knowledge of trends and sequences

Knowledge of the processes, directions, and movements of phenomena with respect to time.

Understanding of the continuity and development of American culture as exemplified in American life.
Knowledge of the basic trends underlying the development of public assistance programs.

1.23 Knowledge of classifications and categories

Knowledge of the classes, sets, divisions, and arrangements which are regarded as fundamental for a given subject field, purpose, argument, or problem.

To recognize the area encompassed by various kinds of problems or materials.
Becoming familiar with a range of types of literature.

1.24 Knowledge of criteria

Knowledge of the criteria by which facts, principles, opinions, and conduct are tested or judged.

Familiarity with criteria for judgment appropriate to the type of work and the purpose for which it is read.
Knowledge of criteria for the evaluation of recreational activities.

1.25 Knowledge of methodology

Knowledge of the methods of inquiry, techniques, and procedures employed in a particular subject field as well as those employed in investigating particular problems and phenomena. The emphasis here is on the individual's knowledge of the method rather than his ability to use the method.

Knowledge of scientific methods for evaluating health concepts.
The student shall know the methods of attack relevant to the kinds of problems of concern to the social sciences.

1.30 Knowledge of the universals and abstractions in a field

Knowledge of the major schemes and patterns by which phenomena and ideas are organized. These are the large structures, theories, and generalizations which dominate a subject field or which are quite generally used in studying phenomena or solving problems. These are at the highest levels of abstraction and complexity.

1.31 Knowledge of principles and generalizations

Knowledge of particular abstractions which summarize observations of phenomena. These are the abstractions which are of value in explaining, describing, predicting, or in determining the most appropriate and relevant action or direction to be taken.

Knowledge of the important principles by which our experience with biological phenomena is summarized.
The recall of major generalizations about particular cultures.

1.32 Knowledge of theories and structures

Knowledge of the *body* of principles and generalizations together with their interrelations which present a clear, rounded, and systematic view of a complex phenomenon, problem, or field. These are the most abstract formulations, and they can be used to show the interrelation and organization of a great range of specifics.

The recall of major theories about particular cultures.
Knowledge of a relatively complete formulation of the theory of evolution.

INTELLECTUAL ABILITIES AND SKILLS

Abilities and skills refer to organized modes of operation and generalized techniques for dealing with materials and problems. The materials and problems may be of such a nature that little or no specialized and technical information is required. Such information as is required can be assumed to be part of the individual's general fund of knowledge. Other problems may require specialized and technical information at a rather high level such that specific knowledge and skill in dealing with the problem and the materials are required. The abilities and skills objectives emphasize the mental processes of organizing and reorganizing material to achieve a particular purpose. The materials may be given or remembered.

2.00 Comprehension

This represents the lowest level of understanding. It refers to a type of understanding or apprehension such that the individual knows what is being communicated and can make use of the material or idea being communicated without necessarily relating it to other material or seeing its fullest implications.

2.10 Translation

Comprehension as evidenced by the care and accuracy with which the communication is paraphrased or rendered from one language or form of communication to another. Translation is judged on the basis of faithfulness and accuracy; that is, on the extent to which the material in the original communication is preserved although the form of the communication has been altered.

The ability to understand nonliteral statements (metaphor, symbolism, irony, exaggeration).
Skill in translating mathematical verbal material into symbolic statements and vice versa.

2.20 Interpretation

The explanation or summarization of a communication. Whereas translation involves an objective part-for-part rendering of a communication, interpretation involves a reordering, rearrangement, or new view of the material.

The ability to grasp the thought of the work as a whole at any desired level of generality.
The ability to interpret various types of social data.

2.30 Extrapolation

The extension of trends or tendencies beyond the given data to determine implications, consequences, corollaries, effects, etc., which are in accordance with the conditions described in the original communication.

The ability to deal with the conclusions of a work in terms of the immediate inference made from the explicit statements.
Skill in predicting continuation of trends.

3.00 Application

The use of abstractions in particular and concrete situations. The abstractions may be in the form of general ideas, rules of procedures, or generalized methods. The abstractions may also be technical principles, ideas, and theories which must be remembered and applied.

Application to the phenomena discussed in one paper of the scientific terms or concepts used in other papers.
The ability to predict the probable effect of a change in a factor on a biological situation previously at equilibrium.

4.00 Analysis

The breakdown of a communication into its constituent elements or parts such that the relative hierarchy of ideas is made clear and/or the relations between the ideas expressed are made explicit. Such analyses are intended to clarify the communication, to indicate how the communication is organized, and the way in which it manages to convey its effects, as well as its basis and arrangement.

4.10 Analysis of elements

Identification of the elements included in a communication.

The ability to recognize unstated assumptions.
Skill in distinguishing facts from hypotheses.

4.20 Analysis of relationships

The connections and interactions between elements and parts of a communication.

Ability to check the consistency of hypotheses with given information and assumptions.
Skill in comprehending the interrelationships among the ideas in a passage.

4.30 Analysis of organizational principles

The organization, systematic arrangement, and structure which hold the communication together. This includes the 'explicit' as well as 'implicit' structure. It includes the bases, necessary arrangement, and mechanics which make the communication a unit.

The ability to recognize form and pattern in literary or artistic works as a means of understanding their meaning.
Ability to recognize the general techniques used in persuasive materials, such as advertising, propaganda, etc.

5.00 Synthesis

The putting together of elements and parts so as to form a whole. This involves the process of working with pieces, parts, elements, etc., and arranging and combining them in such a way as to constitute a pattern or structure not clearly there before.

5.10 Production of a unique communication

The development of a communication in which the writer or speaker attempts to convey ideas, feelings, and/or experiences to others.

Skill in writing, using an excellent organization of ideas and statements.
Ability to tell a personal experience effectively.

5.20 Production of a plan, or proposed set of operations

The development of a plan of work or the proposal of a plan of operations. The plan should satisfy requirements of the task which may be given to the student or which he may develop for himself.

Ability to propose ways of testing hypotheses.
Ability to plan a unit of instruction for a particular teaching situation.

5.30 Derivation of a set of abstract relations

The development of a set of abstract relations either to classify or explain particular data or phenomena, or the deduction of propositions and relations from a set of basic propositions or symbolic representations.

Ability to formulate appropriate hypotheses based upon an analysis of factors involved, and to modify such hypotheses in the light of new factors and considerations.
Ability to make mathematical discoveries and generalizations.

6.00 Evaluation

Judgments about the value of material and methods for given purposes. Quantitative and qualitative judgments about the extent to which material and methods satisfy criteria. Use of a standard of appraisal. The criteria may be those determined by the student or those which are given to him.

6.10 Judgments in terms of internal evidence

Evaluation of the accuracy of a communication from such evidence as logical accuracy, consistency, and other internal criteria.

Judging by internal standards, the ability to assess general probability of accuracy in reporting facts from the care given to exactness of statement, documentation, proof, etc.
The ability to indicate logical fallacies in arguments.

6.20 Judgments in terms of external criteria

Evaluation of material with reference to selected or remembered criteria.

The comparison of major theories, generalizations, and facts about particular cultures.
Judging by external standards, the ability to compare a work with the highest known standards in its field—especially with other works of recognized excellence.

II:13 A condensed version of the affective domain of the taxonomy of educational objectives

Summary (See p. 281)

1.0 Receiving (attending)

At this level we are concerned that the learner be sensitized to the existence of certain phenomena and stimuli; that is, that he be willing to receive or to attend to them. This is clearly the first and crucial step if the learner is to be properly oriented to learn what the teacher intends that he will. To indicate that this is the bottom rung of the ladder, however, is not at all to imply that the teacher is starting *de novo*. Because of previous experience (formal or informal), the student brings to each situation a point of view or set which may facilitate or hinder his recognition of the phenomena to which the teacher is trying to sensitize him.

The category of *Receiving* has been divided into three subcategories to indicate three different levels of attending to phenomena. While the division points between the subcategories are arbitrary, the subcategories do represent a continuum. From an extremely passive position or role on the part of the learner, where the sole responsibility for the evocation of the behavior rests with the teacher—that is, the responsibility rests with him for 'capturing' the student's attention—the continuum extends to a point at which the learner directs his attention, at least at a semiconscious level, toward the preferred stimuli.

1.1 Awareness

Awareness is almost a cognitive behavior. But unlike *Knowledge*, the lowest level of the cognitive domain, we are not so much

Krathwohl D. R., Bloom B. S., Masia B. B., *Taxonomy of educational objectives: the classification of educational goals—Handbook II: Affective domain*, David McKay Co., 1964, pp. 176–185 (Appendix). Reprinted by permission.

concerned with a memory of, or ability to recall, an item or fact as we are that, given appropriate opportunity, the learner will merely be conscious of something—that he take into account a situation, phenomenon, object, or stage of affairs. Like *Knowledge* it does not imply an assessment of the qualities or nature of the stimulus, but unlike *Knowledge* it does not necessarily imply attention. There can be simple awareness without specific discrimination or recognition of the objective characteristics of the object, even though these characteristics must be deemed to have an effect. The individual may not be able to verbalize the aspects of the stimulus which cause the awareness.

Develops awareness of aesthetic factors in dress, furnishings, architecture, city design, good art, and the like.
Develops some consciousness of color, form, arrangement, and design in the objects and structures around him and in descriptive or symbolic representations of people, things, and situations.*

1.2 Willingness to receive

In this category we have come a step up the ladder but are still dealing with what appears to be cognitive behavior. At a minimum level, we are here describing the behavior of being willing to tolerate a given stimulus, not to avoid it. Like *Awareness*, it involves a neutrality or suspended judgment toward the stimulus. At this level of the continuum the teacher is not concerned that the student seek it out, nor even, perhaps, that in an environment crowded with many other stimuli the learner will necessarily attend to the stimulus. Rather, at worst, given the opportunity to attend in a field with relatively few competing stimuli, the learner is not actively seeking to avoid it. At best, he is willing to take notice of the phenomenon and give it his attention.

Attends (carefully) when others speak—in direct conversation, on the telephone, in audiences.
Appreciation (tolerance) of cultural patterns exhibited by individuals from other groups—religious, social, political, economic, national, etc.
Increase in sensitivity to human need and pressing social problems.

1.3 Controlled or selected attention

At a somewhat higher level we are concerned with a new phenomenon, the differentiation of a given stimulus into figure and

---

* Illustrative objectives selected from the literature follow the description of each subcategory.

ground at a conscious or perhaps semiconscious level—the differentiation of aspects of a stimulus which is perceived as clearly marked off from adjacent impressions. The perception is still without tension or assessment, and the student may not know the technical terms or symbols with which to describe it correctly or precisely to others. In some instances it may refer not so much to the selectivity of attention as to the control of attention, so that when certain stimuli are present they will be attended to. There is an element of the learner's controlling the attention here, so that the favored stimulus is selected and attended to despite competing and distracting stimuli.

Listens to music with some discrimination as to its mood and meaning and with some recognition of the contributions of various musical elements and instruments to the total effect.
Alertness toward human values and judgments on life as they are recorded in literature.

2.0 Responding

At this level we are concerned with responses which go beyond merely attending to the phenomenon. The student is sufficiently motivated that he is not just 1.2 *Willing to attend*, but perhaps it is correct to say that he is actively attending. As a first stage in a 'learning by doing' process the student is committing himself in some small measure to the phenomena involved. This is a very low level of commitment, and we would not say at this level that this was 'a value of his' or that he had 'such and such an attitude'. These terms belong to the next higher level that we describe. But we could say that he is doing something with or about the phenomenon besides merely perceiving it, as would be true at the next level below this of 1.3 *Controlled or selected attention*.

This is the category that many teachers will find best describes their 'interest' objectives. Most commonly we use the term to indicate the desire that a child become sufficiently involved in or committed to a subject, phenomenon, or activity that he will seek it out and gain satisfaction from working with it or engaging in it.

2.1 Acquiescence in responding

We might use the word 'obedience' or 'compliance' to describe this behavior. As both of these terms indicate, there is a passiveness so far as the initiation of the behavior is concerned, and the stimulus calling for this behavior is not subtle. Compliance is perhaps a better term than obedience, since there is more of the element of reaction to a suggestion and less of the implication of resistance or yielding unwillingly. The student makes the response, but he has not fully accepted the necessity for doing so.

Willingness to comply with health regulations.
Obeys the playground regulations.

2.2 Willingness to respond

The key to this level is in the term 'willingness,' with its implication of capacity for voluntary activity. There is the implication that the learner is sufficiently committed to exhibiting the behavior that he does so not just because of a fear of punishment, but 'on his own' or voluntarily. It may help to note that the element of resistance or of yielding unwillingly, which is possibly present at the previous level, is here replaced with consent or proceeding from one's own choice.

Acquaints himself with significant current issues in international, political, social, and economic affairs through voluntary reading and discussion.
Acceptance of responsibility for his own health and for the protection of the health of others.

2.3 Satisfaction in response

The additional element in the step beyond the *Willingness to respond* level, the consent, the assent to responding, or the voluntary response, is that the behavior is accompanied by a feeling of satisfaction, an emotional response, generally of pleasure, zest, or enjoyment. The location of this category in the hierarchy has given us a great deal of difficulty. Just where in the process of internalization the attachment of an emotional response, kick, or thrill to a behavior occurs has been hard to determine. For that matter there is some uncertainty as to whether the level of internalization at which it occurs may not depend on the particular behavior. We have even questioned whether it should be a category. If our structure is to be a hierarchy, then each category should include the behavior in the next level below it. The emotional component appears gradually through the range of internalization categories. The attempt to specify a given position in the hierarchy as *the* one at which the emotional component is added is doomed to failure.

The category is arbitrarily placed at this point in the hierarchy where it seems to appear most frequently and where it is cited as or appears to be an important component of the objectives at this level on the continuum. The category's inclusion at this point serves the pragmatic purpose of reminding us of the presence of the emotional component and its value in the building of affective behaviors. But it should not be thought of as appearing and occurring at this one point in the continuum and thus destroying the hierarchy which we are attempting to build.

Enjoyment of self-expression in music and in arts and crafts as another means of personal enrichment.
Finds pleasure in reading for recreation.
Takes pleasure in conversing with many different kinds of people.

3.0 Valuing

This is the only category headed by a term which is in common use in the expression of objectives by teachers. Further, it is employed in its usual sense : that a thing, phenomenon, or behavior has worth. This abstract concept of worth is in part a result of the individual's own valuing or assessment, but it is much more a social product that has been slowly internalized or accepted and has come to be used by the student as his own criterion of worth.

Behavior categorized at this level is sufficiently consistent and stable to have taken on the characteristics of a belief or an attitude. The learner displays this behavior with sufficient consistency in appropriate situations that he comes to be perceived as holding a value. At this level, we are not concerned with the relationships among values but rather with the internalization of a set of speci-fied, ideal, values. Viewed from another standpoint, the objectives classified here are the prime stuff from which the conscience of the individual is developed into active control of behavior.

This category will be found appropriate for many objectives that use the term 'attitude' (as well as, of course, 'value').

An important element of behavior characterized by *Valuing* is that it is motivated, not by the desire to comply or obey, but by the individual's commitment to the underlying value guiding the be-havior.

3.1 Acceptance of a value

At this level we are concerned with the ascribing of worth to a phenomenon, behavior, object, etc. The term 'belief,' which is defined as 'the emotional acceptance of a proposition or doctrine upon what one implicitly considers adequate ground' (English and English, 1958, p. 64), describes quite well what may be thought of as the dominant characteristic here. Beliefs have varying degrees of certitude. At this lowest level of *Valuing* we are concerned with the lowest levels of certainty; that is, there is more of a readiness to re-evaluate one's position than at the higher levels. It is a position that is somewhat tentative.

One of the distinguishing characteristics of this behavior is consistency of response to the class of objects, phenomena, etc. with which the belief or attitude is identified. It is consistent enough so that the person is perceived by others as holding the belief or value. At the level we are describing here, he is both sufficiently consistent that others can identify the value, and sufficiently committed that he is willing to be so identified.

Continuing desire to develop the ability to speak and write effectively.
Grows in his sense of kinship with human beings of all nations.

3.2 Preference for a value

The provision for this subdivision arose out of a feeling that there were objectives that expressed a level of internalization between the mere acceptance of a value and commitment or conviction in the usual connotation of deep involvement in an area. Behavior at this level implies not just the acceptance of a value to the point of being willing to be identified with it, but the individual is sufficiently committed to the value to pursue it, to seek it out, to want it.

Assumes responsibility for drawing reticent members of a group into conversation.
Deliberately examines a variety of viewpoints on controversial issues with a view to forming opinions about them.
Actively participates in arranging for the showing of contemporary artistic efforts.

3.3 Commitment

Belief at this level involves a high degree of certainty. The ideas of 'conviction' and 'certainty beyond a shadow of a doubt' help to convey further the level of behavior intended. In some instances this may border on faith, in the sense of it being a firm emotional acceptance of a belief upon admittedly nonrational grounds. Loyalty to a position, group, or cause would also be classified here.

The person who displays behavior at this level is clearly perceived as holding the value. He acts to further the thing valued in some way, to extend the possibility of his developing it, to deepen his involvement with it and with the things representing it. He tries to convince others and seeks converts to his cause. There is a tension here which needs to be satisfied; action is the result of an aroused need or drive. There is a real motivation to act out the behavior.

Devotion to those ideas and ideals which are the foundations of democracy. Faith in the power of reason and in methods of experiment and discussion.

4.0 Organization

As the learner successively internalizes values, he encounters situations for which more than one value is relevant. Thus necessity arises for (a) the organization of the values into a system, (b) the determination of the interrelationships among them, and (c) the establishment of the dominant and pervasive ones. Such a system is built gradually, subject to change as new values are incorporated. This category is intended as the proper classification for objectives which describe the beginnings of the building of a value system. It is subdivided into two levels, since a prerequisite to interrelating is the conceptualization of the value in a form which permits organization. *Conceptualization* forms the first subdivision in the organization process, *Organization of a value system* the second.

While the order of the two subcategories seems appropriate enough with reference to one another, it is not so certain that 4.1 *Conceptualization of a value* is properly placed as the next level above 3.3 *Commitment*. Conceptualization undoubtedly begins at an earlier level for some objectives. Like 2.3 *Satisfaction in response*, it is doubtful that a single completely satisfactory location for this category can be found. Positioning it before 4.2 *Organization of a vaue system* appropriately indicates a prerequisite of such a system. It also calls attention to a component of affective growth that occurs at least by this point on the continuum but may begin earlier.

4.1 Conceptualization of a value

In the previous category, 3.0 *Valuing*, we noted that consistency and stability are integral characteristics of the particular value or belief. At this level (4.1) the quality of abstraction or conceptualization is added. This permits the individual to see how the value relates to those that he already holds or to new ones that he is coming to hold.

Conceptualization will be abstract, and in this sense it will be symbolic. But the symbols need not be verbal symbols. Whether conceptualization first appears at this point on the affective continuum is a moot point, as noted above.

Attempts to identify the characteristics of an art object which he admires. Forms judgments as to the responsibility of society for conserving human and material resources.

4.2 Organization of a value system

Objectives properly classified here are those which require the learner to bring together a complex of values, possibly disparate values, and to bring these into an ordered relationship with one another. Ideally, the ordered relationship will be one which is harmonious and internally consistent. This is, of course, the goal of such objectives, which seek to have the student formulate a philosophy of life. In actuality, the integration may be something less than entirely harmonious. More likely the relationship is better described as a kind of dynamic equilibrium which is, in part, dependent upon those portions of the environment which are salient at any point in time. In many instances the organization of values may result in their synthesis into a new value or value complex of a higher order.

Weights alternative social policies and practices against the standards of the public welfare rather than the advantage of specialized and narrow interest groups.
Develops a plan for regulating his rest in accordance with the demands of his activities.

5.0 Characterization by a value or value complex

At this level of internalization the values already have a place in the individual's value hierarchy, are organized into some kind of internally consistent system, have controlled the behavior of the individual for a sufficient time that he has adapted to behaving this way; and an evocation of the behavior no longer arouses emotion or affect except when the individual is threatened or challenged.

The individual acts consistently in accordance with the values he has internalized at this level, and our concern is to indicate two things : (a) the generalization of this control to so much of the individual's behavior that he is described and characterized as a person by these pervasive controlling tendencies, and (b) the integration of these beliefs, ideas, and attitudes into a total philosophy or world view. These two aspects constitute the subcategories.

5.1 Generalized set

The generalized set is that which gives an internal consistency to the system of attitudes and values at any particular moment. It is selective responding at a very high level. It is sometimes spoken of as a determining tendency, an orientation toward phenomena, or a predisposition to act in a certain way. The generalized set is a response to highly generalized phenomena. It is a persistent and consistent response to a family of related situations or objects. It may often be an unconscious set which guides action without conscious forethought. The generalized set may be thought of as closely related to the idea of an attitude cluster, where the commonality is based on behavioral characteristics rather than the subject or object of the attitude. A generalized set is a basic orientation which enables the individual to reduce and order the complex world about him and to act consistently and effectively in it.

Readiness to revise judgments and to change behaviour in the light of evidence.
Judges problems and issues in terms of situations, issues, purposes, and consequences involved rather than in terms of fixed, dogmatic precepts or emotionally wishful thinking.

5.2 Characterization

This, the peak of the internalization process, includes those objectives which are broadest with respect both to the phenomena covered and to the range of behavior which they comprise. Thus, here are found those objectives which concern one's view of the universe, one's philosophy of life, one's *Weltanschauung*—a value system having as its object the whole of what is known or knowable.

Objectives categorized here are more than generalized sets in the sense that they involve a greater inclusiveness and, within the group of attitudes, behaviors, beliefs, or ideas, an emphasis on internal consistency. Though this internal consistency may not always be exhibited behaviorally by the students toward whom the objective is directed, since we are categorizing teachers' objectives, this consistency feature will always be a component of *Characterization* objectives.

As the title of the category implies, these objectives are so encompassing that they tend to characterize the individual almost completely.

Develops for regulation of one's personal and civic life a code of behavior based on ethical principles consistent with democratic ideals.
Develops a consistent philosophy of life.

Reference

English, H., and English, A. C., *A comprehensive dictionary of psychological and psychoanalytical terms*, New York, David McKay, 1958.

Robert M. Gagné

II:14 Learning theory, educational media, and individualized instruction

Gagné brings together some of the major findings from learning theory which have a bearing on the design of conditions of learning to carry out curriculum objectives. Learning theory as it exists today is a highly inelegant and unfinished entity, according to Gagné, but nevertheless the work of N. E. Miller, B. F. Skinner, D. P. Ausubel and Gagné provides useful guidelines. The importance of individualized learning is stressed and the role of non-human media in the performance of instructional functions is discussed.

Instruction of college and university students is an activity not customarily derived in a deliberate fashion from theories about learning. Most college instructors set about their initial task of teaching courses by using a model derived from their own college experiences; in other words, they try to emulate their own professors. The new instructor may spend many hours in selecting a text and other references, in planning what he will say to his class of students, in seeing how certain topics will 'fit' a semester of so many weeks. But the question of just what the students are going to be doing during these weeks, and how their activities are going to affect their capabilities, is not likely to be given a great deal of thought.

In proceeding in this manner to face the task of college instruction, it is obvious that the new instructor is perpetuating many traditions. He is planning his work in terms of the content of knowledge to which students will be exposed, the kinds of communication he will make to them in lectures. He is selecting for students a minimal set of readings and oral communications to which they

Paper given at faculty seminar, Bucknell University, 16–17 November 1967 and published in *Educational Broadcasting Review*, 1970, vol. 4, 49–62. Reprinted by permission of the author.

will be 'exposed'. He is thinking in terms of how much reading material and orally-presented material his students may be expected to 'absorb' during a given period of weeks. All of these activities are traditional in the sense that they are the same ones he himself was subjected to; they resulted in the framework for instruction as he experienced it.

It is also true that this traditional system may be said to 'work'. The young instructor knows that, because it has worked for him and for most of his fellow students. Why does it work? Under what circumstances does it work? One suspects that it works within the confines of two major conditions: (1) first, that students attending college are highly selected to accomplish learning in just this fashion; and (2) second, that what they are expected to accomplish represents a limited set of educational goals.

To treat these questions fully, and to deal with all of their implications would require a different direction than the one this paper is supposed to take. I shall therefore have to be content to suggest the lines of questioning that seem to me to be opened up by identifying these limiting conditions of traditional college instruction. Do we want to select just those students for college who are most able to learn by traditional means? By our selection procedures, are we simply perpetuating patterns of thought and learning that are first laid down in high school and earlier? Are we in danger of screening out by such procedures many individuals whose potential contributions to our culture are the most unusual? Are traditional methods of instruction best adapted to prepare the student for the activities of graduate school, where greater independence of thought is expected? Are these methods, in fact, preparing the student to be both an independent thinker and a continuing learner?

If one admits these kinds of questions into his thinking about the nature of college instruction, one faces the problem of understanding the nature of instruction itself, and in particular, what instruction has to do with human learning. One is led to examine the ways in which things, events, and ideas about them are presented to the human learner; in fact, the ways in which relevant stimulation impinges upon the learner from his environment. Further, one is led to a consideration of what happens to this stimulation when it reaches the nervous system of the learner—in other words, what kinds of transformations it undergoes. For we know that this environmental stimulation is processed in at least several different ways: this is the kind of inference we make when we say that the human individual has changed in the sense that he has learned something.

MEDIA. The first of these problems of stimulating the human learner, represents the area of media of communication. Generally, we tend to describe media in terms of the material things that provide the vehicles for the 'messages'—as, textbooks, newspapers, blackboards, motion picture projectors, television systems. However, for the purposes of considering their effects on learning, there are advantages to attending instead to the kinds of channels they offer. Considered in this way, one may conveniently describe media in several major categories as follows:

(1) actual objects and events
(2) veridical pictures (static and moving)
(3) diagrammatic pictures
(4) printed language
(5) auditory language.

These are the different ways in which the learner is affected by media. He may be stimulated by actual objects and events, and a reasonable portion of his learning results from such stimulation. Once he has learned how, in his early years, the learner may be stimulated with apparently equal effect by pictures, whether he sees them in a textbook, on a movie or television screen. Again, following some early learning, he responds to diagrammatic pictures, which are of several varieties. He responds to a two-dimensional representation of a cube as if it were a cube, for example; and in a more abstract way, he comes to understand the communication of a bar chart or line graph. As schooling proceeds, learning comes to depend increasingly on the stimulation provided by printed language. There is surely much truth in the definition of a university as a collection of books; even though one recognizes this to be an ironically partial truth nowadays. Auditory language has always been another major source of information for use in learning, whether presented by itself as in a lecture, or combined with the pictorial mode as in a motion picture or television program.

LEARNING THEORY. These are the ways, then, that stimulation is presented to the human learner. The second part of the problem to be considered concerns what happens to this stimulation when it reaches the learner. How is it transformed in such a way as to change *his* capabilities from one state to another? What kind of processing does it undergo in leading his professors to conclude that he has learned?

Obviously, this is the area of learning theory. Psychologists have studied, experimented upon, speculated about, and generally tried to understand learning for many years. Progress has not been rapid, but it surely appears to have been speeded by the application of experimental methods in use for about the last sixty years. As is not unusual with phenomena of living things, learning is a complicated process, occurring in many varieties, forms, and situations. It is necessary first, therefore, to recognize that learning theory as it exists today is a highly inelegant and unfinished entity. Nevertheless, there do appear to be some fairly fundamental and stable principles which serve to tell us what learning is *not* like, and to suggest the outlines of what it *is* like.

Sorting out the general principles from the more specific ones in learning theory is by no means an easy task. Similarly, selecting those principles of learning which are most highly relevant to the practical problem of instruction is not a self-evident procedure. The reason for this is that modern learning investigators have chosen different models to study, and they are intent on accounting for these models. Sometimes, these models resemble the learning of the school child, or the college student, and sometimes they do not. For example, the prototype learning situations represented in a recent influential book on *Categories of human learning* (Melton, 1964), are approximately as follows:

(1) Conditioning: Learning to blink the eye to a signal
(2) Rote learning: Learning to memorize pairs and lists of words
(3) Probability learning: Learning to choose a correct alternative from a set of words or objects
(4) Short-term memory: Initial reception and storage of information, usually a syllable or word
(5) Concepts: Learning of simple object properties by young children
(6) Perceptual-motor skill: Learning to make continuous tracking movements
(7) Problem solving: Discovering a principle which achieves a stated goal.

Obviously, not many of these prototype learning situations, in and of themselves, sound much like 'learning the facts of history from a textbook', or like 'learning to demonstrate Coulomb's Law in the laboratory'. Nevertheless, at some level of generality, these models all contribute to learning theory. For example, short-term memory, the initial reception of information, *is* an important part of every learning act. In considering how such principles apply to practical learning situations, it is mainly a matter of deciding *what can be assumed to be going on without a hitch,* as contrasted with *what requires critical planning and arrangement.*

The design of effective instruction, then, has these two areas of knowledge to call upon. Instruction needs to be arranged so that it will bring about the kind of change in a student which is called learning, and this requires a consideration of learning theory. In attempting to bring about such a change, the act of instruction is a matter of stimulating the student in certain ways—and here one has a choice of media to work with. Putting ideas together from these two domains of knowledge can yield some techniques and procedures of instruction which should make the process of learning an optimally effective one.

Suggestions from learning theory

What specific suggestions about instruction can be derived from learning theory? As I have already noted, these are not self-evident. There are many learning theories, and most of them are micro-theories, designed to provide models of some relatively specific kinds of learning. Accordingly, a selection must be made among them, keeping in mind the purpose of orientation toward the learning of young adults, or college students, and with an awareness of the variety of media available.

I believe there are four different learning theorists who have presented ideas of major importance to the design of instruction. These are Miller, Skinner, Gagné, and Ausubel. I intend to describe these ideas briefly here, before going on to elaborate on their implications. It will be apparent that the suggestions of these theorists vary in their specificity, and I have ordered them along this dimension. Miller's ideas are the most general, applying to a great variety of learning situations. The specificity of suggestions increases progressively through the theory of Ausubel, who attempts to deal in a highly concentrated manner with the problem of acquiring meaningful, organized knowledge.

N. E. MILLER. Miller's views regarding the implications of learning theory for instruction are presented in a volume of the *Audio-Visual*

Communication Review, entitled *Graphic communication and the crisis in education* (1957). The four principles he describes are suggested by the words: motivation, cue, response, reward. It is Miller's contention that an effective sequence of instruction, in any medium, must include provision for these four conditions.

First, motivation: the student must want something. The motivational effects of a 'lesson' depend upon motivation which has already been learned. To be most effective, the motivations aroused by instructional materials must build upon those that are already in the life experiences of the student. In other words, instructional materials cannot in themselves be expected to generate brand-new sources of motivation; but what they can and should do is to capitalize upon, and add to, the kinds of motivations that are already there. Various kinds of motivation may be called upon, including some presumably fundamental ones such as intellectual curiosity and the desire to achieve. For students in college, learned motivations which form a part of the individual's life goals, and which may exhibit themselves as identification with admired people, as well as with choices leading to social approval, are possibly of special importance.

Second, there must be a cue: the student must notice something. Materials for instruction, whether verbal or pictorial, need to distinguish the relevant cues. Instructional materials are better to the extent that they facilitate the discrimination of cues. Printed materials may do this in a variety of ways—by varying type, by the use of color, but particularly by means of their organization. Lecturers have a variety of ways of distinguishing cues in auditory language—by differences in loudness and emphasis, and again by the organization of material. Pictorial presentations obviously have used a variety of ingenious techniques of distinguishing cues—by simplification, by the addition of pointers and markers, by the use of color and contrast. The general point is that instruction will be enhanced when the stimuli relevant to learning are readily discriminated by the student.

Third, response: the student must do something. Many studies of learning have indicated the importance of student participation. Of course, the doing may be a matter of internally conducted thinking or rehearsal. But whatever form they may take, responses to instructional materials are an essential element in learning. Instructional effectiveness will be increased to the extent that the materials involve the student in doing something with his just-acquired knowledge—transforming it, applying it, using it.

Four, reward: the student must get something he wants. Various techniques may be used to bring about satisfaction of this sort. Immediate rewards are presumably more effective than delayed ones. Instruction needs to reinforce the rewards learned in real life. For the student who is motivated to solve problems and to achieve some learning goal, finding out that he has done well is an important reward. Instruction will be improved in effectiveness to the extent that some desired aim can be achieved, and that knowledge of this achievement is given.

Obviously, these four principles described by Miller are considered to have highly general applicability to the design of instruction. They are relevant to the learning of all kinds of students, and presumably to all kinds of learning tasks. These principles may be put to work regardless of whether one is considering the task of a first-grader in learning to print letters, or to the task of a graduate student in understanding a scholarly article on Roman architecture.

The generality of these principles is also the key to their limitations in practical usefulness. To the skilled teacher or designer of instruction, they seem obvious, and such a person would likely aver that he *always* uses such principles. Most instruction, in fact, could probably be shown to incorporate these four principles in some degree. Even when one or another is not strongly exhibited by instructional materials, it may be expected that an experienced learner (like a college student) will often arrange his own learning conditions to include these principles. He comes with his own motivation, he makes responses to what he reads, sees, or hears, and he arranges his studying objectives so that some achievement will be noticeable. Miller's principles are surely important to instruction, but it is questionable whether they are often violated even in the most traditional instruction.

SKINNER. The views of Skinner on instruction are contained in a variety of articles, particularly those on teaching machines (Skinner, 1957, 1958, 1965). Valuable analyses are also contained in books and articles by his students (Gilbert, 1962; Green, 1962). At the most general level, it may be said that no great disagreement can be found with the principles of Miller. Skinner's analysis of instruction assumes that motivation must be present, that the student must make a response, and that this response needs to be rewarded, or 'reinforced'. The increased specificity of Skinner's suggestions centers around the principle of *stimulus control*, or the ways in which re-inforcement may be used to establish both more precise and more elaborate learnings by manipulation of the stimuli impinging on the learner. In this sense, Skinner's views are most highly related to Miller's principle about the importance of the *cue* in learning. It is possible to interpret Skinnerian principles of instruction as a more extensive account of what must be done to present cues (or stimuli) in such a way as to optimize learning.

Several relatively specific ways of controlling the learning process by suitable sequencing of stimuli and reinforcement are suggested by Skinner's theory. One is the principle of *shaping*, applicable to the learning of motor acts. As the individual practices a motor re-sponse of some sort, reinforcement is given selectively so that the response which is originally only a crude copy of what is acceptable comes by a gradual process to be more and more exact. Such a principle applies, for example, to learning to pronounce an unfam-iliar language sound, such as the German umlauted ü, or the French uvular r. A second principle, somewhat similar, is that of *successive approximation* of stimulus control, in which a response which is originally 'prompted' comes to be given properly even when the prompt has been progressively 'faded'. Initially, a student may need many contextual prompts, for example, to remember what the Constitution says about the powers of the President, but as he continues to practice recounting these powers, he can do it without these extra cues. A third Skinnerian principle is *chaining*, which describes the conditions of reinforcement by means of which a lengthy procedure is learned. Essentially, the steps in the procedure, which might be a computational procedure in mathematics, for example, are put together in a step-by-step fashion, insuring that the final step is always connected with the others which precede it (cf. Gilbert, 1962).

Thus it may be seen that the learning theory of Skinner leads to some relatively specific suggestions about the design of instruction. It gives us practical procedures for shaping motor responses, for establishing discriminations by successive approximations of stim-uli, and for chaining together the steps in complex procedures. For certain kinds of learning tasks, these procedues are indeed specific and undoubtedly successful.

In my view, these principles are still only of general applicability to the learning of certain other kinds of tasks, particularly concepts and principles. For example, if one is concerned that a student acquire an understanding of the principle of separation of powers as defined by the Constitution, or an understanding of the principle of centrifugal force, the notion of successive approximation provides only a very general prescription for instruction. It says one must bring such behavior under finer stimulus control, but it does not specify how to do this. It does not say how to select the stimuli which will accomplish this purpose. It seems to me, therefore, that although some specificity about instruction in certain tasks is definitely gained from Skinnerian theory, for certain others of particular importance in college-level instruction, the suggestions remain highly general.

GAGNÉ. The ideas of this theorist regarding the learning process are contained in a book entitled *The conditions of learning* (1965), and their applicability to instructional practice is discussed in a chapter of another recent book, *Instruction: some contemporary viewpoints* (Siegel, 1967). The suggestions to be derived from this view of learning are more specific for instruction than are those previously described.

The first principle deserving emphasis is that of *distinctive conditions* for different kinds of learning. Gagné distinguishes seven major kinds of mental processing which are called learning, each of which has a different set of conditions for its optimal occurrence. The seven kinds are called signal learning (classical conditioning), S–R learning, motor and verbal chain learning, multiple discrimination, concept learning, principle learning, and problem solving. He considers that the typical learning of young adults, high-school and college students, may partake of any or all of these types of learning, but that some are much more frequent than others in the school environment. For example, certain motor and verbal chains may need to be learned in tackling a new foreign language, but these types of learning would probably never be encountered in courses in history, government, or English composition. Most subjects in high school and college include primarily the kinds of learning described as concept learning, principle learning, and problem solving.

Although all types of learning may require certain general conditions for their establishment, such as those of contiguity, repetition, and reinforcement, emphasized by most learning theorists, the *specific* conditions for establishment of concepts, principles, and rules are in addition to these. Furthermore, they are distinguishable for each type: learning complex principles through problem solving demands a different set of conditions than does learning a new concept like 'cell', 'neuron', or 'central nervous system'. The external conditions for each particular type of learning form the basis for instruction. The internal conditions are retained capabilities of the student which have been established by previous learning.

The second principle of importance for instruction may be called *cumulative learning*. This is the principle that the learning of any new capability builds upon prior learning. According to this theory, there is a specifiable minimal prerequisite for each new learning task. Unless the learner can recall this prerequisite capability (or some other which can serve the same purpose), he cannot learn the new task. As a very simple example, unless a learner can recall how to factor numbers, how to divide, and how to multiply, he cannot learn to find a lowest common denominator, and thus to add fractions. This principle has a deceptive simplicity about it, and may readily be dismissed as either obvious or trivial. In actuality, it is neither. It does not say, before the learner undertakes to learn how to add fractions, he must have 'had' or 'been through' the factoring of numbers. Instead, it says he must have *mastered* and must *be able to recall* the factoring of numbers in order for the desired learning to take place at all. This principle is considered to have broad applicability to the learning of principles, whether they be the origins of the American Revolution, the generation of induced electric current, or the constancy of perceived size. In all of these instances, there are specific minimal prerequisite learnings, before the new learning task is undertaken.

AUSUBEL. The views of this learning investigator may be sampled in *The psychology of meaningful verbal learning* (1963), and also in an informative chapter in the book *Instruction: some contemporary viewpoints* (Siegel, 1967).

Ausubel insists, first of all, that school learning is meaningful learning and that this process is distinctly different from what is usually called rote learning. Thus he comes to grips directly and specifically with the learning of facts and principles, and is not particularly concerned with other forms of learning such as motor and verbal chains. In this theory, the most important principle is called *subsumption*. Meaningful learning takes place, according to this theory, when a new idea is subsumed into a related structure of already existing knowledge. The result of this process is the acquisition of a set of new meanings.

There are a number of implications of this view for instructional practice. For example, one is the importance of providing the learner with a meaningful structure before he attempts to learn a new principle—an *organizer*, which bears a logically superordinate relation to what will be learned. Putting this in a somewhat over-simplified form, it means that if the learner is expected to learn about coal and oil and gas, one must tell him ahead of time that he is going to learn about 'the different forms of fuel'. A second principle is that any subject should be presented by *progressive differentiation* of content, the most general and inclusive ideas first, and then the more detailed and specific ones. Ausubel states that although this seems a self-evident principle, it is rarely followed in actual teaching procedures or in textbooks.

Still a third principle of importance is called *consolidation*. This means the insistence on mastery of ongoing lessons before new material is introduced. This proposition is at least highly similar, if not the same, as Gagné's principle of cumulative learning. Another Ausubel principle of great importance would seem to be *integrative reconciliation*. By this he means that new ideas, once introduced, need to be deliberately related to old ideas, significant similarities and differences pointed out, real or apparent inconsistencies reconciled. Again, Ausubel finds this a practice followed scarcely at all by textbook writers.

These principles add up to a pretty strong specification of how instructional materials should be organized and presented for most effective learning. While one finds only very general guidance for the construction of programs of instruction, texts, or educational films by following such principles as Miller's, it is evident that Ausubel's principles are pretty specific. They tell an instructional designer what to do first, what sequence of ideas to follow, what to do to ensure remembering. and what kind of outcome to expect. Note that I do not maintain that Ausubel's theory is entirely correct—only a good deal more experimentation will determine that. But his ideas lead to very concrete suggestions about how to conduct instruction.

Here then we have four theories of learning, each of which has something to say about how to design instruction. Virtually no in-structional materials, texts, or films in existence today have deliber-ately been prepared on the basis of these principles. Today's instruc-tion simply does not reflect these principles, but appears instead to be based upon an older set of principles derived from quite different considerations. Could instructional materials be designed to take these principles into account? I see no reason why this could not be done. It would be an expensive undertaking, even to design a single course this way. I am unable to estimate cost effectiveness—indeed this may not even be possible until someone has tried to do it once.

Otherwise, the kinds of principles I have been talking about can even now be put into effect in at least a partial fashion by, first, the instructor, and second, the student. For example, the instructor can use the principle of organizers, and the principle of integrative reconciliation, even though he may not be able in any immediate sense to rewrite the textbook or redesign the television lesson. The student is also able to put many of these principles into effect himself. In fact, it seems probable that what is meant by a sophisticated learner, as opposed to a novice, is one who imposes his own organizations on presentations of material, arranges his own distinctive conditions for learning different kinds of tasks, carries out his own integrative reconciliation of new and old ideas. Learning to do these kinds of intellectual activities, to carry out these kinds of strategies, may represent an educational goal of more fundamental importance than the learning of any particular set of facts, rules, or principles.

Learning and the individual

This possibility of the learner's contribution to his own learning suggests an even broader theme than any which has been specifically defined by learning theories. Perhaps it may become the most general principle of all. It may be said, surely, that the great majority of modern studies of learning, of a variety of types, provide an accumulating body of evidence for this principle: Learning and remembering require the imposition of an active intellectual process by the learner on the material presented to his senses. One simply cannot account for learning by specifying only what is presented and the level of 'intelligence' of the learner. Apparently, some specific sort of processing is always contributed by the learner himself....

So far as theories of the learning process are concerned, the learning of any set of materials depends importantly upon individual contributions from the learner himself. Learning is an individual matter. In a fundamental sense, it is determined by what the learner does, and not by what the material does or what the teacher does. One can even go a step farther, in drawing implications for education. If one is concerned about how to make learning efficient, the focus of emphasis must be the student. The design of efficient conditions for learning demands that learning be conceived as an individual matter.

Now, there are conflicting views on this question. Some psychologists, looking at the educative process as typically involving a teacher and a class, have emphasized the teacher–student interaction, or what is sometimes called the teaching-learning process. Jackson (1966), for example, distinguishes between teacher–student dialogues which are private (as in a tutoring situation), those which are public (as in a classroom), and those which might be called semi-private, in which the teacher works with a single student while others engage in some other activity. He correctly notes that learning theorists have seldom if ever contributed to an understanding of the public teaching situation. Another theorist about teaching is Thelen (1967), who has carried out a series of most interesting studies of teacher–student interactions, seeking ways to find a 'fit' between teachers and groups of students. The absence of change in the school's output resulting from changes in administrative procedures such as class size, team teaching, ability grouping, as well as instructional procedures like discussions vs. lectures, leads Stephens (1967), to the conclusion that as long as a teacher has a strong interest in his subject, what he does is relatively unimportant.

For many legitimate purposes, there is surely much to be gained by studying the activities of the teacher, and theorizing about how he interacts or should interact with a learner. But such studies can tell us little about how learning occurs, or how to make it efficient. If we wish to find out about learning, we must begin and end with the human individual who is the learner. We must, in other words, find out what the learner is like, what he needs to know to begin the learning process, and what he needs to do to carry it out. The site of learning is not in a group, nor is it in a relationship between instructor and student. The site of learning is the individual's central nervous system. For this fundamental and unarguable reason, learning *is* individual. Efficient instruction is designed for the individual learner.

The recognition of the individual character of learning need not blind us to some of the necessities of public communication, with both teachers and other students. Schools and colleges are concerned with the transmission of public knowledge. There is, of course, such a thing as strictly private knowledge, as for example that exhibited in artistic accomplishment. But the schools cannot transmit this private experience, by definition. The communications of knowledge become refined, sharpened, and clarified by public discussion. In schools, therefore, public discussion serves the same highly essential purpose as it serves in other settings in the larger community. In a university setting, there is a great deal of public discussion, and it is highly important for the clarification and refinement of the 'messages' that are to be transmitted. Often, discussion takes place in a classroom, among students, and between students and teachers. Much discussion takes place among faculty members. And obviously, a great deal takes place outside of class among students. I believe discussion is a highly important part of school learning. Unfortunately, it must be said that we have no theory as yet of the role of discussion in learning. Such a theory, it may be expected, will not be opposed to a theory of individual learning, but will supplement it.

Instruction and the individual learner

It is possible, then, to bring to bear upon the design of instruction some principles of learning theory. These principles range from those which are quite generally applicable to all forms of learning to those which apply specifically to the learning of concepts and principles of the sort which characterize the bulk of knowledge taught in the schools. In addition, modern studies of learning suggest the clear implication that some idiosyncratic processing of information is done by the learner. This provides a fundamental reason for viewing learning as an individual process, and strongly suggests that individualized instruction represents the route of efficient learning. If arrangements for individual learning are not deliberately made by the system, they presumably will be made by the learner himself. In doing this, he will presumably use whatever media are available, although some may be better adapted for some purposes than are others.

The 'arrangements' of the external environment for purposes of efficient learning are what constitute the events of instruction. One should not lose sight of the fact, though, that learning in the sense used here also includes remembering and transfer of learning, since it is these less immediate outcomes that are the true concerns of an educational system. Assuming that these are included, what are the events of instruction that must take place in order for learning to occur?

In framing an answer to this question, I should first point out that according to Gagné's (1967) conception, the conditions of instruction differ with the type of learning being undertaken. Thus one does not design instruction on using a key-punch machine to be the same in its formal characteristics as instruction on how the mechanism of a key-punch machine operates. Or, in learning a foreign language, one does not design instruction on pronouncing words to be the same as instruction on understanding spoken sentences. There are some important distinctions here which should not be overlooked. However, for purposes of the present paper, I shall not elaborate them further. Instead, I shall speak only about the events of instruction applicable to the learning of principles, including facts, generalizations, and rules.

What appear to be the most important events of instruction are the following:

1 Gaining and maintaining attention. Obviously, in order for learning to occur, attention must be attracted in the first place, and then maintained. Many of the stimulation conditions that attract attention have been known for a long time, including such things as change, novelty, appeal to dominant interests. Concerning the maintenance of attention, we know somewhat less. Some clarification has surely been gained by Travers' (1964) demonstration that we only attend to one thing at a time, regardless of how many media channels may be bombarding us. Presumably, maintaining attention is a matter of achieving a set, related to one or more individual goals, which makes the learner return again and again to the task at hand. Manipulating external stimuli is probably ineffective over the long pull, and one must instead seek ways of reinforcing the motivational state of the learner.

2 Ensuring recall of previously acquired knowledge is another important function of instruction. We have seen that recall of prior knowledge is considered an essential condition of learning by both Gagné and Ausubel. When the learner undertakes to learn something new, he must first be reminded of what he already knows which is relevant to that learning.

3 Guiding the learning is done in instruction by verbal or pictorial material that provides 'cues' or 'hints' to new principles, usually

without stating them fully in verbal form. In part, the 'organizers' mentioned by Ausubel perform this instructional function. In part, it is done by questions, as Rothkopf's work illustrates. The skilled self-learner, of course, provides his own questions.

4 Providing feedback to the learner on his accomplishments is another function of instruction. One of the surest ways, it seems to me, is by defining the objectives of instruction clearly to the learner, so that he will become aware immediately when he has attained each specific goal. Again, the skilled learner may usually do this himself. Textbooks and other media often seem to neglect badly this essential instructional function.

5 Establishing conditions for remembering and transfer of learning would surely be counted as one of the essential functions of instruction. For purposes of transfer, there needs to be a carefully designed series of problems to which application of the newly learned principle is made. Probably also having this function is the process Ausubel calls 'integrative reconciliation', in which new ideas are compared and contrasted to related ones previously learned. For remembering, there needs to be provision for spaced review, which has often been shown to be an effective technique (cf. Davis, 1966, pp. 55–71).

6 Finally, there should be mentioned still another instructional function, often neglected. This is the assessment of outcomes. The outcomes of learning and remembering need to be assessed frequently. The administration of a final test or examination for purposes of determining a grade seems often to be a way of consolidating an onerous task which because of its unmanageable scope ends up avoiding the very assessment that should be done. Learning of the specifics needs to be assessed, perhaps more so than learning of the generalities. The five-minute daily or weekly quiz has much to recommend it. For the skilled learner, this function can often be performed with some success by himself. But to test oneself is indeed a highly sophisticated thing to do, and instructional materials should provide as much help as possible in this function.

There are, then, these six major functions that take place in instruction. It may be noted that learning theory does not, in and of itself, say exactly how these are to be put together in the great variety of specific instances to which they are applicable. What learning theory tells us is that when certain of these conditions are present, learning will occur, and when certain ones are not present, learning is improbable. Beyond such theory there must of course be both technology and artistry, whether this be exhibited by the textbook writer, the film-maker, or the master teacher. And to a considerable extent, at least, we should expect effective technique of self-instruction to be present in the young adult.

What can media accomplish?

It can readily be seen that most media of communication can readily perform most of these instructional functions. They can be performed by pictures, by printed language, by auditory language, or by a combination of media. So far as learning is concerned, the medium is not the message. No single medium possesses properties which are uniquely adapted to perform one or a combination of instructional functions. Instead, they all perform some of these functions well, and some not so well. The arrangement of instructional conditions is still the key to effective instruction, regardless of the medium or media employed.

One key to the question of which media is to be found by considering the learning task, that is, the objectives of the learning. A properly defined set of objectives provides information on the nature of stimuli to which the learner is expected to respond, after he has learned. Consider a few examples:

1 An objective in a course in physics might be, 'demonstrating Ohm's Law'. If one expects the student to show how resistance in an electric circuit varies with the current and voltage, there would seem to be considerable justification for using actual objects and events as the medium for instruction. In other words, one might set up instruction in a laboratory. If the student has sufficient prior acquaintance with such actual objects and events, a pictorial presentation may perform the same functions.

2 An objective in a course in English might be, 'editing composed written paragraphs for correctness of structure and optimal clarity of expression'. Obviously, what has to be presented here initially are incorrect and non-optimal paragraphs. Printed language has to be the medium. However, it may be of considerable importance in such an instance to arrange for frequent and prompt feedback to the learner as he makes his corrections. Thus one might choose to have a teacher convey this feedback in the presence of printed language given in a text or projected on a screen.

3 In a foreign language course, an objective might be, 'making appropriate responses containing personal biographical information to questions asked by a speaker in the foreign language'. Here again, the medium required is quite evident—it is auditory language. The learner must be presented with these questions in an auditory form, and the printed form will not be an adequate substitute.

Consideration of these examples, and others like them, leads to the following generalizations concerning the use of media for instruction. These seem to me to be more or less self-evident principles with which one must begin to think about media. They are not 'the answers', but merely the basis for further investigation of the uses of media.

1 First, no single medium is likely to have properties that make it best for all purposes. There is, so far as we know, no special magic in any particular medium.

2 Second, the most important single criterion for a choice of medium is often the nature of the learning task itself—that is, the objective of the instruction. If the learner is going to respond to real objects, these need to be used at some point in instruction. If he is going to respond to auditory language, then this form of communication needs to be used at some point in his instruction. However, it should be noted that this criterion doesn't solve the whole problem, by any means. The reason is that for many objectives, one medium is as appropriate to the task as another. For example, the principle relating the sides and hypotenuse of a right triangle can be presented in printed words, in mathematical symbols, or in diagrammatic pictures. Or, the events leading up to the Boston Massacre can be described in a printed text or shown in dramatized pictorial form. In these instances, nothing in the instructional objective itself provides a clue as to which medium will be best.

3 Third, when one considers the six functions of instruction (controlling attention, stimulating recall, etc.) previously mentioned, it is evident that any given medium may perform one of these functions best at a given time during a period of instructing, while another medium may perform an instructional function best at another time. That is to say, the precise answer to the question of 'which medium' is not to be found by matching courses with media, or even topics with media, but rather in matching *specific instructional functions* with media. Within a given topic, for example, attention

might best be maintained by the introduction of pictures, whereas guiding learning might best be accomplished by printed verbal instructions, and feedback might be best performed by auditory language. This line of reasoning is developed more fully by Briggs *et al.* (1967), in a monograph on *Instructional media*. When one chooses a particular medium for a whole course, or even for the development of an entire topic, one is usually making a judgment that such a medium will be best suited 'on the average' for the various instructional functions it must perform.

4 Finally, there is another suggestion to be derived from these considerations about the instructional functions of media. It may be that the most striking effects of instructional planning are to be sought in various *combinations* of media, where each may perform a particular function best. This does not mean reverting to the idea which Travers' (1964) work calls into question, that simultaneous auditory and visual presentations are superior to either alone. What it means instead is that any given medium might be used alternately with others over relatively short periods of instructional time.

Consider, for example, an instructional situation in which the student reads from a printed text and responds to it by writing problem answers. When the occasion demands, pictures or diagrams are presented to perform the functions of stimulating recall and guiding the learning. Now, as the student works along in this fashion, every so often, when a new subtopic is to be introduced, or special emphasis is to be given, a taped auditory message is introduced, having the primary purpose of controlling attention. Frequent questions are included in the printed text for self-assessment, and feedback is also provided in an auditory form. What would be the effectiveness of this kind of combination of media?

I do not know the answer to this question, and there is no research to provide it. Yet this kind of instructional arrangement, only roughly described in this example, may hold the key to effective instruction, particularly the sort of instruction which depends upon the individual to do a large part of the establishment of learning conditions for himself. Obviously, a good deal of testing of practical alternatives is needed before we can feel confident about the outcome of such plans for instruction.

I have been led in this paper to consider first how learning theory relates to the practical events of instruction. There is little doubt that this relationship can be demonstrated. Depending upon which

learning theory one chooses, the suggestions for practical application to instruction are more or less specific. And running through all
theories is the theme that learning is, after all, an individual matter,
in which essential idiosyncratic elements must be supplied by the
learner himself.

As a practical matter, the events of instruction encompass more
processes than are included in learning theories themselves. Instruction involves gaining and controlling attention, stimulating recall,
guiding the learning, providing feedback, arranging for remembering, and assessing outcomes. It is these functions that are performed
by various media of instruction, and to a considerable degree by the
learner himself. One should not expect, I think, to find that a single
medium is best fitted to do all of these things. Instead, it seems likely
that carefully designed combinations of media may be required to
achieve the kind of instruction that is most effective, and which at
the same time exploits the properties of media to fullest advantage.

References

Ausubel, D. P. *The psychology of meaningful verbal learning.* New York:
    Grune and Stratton, 1963.

Ausubel, D. P. 'A cognitive-structure theory of school learning.' In L. Siegel
    (ed.), *Instruction: some contemporary viewpoints.* San Francisco: Chandler,
    1967, pp. 207–257.

Briggs, L. J., Campeau, P. L., Gangé, R. M., and May M. A. *Instructional media.*
    Pittsburgh: American Institutes for Research, 1967. (Monograph No. 2).

Davis, R. A. *Learning in the schools.* Belmont: Wadsworth, 1966.

Gagné, R. M. *The conditions of learning.* New York: Holt, Rinehart, and
    Winston, 1965.

Gagné, R. M. 'Problem solving.' In A. W. Melton (ed.), *Categories of human
    learning.* New York: Academic Press, 1964.

Gagné, R. M. 'Instruction and the conditions of learning.' In L. Siegel (ed.),
    Instruction: some contemporary viewpoints. San Francisco: Chandler, 1967,
    pp. 291–313.

Gilbert, T. F. 'Mathetics: the technology of education.' *Journal of Mathetics,*
    1962, vol. 1, 7–73.

Green, E. J. *The learning process and programmed instruction.* New York:
    Holt, Rinehart, and Winston, 1962.

Jackson, P. W. 'The way teaching is.' In *The way teaching is: report of the
    seminar on teaching.* Washington, D. C.: National Education Association,
    1966, pp. 7–27.

Jenkins, J. J. 'Mediated association: paradigms and situations.' In C. N. Cofer
    and B. S. Musgrave (eds.), *Verbal behavior and learning.* New York:
    McGraw-Hill, 1963.

Katona, G. *Organizing and memorizing*. New York: Columbia University Press, 1940.

Kendler, H. H. 'The concept of the concept.' In A. W. Melton (ed.), *Categories of human learning*. New York: Academic Press, 1964.

Melton, A. W. 'Implications of short-term memory for a general theory of memory.' *Journal of Verbal Learning and Verbal Behavior*, 1963, vol. 2, 1–21.

Melton, A. W. (ed.) *Categories of human learning*. New York: Academic Press, 1964.

Miller, N. E., *et. al. Graphic communication and the crisis in education*. Washington, D. C.: Department of Audio-Visual Instruction, National Education Association, 1957 (*Audio-Visual Communication Review*, vol. 5, no. 3).

Rothkopf, E. Z. 'Some theoretical and experimental approaches to problems in written instruction.' In J. D. Krumboltz (ed.), *Learning and the educational process*. Chicago: Rand-McNally, 1965, pp. 193–221.

Siegel, L. (ed.) *Instruction: some contemporary viewpoints*. San Francisco: Chandler, 1967.

Skinner, B. F. *Verbal behavior*. New York: Appleton-Century-Crofts, 1957.

Skinner, B. F. 'Teaching machines.' *Science*, 1958, vol. 128, 969–977.

Skinner, B. F. 'Reflections on a decade of teaching machines.' In R. Glaser (ed.), *Teaching machines and programmed learning: II. Data and directions*. Washington, D. C.: National Education Association, 1965, pp. 5–20.

Stephens, J. M. *The process of schooling*. New York: Holt, Rinehart, and Winston, 1967.

Thelen, H. A. *Classroom grouping for teachability*. New York: Wiley, 1967.

Travers, R. M. W., *et. al. Research and theory related to audiovisual information transmission*. Salt Lake City: Bureau of Educational Research, University of Utah, 1964.

Fred T. Wilhelms

II:15 Evaluation as feedback

*Evaluation is a central component of the educational
process. Properly handled, it feeds back into the
functioning of the system and redirects it. Wilhelms lists
a number of basic criteria which test the value of a
school's mechanisms for evaluation. Measured by these
criteria, the evaluation mechanisms of most schools
come off badly.*

The great breakthrough in technology—the one commonly called
'automation' and, even more, the one called 'cybernation'—is the
offspring of feedback. The scientists and engineers learned how to
build right into a machine the capacity to gather data from what
the machine had just done and what had happened as a result, and
feed those data back into a decision system controlling what the
machine should do next.

That basic invention opened up a whole new world of technology. At the peak of that technology stands the computer. It can
be programmed to 'keep in mind' a complex set of purposes, criteria, rules and policies—the background factors that must lie behind any specific action. Then a constant stream of data, arising out
of the ongoing process, is fed back into its calculations. 'Considering' these data in terms of the background factors, the computer
constantly 'decides' what needs to be done next. It keeps making
whatever adjustments are necessary to keep the whole process
moving forward toward its goal.

But human beings—all organisms, for that matter—had anticipated technology by thousands of years. In some ways even the
brain of a pigeon is 'better' than the most complex computer yet
developed. People have always operated on feedback. Sometimes
they do it deliberately. Then they reflect upon their basic purposes
and the values they hold dear; they ponder over how a situation has
worked out to this point and the problems they have to solve to
achieve their goal; finally, either slowly or in a flash, they make up
their minds as to what is the best thing to do next. They could not

Wilhelms, F. T. (ed.), *Evaluation as feedback*, 1967 Yearbook, pp. 2–16. Assn.
for Supervision and Curriculum Development, Washington, D. C. Reprinted
by permission.

do this well if they lacked a basic sense of direction, of purposes and values and criteria to judge by; but neither could they do it with growing precision if they did not have a constant stream of information feeding back into their minds out of what was going on and how it was working.

More often—all the time, in fact—people are gathering data without even knowing it and taking the next step that just seems to come naturally. The background factors are taken for granted—one knows he intends to drive to the office—and the sensory data come in unnoticed, to keep him on his course. But always feedback is coming in, and the quality of the next step depends on how well that feedback is blended with basic purposes and converted into decisions.

For as long as there have been social organizations, they, too, have used feedback. On occasion they do it thoughtfully and wisely, reflecting upon their long-term objectives and analyzing their current data; more often they do it crudely and half-intuitively. But, at least in some vague, inchoate way, every community, family, or school system is forever sizing up how things are going and making up its mind what to do next.

Schools organize a special variety of feedback. They call it *evaluation*. Most of its goes on informally, half-intuitively; the most visible—but not necessarily the most important—part of it goes on through a complex of quizzing and testing and examining and comes out in a system of grades and marks and credits.

Yet regardless of whether the evaluation is formal or informal—and equally regardless of whether it is 'good' or 'sensitive' or 'adequate'—it has one thing in common with every other system of feedback: When it has been blended into the background system of purposes and values and policies, *it controls the next step*. This is simply a fact of life; all our decisions are conditioned by perceptions of how we are doing in terms of what we hope to do. . . .

Feedback has many consumers

Much of the real evaluation, too often unnoticed, goes on within the individual pupil, as he is constantly 'aware-ing' himself and the situation around him, sizing up the value of what the school offers him, and making his decisions—conscious or unconscious, but in either case *plenary*—about his next investments of energy. A first criterion of evaluation must be how well it is converted into genuine feedback to the pupil, whether it leads him steadily toward sharper, more valid perceptions, and therefore toward wiser decisions and actions.

Much of evaluation is centered in the teacher. He is constantly using his personal sensitivity plus whatever diagnostic aids he can devise to calibrate his next choice of subject matter and method. This is the sector of evaluation most commonly noticed and worked at. As the teacher proceeds with his work, he is expected to listen and watch and test—to search in every way for the data that arise out of the process. The question still remains whether his total system of searching yields him the feedback he needs to guide him to the wisest adaptations.

Important parts of evaluation are lodged in the school's bigger organizational centers—among the supervisors and curriculum workers, in the principals' offices, in the headquarters of the superintendent, or at the level of the county, the state, or the federal authorities—as well as in the general public. These parts lead to large, sweeping decisions about what to emphasize in the curriculum, about facilities to build, about schemes of organization to adopt, and about the allocation of financial support. Here, again, as in the case of the individual pupil, the use of evaluation is too often unnoticed. Judgments *are* made and profoundly important decisions are based upon them—but they are far too often the judgments of hunch and impression and rumor and even prejudice, because an organized flow of significant feedback has been neglected.

The essential, unremitting fact is that at every level it is *evaluative feedback*—and, again, regardless of whether it is 'good' or 'sensitive' or 'adequate'—whether it is based on the reasoned analysis of sound data or only on some vague impression—that conditions what happens next. It conditions what pupils do, what teachers do, what school officials do, and what the supporting public does.

Evaluation must meet multiple criteria

Of course, the feedback system which exerts all this force involves an enormous complex. . . . At one end of the scale, much of it lies within the private world of each child or teacher; at the other end of the scale much of it is hidden in the subtle interaction of public opinion. In a very real way it is all relevant to the evaluation which schools carry on, but it is not all accessible to an organized program—and it would be too bulky to handle, anyway. . . .

Yet, no matter where one draws the line, the test of an evaluation system is simply this: *Does it deliver the feedback that is needed, when it is needed, to the persons or groups who need it?*

If any system of evaluation is to meet this test, it must satisfy several basic criteria:

1 *Evaluation must facilitate self-evaluation.* The most fundamentally important outcome of evaluation is what happens within the learner himself. In the narrower terms of subject matter he needs to understand with some precision what is to be learned and 'what it is all about' (i.e., why it is important, how it relates to other subject matter and to himself). To whatever extent he has succeeded, he needs to know about it, for a sense of success contributes energy for the next task; to whatever extent he has not yet achieved mastery, he needs to know what the gaps are, so that he can figure out what to do about them. In some degree he has to be equipped to be his own diagnostician, because in the final analysis he will be his own diagnostician anyway—he is the person who is in control of his learning energies—and it is better that he do the job well.

In the broader terms of the learner's development as a person, it is essential that evaluation help him steadily toward a valid and healthy image of himself. It is especially important for him to learn about his strengths and resources, in a way that genuinely leads him to incorporate these into his self-concept. It is also essential that evaluation should enrich his conception of the life-space he has to operate in, by expanding his vision of the opportunities and the choices that can be open to him and by enriching his background perceptions of purposes and values to judge by. Of course, it is also important to help him appraise realistically his residual weaknesses and the limitations of his resources, if this can be done in such a way as to create a genuine challenge. But most evaluation probably rushes in too soon and concentrates too much on the catching of 'failures'. Youngsters who accumulate a sense of strength and resource and opportunity gain the psychological freedom to look with clear eyes at their remaining problems. Those who are overwhelmed by a hopeless sense of failure are forced, for their own self-preservation, to distort the evidence, and never become good diagnosticians.

Taken altogether, the kind of feedback which a young person receives from a system of evaluation is crucial in his learning and development. It can lead him forward to precisely calibrated learning efforts on an ever-broadening front as well as to an enriched conception of himself and of his purposes and values and ultimate goals. Or it can strain and distort him, narrow his vision and purpose, and bring him little but a sense of defeat.

2 *Evaluation must encompass every objective valued by the school.* We are talking here of the *total* evaluation system, which includes much that depends on personal sensitivity and intuition, not merely of the testing-and-marking system, which may have to be more limited. Nevertheless, we cannot shake off the fact that it is the feedback generated by evaluation which conditions what everybody does next. And there cannot be thoughtful improvement on lines where there is no feedback.

If a history teacher says he is aiming for big generalizations but organizes his evaluative feedback in terms of the memorization of facts, his students will soon attend to the facts—and so, eventually, will he. Nothing will true up their learning and his teaching better than a widening of his evaluation. One fact is that he cannot improve his procedures unless he knows the results of what he has already been doing. Another fact is that unless there is something to deepen his awareness of a line of effort, he will slack off in the effort itself, shifting his energies toward those outcomes of which he *is* aware.

If the goals of a school include—along with the mastery of subject matter—such important 'side effects' as a spirit of inquiry, sensitivity to beauty, and a moral commitment to conscientious citizenship, then these must steadily be within the view of the school's evaluation, too. The obligation is virtually a moral one: Whenever an institution commits itself to any purpose, it takes on the obligation to keep finding out how well it is achieving that purpose. Otherwise it cannot improve its efforts. The obligation is also a pragmatic one: Unless the school keeps trying to find out how well it is succeeding with a purpose, the purpose itself is likely to atrophy. Any school which hopes to maintain a balance among its multiple objectives—to maintain this balance in the instruction teachers provide and in the learning students devote energy to—must strive first of all for breadth and balance in its evaluation of those objectives. . . .

The best guide to curriculum improvement is evaluation; and to be an adequate guide the system of evaluation has to be as 'big' as the purposes of the curriculum development itself.

3 *Evaluation must facilitate learning and teaching.* Instructional

diagnosis lies at the very heart of good teaching. After each bit of evaluative data comes in, the teacher should be a little surer of how to proceed next. The all-too-common confusion of evaluation with grading tends to produce an image of evaluation as a terminal thing. But its far more significant function is a constant probing for the best way to move forward.

It is not the teacher alone who needs the diagnosis. After each bit of evaluation, the student, too, should know better where he stands and how to move ahead. And this purpose of diagnosis should be so apparent in the evaluative devices used that the student will see diagnosis as an aid, not as a trap set to catch him in failure.

4 *Evaluation must produce records appropriate to the purposes for which records are essential.* We intend to raise serious questions about the present system of grades and marks and credits—questions so grave that *they force us to propose that the system by discarded.* But the proposal does not stem from our taking the record-generating function of evaluation lightly; quite the contrary, we consider it terribly important that the records be so good that whenever they are needed they can deliver exactly that information which is truly significant.

Obviously, classroom teachers need some kinds of records purely for their own private purposes, as an aid to their instruction. These can and should vary with the nature of the subject matter and situation, as well as with the teacher's personal style. There is no particular need for uniformity, and anything that 'works' for a given teacher is fine.

To experienced educators the phrase *evaluation for the record* immediately creates an image of the transcripts and other records we send to another school when a student transfers or to a college when he graduates; transcripts made up of grades and credits and test scores and the like. These records are enormously important at critical times in a student's life. Here, at least, the school is reporting to other professionals, who presumably know how to read the records. Even so, the question remains whether the reports we send are actually good stewards of the data we wish to convey—and also whether those data are, in fact, the most significant things we could pass on.

But schools also report to employers, whose need for information may be very different and whose ability to interpret the typical record may be questionable. Furthermore—and more fundamentally important—teachers and other staff members need to bring the learner himself into interaction with the evaluative process. The records which a teacher or counselor needs in order to communicate meaningfully to him may be very different again from a mere list of grades. And the record of the interaction itself may later be highly significant. Finally, there is great need to communicate clearly to parents—and, once more, the kinds of records that will help most may have their own peculiarities.

We are not trying to create an image of a vast volume of records. We are trying to say that records are used in a variety of ways, and that there probably needs to be a variety of kinds. In every case the essential thing is that the records be able *to say what really counts* and say it in a way that genuinely communicates.

5 *Evaluation must provide continuing feedback into the larger questions of curriculum development and educational policy.* It is one thing for a history teacher to organize a continuing feedback to guide him in teaching his class. It may take quite a different order of evaluation to tell whether his history teaching would be more effective if he injected more economic and anthropological content into it. It may require still something more to guide a school's relative investment in the social studies as against the sciences and the humanities.

It is one thing to measure results and establish that the audio-lingual way of teaching a foreign language produces better speakers of that language than does a grammatical approach. It is another thing to find out whether the audio-lingual system aids or hinders the students' understanding of the culture behind the language or their appreciation of its literature. The school is full of such situations, where even the most precise measurement along one line may leave untouched larger questions of ultimate total effect.

It is important to emphasize that evaluation must concern itself with all the important objectives of a school rather than only a narrow band out of the total spectrum. In a curious way, however, it is even necessary on occasion for evaluation to 'get outside of' the established objectives and raise still larger questions. Why, after years of instruction in composition, do so many adults 'freeze up' when they face even the simplest writing task? Does cultural relativism in the social studies lead students to an 'anything goes' philosophy? The most important educational choices often involve whole blocks of curriculum, or programs differing in *kind* rather than in detail; if evaluation is to live up to its responsibilities, it must provide data for this order of choices, too.

Typically, decisions of this order are not made within the individual classroom, perhaps not even within the individual school. They are made by curriculum committees, administrators, and boards of education. This raises the problem of organizing data and channeling them so that they will be available to the persons or groups that actually make the choices. Since these are among the most important decisions made in any school, it is obviously crucial that they be based on genuinely evaluative feedback.

Time out, to dream a little

In this imperfect world it is not likely that any school system will ever devise a program of evaluation that will meet all five of these criteria perfectly. But suppose it could. What would be the results?

Every teacher would soon be teaching with greater precision, because he would be getting data constantly on what was 'working' and what was not, what was already mastered and what remained to be learned. The ideal of 'diagnostic teaching' would be close to fulfillment. Meanwhile the student himself would be channeling his own efforts with greater precision for he, too, would have a clear sense of direction.

When a student is transferred to other teachers or another institution, the new institution or teachers could pick him up smoothly and move forward with him, for they would have ways of knowing the things that really matter about him. Parents could be helped to become superior counselors to their children, for the school could help them toward true insight. Employers could choose their employees with more discernment and give them assignments fitted to their capacities and interests.

But in the long run even these great gains might be overshadowed by still greater ones. The public and the profession would be in position to make wiser fundamental decisions about changes in the educational program as a whole—or large parts of it. Fresh, daring questions could be raised, and there would be at least some ways of getting at evidence with which to answer them creatively. Because a wide spread of educational purposes could be kept constantly in clear view, it would be difficult for partial and narrow-based efforts to be substituted for the whole.

Perhaps the greatest gains of all would occur within the young person himself. As he learned not only to see his academic progress with clear eyes, but also to appraise himself validly, he would be more and more in position to take charge of his own life space and guide his own learning energies. The whole spirit of a school constantly guided by thoughtful evaluation would be healthy and constructive. For, as everyone became more and more aware of purposes and progress, and as diagnosis came to be seen as an ally, the old lines of antagonisms and cross-purposes must surely be erased.

An idealistic picture? Yes, but only because educators cannot yet produce such perfect evaluation—not because it would not realistically have such effects if we could produce it. There is no more realistic fact in the realm of human life than that we are all governed by our perception of the feedback we receive—and the nearer we come to having the feedback we need, the more nearly we approach wisdom at the next step.

All this is another way of saying that there is a great deal more to evaluation than first meets the eye. All too commonly it has been seen as if it were only measurement—a way of getting at marks and grades and credits. But when we view *evaluation as feedback* we instantly see how it resonates back through every stage of the educational process. Good evaluation has a way of stimulating deliberate thought about basic purposes and values and goals. One cannot measure progress toward a goal without knowing what that goal is. And every thoughtful effort to measure such progress brings the goal itself into renewed visibility.

If the evaluation is of sufficient scope and if it is handled through an interactive process, it has this clarifying, renewing effect upon learners, teachers, higher educational officers, and public alike. It helps everybody who is involved to think more clearly about what he is after and how he is getting along. In the long run, then, a high-quality evaluation program is the surest guarantee a learner, a teacher, or a school system can have of the ability constantly to envision valid objectives, plan for their achievement, look successes and failures in the eyes, and develop new plans as these are needed.

How does reality compare with the dream?

How does the system of evaluation we now have stand up in the light of such a description? Even to ask the question is to have a quick and woeful perception of how very far it falls short. Yet perhaps it is unfair and unprofitable to judge any human institution against an absolute ideal. Let us, instead, try to size up realistically how well the typical system of evaluation does the five essential jobs.

1 *Does the system we have facilitate self-evaluation?* Not very well, by and large. One has to be careful here, for it makes an enormous difference in what school or what classroom the youngster finds himself. (Having said that, let us add a more general acknowledgment: We recognize that in speaking of 'the system we have,' we are implying a uniformity which does not exist. We trust the reader to recognize this also and to bear in mind that we are talking about certain fairly general characteristics which tend to run through a variety of patterns.) If a pupil is working with warm, sensitive teachers in a school that is open and friendly, he will have many chances to catch glimpses of his true potential.

But, by and large, the system is simply not geared to making significant feedback available to the pupil. Particularly those portions which to the pupil are most prestigious and important (i.e., the quizzing, testing, grading and marking, which have such weight in his life) have serious flaws.

For one thing, these measures are largely confined to the intellectual mastery of subject matter, tending to make all else seem extraneous. Almost worse, they generally interpret such mastery in terms of a bare memorization of factual details, ignoring the more fundamentally important generalizations, appreciations, and creative ideas. If the results tell the student anything about himself it is a bare sort of message.

Furthermore, even within these limits, the climate of formal evaluation is often so threatening as virtually to close out honest self-appraisal. Especially to the less able student, the main thrust of the effort may seem to be to 'catch him out,' to reveal as many as possible of his weaknesses, errors and failures. Human beings are so constituted that they can look at themselves with clear eyes only when they are in a relaxed, supportive situation. When they feel themselves persistently threatened they distort the feedback offered them to make it match the self-concept they need.

Finally, in most formal evaluation situations, it was never the intention of the school to involve the student cooperatively and to develop his powers of self-diagnosis. The teacher does the diagnosing and returns a mark and a scatter of red ink. Even if the teacher's diagnosis is perfectly sound, the student is unlikely to understand it as the teacher does—and even less likely to learn the process of diagnosing himself.

All in all, the evaluation system most learners experience may lead about as often to self-distortion as to perceptive self-appraisal. This is probably less true—or at least it may be less damaging—in the case of bright, attractive youngsters who are constantly receiving good news both through the formal media of marks and grades and through the personal cues supplied by their interactions with their peers and teachers. It is terribly true in the case of the less able and less attractive.

No human being can be expected to continue to 'take' the volume of negative information such youngsters receive through their grades and marks and the way others treat them. They are literally forced to distort the cues into some kind of congruence with a bearable self-image. It is no wonder at all if they withdraw into private despair or flare out in public rebellion. In the process they lose the opportunity to learn about their real strengths and resources. The evaluation we have has a great deal to answer for, in its destruction of potentially sound human beings. No school system with a commitment to mental health and self-actualization ought to tolerate the sheer immorality of such a process.

2 *Does the evaluation we have encompass every objective valued by the school?* Obviously not—at least not in any balanced way. Here and there some scattered attention may be given to the more remote objectives, such as the development of a personal system of values. But at the same time such overwhelming weight is placed on a narrow range of purposes that the others virtually disappear from view.

Of course, the egregious fact in this connection is the constant testing of what is easiest to measure : memory of factual detail and manipulation of mechanical skills. In the crisis points of his academic life—when his 'success' or 'failure' is at stake—the student is taught by the tests set before him that survival depends on such memorization and manipulation. Small wonder if he concentrates his attention there, if he neglects the larger ideas or falls away from active questioning and creative divergence!

And it is no trivial side effect that over time, in some subtle way, the teacher's own efforts will also follow where his own tests—and those external tests which he is asked to administer—lead him. If he tests for facts he will teach facts; if he were to test for creativity he might at least try to teach toward it.

This is no small thing. It leads to massive distortion of energy input by both students and teachers. In recent years valuable new programs of science and mathematics have been 'sold' on their ability to get away from rote memorization and manipulation, to create a new spirit of inquiry and sense of discovery, to build a new level of divergent thought and creativity. Yet if the measures used to evaluate them do not themselves highlight these great values—if they regress to the old narrow emphases—then it is a cinch that the programs, too, will regress.

The disease is endemic. We have courses ostensibly dedicated to the building of good citizenship—and measured in terms of knowledge of government structure. We have courses devoted to the 'appreciation' of literature—and evaluated by knowledge of authors' names and movements and literary types.

But if the evaluation focus is stultifyingly narrow even within the range of *academic* goals, it is doubly dangerous in its exclusion of more personal variables. It is bad enough when the paraphernalia of tests and grades diminish attention to insight and understanding in favor of bare knowledge. It is even worse if they foreclose attention to ideals and values and personal traits in favor of the coldly intellectual.

The net result, over time, is that not only pupils and teachers but also parents and the general public make judgments and decisions affecting the entirety of education on the basis of evidence from one skimpy sector.

3 *Does the evaluation we have facilitate learning and teaching?* Here, especially if we confine ourselves to the teaching and learning of a set body of academic subject matter, the answer is considerably more positive. Particularly from the teacher's point of view. Good teachers commonly combine an intuitive discernment with fairly sensitive measures to assess what is going on and to calibrate their next steps. If few of them achieve the high ideal implied by the phrase 'diagnostic teaching,' many do maintain a running evaluation that tells them much about what to do.

From the learner's point of view the answer probably can not be quite so positive. Even if this teacher has a pretty good running diagnosis, *he* may not be sharing in it. When the teacher painstakingly marks his English composition with red ink, the teacher may arrive at an excellent analysis of what is needed; when the discour-

aged student glances at his ink-splashed effort, he may only learn
that he is a poor writer. Still, even this student does get a fairly good
running account of his mistakes and sometimes of his successes. The
evaluation we now have is probably at its best in shaping the internal decisions within each classroom.

But even this is true only if the curriculum is confined to the
regularized learning of a set body of subject matter, with limited
objectives. In the very process of guiding that reasonably well, the
intra-classroom evaluation program may be damping down attention to larger, more fundamentally important goals. Thus, the English teacher who so conscientiously took time to edit the composition just mentioned probably spent nearly all that time to mark
errors in an effort to teach *correctness of form*. He may have paid
almost no attention to *what the student had to say*. In his zeal for
one set of purposes, he passed up the opportunity to help the student
consider his logic or his implied values or his adherence to the truth.
Evaluation has been so tragically successful in concentrating attention and energy on the narrowest objectives that marks and grades
based on those objectives become almost an obsession. And all that
falls outside the marking-grading system suffers.

This last point needs further extension. We have developed a
preoccupation with everlastingly grading everything in sight. (There
is even a case on record of a teacher who graded the sympathetic
letters her pupils wrote her while she was ill!) Many teachers
almost automatically look at every pupil product in terms of the
grade it deserves. And so, all too naturally, students have come to
see their purpose as 'working for a grade'. The obsession virtually
blots out their real purposes. Parents pick up the message and add
their pressure. Because the mode is so prevalent, many adults, both
lay and professional—and even many children—cannot really conceptualize a pupil's doing purposive work except under the compulsion of 'getting a grade'. There can be no question but that this side
effect of the evaluation system we have now is a major deterrent to
genuine teaching and learning.

4 *Does the evaluation we have produce records appropriate to the
purposes for which records are essential?* That the system generates
records in considerable volume is not to be questioned. Thus, when a
student has come through to the twelfth grade, a well organized
high school is in position to tell a prospective college a great many
facts about him. It could supply a good many vital statistics such as

age, height, weight, a health record, and a record of attendance, along with at least one score indicating general academic aptitude. It could furnish some indications of the student's record of 'citizenship' and of his participation in student activities. What it could do best of all is to record how much time the student has spent in each subject, and what grades he has earned. On the basis of these grades it could compute his rank-in-class. In addition, it might offer a considerable number of scores on various standardized tests.

These records are not to be sneered at. In the hands of an expert counselor who adds interpretive comments, such a record can be highly revealing. It is significant that many colleges consider the record inadequate and ask for a record of performance on something like the College Entrance Examination Board's special tests; but then it is also significant that the student's grade-point average is usually considered a better predictor of his college performance than the examination scores are—though the two together are still better. It is significant, too, that when research is contemplated the grade records are rarely thought adequate; nearly always the researcher substitutes measures which he hopes will be more precise.

Undoubtedly, if we measure the records a school can ordinarily supply against the absolute ideal that it ought to have to be able to paint a highly revealing portrait of him—to tell whatever is truly significant—the records will seem mechanistic and unrevealing. Nevertheless, it may well be true that the records themselves are less to be criticized than the process of getting them. The fact is that the process of accumulating those records has constituted an enormous preoccupation among teachers and pupils alike. The most trivial papers have been treated as if they existed largely to create a record. The student has been marked and graded day after day until the getting of good marks has become a goal in itself, with intrinsic learning left a very bad second. There is evidence that on the average the best way to get those marks is to think convergently, to do the standard task in the expected way; the creative student who persists in thinking divergently often comes off second best.

Furthermore, as already pointed out, the records school people typically create are those which will be meaningful and useful to other professional educators. In the process they have largely ignored other kinds of records: the kinds needed by a teacher—or counselor—in planning for groups or individuals; the kinds that would be meaningful to the youngster himself, or to his parents; the kinds that would be really significant to employers.

5 *Does the evaluation we have provide continuing feedback into the larger questions of curriculum development and educational policy?* The answer is a resounding *no!* Oh, there cannot help being a certain intuitive formation of opinion out of experience, which is not entirely without validity. When experienced teachers grow discontented with one approach and choose to try another, their opinion certainly deserves weight even if they cannot mobilize hard data.

Yet there are dangers in this. The shifts that result from changing styles of opinion often rest on about as much rationality as the annual decrees from Paris on the length of a woman's skirts. A clever writer decides that phonics are the *open sesame* to all reading and the public puts on the heat; some college professors who have not been inside a school for a decade argue for a different choice of literature; a new administrator parlays a personal hunch into a new curricular organization. In case after case sweeping decisions are made because nobody can adduce any really cogent evidence. And when those who have created an innovation look back, they remind one of Genesis: 'And God saw everything that He had made, and behold, it was very good.'

The 'new' programs in mathematics and science are not really so new any more. They were 'sold' not merely on the claim that they represented more important content but equally on the argument that they would build a new spirit of inquiry and creativity, a new surge of genuinely scientific attitude. Who knows whether they are actually achieving these things—or whether some of them are doing it better than others? After all these years, how much is really known on the crucial question of what is sound preparation for vocational life? The cold fact is that the evaluation system we now have puts great energy into grading students and considerable energy into guiding day-to-day teacher-and-pupil conduct within a classroom and within a set course of study, but it yields little evidence on which to assess the longer-range choices of curriculum and policy.

Furthermore, even when evaluation does yield evidence that might be useful in such choices, there is rarely any systematic channeling of the information to the points where the decisions are made. The fact that data exist does not automatically convert them into feedback. That depends on their converging systematically and steadily to the decision points. It is an anomaly that educators work so hard to true up the relatively 'little' intra-class decisions and rest content to play the big ones by ear. It will take great revision of our evaluative efforts to produce data that bear on the large choices; it may take even more work to build a system that will convert these data into functioning feedback.

This analysis leads to radical conclusions

Taken all in all, when it is measured—even rather tolerantly— against our five basic questions, the evaluation we now have comes off badly. On the first and last questions it comes off very badly indeed, for it is most grossly inadequate in providing valid feedback to the individual learner himself and to the larger units of the school system. But it is equally to be condemned for the narrowness of its focus, because in its gross exaggeration of the more mechanical, easier-to-measure features of education, it virtually blots the broader, more fundamental objectives out of sight. The end result is not simply bad evaluation; it is distorted teaching and learning.

We believe that much of the trouble goes back to the marking-grading system and the kinds of records which it produces. The records are themselves inadequate; even the narrative record and the parent conference at the elementary level tell far too little of what is most significant. But the process of getting those records—the eternal preoccupation with marking and grading now spreading even in elementary schools—is even worse. Here the problem is not mere inadequacy but real destructiveness and distortion.

Lawrence Stenhouse

II:16 The humanities curriculum project

The director of the Schools Council Humanities Project, Lawrence Stenhouse, describes the objectives and approach of the project. The project is aimed at developing materials for children of average and below average academic ability, with the emphasis on enquiry and interdisciplinary work. The role of the teacher is radically transformed from information-transmitter to debate-leader.

The project has been funded for three years jointly by the Nuffield Foundation and the Schools Council, and has been given the following remit:

'To offer to schools and to teachers such stimulus, support and materials as may be appropriate to the mounting, as an element in general education of enquiry-based courses, which cross the subject boundaries between English, history, geography, religious studies and social studies. The project is expected to concentrate on such support as will in particular meet the needs of adolescent pupils of average and below average academic ability.'

This is essentially a *curriculum* project, that is to say, it is primarily concerned with the content of education. Any observations about classroom strategies and methods must be seen in the setting of the content, from which they logically derive.

We understand by the humanities the study of both human behaviour and human experience. The study of human *behaviour* is broadly the concern of the social sciences: history, human geography, psychology and sociology. In some sense, these studies aspire to examine human behaviour objectively, viewing it as caused or as dictated by purposes which can be understood from observation rather than detailed subjective analysis. The study of human *experience* is reflected in the arts and in the biographical aspect of history. It is concerned with the subjective or existential

Journal of Curriculum Studies. vol. 1, no. 1, 1969, pp. 26–33. (Published twice-yearly by William Collins Sons & Co. Ltd.) Reprinted by permission.

aspects of human life, and one important criterion by which judgment of the arts are made is fidelity to human experience.

The claim of the humanities in education rests upon the assertion that their study enhances understanding and judgment in those areas of practical living which involve complex considerations of values and cultural traditions. This claim has commonly been made for a classical education, and R. S. Peters has recently stated it in a form which sharpens its relevance to a project such as ours:

'But surely the strongest case for Classics is that it is a field combining *many* forms of understanding and appreciation. At a time when all sorts of rather artificial attempts are being made to contrive an integrated curriculum in which due attention is paid to "the whole man", Classics stands as a well-established field of study which satisfies most of the criteria laid down by such educational theorists.'[1]

It has also been asserted that the study of certain academic disciplines can provide a general education for living. This claim also seems justified though perhaps only at high levels of study. It rests upon the assertion that academic disciplines involve thought structures, methodologies and criteria which can be deployed in a variety of situations. In other words, academic disciplines, systematically taught, make possible a flexible transfer of learning because of their high level of generalisation. Observation would suggest that there are severe limitations to this doctrine. The academic disciplines are easily justified in terms of the organisation and advancement of knowledge; but if one sought an example of education informing and giving grace to living, one would not necessarily choose the society of a university common room.

However, the academic disciplines have their relevance to a curriculum broadly conceived in terms of the humanities. To cross subject boundaries successfully one must grasp—or at the least see the need for—standards of quality in each of the subject fields involved. One must also understand that a logic relating the different fields has to be explored. To conceive a curriculum for general education in terms of the humanities is to commit oneself to an attempt to work out this overall logic in the setting of an application to significant human issues.

A curriculum which focuses on significant human issues runs some risk of degenerating into incoherence precisely because it has relinquished the support of traditional subject structures. The areas of study must be carefully chosen according to explicit criteria and must meet some structural requirements. Part of the task of this project will be to explore problems of logic and structure in a humanities curriculum, and any observations must at this stage be provisional.

The selection of areas of study should probably not need to be justified in terms of transfer of learning. If we wish students to be able adequately to meet important human issues, these issues must themselves be the stuff of the curriculum. We must deal in areas where complex and informed decisions ought to be made by almost everyone. Such topics as family relationships, relations between the sexes, the position of adolescents in society, problems of war and peace and racial prejudice seem immediately to establish a claim to attention. Others, such as law and order, power and ambition, living in cities or human dereliction, though perhaps less compelling, seem to offer rich possibilities. Topics such as transport, water or local government seem difficult to justify in a humanities curriculum; they are derived from a different logic, perhaps that associated with the teaching of the conventional school subjects across disciplines on a project or enquiry base. Moreover, they raise too few issues of value, and deal rather in facts and techniques.

Such distinctions as those made above are important. There are many different curricular experiments afoot, and if they are to make their maximum contribution, each must be clear about its own frame of reference.

Areas of study should have an internal logical coherence, and should not be based on casual associations. Thus, the juxtaposition of political power and power as energy in the physical sense is unsatisfactory, as is the association of irrigation, boiling kettles, swimming and water on the knee in a unit on 'water'. Themes should probably seem inevitable, rather than clever. All areas of study selected for a humanities course should lead students not only to a consideration of human behaviour in an objective frame of reference, but also to an imaginative sympathy with subjective human experience.

There is a tendency to conceptualize curricula which cross subject boundaries in terms of the needs and interests of students. This does not seem a helpful approach. Of course, the curriculum must be interesting and relevant to the students, but these are not sufficient reasons for the selection of material. In a humanities curriculum one selects for adolescents those topics which are of enduring human interest because of their importance in the human situation. The school can make a contribution in these areas precisely because of their central importance in our cultural tradition. No concession is being made: the teachers may be expected to share these interests with their students.

In a curriculum development conceived in these terms, what is the place of a central team?

Its main tasks would appear to be:

(1) to help to found a tradition which will support teachers working in this curriculum by helping them to select materials, by increasing their confidence in appropriate classroom strategies and by making secure their judgments of the quality of students' work;

(2) to provide, as examples, materials for use in the classroom which express this tradition and embody its standards;

(3) to evaluate the impact of its curriculum materials on the classroom situation, and the strengths and weaknesses of the teaching tradition developing round them.

It is important that the limitations of a central team should be recognized, both by the team and by those who may call upon it for service or advice.

A central team can appropriately provide materials, information and suggestions, but it should not intrude upon policy decisions. Even in an open style of teaching the school will reflect values, and the responsibility here lies with the head. The balance of the curriculum in a school and details of timetabling are also matters in which a central team should not intrude (except perhaps in the special case of trial or development schools). The team's job is to broaden, not to constrict, the range of choice open to policy-makers.

Moreover, a central team cannot in the nature of the case provide materials or suggestions for local and environmental studies or for school visits. These are intimately linked to local settings, and accordingly work at this level requires to be done in local teachers' centres. Work done by a team such as ours must evoke an energetic local response if it is to yield maximum dividends.

Finally, a team with a limited life, directed to conceive its task in terms of a specified number of years, cannot aspire to produce topical material. This is bound to fall to teachers' groups in development centres, whose efforts will, one hopes, be supported and supplemented by the enterprise of such agencies as publishers, television companies and makers of audio-visual materials of all kinds.

All too often curriculum innovation is seen as a problem of diffusing 'good' ideas. It is therefore worth stressing that in our view the approach to problems of curriculum development should be experimental. Until the project is in an advanced stage we shall have nothing to recommend to schools.

Working Paper No. 11 revealed that there are up and down the country groups of teachers experimenting or disposed to experiment with teaching in the broad area of the humanities. The central team has made contact with some forty development schools in which experiments of this kind will be mounted. The immediate task undertaken by the team is to support and co-ordinate the experiments in these schools so that they can yield the maximum of information for other teachers.

Two main positions will characterize these experiments.

First, they are an attempt to develop in the humanities a core curriculum element for average and below average adolescent pupils which unites them with the rest of mankind rather than separates them off, and which has about it a prospect of quality which will demand of these pupils the highest standards of work they will attain during their school careers. We are pursuing significance of content and quality of work.

Second, the teaching strategy will be enquiry-based. We take this to imply groups of pupils discussing issues in the light of evidence and under the guidance of the teacher. Distinctions may be drawn between instruction-based, discovery-based and enquiry-based teaching. Instruction-based teaching implies that the task in hand is the teacher's passing on to his pupils knowledge or skills of which he is master. In discovery-based teaching the teacher introduces his pupils into situations so selected or devised that they embody in implicit or hidden form principles or knowledge which he wishes them to learn. Thus, Cuisenaire rods embody numerical principles, and certain scientific 'experiments' used in educational settings reveal scientific principles. Instruction and discovery are appropriate in the classroom whenever the desirable outcome of teaching can be specified in some detail and is broadly the same for every pupil.

Where a curriculum area is in a divergent, rather than in a convergent, field, i.e. where there is no simple correct or incorrect outcome, but rather an emphasis on the individual responses and judgments of the students, the case for an enquiry-based approach is at its strongest. This is the situation in the humanities.

This basic strategy of classroom procedure can be argued, we maintain, from the nature of the content area. Considerations of professional ethics are also involved.

Each of the areas of study we have chosen involves highly controversial value judgments of a kind which divide opinion in our society, and this is bound to be so. It is just this controversial aspect of the work which offers the prospect of live significance; and conscientious teachers will quite properly feel diffidence in entering these areas unless their classroom strategy gives some assurance that the pupils will not have their horizons limited by their teacher's biases. Moreover, teachers are bound to find themselves working in areas of knowledge outside their own specialist qualifications and they ought to feel some reserve about playing an instructional role in this situation. A further consideration is that many of the subjects proposed for study may well be just those most likely to exacerbate the inter-generational and the inter-social class conflicts between teacher and pupil to which recent studies have drawn attention.

On all these grounds, it seems reasonable to assert that an enquiry-based strategy is demanded in the classroom when the school adopts a humanities curriculum as we have defined it. In short, enquiry is not simply a dispensable means to an end which could be reached by other routes.

The classroom strategy of enquiry is by no means new. Many of the ideas behind it can be seen in project work, for example. It is our view, however, that enquiry-based learning has seldom been entirely successful. Certainly, in the past, its adoption in the schools in response to fashion has sometimes led to a deterioration of quality. Teachers whose judgments were secure while they were working within an academic and instructional framework, have suffered from the lack of supporting tradition when they moved over to a different style of teaching. The pattern of traditional academic teaching is so familiar that it is easy to forget the profound theoretical roots which lie beneath it.

Even the shift of role which is asked of a teacher as he moves from instruction to enquiry and discussion is likely to prove demanding. The teacher has to abandon his role as imparter of information and the dominant and didactic style which often goes with it. Instead he is asked to become the chairman of a committee of enquiry or a discussion group. We have enough experience of student complaints about the conduct of seminars in higher education to be aware that the role of a rigorous, but patient and unobtrusive, critic is a difficult one for the instructor or lecturer to fill.

Given the enquiry base, and the difficulties it presents, we believe that the best chance of developing a core tradition of disciplined teaching lies in the exploration of the possibilities opened up by a type of discussion which is not so much an exchange of views as an interpretation of evidence. We start therefore from a model of the classroom situation in which the input of information comes not through the teacher, but through materials which demand critical interpretation. We hope that the close interpretation of evidence can strengthen and stiffen discussion so as to provide a group experience which is a firm centre for an enquiry-based approach. That established, we can explore the possibilities offered by individual and group investigations which feed into discussion, and various types of pupils' work which can develop out of it.

It is almost impossible for teachers to accumulate rapidly enough evidence to support work of this kind. Hence our emphasis on the provision of materials as the second task of the project.

A carefully indexed store of materials is being accumulated, and lessons in material-gathering, storage and indexing have already been learnt. It is hoped that by the end of the project this work will have led to the development of a model for the organization of resources centres in teachers' centres and in schools.

From this growing archive, collections of material will be selected and edited for the use of development schools. The collections will include factual prose, maps, statistical tables, diagrams, fictional prose, poetry, drama, photographs, reproductions of paintings, cartoons and tape-recordings. Such collections will constitute banks of material on which the teachers can draw as they embark upon this style of teaching; but they are banks which ask for further deposits of materials found by the teachers themselves. They will provide the teacher with resources for experimentation, opening up a range of possibilities rather than confining.

The structuring of these collections of material is of great importance. The collections must be logically coherent, adapted to the proposed classroom strategy and yet flexible. We hope to break down each of our areas of enquiry into a number of points for discussion which evoke interest in the classroom and are also significant and appropriate. One or two pieces of material will raise each point, and these will be surrounded by a balanced collection of relevant evidence bearing on the point.

Cinema film is important in this kind of teaching, and is probably essential for average pupils. A film hire service is being built up, carefully keyed into the structure of the collections to be offered to schools.

One of the most acute problems is that of controlling the suitability of the materials, bearing in mind the age and wide range of ability of the pupils with whom we are concerned. First, there is the problem of understanding, which is crudely expressed as that of reading levels. Second, there is that of handling sensitive material, which expresses itself crudely as the problem of censorship. At the experimental stage, some, but not too much, of our material ought really to be too difficult for the ablest of our pupils. Only in this way can we establish a ceiling. By the same token, some of our offerings must be censored by the majority of teachers.

In the case of reading difficulty the problem is made more acute by a wide divergence of view among experienced teachers and by the practical problem of finding enough simple and direct evidence in the time at our disposal. In the face of these problems, we have adopted a compromise strategy. First, we hope to aim initially at the average—at CSE and immediately below—and subsequently to enlist the help of a large number of teachers in order to adapt down the ability range as far as we can while maintaining acceptable quality. Second, we hope to include a wide range of levels of difficulty in our trial materials.

In 1968–9 development schools will begin to work with the first collections on war; education; the family; and relations between the sexes. As soon as work begins in the schools we shall face the problem of reporting and evaluating it.

This problem has three main aspects. Feed-back evaluation of the materials and the teaching strategy must reach the project team so that they can adapt their work in the light of experience. Evidence must be presented to teachers so that they can evaluate what is offered to them and decide whether it has a potential in their own school setting. In particular, they must answer for themselves three key questions: (1) What range of opportunities do the materials open up in the classroom? (2) What difficulties and dangers do they present? (3) What outcomes in children's work are appropriate? Finally, we must at least point the way towards the objective measurement of some of the effects of this style of humanities teaching.

Feed-back to the team is fairly simply arranged. Teachers will be asked to complete a form on each piece of material they use. A schools liaison officer will keep the team informed of major developments and problems in teaching. Members of the team will visit schools using the materials.

The problem of reporting the experiment in a form which makes it accessible to teachers' professional judgment will be handled by a schools study officer. He will mount himself and commission from others case studies of as many of the trial schools as can be covered. These case studies will report both administrative arrangements and teaching strategies. Children's work, bad as well as good, will be collected. Tape-recordings will be used and transcribed and video-tape observation of classrooms will be mounted. The case studies will, it is anticipated, be published as a series and supported by films made from video-tape.

This will expose the work of the project to public criticism on the part of teachers.

On the basis of the close study of the teaching process and of the questions which teachers pose, it is hoped to formulate hypotheses about the range of effects in the classroom, and to make specific recommendations regarding testing. It is not possible to go farther than this within the three year span of the project. Tests in trial schools are of doubtful validity as a basis for prediction of results once the materials are used by schools not in contact with the project team.

The evaluation procedures adopted will have to be reported and discussed more fully at a later date. Complex theoretical issues are involved, particularly in our reserve about the measurement of effects against objectives specified by the central team. This is not the occasion to examine them in detail.

It is worth emphasising, in conclusion, the experimental and hypothetical nature of the project. We are working in a difficult and complex area where relatively high risks are justified by the prospect of substantial rewards. It will often be necessary to co-operate with teachers in the definition of problems before it is possible to set about solving them. The appropriate attitude for the task is tentative, sceptical and experimental. In short it is important to assert without apology, that the project is concerned with *research*.

Reference

1 Peters, R. S. 'A theory of classical education.' *Didaskalos*, vol. 2, no. 2, 1967, pp. 3–11.

Robert Glaser

II:17 Adapting the elementary school curriculum to individual performance

The director of the Learning Research and Development Center at the University of Pittsburgh, Robert Glaser, describes the curriculum development project which the Center has been undertaking in a local Pittsburgh elementary school. The focus of the project is on the individualization of instruction. Glaser looks in detail at the following components of the project: (1) the analysis and definition of a continuum of educational objectives; (2) the development of assessment and diagnostic procedures to monitor individual learners' progress through the individualized curriculum; (3) the design of appropriate instructional materials in various media.

One of the programs of the Learning Research and Development Center at the University of Pittsburgh (one of the R & D centers primarily sponsored by the U.S. Office of Education) has been attempting to design procedures, materials, and an environment in an elementary school so that both research and development can take place on the process of adapting to individual differences. Over the past few years, under the direction of John Bolvin, the initial procedure which is under constant revision has come to be called 'individually prescribed instruction'. In this paper I should like to describe our beginning approach.

In general, it is assumed that certain requirements for adapting to individual differences have to be met for the design of an individualized system. These requirements are the following:

1 The conventional boundaries of grade levels and arbitrary time units for subject matter coverage need to be redesigned to permit each student to work at his actual level of accomplishment in a

subject matter area, and to permit him to move ahead as soon as he masters the prerequisites for the next level of advancement.

2 Well-defined sequences of progressive, behaviorally defined objectives in various subject areas need to be established as guidelines for setting up a student's program of study. The student's achievement is defined by his position along this progression of advancement.

3 A student's progress through a curriculum sequence must be monitored by adequate methods and instruments for assessing his abilities and accomplishments so that a teaching program can be adapted to his requirements.

4 Students must be taught and provided with appropriate instructional materials so that they acquire increasing competence in self-directed learning. To accomplish this, the teacher must provide the student with standards of performance so that he can evaluate his own attainment, and teaching activities must be directed by individual learner accomplishment.

5 Special professional training must be provided to school personnel so that they can accomplish the evaluation, diagnosis, and guidance of student performance that is required to organize instruction for individualized learning—as contrasted to the total-class management of learning.

6 The individualization of instruction requires that the teacher attend to and utilize detailed information about each student in order to design appropriate instructional programs. To assist the teacher in processing this information, it seems likely that schools will take advantage of efficient data-processing systems.

The technicalities for designing and implementing a system with these requirements and the necessary teacher, administrative, and material needs, are demanding. The questions involved in measuring individual differences in learning and performance, making adequate student diagnoses, building appropriate learning materials, and matching student differences to instructional alternatives need to be formulated and answered. With this in mind, I shall discuss some major aspects and indicate some of the questions that have been raised in our attempts to individualize an elementary school curriculum.

First, some things need to be said about the analysis and definition of a continuum of educational objectives. While the objectives of our curriculum designer may not be another's, one of the most important factors that can contribute to improvement in educational attainment in an individualized system is the analysis and specification of the desired outcomes of learning. In the interest of brevity the following points concerning this first step are made without elaboration :

1 The definition of instructional objectives instructs the curriculum designer and the teacher how to proceed. Vague specification of the desired competence level leaves the teacher with little concrete information about what to look for in student performance and about what to provide to the student to attain or surpass this performance.

2 The interaction between the specification of objectives and experience in teaching frequently provides a basis for a redefinition of objectives. The process of clarifying goals, working toward them, appraising progress, reexamining the objectives, modifying the instructional procedures to achieve goals, and clarifying the objectives themselves in the light of experience and data, should be a continuous process.

3 Regardless of the way a subject matter is structured, there is usually present some hierarchy of subobjectives which indicates that certain performances must be present as a basis for learning subsequent performances. Absence of the specification of prerequisite competence in a sequence of instruction dooms many students to failure.

4 Knowledge of objectives by the student gives him a goal to attain; such knowledge is instructive and motivating. It permits the student to monitor his partial successes and failures and to adjust and organize learning resources for himself.

5 As in other lines of endeavor, teachers require frequent information about the results of their work so that they can adjust their practices accordingly. Teachers need standards by which to judge themselves and by which society can judge their effectiveness.

6 The exercise of specifying objectives points up the inadequacies and omissions in a curriculum. The fear of many educators that the detailed specification of objectives limits them to only simple behaviors which can be forced into measurable and observable terms is an incorrect notion. If, indeed, complex reasoning and open-

Table 1 : Description of Sele

Unit No.	Level	Unit Label	Short Description	Approximat Conventiona Grade Leve
1	A	Numeration	Counting to ten.	
2	A	Addition	Addition of sums of six.	
3	A	Fractions	Identification of $\frac{1}{2}$ of sets.	1
4	B	Numeration	Counting to 100; ordinals to 10th.	
5	B	Addition	Addition to sums of 12.	
•				
11	C	Numeration	Counting and skip counting to 200.	
12	C	Place Value	Recognizes place values and concepts of 'greater than; less than'.	
13	C	Addition	Two-digit sums without carrying.	2
14	C	Subtraction	Two-digit differences without borrowing.	
15	C	COP*	Selection of operation to solve problems.	
•				
23	D	Numeration	Counting and skip counting to 1,000.	
24	D	Place Value	Makes place value charts to thousands.	
25	D	Addition	Begins addition with carrying.	
26	D	Subtraction	Begins subtraction with borrowing.	3–4
27	D	Mult†	Begins multiplication as repeated addition with factors to 5.	
28	D	Division	Begins division as partition with divisors to 5.	
29	D	COP*	Problems requiring many processes.	
•				
37	E	Numeration	Identifies odd and even numbers; converts mixed decimal fractions.	
38	E	Place Value	Place value to millions; begins exponents.	
39	E	Addition	Addition with carrying to 4 digits.	
40	E	Subtraction	Subtraction with borrowing to 3 digits.	4–5
41	E	Mult†	Uses associative and distributive principles and does simple multiplication with carrying.	
42	E	Division	Uses ladder algorithm for division.	

* COP stands for Combination of Proces

Unit No.	Level	Unit Label	Short Description	Approximate Conventional Grade Level
43	E	COP*	Solves problems using n̲ as variable.	
.				
.				
.				
51	F	Numeration	Round numbers; identifies prime numbers.	
52	F	Place Value	Manipulates exponents to ten cubed.	
53	F	Addition	Adds large sums to seven digits.	
54	F	Subtraction	Subtracts to seven digits.	
55	F	Mult†	Multiplication with 3 digits.	5–6
56	F	Division	Division algorithm with no remainders; simple division with remainders.	
57	F	COP*	Performs multiple operations with number pairs.	
.				
.				
65	G	Numeration	Uses prime numbers to factor composite numbers; operations in bases 5 and 10.	
66	G	Place Value	Charts numbers by place value in base 5.	6
67	G	Addition	Adds positive and negative numbers.	
68	G	Subtraction	Subtracts negative and positive numbers.	
69	G	Mult†	Multiplies numbers in exponential form.	
.				
.				
76	H	Numeration	Identifies numerals in base 2, 3, and 8.	
77	H	Place Value	Place value charts in other bases.	
78	H	Add & Sub Other Bases	Adds and subtracts in bases 2, 3, 5, 8.	
79	H	Addition	Adds with negative powers of ten.	
80	H	Subtraction	Subtracts with negative powers of ten.	
81	H	Mult & Div Other Bases	Multiplies and divides in bases 2, 3, 5, 8.	7
82	H	Mult†	Multiplies with decimals and negative numbers.	
83	H	Division	Divides decimal numbers, positive and negative numbers; calculates square roots.	
84	H	COP*	Solves word problems with skills learned.	
.				
.				
.				
5				

lt. stands for Multiplication

endedness are desirable aspects of human behavior, then this needs to be a recognized and measurable goal. Overly general objectives may force us to settle for what can be easily expressed and measured.

In our project, also frequently referred to as the 'Oakleaf Project' after the name of the elementary school in the Baldwin–Whitehall school district in suburban Pittsburgh where we started the procedure of individually prescribed instruction, the kindergarten through sixth-grade mathematics curriculum has identified 430 specific instructional objectives. These objectives are grouped into 88 units. Each unit comprises an instructional entity which the student works through at any one time; on the average there are 5 objectives per unit, with a range of 1 to 14. A set of units consisting of different subject areas in mathematics comprises a level; levels are labeled with letters A through H, and can be thought of as roughly comparable to a school grade level. Table 1 provides a content outline of the organization of the curriculum units. . . .

A second major requirement in an individualized program is assessment and diagnosis of student performance so that the amount and kind of instruction can be adapted to the student's particular requirements. From this point of view, testing and teaching are inseparable aspects and not two different enterprises as one might be led to believe by current practices in education. Frequent information about student performance is used as the basis on which the teacher decides on the next instructional step; and equally important, it also serves as feedback to the student. It is also invaluable data for the design and redesign of teaching materials.

The kind of measurement required for these purposes forces a distinction between performance measurement and aptitude measurement. The instruments used to measure performance are specifically concerned with the properties of present behavior as they are related to the requirements for deciding on subsequent instructional steps. It seems easier, in a sense, to predict the next moment in time in a lesson sequence than to predict long-range performance, which is a task usually set for aptitude measurements. It is possible that measures predictive of immediate learning success are different from those employed for more long-range prediction; as an example, some of the factor studies of changing ability constellations over learning suggest that this may be the case.

The testing procedure so far designed under the direction of

Richard C. Cox, with the evaluation back-up of C. M. Lindvall, is oriented toward subject matter mastery. For every unit in mathematics there is a pretest and a posttest. A pretest samples the various objectives in the unit and is diagnostic enough to pinpoint mastery or the lack of it in the various component skills. A posttest assesses the material that a student has been taught and is essentially an alternate form of the pretest. For each objective within the unit there is a curriculum-embedded test which is part of the instructional sequence. These curriculum-embedded tests measure performance not only on the objective on which the student has been working, but also include test exercises on the next objective that the student is likely to work on. The notion here is that if a lesson is taught well, the student will learn not only the present lesson, but will be able to master exercises in the immediate subsequent skill. It is a special challenge for lesson writers to make this 'testing out' of an objective as frequent an occurrence as possible.

At the beginning of a school year, a student takes one or more wide-band placement tests which consist of sample items measuring the objectives in each of the units within a level of work. On the basis of his last year's performance, an approximation is made of the student's level of achievement, and testing begins from there. The student is tested over a range from what he knows to what he has not yet learned. Depending on his background, and depending to some extent on how hierarchical the achievement objectives in a subject matter are, the student's performance may be more or less cumulative. In the first year at Oakleaf, the achievement assessed by the placement tests was spotty, that is, areas of mastery and areas of weakness ranged up and down the continuum. The data from the placement tests in subsequent years show a more cumulative pattern of achievement, this may be a function of the individualized curriculum.

Tests are seen as part of instruction, and the students look forward to them because they get immediate information about whether they need additional work in a unit or can move on to new work. The overall philosophy of this built-in testing program is that at any point in time the student's performance is so monitored that a detailed assessment is available of his performance and progress. The continuous recording and updating of this performance data seems to make special testing procedures unnecessary. As we get better in designing a curriculum which adapts to individual differences, I suspect that the test-taking aspects generally present in education will diminish, as perhaps will the test-anxious or test-sensitive student.

Consider now some of the questions about testing that arise and that need to be answered: one point is that initial placement tests take an undue amount of time to administer, especially to new students entering an individualized program. Some form of sequential testing should be helpful here, considering procedures with and without the use of a computer terminal. More fundamental than this, however, is the question of analysis of the dimensions of individualization that can be measured and are useful for instructional decision-making. At the present time, the measures obtained in the mathematics curriculum are measures of achievement in the various units and objectives, with some further indices of the rate at which a student has been achieving mastery and the amount of practice and review he has required. Little use is made, at present, of measures of general intelligence or aptitude which have seemed difficult to relate to instructional decisions in the elementary school. From the placement tests no measures are obtained of subtle aspects of learning style, but perhaps reliable measures of this can be found. It is our general contention that the most useful measures of learning characteristics related to instructional decisions will result from indices obtained from monitoring the student's learning characteristics and performance over a period of time in the curriculum.

Another problem is the following: as a student goes through the units in the mathematics curriculum, a posttest mastery criterion of 85 percent is employed, that is, a student must achieve this level of performance before he moves on to the next unit. The setting of a criterion level, however, is an experimental question which needs investigating. The question is, assuming a reasonably cumulative curriculum where new learning depends upon previous learning, do different units and differing students require a uniform level of proficiency? If too high a criterion is set, a student can spend too much time mastering fine points of one unit, while he might be beginning the next. A bright student might begin to learn multiplication while still becoming proficient in the fundamentals of addition and subtraction, and in this way develop a richer concept of addition; another student may require more detailed mastery of fundamentals before he moves on. The questions involved seem more complex than we had originally supposed.

The accumulation and maintenance of the day-to-day records required for individualized instruction is a sizable enterprise for a school. In the initial years of the Oakleaf project, we have been accomplishing this by hand. Each teacher has the assistance of an aide for individualized classes, and there is a data-processing room with a staff of clerks who receive information from teachers and teacher assistants, process it, and return it to the classroom. After using this simulated computer system for two years, we designed an initial computerized data-processing system. At the present time, in cooperation with the General Learning Corporation, we are investigating a computer management system to assist in researching and implementing individualized instruction. In its initial operation there is a teacher terminal at the school which the teacher can interrogate for information; there is a terminal back in the laboratory which can be used to write programs, to analyze various aspects of student performance, to try out various data-reduction routines, and to analyze the instructional effectiveness of various curriculum units so that they can be revised when necessary. The particularly challenging research aspect of a computer management system is the task of matching relevant measures of student performance with appropriate curriculum methods and materials in order to provide the teacher with assistance in preparing instructional prescriptions for each student....

So far, the components of a system for adapting to individual differences that have been listed are specification of objectives, measurement and assessment of these objectives, and the monitoring of student performance and progress. The system also requires learning and teaching. The primary task to be faced here is that instruction involves teaching to the student and not to the classroom group. That the problem is not a trivial one is attested to by statements of teachers who participate in individualized instruction; these teachers express some frustration when they point out that they have been trained to teach a class and have had much less experience in teaching individuals. Another sign of the problem involved is that instructional materials, especially in the elementary school, consist of texts and workbooks designed to be used with group directions and group-paced exercises.

Adapting instructional materials and procedures to individual differences is a function of both student behavior and the nature of the subject matter being taught. It is important to emphasize at this point that individualization is accomplished by designing a particular curriculum for the needs of a student, the word 'needs' being used operationally in terms of student characteristics that we can reliably assess and that are relevant to instructional decisions. Adapting to individual requirements does not at all imply that a student necessarily works alone or in any particular mode or setting. In the course of individualized instruction, students may be taught by lecture, by programmed texts, by group discussion, by group projects, or by teaching machines. The essential notion is that individual requirements are matched to appropriate instructional procedures. For much of mathematics a self-instructional situation may be suitable; it may be less suitable for various components of the social studies and the language arts. The individualization of instructional procedures certainly involves a variety of modes of learning.

In the elementary school, general education curriculum objectives are more or less the same for all students so the differentiation of learning goals may not be an appropriate procedure for adapting to individual differences. While the goals are the same, the pattern of the specific subgoals may differ to the extent that different students may work through a sequence of different topics to reach the same goal. In this way, some adaptation can take place by individualizing instructional tasks. Individualization also takes place by allowing for different learning rates involving different amounts of repetition, and materials which permit smaller or larger instructional steps. These two modes of individualization are the easiest to implement on the basis of student performance. Other modes of adapting to individual differences involving different media and different instructional methods are more difficult to implement because we know very little about the relationship between measures of student behavior and the learning effectiveness of these various means and media of instruction.

However, I should like to suggest that a basic principle in designing instructional materials and environments for individualized learning is to provide situations which are highly responsive to the behavior of the student. It is well-known that learning occurs because the learner acts on his instructional environment, changes it, and is changed in turn by the consequences of his actions. As learning proceeds, new consequences in the environment are established with which the learner interacts. It is the management of the contingencies between student performance and environmental change that is the fundamental task of the teacher and the tools with which he is provided. This intimate dynamic relationship has been the aspiration of the work in programmed instruction and should be the goal of systems for individualizing instruction. An environment highly responsive to the student's endeavors seems to be capable of resulting in the effective attainment of competence, but is also motivating in the sense that it reinforces the kind of behavior that is alluded to when we use words like 'developing a sense of exploration and curiosity', 'a sense of inquiry', and 'a sense of control over one's own education'. To date at the Oakleaf school, teachers have been provided with an initial set of materials and procedures from which they can select in prescribing a student's instruction. By selecting these instructional means on the basis of the student's performance record and general behavior, the teacher, in essence, can make up a unique set of activities for each student. The decision process intervening between student assessment and the assignment of instructional activities is the essential task of individualized instruction that needs to be studied and understood.

Alice Miel

II:18 Reassessment of the curriculum—why?

Education is dominated by fashions—team teaching, the project method, etc.—which come and go continuously. The curriculum designer would be helped if some pattern could be discerned in these movements of educational thought. Alice Miel puts forward three possible patterns: (1) movement down a long road, as exemplified in statements such as education is moving from emphasis on the group to emphasis on the individual; (2) the swing of the pendulum; (3) movement in a spiral. Miel concludes that the spiral pattern is the most useful and most accurate.

There seems to be enough confusion about education today to warrant a careful reassessment of past events and current happenings. Such an appraisal should aid curriculum specialists in planning strategies in the years ahead. Let us, then, examine the phenomenon of educational thought moving from emphasis to emphasis. Hopefully, by gaining perspective, we may obtain guidance in making our individual decisions.

How new is the phenomenon?

First, are we dealing with a new or a familiar phenomenon? In this connection, there comes to mind a cartoon appearing in the *Michigan Educational Journal* in the twenties. A hapless educator is pictured as an Arab riding on a camel through a desert, with various inviting mirages—the Herbartian steps, the socialized recitation, the project method—appearing ahead of him. The viewer of the cartoon is invited to believe that each highly advertised idea in education fades away without a trace as surely as a mirage disappears when one draws near. Although his pessimism seems unwarranted, our cartoonist of forty years ago apparently was quite familiar with shifts in emphasis on the educational scene.

As one reads convention proceedings and reports of educational commissions in this century, he gains the impression of concentrated attention, first here, then there. Economy of time, scientific movement, aims and objectives, activity movement—these are labels for consuming interests of various educators for a decade or more. Any search of *Education Index* will quickly show up peaks of attention in the literature to one facet of education after another. Intercultural education waxed and waned in the forties. Articles on team teaching may show a similar rise and fall in the sixties.

It is not new for people in our profession to attempt to redress a balance by compensating for an underemphasis or correcting an ensuing overemphasis.

Who is responsible?

Who is responsible for the phenomenon of movement from emphasis to emphasis? Kircher believes that the school of education is the source. In a recent address he declared:

'There appears to be a tendency for professional schools of education to be overcome by recurrent cycles of certainty. For a period of time they exaggerate the adequacy of some illuminating insight to correct the ills of their infinitely complex enterprise. Some of these grow into movements, some simply become prevailing ideas in the profession for a time, but every decade or so the climate of teacher education appears to be changed by them. They all have one characteristic in common. They oversimplify our problem and thereby catch the popular imagination.'[1]

The speaker goes on with a long list: 'We have had the project method, the child-centered school, the community-centered school, correlated studies, unified studies and the core curriculum. ...' He brings his review up to the present with 'the teaching machine and team teaching'.

There is no doubt that professors of education did do a lion's share of the lecturing and writing in the first half of this century. They both reflected and influenced the successive shifts in emphasis to which Kircher refers. Increasingly in the last ten years, however, education professors have been joined by two other groups urging their own reforms in education. One group contains professors in the academic fields reasserting their interest in the curriculum. The other group is made up of speakers and writers addressing themselves to the public, usually through one of the media of mass communication.

This change in the cast of characters calling for a look at a favorite concern in education has had two observable results already. First, the demands for attention are coming thicker and faster and with more force because of saturation techniques familiar in the field of advertising. The layman in particular tends to oversimplify the problems to which he responds even as Kircher has accused the school of education of doing. Second, the professor of education and his colleagues in educational organizations and in state and local school systems are finding it more difficult to be heard, either because the competing voices are so loud and numerous or because their own voices may not be carrying ringing messages just now. The two results add up to considerable confusion for both educators and the public.

Is there an understandable pattern?

Is there a pattern in all of this movement? If so, we shall be helped with prediction and individual decision-making through grasping the nature of the pattern. Three alternatives seem worth exploring.

Movement down a long road

One possible view is that change of emphasis in education is like movement down a long road, whereby arrangements or practices once considered adequate are left behind forever. All that is abandoned becomes the traditional. The new which is in sight is the progressive or modern or right way.

This view reflects the either-or type of thinking so difficult to avoid in human affairs. It was especially prevalent in the thirties when there was a determined revolt against the rigid and the meaningless in the curriculum. A small pamphlet, *Curriculum trends*, published in 1935, offers a fitting illustration of the point.[2] In a two-column arrangement are shown the traditional practices being left behind and the progressive practices being approached. On the facing page are a few items chosen for illustration.

Even though these selections are not entirely fair to the pamphlet as a whole, they do give evidence that educators attempting to influence thought in the thirties fell into the error of believing that it was necessary to be *against* one item of a pair in order to be *for* the other. Perhaps it is easier for us today to see that we do not have to give up content values, the learning of skills, or scheduled reading

FROM:	TO:
Content values of curriculum	Process values of curriculum
Learning skills	Building up appreciations and enjoyments
Curriculum based on subject matter	Child interest; experience leading to new purposes, meanings, insights, skills, integrations
Perfection emphasized	Emphasis on the growing process
Over stimulation and overmature content	Growth needs and corresponding maturity levels; avoidance of evil effects of failure, strain, fatigue
Dictated, prescribed and controlled learning	Self-planning and self-direction; freedom to discover, explore, think, play
Scheduled reading periods	Leisure reading and story hour for social enjoyment
Arithmetic texts and workbooks	Much informal practical arithmetic based on experience
Mass teaching	Developing creative, dynamic, integrated personalities; development of individuality
Subject matter and skills	Growth in behavior and conduct
Question-answer recitation	Children taking initiative, making and carrying out plans; group discussions, conferences, conversation on common interests
Organization of curriculum into school subjects	Organization of curriculum to promote the most effective learning procedures even though it means abandonment of present school subjects

periods in order to achieve process values, appreciations, purposeful experience, and leisure time reading.

We have not entirely outgrown either-or thinking, however. The same format of *from* and *to* is used to make a point in *Schools for the Sixties*, recently published by the Project on Instruction of the NEA. Harold B. Gores is quoted as having given 'an interesting progression in educational emphases that underlie new concepts of space [in designing school buildings]'.[3] Again the reader is asked to choose *either* this value *or* that.

Examples are:

FROM:	TO:
The group	The individual
Memory	Inquiry
Self-contained classroom	Self-contained school
Scheduled classes	Appointments and independent learning
Teacher as general practitioner	Teacher as clinical specialist (member of team)
Teaching as telling	Teaching as guiding

The view that we move *from* one emphasis *to* another with no return for a second look does not seem to describe events with any accuracy. It does not account for the fact that items on both sides of a pair seem to come back periodically for serious reconsideration, that the traditional and the progressive have a way of changing places over the decades. For example, the self-contained classroom was a hard-won innovation in the elementary school not too many years ago, while departmentalization was the outmoded arrangement that forefront educators worked to discredit. Now the self-contained classroom is dubbed a back number as team organization becomes the favorite. The view of movement down a long road with no return would have us believe that both the departmentalized elementary school and the school organized around the self-contained classroom have had their last chance to be considered as components in a solution to an educational problem.

The swing of a pendulum

A second and favorite way of picturing the movement of educational thought is to liken it to the swing of a pendulum back and forth in the same groove. According to this view the weight of opinion may go from all phonics in teaching to no phonics and back again to all phonics. Opinion may shift from favoring homogeneous grouping to heterogeneous grouping and back again to the same original position with no variation and no learning from previous experience. At first glance this view appears to be near to the truth, providing as it does for reconsideration of an abandoned position in education. However, upon closer inspection, it becomes clear that educational thought does not move in the same well-worn rut. Even though attention seems to refocus on an old position, more careful investigation will show that the new version is different in many ways. Thus, the pendulum swing is too crude an analogy to describe actual patterns of movement. Furthermore, this view, too, rests upon either-or thinking.

The upward and outward spiral

A third way of viewing the path of change in educational thought is to think of a spiral which ascends, enlarging as it climbs. In common with the pendulum swing, this view allows for renewed attention to a problem and line of solution which have been neglected for a time. The difference in the spiral view is that it accounts for the fact that proposals made at a later point in educational history usually are much more refined, with wisdom distilled from experience at both sides of the spiral built into them. At each new point on the upward and outward spiral the concepts are clearer and the language of education is more precise.

While it would be possible to trace any number of specifics around this spiraling path, we may use as a clarifying illustration an earlier example—the swing from emphasis on phonics to de-emphasis of this approach in teaching reading. At present phonics is again strongly in the picture, but this time it is taking its place *along with other approaches*. Much was learned from trying out various ways of teaching children to read in the period when educators were rebelling against overdependence on phonics. As a result, the teacher of reading has a much broader repertoire now that renewed attention is being given to finding an appropriate place for phonics in the whole scheme.

Because this way of picturing the pattern of movement from emphasis to emphasis in education squares most closely with observed events, it is adopted for purposes of analysis here.

It is important to recognize at once that any analogy will fail to cover all features of the reality to be explained. In this case, there is the added limitation that the analogy is a deliberate abstraction of a direction of movement from a mass of details. We are talking about the net effect of having a preponderance of attention from many speakers and writers focused on a common concern whether they are for or against a particular solution. We are omitting the minority voices asking for equal time for another concern. Accordingly, the possibility of error through over-simplification is sizable. Nevertheless, the value of perspectives in understanding the present and in predicting the course of events is so great that the risk seems worth taking.

Testing the spiral pattern

If a spiral pattern is accurate as a view of movement of educational thought, it should lend itself to being tested with the major curriculum threads. ... Let us proceed with such a test, confining ourselves largely to events in the twentieth century. Throughout, it must be remembered that positions popular in the literature were not carried out to the same extent in actual practice.

Knowledge and the curriculum

One thread which may be traced up the spiral is the way knowledge has been organized at various stages of curriculum development. Over centuries the educators preceding us had labored to organize subject matter into teachable subjects, ordered into sequences and packaged for teaching to young people of various ages. For the greater part of our educational history the separate subject has been the only known way to organize the curriculum. It was not until the end of the last century that there was any real attempt to grope toward other patterns of organization. The first proposal was to correlate subjects similar in content, while maintaining the boundaries around each subject. After 1915 came the suggestion to break down barriers between allied subjects and to create broad fields such as social studies, general mathematics, and general science. By the nineteen thirties the unit of work cutting across subject boundaries was being highly recommended, and an influential book, *Integration*, was published in that decade.[4]

During the period when curriculum integration was the keynote of the day, the separate, logically organized subject was in ill repute.

Teachers were urged to draw on the various subjects for material 'to solve the problem of the unit'. On several counts the forms of curriculum integration advocated in this period were somewhat impractical. First, knowledge was not organized in such a way that it was easy to draw upon it for problem solving. Second, skills of helping young people build order and system out of scattered knowledge, were not well developed. Third, there was confusion between 'external' integration, or unification of subject matter, and 'internal' integration, or integration of personality. Nevertheless, it was useful to have this experience with different approaches to integration. One of the most important gains from this period was the insight that the individual can deal with many separate experiences and put them together into meaningful and orderly wholes if he has the right kind of help. Educators could return to consideration of the separate subject without feeling extreme guilt.

The swing onward toward interest in the separate disciplines which we are seeing today had its roots in the unrest among subject specialists and certain curriculum generalists who were not being listened to during the thirties and forties. One protesting voice was that of Isaac L. Kandel, who wrote as follows in concluding a forty-page *History of the Curriculum* in 1935:

'How integration takes place psychologically is not yet clear nor has a case been made out for maladjustment of normals due to compartmentalization of subjects. Integration seems to be advocated as a general method at a time when the value of general method seems to have been discarded and when the theory [is] that each subject or body of content has its own characteristic method. These criticisms do not exclude the possibility of integrating allied subjects from time to time, but to talk in general of activity programs or of integrated curricula is to perpetuate and to continue the defect with which American education is too frequently charged—that it has emphasized methods and external mechanics rather than content.'[5]

Even before Sputnik there were beginning attempts to secure better understanding of separate disciplines on which school subjects were based. At the present time, when we are, as it were, on the 'separateness' side of the spiral once more, the concerns are not the same as at the lower level when the separate subject was in favor. The work currently in progress on the essential nature and the key concepts of the separate disciplines may well supply the help missing when pioneer attempts at curriculum integration were being made in the thirties. When the separate disciplines are better understood, there may be a sounder basis for helping individuals discover systems of thought and new interrelationships.

The foundation is now being laid for a new stage as yet unnamed but which will represent new attempts at a curriculum synthesis. When the swing completes a half circle to a predicted point where the fitting together of a total curriculum is once more a prime concern of many, it will be possible to build upon the former experience with integration together with the new understanding of the nature of the separate pieces making up the whole of knowledge.

The individual and the group
A second thread which has had a long history is a swing of emphasis from individual to group in teaching methodology. In the early nineteenth century it was common for teachers to prepare copies of practice material for each pupil and to hear lessons individually. Of course, the teachers of that day could not be credited with many concessions to individual differences. The invention of the blackboard opened up a period of group teaching, which led eventually (if we may take a bird's-eye view of only mountain peaks and valleys) to such abuses of mass teaching that there were many protests. Attention began to swing once more toward teaching the individual. By that time the field of educational psychology had developed to such an extent that the profession had at its disposal considerably more information on the nature of individual differences. Useful ways to teach children in groups, which had been discovered, were also carried forward in the proposals made. Thus the new emphasis on the individual was at a higher level than before.

During the depression years, when interest developed in helping children become more skilful, involved members of groups, new information on the dynamics of groups was available. The profession also could carry into the new movement better understanding of the individual within the group. At each new turn of the spiral the practices advocated could be more sophisticated, for educators could look back on the experiences had at previous positions on the lower levels of the spiral and could build into a new whole the useful residue from each previous stage.

The individual and the society
A third thread has been a swing in emphasis in the curriculum between concern for the individual and concern for the society. One can trace a swing toward and away from the child-centered curriculum thus: subject-centered (with the purpose of preserving the

cultural heritage) to child-centered (with the purpose of meeting the needs and interests of the whole child) to society-centered (with the purpose of promoting social reconstruction). . . .

How may the spiral view be used?

If it is accurate to picture the general trend of educational thought as moving in such a spiral pattern, at the very least we are aided in seeing some interconnectedness and indeed some progression in events in a single series. By placing several series on the same spiral, with an eye to chronology, we might arrive at a spiral-shaped time line. Such a time line might have the same usefulness to the curriculum specialist that the map does to the geographer in that relationships not hitherto perceived might become apparent. The new currents moving in to influence the course of events and the mutually inconsistent cross currents ever competing for the limelight might show up with new clarity.

By examining recurring emphases in a systematic way, we may be helped to locate persisting problems in need of intensive study and may gain new insights as to promising lines of solution. The curriculum field would benefit from the development of a sound conceptual framework which might move us toward a consistent theoretical base for our operations.

The spiral view should also be useful to the individual educator who wishes to influence the course of events and is trying to decide where and how to invest his own time and energy. Three overall stances seem feasible. A person may decide, in general, to swing with the major currents of thought, thus having experience in developing positions on both sides of the spiral. Such a decision might mean, for example, willingness to be strongly committed to efforts to improve school organization in one period and curriculum organization in another, with a readiness to turn attention once again to new proposals on school organization in still a third period of time. Within such a stance, it would be possible to be a pioneer, leading the procession, or to be one who rushes to join the procession as soon as it becomes clear that the movement is a safely popular one, or yet to be one who follows along with only moderate commitment, for any number of defensible or not so defensible reasons.

A second stance might be to adopt one side of the spiral to which to maintain general loyalty. For example, an educator might choose always to support efforts to keep an eye on the individual to be educated whatever may be the nature of the proposals in current favor. Within such a stance also, it is possible to be a leader, preparing the way for the next swing to a higher level. But a person may choose instead to be a diehard, hanging on grimly to a consistently held position and refusing to reconsider it in any major way.

It may be noted that within *each* stance it is possible to exhibit either-or thinking. The individual who clings to a position and merely waits for a return to his way of solving problems is denying the worth of any developments not in obvious harmony with his own views. He prefers to disregard intervening events and thus will be unprepared to understand the new form his own position will be assuming when it reappears on a higher level of the spiral. The individual who abandons all interest in a position as soon as it grows unpopular and becomes completely absorbed in a new cause will also be having an incomplete experience, ignoring as he does the wisdom accumulated at the preceding stage. He, too, is *excluding* important factors from consideration.

It is also possible, within *each* stance, to take an approach which *includes* consideration of the best thinking from both sides of the spiral. An individual may move with the procession, trying out new approaches but always including consideration of the most useful ideas earned at preceding stages. Or he may hold to a position at a currently unpopular side of the spiral, at the same time watching developments and finding ways of including what is being learned wherever the procession is. This individual puts his efforts toward pulling attention back to the object of his loyalty but he is thrusting upward to be ready with an even more inclusive position as the procession swings back in his direction.

Either stance is useful so long as it is based on respect for a broad spectrum of experience and so long as there is an attempt to see how much latitude can usefully be included in a new educational proposal. There is need for educators to take each of these two stances, for this situation is a source of fruitful dialogue and here lies hope for developing and making use of educational criticism.

A third possible stance is to stay clear of commitment to either side of the spiral but still to become immersed in the swirl of events and ideas and to seek the creative new patterning of thought that will transcend all former positions. Those who take this stance may seem like impractical dreamers for periods of time but they are a source of fresh leaps in education. Those taking an including position within the first two stances will proceed more or less logically while those taking the third stance will operate more intuitively. All three are useful stances in that there is intent to influence the course of events rather than to be tossed about by the force of circumstances.

Whatever the stance chosen, it is essential to have a central support for the top-heavy educational spiral; otherwise it cannot stand. That central support must be the individual in a society and in the midst of knowledge. If this is maintained as the center around which we spiral, our swings hopefully cannot go too far afield.

Conclusion

What have we said about the why of curriculum reassessment? We have made the point that educational thought keeps moving in some sort of pattern. Gaining understanding of the pattern may help in two ways, (1) by pointing up the key matters which must be accounted for in a curriculum theory and (2) by helping the individual curriculum specialist decide upon his particular stance. The overarching answer to why? is the need to be in command of a field rather than to be a puppet responding to whims of those within or outside of the field.

References

1 Everett J. Kircher, 'The role of philosophy of education in undergraduate education,' address given before the Advisory Council of the Association of Organizations for Teacher Education meeting in Columbus, Ohio, May, 1963.
2 Laura Zirbes, (ed.), *Curriculum trends*. (Washington, D.C., Association for Childhood Education), 1935.
3 *Schools for the sixties*. New York, McGraw-Hill Book Co., 1963, p. 117. Quoted from 'The big change', an address delivered to the 43rd Annual Convention of the New York State School Boards Association, December 1962.
4 L. Thomas Hopkins and others, *Integration: its meaning and application* (New York, D. Appleton–Century Company, 1937).
5 Isaac L. Kandel. *History of the curriculum*. 1935. Experimental edition, mimeographed.

Part III

Development of the curriculum

Introduction

Curriculum design becomes curriculum proper when it is adopted and adapted in the classroom. The curriculum designer becomes the curriculum developer—a strategist of innovation. Hoyle (III:1), Brickell (III:2) and Hooper (III:3) examine strategies of innovation and the constraints operating on change in education. Nisbet (III:4) and Banks (III:5) describe the strategies of curriculum development at national level in Scotland, and England and Wales. Lawton (III:6), Bassett (III:7) and Midwinter (III:8) describe curricula that have been produced nationally and locally in primary and secondary education.

'... we know too little at the present about the process of educational innovation ...' (Hoyle, III:1). The absence of a coherent explanation of the process of educational innovation means that the literature on the subject veers from banality dressed up as theory at one extreme to unresearched 'tips for teachers' at the other. Yet it is possible to draw out of the work done in this area an idea of the sort of factors that might speed the success of a curriculum innovation and the sorts of obstacles that innovation is likely to encounter—and from these derive strategies of innovation.

What factors facilitate innovation? Hoyle (III:1) identifies some of the characteristics of the innovative school. 'Genuine innovation does not occur unless teachers become personally committed to ensuring its success ... it is clear that destreaming introduced by fiat and without the commitment of the teachers is likely to prove ineffective.' The organizational health of the school, the leadership role of the head, the administrative structure, participation by teachers in decision-making, are key factors, alongside the more practical issues of financial provision, and availability of supporting teaching materials. Hoyle summarises Carlson's research on the relationship between the 'social characteristics' of US school superintendents (roughly equivalent to chief education officers in Britain)

and the rate at which the school systems adopted modern maths:
'. . . the early adopting systems had superintendents who had a high
social network involvement with other superintendents and who
also had a high social status vis-à-vis other superintendents' (III : 1).

The problem of innovation can be approached from the other
direction by examining the obstacles in its path. Hooper (III : 3)
diagnoses the failure of a particular innovation in American education—educational technology. The causes are multiple and interlocking. Blaming everything on the conservatism of education is too
simplistic. The role and posture of the innovators themselves are
often major obstacles to the acceptance of the innovation. This is
compounded by the questionable behaviour of some of the commercial interests which have concentrated on profitable gadgetry to
the exclusion of less profitable programmes for use with the gadgets.
The classroom teacher is pilloried for resisting new instructional
materials when the materials are often difficult to get hold of,
evaluate and use. A persistent cause of failure underlying many of
the other causes is the absence of a coherent theory of learning to
guide the design of instructional materials in different media. 'At
one time or another, radio, motion pictures, filmstrips, TV, language
labs, and teaching machines have been hailed as the saviours of
education. So have large classes, small classes, seminars, tutorials,
independent study, years abroad, work-study programs, mid-winter
reading periods, and year-around operation. None of these is either
as bad as detractors assert or as good as zealots claim. Lacking an
adequate theoretical framework in which to place these innovations, the pendulum continues to swing wildly from euphoria to
cynicism' (Gustad quoted in Hooper, III : 3).

To be successful, a strategy of innovation must take a comprehensive, not piecemeal, approach. The strategy which considers only
some of the interlocking problems of change is likely to be destroyed
in time by the problems that were not considered. Curriculum innovations which concentrate on subject matter to the exclusion of the
problems of school organization—or vice versa—are not likely to
succeed. In the British primary school, where curriculum innovations have been increasingly successful, '. . . the interdependence of
different innovations is being more thoroughly recognized. Changes
in curriculum, in methods of teaching and examining, in school
organization, and in school buildings, are all interrelated . . .' (Bassett,
III : 7). The strategy must work on different levels of the educational
hierarchy—at the level of the classroom the teacher needing guid-

ance, encouragement and a sense of involvement and at the top
level of educational management where decisions about the allocation of resources are made. 'Without top-level commitment there
will be no favourable climate in which change can happen and no
favourable organization of time, space, and money inside which the
teacher may be able to make the change' (Hooper, III:3).

Henry Brickell (III:2) outlines in detail two specific strategies of
innovation—one for schools wishing to 'invent' their own innovation, one for schools adopting an innovation developed elsewhere.
Local invention by a school or schools requires the collection of a
team of people with different skills and interests, the allocation of
considerable time to their work, the finding of a temporary home
perhaps away from the school setting altogether, the participation
of high quality subject matter specialists, the development of instructional materials to carry the subject matter, facilities for pretesting the innovation in real situations. These requirement are unlikely to be met, Brickell points out, by many schools and that is the
reason for so much national curriculum development. Adoption of
curricula produced outside the adopting school requires the involvement of the public, an administrative staff which shows '... positive
desire for the change, not merely a neutral acceptance ...' (III:2),
and the release of resources. 'Some innovations require more space;
some require new subdivisions of old space; some require more flexible allocations of it from day to day. Whatever the situation ... it
must be made clear to prospective users that they will not be expected to cram the innovation into an unsuitable location. If the
innovation requires more operating time, or a shift in time placement, or more flexible time-scheduling, arrangements for accommodating it should be planned in advance' (Brickell, III:2). Staff must be
encouraged to visit schools where the innovation is in operation and
provision for teacher-training is essential. A delicate balance has to
be struck between identifying for the teachers the familiar aspects
of the innovation and its distinctive features. The professional
associations to which the teachers belong need to endorse the innovation. Teaching materials should be made available for early inspection and some form of pilot experiment put into operation.
Perhaps most important of all '... it must be shown that the innovation is addressed to an area of learning in which the local school
itself has located an unacceptable gap' (III:2). In other words the
need for change must be precisely identified and agreed on.

Paul Mort's research into the time taken by school systems to adopt an innovation (quoted by Hoyle, III : 1) revealed a very slow rate of diffusion. Typically there was a fifty-year time lag between the appearance of a need and the appearance of an innovation to meet the need, a further fifteen years before the innovation was adopted by three per cent of school systems, followed by a rapid period of adoption. The problem is that 'Schools and colleges too often take on the outward appearance of innovation, but not its substance' (Hooper, III : 3). The curriculum innovations described by Nisbet, Lawton, Bassett and Midwinter raise a number of interesting questions. Why, for example, has the primary school been so much more innovative both in content and methods than the secondary school? Why have the basic disagreements about secondary curricula—discipline-centred *vs.* interdisciplinary, common curriculum for all *vs.* special curriculum for the 'average' child—not been reflected in the primary school? Why are interdisciplinary, topic-centred approaches acceptable in the primary school but not in the secondary school? To what extent does the departmentalization of teaching and learning in secondary and higher education block innovation? Why have the curriculum innovations in the secondary school been virtually restricted to the Newsom children, barely affecting the academic streams? What is the role of external examinations in resisting or accelerating change? Why is the Schools Council strategy for curriculum development not acceptable in Scotland? How can *local* agencies of diffusion like teachers' centres be strengthened without losing the advantages of economies of scale? To what extent are the basic disagreements about the nature and objectives of secondary education (Lawton, III : 6) actually responsible for innovations being resisted? To what extent is change in education only brought about by crisis situations—for example the raising of the school-leaving age? What is the role of teacher training—both pre- and in-service—in promoting change?

Some answers need to be found to these questions if the curriculum revolution that has begun in the United Kingdom is to persist and make worthwhile contributions to the educational system. Looking ahead, certainly in the secondary school, the opportunities and requirements for change seem almost limitless. '. . . in the long run . . . there is no substitute for a re-thinking of the entire secondary school curriculum. The raising of the school-leaving age should therefore be seen not as one isolated problem, or a gap to be filled, but as part of a complex of reform measures. The complex will include, for example, how to organize comprehensive schools so that they do not become grammar and secondary schools under a single roof; how to unstream schools and yet preserve opportunities for individual fulfilment at the highest possible level; how to cope with the explosion of knowledge by a policy of adequate coverage, plus a balanced curriculum; how to avoid early specialization; how to organize sixth forms in order to cater for pupils who are not only destined for higher education, and for whom A level courses may not be entirely appropriate. This may seem to be an enormous set of problems for schools to solve, but taken together they may even be seen as more manageable than if attempted one at a time. Piecemeal reform almost inevitably results in fragmentation of the curriculum, whereas the indications are that what is really required in English schools in the 1970s is far-sighted, long-term planning which would give the curriculum some kind of logical structure and unity' (Lawton, III:6).

Eric Hoyle

III:1 How does the curriculum change?

*Eric Hoyle brings together the key findings from
sociological research into the process of curriculum
change. Four topics are selected for consideration:
(1) the relationship between social change and curriculum
change; (2) the diffusion of innovation in education;
(3) factors determining the innovativeness of the school;
(4) strategies of planned curriculum change.*

[PART I]

Curriculum change is a variety of educational change which, in
turn, is one form of social change. By and large sociologists have
been more successful in carrying out static analyses of social institutions, focussing upon the 'functional' contributions which the parts
make to the whole, than in analysing their dynamic aspects. One
student of social change has commented with some justification that
the study of social change is an area 'where only fools rush in and
authentic angels have not yet trod',[1] and it must be conceded that
the sociological study of education has concerned itself with change
neither more nor less than other branches of sociology. The contribution which sociologists have made so far has been to analyse
changes in the structure of education rather than in the content of
education (although this is not a true dichotomy). The emerging
curriculum movement is thus a challenge to the sociologist of
education not to found a new subdiscipline which might be termed
'the sociology of the curriculum', but to extend current modes of
sociological analysis to a new set of problems.

The term *curriculum change* in the title has been deliberately
preferred to the more common term *curriculum development* since
the sociologist is not only concerned with the rational processes of
curriculum planning which are implied in the term *development*,
but also with the relatively unplanned and adaptive 'drift' which

Journal of Curriculum Studies, vol. 1, no. 2, 1969, pp. 132–141; and vol. 1,
no. 3, 1969, pp. 230–239. (Published twice-yearly by William Collins Sons &
Co. Ltd.) Reprinted by permission.

has characterised so much curriculum change in the past, and still remains a significant form of change. The following are some of the aspects of curriculum change which are of interest to the sociologist:

The relationship between socio-economic change and curriculum change.
The determinants of long-term evolutionary change in the curriculum.
The cumulative and/or cyclical nature of curriculum change.
The strategies of planned curriculum development.
The diffusion of innovation in education.
The school's response to outside pressures for curriculum change.
The factors which generate an impetus towards change within a school.
The short-term and long-term effects of curriculum change—both intended and unintended.

He is thus concerned with the large-scale and the small-scale, the

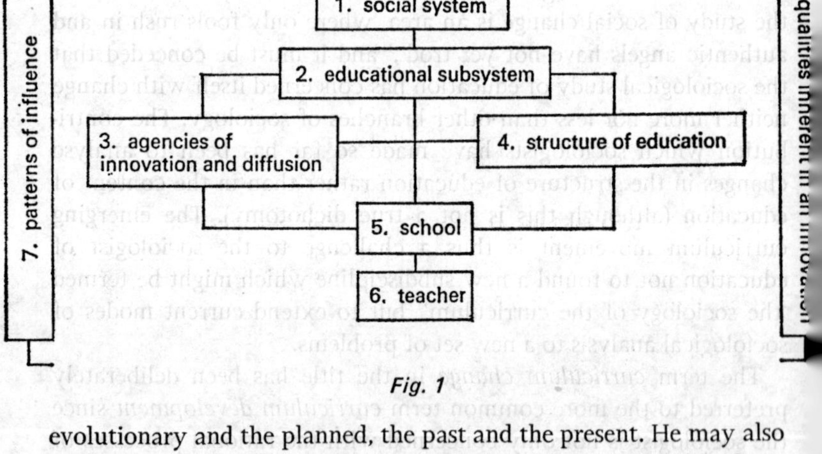

Fig. 1

evolutionary and the planned, the past and the present. He may also play a role at some point on a continuum which stretches from detached analysis to active involvement where the sociologist himself acts as an agent of change.[2]

It would be impossible ... to discuss all the potential areas of sociological research into curriculum change. Four topics have therefore been selected for consideration: (a) the relationship between social change and curriculum change; (*b*) the diffusion of innovation in education; (*c*) factors determining the innovativeness of the school; (*d*) strategies of planned curriculum change. In discussing different levels of analysis, patterns of interaction, and clusters of variables, reference will be made to Fig. 1.

It must be emphasised, however, that this diagram cannot be regarded either as a model or a paradigm. The lines which connect the boxes indicate a reciprocal relationship, but not the direction of the flow of influence. Models could be constructed to indicate the systematic relationship between some of the variables suggested, but we know too little at the present time about the process of educational innovation to construct a single overarching model.

Social change and curriculum change

Society (represented here in Box 1 as *the* social system)[3] has two major dimensions:

(*a*) *institutional*—consisting of economic, political, religious, educational, and other institutions,

(*b*) *normative*—consisting of the values and norms which pervade the social system and its institutions.

The degree of 'necessary' integration between the different institutions of society, and the 'necessary' degree of value consensus within society, are fundamental questions still very much in dispute amongst sociologists. But it is sufficient for our purpose here to affirm the relationship between education (represented in Box 2 as a subsystem) and other institutions of society, and between the values pervading education and the values pervading other parts of society. We know little about the nature of these relationships, yet they are crucial for an understanding of the process of curriculum change. Potentially, the role of education can range from *initiation* to *adaptation* on both the normative and institutional dimensions, and these possibilities suggest a number of important questions, e.g.:

Is education inevitably adaptive to economic and technological change, or can education itself generate change in these areas?

Does the class structure inevitably shape the structure and content of education, or could educational change alter the class structure?

If, at the present time, we are experiencing a shift from élitist to egalitarian values, and from ascriptive to achievement values in education, to what extent is this a reflection of such value shifts in society as a whole? And are these normative shifts themselves a response to economic and technological pressures?

To what extent are changes in educational philosophy generated within the educational system independently of broader normative and institutional changes? What, for example, is the relationship between the growing emphasis on flexibility and open-endedness in the curriculum and the economic demand for flexible and creative manpower? Are these trends independent and their complimentariness a happy coincidence? Or is the economic demand being exploited by educationists as an argument for institutionalising ideas which have long appealed to progressives, but which have not been institutionalised hitherto because they have offered no economic pay-off?

The answers to such questions can only emerge from a careful analysis of institutional and normative change in society and in education.

Contributions to the analysis of social change and curriculum change have come from many sources. British sociologists have tended to concentrate their attention upon institutional structures, and have produced excellent case studies of the relationship between socio-economic factors and the social function of different sorts of educational institutions. Clearly structure and content are very closely related and studies such as those of Banks,[4] Cotgrove,[5] Halsey,[6] Taylor[7] and Blyth,[8] have considerable significance for the understanding of curriculum change in the different institutions with which each one deals. There have been a number of attempts, especially in the United States, to take a broad view of curriculum development which have included a consideration of sociological influences on the curriculum, e.g., Smith, Stanley and Shores,[9] Taba[10] and Saylor and Alexander.[11] Another approach, especially strong in the United States, has been through the analysis of the values pervading society and their influence upon the content of the curriculum, e.g., Riesman,[12] Spindler,[13] Getzels,[14] Callahan[15] and Hofstadter.[16] A fourth approach, which is being strongly pursued in both this country and the United States, is through the study of the social determinants of educability. Clearly socially-induced handicaps to learning must enter into any consideration of curriculum objectives or teaching methods. Studies have been made of the ecological, material and cultural correlates of educability, e.g., Bernstein,[17] Wiseman,[18] Douglas,[19] Swift,[20] Kahl,[21] Turner,[22] Herriott and St John,[23] and there is a growing number of American studies which deal in a pragmatic way with the educational problems of deprived social groups, e.g., Reissman,[24] Passow,[25] and also the British Plowden Report.[26]

The relationship between educational change and social change is a highly complex one and there is a variety of different ways of approaching the problems involved. It is incumbent upon those who are engaged in curriculum development to draw appropriate inferences from the institutional studies of the sociologists of education and to relate these to their own pursuit of objectives and strategies of change. For their part, sociologists of education can make further contributions to curriculum development by increasing the attention which they pay to the sociological determinants of the *content* of education. This presupposes the existence of a theory of educational change which we do not yet have. However, a recent attempt has been made by McGee[27] to develop a paradigm for identifying the nature of educational change which is a useful starting point. He proposes a distinction between education as an *agent* of social change (i.e. where social changes are brought about through education), as a *condition* of change (i.e. where changes in education are necessary to broader social changes), and as an *effect* of change (i.e. where educational institutions adjust to changes occurring in other social institutions). He also proposes that these different functions of education in the process of social change should each be related to three major factors: economic, technological and ideological. The categories in this paradigm do not, of course, occur independently, but the analytical distinction can be made in the interests of collecting the data on educational change upon which a theory might be built.

The diffusion of curriculum innovations

In this section we turn from the general relationship between social change and educational change to one aspect of the change process itself, i.e., how new ideas and practices spread. Innovation is defined as:

'(1) acceptance, (2) over time, (3) of some specific item—idea or practice, (4) by individuals, groups or other adopting units, linked by (5) specific channels of communication, (6) to a social structure, and (7) to a given system of values or culture.'[28]

An analytical distinction can be made between *innovation* and *diffusion*. An *innovation* is an idea or practice which is perceived as new by the potential adopting unit. *Diffusion* is the process whereby this new idea or practice spreads through a social system. It must be admitted, however, that the term *innovation* is also frequently used to indicate the process as well as the idea or practice. An innovation is almost always a development of some existing form, and it is not easy to trace cases back to the point of creation. Undoubtedly many new ideas originate with creative teachers who develop them to meet their own particular problems, and are then diffused through informal channels of communication via teachers, head-teachers, local inspectors, college lecturers and others, and perhaps in a more formalised way through locally-sponsored courses or through articles in the teachers' journals. Other innovations, especially those requiring capital outlay, are developed outside the schools and promoted amongst teachers through a variety of organisations. We know almost nothing about the sources of new ideas in education, whether these are largely conceived in the schools to be taken up or promoted by outside bodies, or whether most of the new ideas in education are generated outside the schools. Although the creation of new materials, methods, teaching aids, forms of organisation and curriculum content is rapidly becoming institutionalised with the progress of the curriculum development movement, it would be worthwhile to study not only these institutionalised forms, but also the sources and pathways of other useful innovations.

The institutional agencies of innovation and diffusion are represented in Box 3 of Fig. 1. They include:

The Schools Council
Private foundations
Commercial agencies (e.g. publishers)
Research units (e.g. N.F.E.R., university units)
Teacher-training institutions
In-service training institutions (e.g. university course, L.E.A. courses)
Professional organisations (e.g. Science Masters' Association, the Physical Education Association)
Her Majesty's Inspectorate
L.E.A. Inspectors and advisers
Examining bodies
Teachers' unions

These agencies differ, of course, in the degree to which they are concerned with innovation and/or diffusion, but in the absence of detailed case studies one cannot range them along this continuum.

These agencies might be studied in the following ways:

(a) The overall analysis of the functions of interorganisational co-operation in curriculum development. Clark[29] has made an approach to this form of study and has summarised the American pattern as follows:

'The pattern of influence sums up as follows: it was set in motion from the top, by a Federal agency and a private national committee. Its object was to affect grass roots educational practice which was seen as a national weakness. This flow of influence is downward, through a chain of independent groups and organisations who find it in their interest to enter the alliance or compact. A federal agency provides the funds; a private non-profit group receives the money and develops a new course; commercial firms carry the new materials to all corners of the existing decentralised structure; dispersed universities and colleges train teachers in all regions of the country to the new materials; existing local authorities adopt the materials and allow their teachers to reshape the local courses. Decision-making in this pattern, right down the line, is heavily influenced by the prestige of expertise. The National Science Foundation was expert and prestigeful; so were the committees, the Institutes, the teachers training in the new materials. The very materials themselves travelled under the same aura.'

There are obvious affinities with the major patterns of diffusion in Britain, and there is considerable scope for studies of the relationships between the various agencies involved in the promotion of curriculum innovation, e.g., between commercial firms and the foundations, between curriculum development units and the teachers' unions.

(b) Studies of the structure and functions of the agencies of innovation and diffusion. A welcome starting point here would be careful descriptions of the work of these bodies using a case approach[30] and beyond this the application of the concepts and techniques of organisational analysis (see on this topic Wilson,[31] Etzioni,[32] Hoyle[33]).

(c) Studies in the key roles in the process of innovation through the use of the concepts and techniques of role analysis (see on this topic Gross, Mason and McEachern, 1958;[34] Gross and Herriott, 1965[35]). Interest might centre upon the role played by particular 'product champion' or upon a role category, e.g., the problems besetting the H.M.I. as a promoter of curriculum change as he seeks to overcome the non-motivating 'punishment-centred' perceptions of his role.

(d) Surveys of the attributes, e.g., age, sex, qualifications, experience, professional mobility, professional aspirations, etc., of those teachers who become involved in curriculum development either as leaders or as consumers.

(e) Sociometric studies of the pathways of innovation in local areas.

Box 4 in Fig. 1 represents the structure of education—local, national, and private. Although L.E.A.'s are both 'target systems' for innovation and also agencies of diffusion, the different levels of the educational structure (and their financial policies, decision-making structures, etc.) are treated here also as an independent cluster of variables. Major questions in this area centre upon the integration of local and governmental authorities in the area of curriculum innovation, the significance of the size of the local authority in relation to its innovativeness, and the relative innovativeness of the public and private sectors of education.

Boxes 7 and 8 represent clusters of variables which are significant at all stages of the diffusion process and can be treated as independent.

Box 7—Patterns of Influence—represents a variety of techniques which individuals and groups can employ in order to facilitate the adoption of an innovation by others. One would be concerned here with the functions of different forms of authority, power, and interpersonal influence, and with the role of the mass media in encouraging the adoption of curriculum innovation. Box 8 represents a recognition of the fact that there are qualities inherent in an innovation which make it acceptable or otherwise to adopting systems. Carlson[36] found differential rates of adoption for different innovations, e.g., modern maths was adopted more readily than foreign language programmes, and although educationists rated team teaching as potentially more diffusible than programmed instruction, this was not found to have happened. Miles,[37] reviewing the literature in this area, found that cost, congruence between the innovation and the values of the adopting system, degree of technical expertise required, availability of supporting teaching materials to be some of the significant factors.

The sociological study of the diffusion of innovation is a relatively under-developed field at the present time. The major work of reference is that of Rogers[38] which discusses concepts and techniques, and reports many substantive studies of the diffusion of new ideas and practices in agriculture, industry, medicine, and education. He reports that typically, where adopting units are categorised on the basis of standard scores, the distribution of adopters over time approaches normality, and that cumulative frequencies conform to an S-shaped curve (thus mirroring the learning curve for individuals). The 'innovativeness' of adopting units, as assessed by their position within the distribution, can be taken as an independent variable and related to a whole variety of correlates. Rogers concludes his work with fifty-two generalisations about the diffusion of innovation based upon the researches of himself and others. A further source of generalisations about the diffusion of innovation, again concerned largely with the diffusion of agricultural innovation, is the work of Lionberger.[39]

A larger number of studies of the diffusion of new ideas in education has been undertaken by the late Paul Mort[40] and his colleagues at Teachers' College, Columbia University (Ross[41]). This work on the adaptability (i.e. innovativeness) of school systems (i.e. local units of educational administration) revealed a very slow rate of diffusion. It was found that typically there was a fifty-year lag between a felt need and the appearance of an innovation to meet that need, a further period of fifteen years before the innovation was adopted by three per cent of school systems, and then a rapid period of adoption followed by a period of deceleration until near-complete diffusion had been achieved. Mort's studies were focussed upon financial rather than on sociological variables, and whilst there is no doubt that for some innovations—though not all—financial provision is a fundamental facilitating or inhibiting factor, to focus upon this factor is to omit from consideration the factors which determine curriculum innovations which cost little, and also the factors which lead to the utilisation of what financial resources are available (e.g., the school's capitation allowance) for changing rather than maintaining the existing curriculum.

Carlson,[42] unhappy with the approach of Mort and his colleagues, undertook a study which concentrated upon sociological variables. He sought to relate the rate at which school systems adopted certain innovations (foreign language teaching, modern maths, accelerated programmes, team teaching, language laboratories and programmed instruction) to the social characteristics of the superintendents of those systems. He was able to demonstrate that the early adopting systems had superintendents who had a high social network involvement with other superintendents and who also had a high social status vis à vis other superintendents. Eichholz (1963[43]; Eichholz and Rogers, 1964[44]), working within the sociological tradition but taking the teacher as the adopting unit, carried out a study of the rejection of electro-mechanical teaching aids. He identified five major forms of rejection (ignorance, suspended judgment, situational, personal and experimental) and linked these with the state of the rejecting teachers (e.g., uninformed, anxious, guilty, doubtful), and their responses.

In order to proceed further with the explanation of the process of diffusion in education, the ordering of data is dependent upon the existence of a viable theory. Guba and Clark put forward the following paradigm for the identification of the different stages of the diffusion process.[45]

GUBA–CLARK SCHEME FOR CHANGE IN A SOCIAL PROCESS FIELD

	Research	Development	Dissemination	Demonstration	Implementation
Objective	To advance knowledge	To apply knowledge	To distribute knowledge	To build conviction	To facilitate action
Criteria	Validity of knowledge produced	1. Feasibility 2. Performance	1. Intelligibility 2. Fidelity 3. Comprehensiveness 4. Pervasiveness	Credibility	1. Effectiveness 2. Efficiency
Relation to change	Provides basis for innovation	Produces innovation	Informs about innovation	Promotes innovation	Incorporates innovation

Finally, Bohla[46] has proposed a theory of diffusion which is intended to have both explanatory and predictive power. This theory can be symbolised as:

$$D = f(CLER)$$

Thus diffusion (D) is a function of configurational relationships (C) between initiators and targets (where configurations include individuals, groups, institutions, and cultures), the nature and extent of the linkages (L) between and within these configurations, the environments (E) in which the configurations are located, and the resources (R) of both initiator and target configurations. Bohla discusses at length the connotation of the concepts used in this theory, ways in which they might be operationalised, and a number of hypotheses which it generates and which might be tested.

Theories of diffusion seek to articulate innovators and targets, and where these targets are schools one can draw upon a wider range of research relating to the nature of schools as social systems and particularly their potentialities as adopting units. . . .

[PART 2]

The innovative school

For any curriculum innovation to become an effective improvement on an existing practice it must 'take' with the school and become fully institutionalized. Genuine innovation does not occur unless teachers become personally committed to ensuring its success. Unless this commitment occurs, new methods and materials may eventually be permanently relegated to store-cupboards, or used only in an unsystematic manner. Organizational innovations are less likely to fall into disuse because the number of people involved ensures some continuity, but these can remain ineffective even when they are nominally operative. Mixed ability grouping is a case in point; for this to be fully effective the teacher must be committed to its success otherwise it is unlikely to be more effective than grouping by ability. The rather ambiguous results of research on the effects of mixed ability grouping are perhaps a reflection of the fact that researchers have focussed their attention only upon the structure of the school and not upon its climate. Yet it is clear that de-streaming introduced by fiat and without the commitment of the teachers is likely to prove ineffective.

This section is concerned with those characteristics of a school which predispose it to innovativeness. This does not assume that innovative schools will indiscriminately adopt anything which is new, but that they will adopt some innovations and reject others dependent upon their relevance to the particular needs of the school at a given time. It does assume, however, that some schools are more open to new ideas than others. It also assumes that schools have a collective quality of innovativeness. Ultimately the individual teacher is the 'adopting unit' who will determine the effectiveness of an innovation, and some teachers have more 'open' minds than others as a function of their cognitive, perceptual and creative skills. But the focus of this paper will be upon the school as the adopting unit partly because many curriculum innovations are school-wide both in their extent and in their consequences, and partly because the behaviour of individual teachers is influenced by the institution in which they work.

In an important contribution to the discussion of the innovative school Miles has used the concept of *organizational health* to denote 'a school system's ability not only to function effectively, but to develop and grow into a more fully-functioning system'.[2] A school in good organizational health is likely to be characterized by an awareness of potential innovation, a continuing willingness to examine its own procedures, and a capacity to adopt innovations in a way which ensures their full effectiveness. Miles makes the following point:

> 'It seems likely that the state of health of an educational organization can tell us more than anything else about the probable success of any particular change effort. Economy of effort would suggest that we look at the state of an organization's health as such, and try to improve it—in preference to struggling with a series of more of less inspired short-run change efforts.'

Extending Miles' medical metaphor we can say that the central problem facing the curriculum development movement is the avoidance of *tissue rejection* whereby an innovation does not 'take' with a school because the social system of the school is unable to absorb it into its normal functioning.

Any appreciation of the innovative potential of a school is dependent upon an understanding of its nature as a social system which includes such dimensions as its formal structure, administrative processes, informal structures and activities, and culture. Little research exists at the present time which would enable us to predict the likelihood of a school being receptive to curriculum innovation nor the strategies which it could employ to induce a greater innovativeness. However, useful inferences can be drawn from the research based upon Halpin's Organizational Climate Description Questionnaire.[3] A factorial analysis of responses to a questionnaire containing items relating to administrative relationships in the school revealed eight major dimensions—four referred to staff behaviour and four to the principal's behaviour. Further analysis revealed that these dimensions yielded six distinct school profiles which are referred to as *organizational climates*. Halpin ranged these climates on a continuum from 'open' to 'closed' which he concedes is based upon his own value preferences. The climates can be briefly summarized as follows:

Open
The head is a leader who works hard himself and thus sets an example. He establishes rules and procedures and is prepared to be critical, but he is also flexible and to a large extent meets the social needs of his staff. He does not monitor the teachers' work too closely and allows leadership acts to emerge from his staff. Morale is high owing to a feeling of accomplishment by the staff and their experience of good personal relationships.

Autonomous
The head gives greater autonomy to his teachers than the 'open' climate head, but does not give them the same degree of positive leadership nor meets their social needs satisfactions to the same extent. He is aloof but gives a free hand, and all the teachers experience a sense of task accomplishment.

Controlled
The head is an authoritarian who controls his staff closely, works them hard, and provides for little social satisfaction. Nevertheless, the staff respond to this militant behaviour and derive satisfaction from their task achievement.

Familiar
The head is centrally concerned with creating a happy family atmosphere in the school. Hence he exerts little leadership or control and is disinclined to be critical. The staff enjoy friendly relationships but their morale is diminished through having little sense of task achievement.

Paternal
The head tries to exert control over his staff with little effect. He is constantly busy within the school but this is regarded as interference rather than leadership. The teachers pay little heed and rather

little is achieved. The head also attempts to fulfil the social needs satisfactions of his staff, but this is characterized in Halpin's terms as a 'seductive oversolicitousness' which is regarded as non-genuine and is therefore non-motivating.

Closed

The head is aloof, controlling, impersonal, arbitrary and unconcerned with teachers as people. He gives no leadership and provides no example. The teachers gain little satisfaction from either their social relationships or their achievements.

Halpin now concedes that this climate dimension is not necessarily linear but feels that at least the open-closed dimension is meaningful.[4] It would appear from Halpin's description of the 'open' climate that such a school could be said to be in a state of 'organizational health' and hence innovative. But in his review of the state of research on school climates he states:

'The blunt truth is that we do not yet know very much about how to change a climate.'

Clearly the willingness of a school to institutionalize curriculum development is very much dependent upon the manner in which the head teacher performs his leadership role; whether he is, in fact, a *leader* in the sense that he attempts to keep the school moving rather than simply ticking over. It is also dependent upon the administrative structure which he creates since communication and decision-making patterns of a school can clearly be motivating or otherwise. Revans,[5] for example, has shown how a measure of pupils' involvement in their school work is correlated with administrative relationships in the school. We are not in a position to say what are the patterns of communication and decision-making which are likely to maximize teacher commitment to curriculum innovation. Sharma[6] reports that teachers' morale is high when there is a close relationship between *desire* for involvement and *actual* involvement, and that teachers express a particular desire for participation in decision-making in the area of the curriculum. As a broad generalization it is probably true to say that schools would be more innovative if teachers played a greater part in decision-making than at present, but there are incompatibilities between certain of the goals of decision making.[7] For example the goals of motivation, quality of decision, and training might point to extended participation. Teachers want to be involved in decisions about the curriculum, but for many at the present time their only participation in decision-making is limited to basic organizational arrangements, with such questions for example, as how best to prevent pupils going 'up the down staircase'. Undoubtedly the curriculum movement itself is creating situations in which teachers are taking more responsibility for decision-making, but the effectiveness of the various structures of decision-making which are emerging in schools have yet to be evaluated.

The effectiveness of any complex organization such as a school is dependent upon *differentiation* (whereby individuals are allocated specialized functions) and *coordination* (whereby these functions are integrated in the service of a common purpose). the coordination of the activities of the personnel of a school requires a balance between order and initiative. Since Max Weber outlined his model of a bureaucracy—characterized by an emphasis on hierarchy, procedures, and predictability—sociologists have been concerned with the viability of this model for different types of organization. This is probably not the place to discuss the degree to which schools can be said to be bureaucracies, but it can be noted that a bureaucratic mode of organization perhaps has certain dysfunctions for schools, particularly in its emphasis on rule-following rather than creative and innovative behaviour. Bidwell[8] has pointed out that schools are characterized by a mixture of authority and autonomy. Within his classroom the teacher has a high degree of autonomy if not over what he teaches at least how he teaches it, but in terms of the overall policy of the school he has relatively little influence. A major problem in all organizations is the prevention of ends becoming superseded by means. This is a particularly potent threat in educational organizations owing to the diffuseness of cultural goals and the great difficulties involved in evaluating procedures. Organizations with diffuse and diverse goals are liable to scale down these goals and sometimes to transform them into much more limited commitments largely concerned with maintaining the school in good running order, the substitution of discipline for education. It is perhaps too much to expect the head to promote a Maoist cultural revolution and shatter his own bureaucracy in the services of promoting the goals of education, but the good head will seek to prevent the structure of his organization repressing the innovativeness of teachers. Corwin[9] has pointed out that teachers can perform their role on a continuum which extends from an *employee* model to a *professional* model. The *employee* teacher follows fixed rules and procedures, his work is characterized by uniformity and lack of innovation, he is primarily concerned with narrow teaching techniques, has a personal commitment to his school and its existing structure and functions, and participates in a 'punishment-centred' administration. The *professional* teacher on the other hand emphasises the uniqueness of problems which he faces, is flexible within the broad policy of the school, adapts readily to changes, emphasizes the importance of curriculum knowledge, gives his loyalty to the wider profession and takes its innovators as his reference group, and participates in a 'representative' administration. Corwin's typology has much in common with Gouldner's distinction between *locals* and *cosmopolitans*.[10]

What sort of teacher-role is most appropriate to curriculum development? Employee? Or professional? Or is there an optimum balance between the two? Arguments have been advanced in favour of a 'teacher-proof' curriculum whereby the class teacher simply accepts a prepared package and goes through teaching procedures in a more or less bureaucratic way.[11] On the other hand there is a strong argument for extending the professionalism of teachers since solutions to educational problems cannot be fully standardized and require the flexibility, adaptability and insight of the professional. The problem ought not, perhaps, to be framed in this way, since it is predicated upon a model of a school and the role of the teacher within it which may be disappearing. Eggleston[12] has pointed out that 'English educational organizations are moving from a situation where their *differentiated* nature is the paramount determinant of the rôles of their personnel, to one where their part in the differentiating process is paramount'. This change is attributed to a number of changes within industrialized society including the breakdown in the traditional distinction between academic and practical curricula, the demand for the generation of new knowledge, the 'personalization' of goals, changes in the concept of ability, societal demand for increasing numbers of personnel with extended education, and the reorganization of institutions to embody these changes. The power of the client is becoming more pronounced and leading to individualized instruction and teacher-pupil rôles based upon cooperation. These changes in organization have much in common with Bernstein's[13] model of an 'open school' characterized by a non-bureaucratic structure, achieved (rather than ascribed) teacher and pupil rôles, and cooperation between teachers. This form of school organization is fully congruent with current curriculum trends. In fact, although we do not yet know the educative power of the school organization, one can hypothesize that to some extent 'the organization is the message' in that the structure and climate of the school have an impact upon the child which is relatively independent of the content of the curriculum and the influence of individual teachers. Yet there remain certain problems to be faced and questions to be answered before it can be affirmed that the open-school and associated curriculum trends can become fully effective. One such question is whether lower working class children are able to profit from a system which is relatively unstructured and throws an increased responsibility for decision-making upon pupils and parents. Evidence from many sources on the socialization of lower working class children suggests that extremely careful strategies will be needed to ensure that these children will gain the presumed benefits of the open school. A similar problem exists for the teachers. The stratification of the teaching profession in recent years has perhaps been antithetical to the open school. Status distinctions, the vested interests of subject teachers, the need to demonstrate personal superiority in order to achieve promotion, and the tendency of many teachers to aspire to posts outside the classroom may tend to inhibit the beneficial aspects of the open system. Perhaps our thinking about the flexible school needs to be coupled with a reconsideration of the career structure in education.[14]

Strategies of change

As Hilda Taba[15] has pointed out, to change the curriculum implies changing people and institutions. The implication of this is that curriculum change cannot be considered independently of planned organizational change founded upon adequate theories derived from the social sciences. This was recognized long ago in a pioneering work edited by Benne and Muntyan[16] which applied some of the extant findings in the area of group dynamics to the problems of curriculum change. Group dynamics is not, however, the only approach to the social science of curriculum change. Chin[17] has grouped strategies of planned organizational change into three broad categories. Power-coercive strategies are, as the term implies, based upon the use of power to alter the conditions within which other people act by limiting alternatives, shaping the consequences of acts and by directly influencing actions. This is currently perhaps the most common form of administrative intervention to secure change. But within education there is a strong sentiment against such strategies founded on the assumption that because of their very nature educational ends cannot be achieved without the commitment of the participants, both teachers and taught. Chin notes that any major innovations which alter the forces in a school will inevitably also alter the power relationships and that the conflict is a normal state of affairs and must be recognized as such. But he also notes that: 'The concurrent strategy of converting these types of conflicts into problem-solving ones is one phase under way in educational circles.' *Normative-re-educative* approaches to effecting change are defined as making use of direct interventions based upon a theory of change and applied to individual behaviour in small groups, organisations and communities. Two main approaches can be identified within this group. One is the problem-solving method in which change strategies are concerned with 'activating forces within the system to alter the system', and in terms of curriculum development this implies a prior self-study of the school as a social system with the object of identifying and solving the problems associated with change. The other approach is the process of attitude change through a study of how one's behaviour impinging on others leads to a greater sensitivity and hence to collaborative behaviour in the change situation. The disciplinary basis of the *normative-re-educative* approach is social psychology and owes much to the pioneering work of Kurt Levin. Currently its major procedures include T-groups, human relations laboratories, and curriculum laboratories. *Empirical-rational* approaches make an intellectual appeal through the demonstration of the greater effectiveness of some new idea or practice over existing ones. Basically the method involves linking innovative processes with research and development[18] often utilizing consultants to establish the link between knowledge and change. This has perhaps been the major approach to curriculum development in this country except that consultants have been largely concerned with the *content* of change rather than with the change mechanisms themselves and have not usually become involved in the change processes *within* the schools.

One of the most explicit statements on the potentiality of planned organizational change is that of Miles[19] who proposes the following six types of intervention: *team training* (i.e. an intact work group such as a school department meets away from the school setting to discuss common problems with the central objective of improving relationships); *survey feedback* (i.e. the use of research on the school as an organization including the attitude and opinions of staff as a basis for decision-making); *rôle-workshop* (i.e. where the incumbents of a particular rôle—such as head teachers—meet to discuss, on the basis of questionnaire data, the problems associated with the rôle with a focus on rôle clarity and an improved fit between rôle and personality); *target-setting* (i.e. regular meetings between, say, the school head and individual members of his staff to arrange 'targets' for the subordinate's work for periods of about six months when a review takes place); *organizational diagnosis* (i.e. residential meetings of a work group focussed less upon improving interpersonal relationships—as in *team-training*—but more upon specific problems and their solutions via established or new procedures); *organizational experiment* (i.e. the conduct of an experiment designed to evaluate some particular innovation and the use of resultant data as a basis for further decision-making). These strategies combine the three approaches outlined above. Miles notes that certain common threads flow through them: self study, an emphasis on personal relationships, increased data flow, norms as a change target, a temporary systems approach and the use of expert consultants. Miles has written at great length about the temporary systems approach.[20] Basically his view is that it is the group which is the unit of change rather than the individual and that one can only change groups by having them meet away from the normal work setting with its pressures, vested interests and specific power relationships. When one considers the phenomenon of the individual who returns from some course or workshop highly enthusiastic about some innovation only to be met by the stony apathy of colleagues who have not shared his experience, one can appreciate the value of Miles' proposal to work through complete work groups preferably in a setting conducive to interaction.

The use of consultants or change agents in the process of curriculum development is likely to meet with considerable resistance in British education owing to the power traditionally exercised by the head and the classroom autonomy of the teachers. Nevertheless, it will perhaps be clear from the discussion so far that not only the curriculum consultants but also behavioural scientists can play a useful rôle in the induction of innovation. Organizational analysis, theory developments, experimentation and evaluation, group leadership, etc., are specialized tasks which are nevertheless important in the change process. The potentialities of a change-agent rôle have yet to be worked out for the British context. These are currently occurring at the practical level as in the North West Curriculum Development Project, but there is also the need to consider the rôle of the change-agent in education from a more theoretical standpoint utilizing the perspectives of behavioural scientists who have been working in these areas in educational and non-educational settings.[21]

Conclusion

One of the striking features of British education at the present time is the institutionalization of innovation. It is now widely accepted that education can never be in a steady state but must constantly be seeking new solutions as new problems are generated by social and educational change. New structures are being developed for the creation and diffusion of innovation, but one of the most pressing problems at the present time is to develop strategies whereby schools are transformed. Miles has rightly pointed out that one-shot innovation is not likely to be successful unless the school is in sound 'organizational health'. Curriculum development is exerting a pressure towards a more open and flexible school with greater freedom for the teacher, perhaps, paradoxically, the freedom to co-operate with other teachers in the organization of his teaching. This process might be accelerated by means of carefully designed change strategies having their initiative both within the school and outside. Again a paradox is apparent in that the initiative which would seek to maximise the creativity of teachers could come from outside intervention. But the paradox is more apparent than real in that it is basic to the theory of consultancy that it is a co-operative relationship in which the consultant helps to remove barriers to changes which the clients themselves come to see as desirable during the analysis of a problem. There is no question of an external agent imposing change upon an unwilling client, both change-agent and client system work together towards a solution to a problem with each party having equal power to influence the other.

In conclusion it should be pointed out that although this paper has been concerned with change it has not been the intention to convey the view that change for its own sake is a good thing. Resistance to change is a natural response and any attempt to force change upon unwilling teachers would bring no benefit to education. Planned change should itself be regarded as an educational enterprise which is essentially a dialogue. One can end with the following point made by Andrew Halpin:

'Social change takes place slowly. To force its growth "out of phase" is to invite unanticipated social consequences that can be damaging. For political reasons some of us may be forced to make rhetorical declamations about change and its happy consequences for everybody. These declamations are like T.V. commercials. I suggest that we recognize such rhetoric for what it is, but that we do not confuse it with reality.'[22]

References

[PART I]

i W. Moore, *Social change* (Englewood Cliffs, N.J.: Prentice-Hall, 1963).

2 W. G. Bennis, 'A new role for the behavioural sciences: effecting organizational change', *Administrative Science Quarterly*, 8.

3 T. Parsons, *The social system* (London: Routledge and Kegan Paul, 1951).

4 O. Banks, *Parity and prestige in English secondary education* (London: Routledge and Kegan Paul, 1955).

5 S. Cotgrove, *Technical education and social change* (London: Allen and Unwin).

6 A. H. Halsey, 'The changing functions of universities', in A. H. Halsey *et al*, *Education, economy and society* (New York: Free Press, 1961).

7 W. Taylor, *The secondary modern school* (London: Faber, 1963).

8 W. A. L. Blyth, *English primary education* (London: Routledge and Kegan Paul, 1965).

9 B. O. Smith, W. O. Stanley and J. H. Shores, *Fundamentals of curriculum development* (New York: World Books, 1957).

10 H. Taba, *Curriculum development: theory and practice* (New York: Harcourt, Brace and World, 1962).

11 J. G. Saylor and W. M. Alexander, *Curriculum planning for better teaching and learning* (New York: Rinehart, 1954).

12 D. Riesman, *Constraint and variety in American education* (New York: Harper, 1958).

13 G. D. Spindler, 'Education in a transforming American culture', *Harvard Educational Review*, 25 (1965).

14 J. Getzels, 'Changing values challenge the schools', *School Review*, 65 (1957).

15 R. E. Callahan, *Education and the cult of efficiency* (Chicago: University of Chicago Press, 1962).

16 R. Hofstadter, *Anti-intellectualism in American life* (London: Cape, 1964).

17 B. Bernstein, 'Social class and linguistic development: a theory of social learning' in A. H. Halsey *et al.*, *Education, economy and society* (New York: Free Press, 1961).

18 S. Wiseman, *Education and environment* (Manchester: Manchester University Press, 1964).

19 J. W. B. Douglas, *The home and the school* (London: McGibbon and Kee, 1964).

20 D. F. Swift, 'Family environment and 11+ success: some basic predictors', *British Journal of Educational Psychology*, vol. 37, (1), 1967.

21 J. Kahl, 'The educational aspirations of "common man" boys' in A. H. Halsey *et al*, *Education, economy and society* (New York: Free Press, 1961).

22 R. H. Turner, *The social context of ambition* (San Francisco: Chandler, 1964).

23 R. E. Herriot and N. H. St. John, *Social class and the urban school* (New York: Wiley, 1966).

24 F. Reissmann, *The culturally deprived child* (New York: Harper, 1962).

25 A. H. Passow, *Education in depressed areas* (New York: Teachers' College, Columbia University, 1966).

26 H.M.S.O., *Children and their primary schools* (London, 1967).

27 R. McGee, 'Education and Social Change', in D. A. Hansen and J. E. Gerstl, *On education: sociological perspectives* (New York: Wiley, 1967).

28 E. Katz, M. L. Levin and H. Hamilton, 'Traditions of Research on the Diffusion of Innovation,' *American Sociological Review*, vol. 28 (2), 1963.

29 B. R. Clark, 'Inter-organizational patterns in education', *Administrative Science Quarterly*, vol. 10 (2), 1964.

30 M. B. Miles, *Innovation in education* (New York: Teachers' College, Columbia University, 1964), Section 1. M. B. Miles and E. V. Lake.

31 B. R. Wilson, 'Institutional analysis', in A. Welford *et al*, *Society: Problems and methods of study* (London: Routledge and Kegan Paul, 1961).

32 A. Etzioni, *A comparative analysis of complex organizations* (New York: Free Press, 1964).

33 E. Hoyle, 'Organizational analysis in the field of education', *Educational Research*, vol. 7 (2), 1965.

34 S. Gross, W. S. Mason and A. W. McEachern, *Explorations in role analysis* (New York: Wiley, 1958).

35 N. Gross and R. E. Herriott, *Staff leadership in public schools* (New York: Wiley, 1965).

36 R. O. Carlson, *Adoption of educational innovations* (Eugene, Oregon, Centre for the Advanced Study of Educational Administration, University of Oregon, 1965).

37 M. B. Miles, *Innovation in education* (New York: Teachers' College, Columbia University, 1964).

38 E. M. Rogers, *Diffusion of innovations* (New York: Free Press, 1962).

39 H. F. Lionberger, *Adoption of new ideas and practices* (Ames, Iowa: Iowa State University Press, 1960).

40 P. Mort, 'Studies in educational innovation from the Institute of Administrative Research: an overview', in M. B. Miles (ed.), *Innovation in education* (New York: Teachers' College, Columbia University, 1964).

41 D. H. Ross, *Administration for adaptibility* (New York: Teachers' College, Columbia University, 1958).

C

20

101

232 ?

336

375

411

444

483

42 R. O. Carlson, 'School superintendents and the adoption of modern maths', in M. B. Miles (ed.), *Innovation in education* (New York: Teachers' College, Columbia University, 1964. See also Carlson (1965), *op. vit.*

43 G. C. Eichholz, 'Why do teachers resist change?', *Theory into practice*, vol. 2 (5), (1963).

44 G. C. Eichholz and E. M. Rogers, 'Resistance to adoption of audio-visual aids by elementary school teachers', in M. B. Miles (ed.), *Innovation in education* (New York: Teachers' College, Columbia University, 1964).

45 E. G. Guba, 'From research into action', a banquet address given at the annual meeting of the Educational Research Association of New York State, October, 1964 (cited by Bohla, see reference 46).

46 H. S. Bohla, 'A configurational theory of innovation diffusion', *Indian Educational Review*, 2 (1), (1967).

[PART 2]

1 [omitted]

2 M. Miles, 'Planned change and organizational health: figure and ground' in *Change Processes in the Public Schools*, Eugene, Oregon; Center for the Advanced Study of Educational Administration.

3 A. W. Halpin, *Theory and research in educational administration* (New York: Macmillan, 1966).

4 A. W. Halpin, 'Change and organizational climate,' *J. Ed. Admin.*, vol. 5, no. 1, 1967.

5 R. W. Revans, 'Involvement in school', *New Society*, vol. 6, no. 152, 1965.

6 C. L. Sharma, 'Who should make decisions?' *Administrators Notebook*, 3, 1955.

7 W. R. Dill, 'Decision-making' in *Behavioural science and educational administration*, 63rd Yearbook of the National Society for the Study of Education, Part II (Chicago University Press, 1964).

8 C. Bidwell, 'The school as a formal organization' in J. G. March (ed.), *Handbook of organizations* (New York: Rand McNally, 1965).

9 R. G. Corwin, *A sociology of education* (New York, Appleton-Century-Croft, 1965).

10 A. W. Gouldner, 'Cosmopolitans and locals: towards an analysis of latent social roles', *Admin. Sci. Quart.*, vol. 2, 1957–8.

11 S. Wayland, 'The rôle of the teacher' in A. H. Passow, *Curriculum crossroads* (Teachers' College, Columbia, New York, 1965).

12 S. J. Eggleston, 'Convergences in the rôles of personnel in differentiated educational organizations.' Paper presented to the European Seminar on Sociology of Education (Noordwijk van Zee, The Netherlands, September, 1968).

13 B. Bernstein, 'Open schools, open society?' *New Society*, vol. 10, no. 259, 1967.

14 E. Hoyle, 'Rôle differentiation and professional stratification in education', *Pedagogica Europaea* 1969.

15 H. Taba, *Curriculum development; theory and practice* (New York: Harcourt, Brace and World, 1962).

16 K. D. Benne and B. Muntyan, *Human relations in curriculum change* (New York: Dryden Press, 1951).

17 R. Chin, 'Basic strategies and procedures in effecting change'. In E. L. Morphet and C. O. Ryan, *Designing education for the future*, No. 3 (New York Citation Press, 1968).

18 M. Young, *Innovation and research in education* (London, Routledge and Kegan Paul, 1970).

19 M. B. Miles, *op. cit.*

20 M. B. Miles, 'On temporary systems' in M. B. Miles (ed.), *Innovation in education* (Teachers College, New York, 1964).

21 See W. G. Bennis, K. D. Benne and R. Chin, *The planning of change* (New York: Holt, Rinehart, Winston, 1966) G. Jones, *Planned organizational change* (London: Routledge and Kegan Paul, 1969) R. Lippett, J. Watson and B. Westley, *The dynamics of planned change* (New York: Harcourt Brace, 1958).

22 A. W. Halpin, 'Change and organizational climate', *J. Ed. Admin.*, vol. 5, no. 1, 1967.

Henry M. Brickell

III:2 Two local change strategies

Two major strategies are described which schools can use to bring about a change in curriculum. One concerns the invention of a new instructional process, the other the adoption and adaptation of one invented elsewhere. The approach is severely practical both in terms of producing the instructional materials and getting them accepted by the teachers in the classroom.

This paper lays out two major strategies a local school system might use to bring about change in its instructional program after it has identified shortcomings in the learning of its students. Both are elaborate. In choosing to deal with change strategies available to those *inside* a school system, it ignores a panoply of forces in the *outside* school environment which are far more powerful than any which can be generated within the school.

The major strategic decision for the local school system, then, is whether it will *invent* a new instructional process or *adopt* one invented elsewhere. Here the main road forks.

In fact, most people would assert a third possibility, namely, *adaptation*. Adaptation, in the conventional wisdom, is superior to the other alternatives—being, as it were, an ingenious blending of invention and adoption. It is almost universally recommended, and most schools claim to use it. My own observations have been that it is indeed a third pathway, usually chartered by wandering aimlessly back and forth between the other two. Most adaptation, as observed, is not so much a shrewd redesigning of an outside program to fit special local contours as it is a matter of knocking the corners off trying to get it through the doors of the school. What gets inside looks like *what the school was capable of understanding and reproducing*—its impressions of the innovation, so to speak—a poor copy rather than an improvement over the original. In any case, *adaptations can be understood as the invention of modifications in what is being adopted and will not be treated separately*.

Rational planning in curriculum and instruction, National Education Association of the United States, 1967, pp. 139–152. Reprinted by permission.

Local invention—a set of conditions

If the school system is actually to invent a new instructional program, it must work out a novel configuration of the building blocks
—teachers, learners, content, materials, methods, time, and space.
To alter the individual components, or the mixture of them, or both,
the school must draw together a group of capable people and
surround them with the conditions conducive to invention.

Few school systems are naturally rich enough in resources or free
enough in atmosphere to provide the necessary fertile conditions.
Faculties are so heavily burdened with the duties of operating
current programs that they cannot concurrently work out better
ones. Thus, the school system seriously intending to develop its own
innovation must deliberately create an invention setting.

Among the required ingredients for such a development, surely
the first is a group of highly intelligent people with differentiated
goals.

It is advisable to create a group rather than to rely on individuals.
This will enhance the opportunity for shared goals, cross-pollination
of ideas, mutual support during failure, reinforced exhilaration during success, the convenience of sympathetic but critical hearing
from fellow workers, and the creation of a cadre devoted to the
spread of the ultimate invention.

To ensure both quality in the innovation and eventual acceptance
by the local system, the inventors should have intelligence, energy,
and orientation to forces and trends outside the locality. Furthermore, they should have the respect and confidence of the school
staff. . . .

It is generally advisable to have a temporary group composed of
people who do not normally work together as a project team because it breaks any fixed circle of expectations and frees ideas and
talent to emerge more easily.

Even a talented, divergent group can deal only with a limited
problem at the time. Success is not likely unless the problem area is
narrowed so that a definite problem emerges which the group can
solve with the time, talent, and funds available to it. It follows also
that considerable working time must be allowed if a true innovation
is sought. So little working time is allotted to most school groups
attempting to innovate that they usually resort to adopting what
exists, making occasional modifications if time allows.

The choice of a work setting in some way separated from the

familiar working environment has certain psychological advantages, too, that enhance the sense of specialness which a successful working party always seems to develop. The creation of a temporary home, whether or not it is geographically distant from the accustomed locations of the members, reinforces identification with and allegiance to the group, underlines the importance of the task, and helps remind the members that new behaviors are expected of them.

Without in any way predetermining the nature of the final instructional program to be produced, it should be clearly established that the working party is expected to come up with a definite body of school practice which can be used to solve a likewise definite problem. A clear expectation of a usable product serves to increase task orientation and add a certain sense of urgency.

It is extremely valuable to infuse into an invention setting fundamental knowledge on which instructional techniques can be based. Principles from psychology, sociology, anthropology, and other behavioral sciences give the innovating group a broad platform on which to erect pedagogical methods. If the group is to formulate something truly new, it will come from basic principles underlying instruction, as well as from their personal experience as practitioners. A point to remember is that there is always more knowledge available to underpin the innovation than there was to undergird *current* programs when they were originally invented.

If the working party is placing subject content into its new program, it is essential for it to have a deep knowledge of the subject selected. There are two reasons why the content of elementary and secondary curriculum grew stale between 1930 and 1950: the passing of textbook authorship from content scholars to pedagogical scholars and the production of local curriculum guides without benefit of help from content scholars. The sharp insularity which resulted cut lower schools off from the frontiers of content scholarship and led in time to the curriculum-reform movement.... If locally sponsored innovation is to compete with nationally sponsored innovation, it must of necessity link itself to content scholarship.

There are several ways of making pedagogical and content knowledge available to practitioners. In the order of probable effectiveness, these are—

1 Choosing scholars as members of the working party,
2 Providing direct consulting help with scholars,

3 Arranging for study in college courses or local workshops, and

4 Supplying professional literature.

Currently there is the tendency for teachers to depend almost exclusively on instructional equipment and materials to carry the subject content and to guide their teaching methods. It is likely, therefore, that a design team would define its ultimate invention in terms of the equipment and materials to be used. It follows that the group must be aware of all the media already on the market and, more important, must have the ability to produce novel equipment and materials. Constituting a separate category of concrete apparata are those instruments which will be used to evaluate the innovation. These should be given separate but, nonetheless, careful consideration.

It is increasingly desirable, although probably not essential, for the innovation team to know how others are attacking similar problems. Duplication of errors can be avoided and duplication of correct steps made deliberate. Because parallel efforts are usually not detailed in the literature, travel to other sites is the only way to get full information. But as this might become an end in itself, it could vitiate some creativity.

Any kind of restriction in an invention setting lessens the chance of getting a truly distinctive answer. Members of the working party inevitably bring to the conference table and the laboratory an elaborate set of assumptions about what kinds of inventions the prospective adopters, who presumably are not all present, would accept and use well. These assumptions grow out of ideas about the competency of proposed adopters, their attitudes toward change, the types of materials and equipment they would be willing to use, the time blocks and spaces in which they work, the maximum acceptable cost of the resulting program, and so on.

It is probably best for the working party not to be guided by such assumptions—at least in the exploratory stages—because it is always conceivable that a new program of superb character could be widely disseminated even if quite distinct from those currently in use. Moreover, as the work advances, accurate knowledge of conditions in the target areas can be gathered and those elements of the new design which might later impede diffusion can be replaced by more promising ones. It is true that there are more reports about possible new programs than action on them.

Designers must be offered locations in which the innovation can be tried repeatedly, redesigned if necessary, and tried again as a part of its actual invention. This kind of tryout must be distinguished from full-scale testing of the final program, which has another purpose entirely. This is laboratory testing in contrast to field testing. It will often involve tiny components, use rough pilot models rather than finished products, require short periods of instruction, involve less than full-size classroom groups, use working members as teachers, be accompanied by immediate and perhaps elaborate evaluation, and in other ways look quite different from a test of the final program. It should be obvious that immediate access to classrooms with little or no advance notice is highly desirable.

Also, most members of invention teams need to believe that if they design a useful program, a use will be found for it. Thus, they should be told at the beginning that there is a prospective group of adopters who can benefit from what the working party designs and that dissemination of the invention is planned.

The prospect of personal recognition if the innovation is successful is another reinforcement. Among the ways of enhancing the expectation of recognition is to tell the invention group that the following arrangements can be made if they so desire:

1 An opportunity for them to announce and present the final program to colleagues in the local school system
2 A chance to take a leading role in actually disseminating the result so that other teachers can use it effectively
3 An opportunity to describe the results at professional meetings and in professional journals so that recognition beyond the local school system is a prospect
4 The opportunity to disseminate the program through commercial channels, with compensation through royalties when allowable.

It is important to present these as options to be exercised when the time is right; otherwise, working members may become fearful that premature display of their product may serve to discredit them.

For most school systems, it would be impossible to create such a set of conditions. And it is precisely for this reason that innovations born and bred at home cannot stand muster with the multimillion-dollar national programs like PSSC physics, SMSG mathematics, BSCS biology, and CHEM and CBA chemistry, which all sprang without exception from just such artificially created conditions.

Local adoption—a set of conditions

Most school systems must adopt their instructional programs. Adaptation, as indicated earlier, can be best conceived as the invention of modifications. It seems reasonable to believe that high-quality modifications can only come out of rich invention settings. To the extent that the school system adapts a program without providing such a situation, to that extent will it be hammering upon a well-engineered machine, blindfolded. Depending upon the magnitude of the change, the following conditions—in a rough chronological sequence—appear to be necessary for authentic adoption and successful use. Some will have been accomplished already if the system is diffusing internally a program which it has itself invented.

Any new program must be in a form which is identifiable, describable, and reproducible. An instructional innovation must be adopted as a body of practice. There may be profound principles or a great guiding spirit behind it, but unless it is reduced to behaviors which the adopter can learn, it cannot be successfully imported. Moreover, it must be in such a form that those using the behaviors will almost assuredly produce the desired product as a consequence. That is, the efficacy of the program must not be attributable to some mysterious quality lent to it by an esoteric group of developers. Adopters must, of course, become acquainted with the principles and spirit underlying the innovation so that they will not use it mechanically, but even intimate knowledge of the rationale is no substitute for an identifiable body of practices with which to carry it out.

Public enthusiasm for the specific innovation is not necessary. A particular innovation may not even have high visibility to outsiders. However, while public neutrality is harmless, public opposition would, in all likelihood, devastate the innovation. Thus, opposition must be prevented even if enthusiasm is not aroused. It seems likely that the attitudes teachers themselves display toward the innovation and the reactions they thereby arouse in students are powerful conditioners of public opinion. . . .

The public must be informed about a change so that it will not come as a surprise and arouse opposition for that reason alone. The customary channels of information such as newspaper reports, letters from the school, and PTA meetings can carry the limited information needed to prevent opposition to most innovations. A major change, however, may require the use of public meetings and special citizens' committees to help explain it.

If any principle is well established, it is that a positive desire for the change, not merely a neutral acceptance, must be displayed by the administrative staff. In the best of circumstances, all the administrative levels which are visible to the target location will join in the call for change. It is especially necessary that the call come from line officers in authority positions, not from staff officers such as curriculum coordinators alone.

The ideal stance for the administrative staff is that the change must be accomplished and that all the resources at its command will be applied assiduously to easing the way for the change. A dramatic way of symbolizing this attitude is to have the school as an institution visibly take up part of the burden in such fashion as—

1 Spending unaccustomed amounts for staff travel to innovation sites,
2 Paying staff members extra for time spent beyond normal duties,
3 Closing school to arrange for in-service training,
4 Allowing salary guide credit for training received, and
5 Supplying meals in conjunction with meetings.

Some of these steps, essential on other grounds, are recommended here for their special psychological value.

Probably the most delicate balance to be struck in the introduction of an innovation is that between pointing out its familiar elements and pointing out its distinctive ones. Indicating familiarity with the ingredients of a new program gives encouragement to teachers by assuring them that they can handle the innovation partly with existing skills. And yet, if these familiar elements are overemphasized, the innovation runs the risk of a too close resemblance to existing procedure, in which event the whole case for change may be lost. The best tactic at the outset would seem to be a sharp delineation of selected familiar elements and the equally sharp delineation of novel elements. *Then as the program moves into use, attention should shift almost entirely to the new ones.*

Staff members belong to professional associations outside the local school system and to other outside groups which can grant them status and prestige. Many teachers respond strongly to the values of outside groups in their community and/or professional associations to which they are affiliated. In addition, they look for approval to outside agencies which are in a position to judge their work, such as the schools which will receive their students subsequently or the employers who will hire them. If the innovation calls for behavior which a staff member thinks unacceptable to the outside group, even if ardently endorsed by his own school, he will resist the innovation. Every opportunity should, therefore, be taken to call to the attention of prospective users the endorsement of the innovation by outside professional leaders, colleges, other highly regarded school systems, and the like.

Since information flows to the staff from many outside sources, it will not always be necessary for the local school to make teachers aware that an innovation exists. When it is, simple awareness can be established by printed material and by references in speeches. A favorable impression can be developed by showing how the innovation is in keeping with traditional local values—'Their philosophy seems to be like ours.' 'Some colleges have expressed an interest in what we are doing.' 'We have been using something similar.' 'It seems to be a practical approach.'

Of course, awareness is not sufficient—actual interest must be developed. Here it must be shown that the innovation is addressed to an area of learning in which the local school itself has located an unacceptable gap. Longer printed or filmed descriptions can be used. However, the ideal form is one which makes further inquiry easy. Correspondence with the producers or with users will go a little way, but conversations are better. Speakers and consultants, preferably those who have worked as producers or users of the innovation, should be invited to speak and to discuss. The staff should be able to confront them in small, informal, semisocial sessions so that the utmost in feedback can be established.

It is at this point that the staff will want to examine the actual instructional equipment and materials. This should, therefore, be made available.

It is highly desirable to have the prospective adopters—the staff—make their own inquiries into the innovation. The strategic problem is to ensure forward movement while allowing the intended users to choose the exact route and modulate the pace. One useful tactic is to couple the prospective users in a group with others who already favor the innovation—including administrators. A second tactic is to supply ample information to all the prospective users, both about the innovation and about the plan of adoption, so they can be certain nothing will happen before they have an opportunity to intervene. A third tactic is to arrange specific opportunities for them to react as things proceed.

The chief questions in the minds of the intended adopters are likely to be, 'What *is* the innovation?' 'How will it affect *me*?' 'Can I learn to do it?' and 'Will I be able to stop it if things go wrong?'

The precipitation of a decision to try the innovation is the great moment in the adoption of the innovation. Events rise to this peak and trail downward from it. The chief *questions* in the minds of the prospective adopters seem to be, 'Is it designed for a setting like my own?' and 'Can I make it work?'

It seems to be established beyond doubt that the best way to answer such questions is to have propective adopters visit a site where the new innovation is in actual use. Certain conditions are necessary if the visit is to be fully effective:

1 There must be a minimum of artificiality and showmanship in the program being demonstrated.

2 Ideally, the demonstration setting should be recognizable to the visitors as *quite similar* to the schools from which they come.

3 There should be no special features of the program which the visitor will regard as essential to success but as unreproducible at home. The presence of extraordinary teachers, elaborate equipment, abnormally high contact with university personnel, and other expensive or unmanageable features will tend to convince visitors that the program is not for them.

4 It should be possible for visitors to talk to teachers and students as well as to sponsors of the program so that they can get the perceptions of those who must live with the program from day to day. . . .

Among the methods used to judge teaching success, pupil achievement test results rank high with the public, administrators, and teachers themselves. Innovations which would reduce pupil scores on highly regarded tests and thereby discredit not only the innovation but the teachers employing it will arouse understandable resistance. Therefore, if a desired innovation does not coincide with school achievement tests, these tests must be made to coincide with the innovation. One alternative is to eliminate tests if none can be found to fit the innovation; another is to continue the old tests to see how the new instructional program affects the results. In the latter case, teachers must be assured that any drop in scores will be attributed to the innovation and not to any lack of competency on their part. It is, therefore, necessary to locate or develop tests which will measure what the innovation seeks to teach. Tests administered by external agencies exert more influence on the school than local tests. It is especially important that these external tests accommodate the proposed innovation. If they do not and cannot somehow be changed, the staff must be told how the school proposes to deal with the pressures which may arise if students do poorly on external examinations because of the new instructional program.

Regulations which might prevent or appear to prevent the adoption of the innovation must be amended, suspended, or otherwise lifted aside so that prospective users can see clearly that those barriers have been or can be removed. Regulations of this kind come from authorities above the prospective users, often from a state agency or legislation which supports and controls the given instructional area. But they can also come from the local school system, especially a large rule-ridden one.

Remember that a barrier is often perceived by the viewer even though it was not intended by the sponsoring agency. The reading of nonexistent prohibitions into regulations comes in part from misunderstanding and probably in part from a search for reasons to maintain the status quo. In any event, an early step in paving the way for the introduction of a novel program is a careful inspection, one not only of the regulations themselves, but also of the local adopters' views of them.

Some innovations require more space; some require new subdivisions of old space; some require more flexible allocations of it from day to day. Whatever the situation, as in the previous strategy discussed, it must be made clear to prospective users that they will not be expected to cram the innovation into an unsuitable location. If the innovation requires more operating time, or a shift in time placement, or more flexible time scheduling, arrangements for accommodating it should be planned in advance.

Among the supremely critical conditions of successful innovation is the ready availability of teaching equipment and materials. The prospect of facing a class empty-handed is unnerving at any time, even to the most skilled of teachers. The prospect of having to do it during the installation of a new program is unbearable. A virtually certain way to reduce anxiety is to have all teaching materials on hand in advance of initiating the new instruction so that teachers can become familiar with them and can be positively assured that they will be on the classroom shelves on opening day.

To change requires more energy than to remain the same. Allowing extra working time to those who are taking on the innovation by reducing normal duties somewhat or paying for additional work time is quite helpful during the very early stages. The relief is in part psychological; it need not be sufficient to cover all the new energy output.

Of all the steps in adopting an innovation, the most consequential one is training the staff to conduct it. This is the key to success, an inescapable requirement of authentic adoption.

Unless new teachers who have been trained elsewhere can be hired to mount the program—which becomes increasingly possible with the growing number of national Institutes—the local school system must arrange for the training. Novel content, as well as novel pedagogy, must of course be taught if the innovation demands both.

It seems that training may be given successfully either before or during the introduction of the program. There is some reason to believe that content might be taught as well or better beforehand but that teaching methods are best interspersed with classroom practice. It also appears to be true that content may be taught through reading or standard courses, whereas methods should be taught in authentic workshops, rather than in formal classes.

In the best circumstances for teaching pedagogical skills, the teacher of teachers knows more about the innovation than those he is re-educating and has himself succeeded in using the program with children. Teachers learning the new approach should use it with their own students over a period of weeks or months and meet periodically with colleagues and outside experts to discuss their classroom experiences. Help should always be on call. It seems quite clear that guided practice over time is the only way to convert an appealing instructional idea into a living body of skills.

All the equipment and materials teachers will need to teach the program should be employed by them during their training. If the program is to be used by a given group in a particular school, all members of the group should probably be trained at the same time. Otherwise, polarization of opinion around user and nonuser groups may occur and inhibit diffusion.

Turnover in school faculties is so high that in-service training in the new approach must be given continuously; otherwise, the innovation can drift out of the schools along with teachers who leave. Moreover, periodic refresher work is good for those who remain.

Courses and workshops are probably less appropriate for this purpose than active supervision of the program, coupled with periodic discussion meetings among those who employ the aging innovation.

Some form of trial before permanent adoption serves as a final reassurance to the staff that the ship can still return to shore if the voyage seems doomed. There are two major forms the trial can take: (a) pilot use in a few selected settings, or (b) universal temporary adoption.

The pilot plan is less visible to outsiders, less expensive, more manageable, less upsetting to the staff, and more likely to succeed (if the settings are hand picked). Its chief drawback is that opposition has ample time to develop and become consolidated so that the innovation may become 'contained' in the pilot settings. This can be avoided in part by having the staff choose the pilot users to represent it in the trial. Thus, they do not become elevated through other means such as administrative appointment and thereby become targets for staff resentment.

Universal temporary adoption does not make apparently invidious distinctions between those chosen to make the maiden voyage and those left on shore, gives everyone a chance to judge for himself, accentuates the urgency of change, gives teachers company during difficult times, and begins the universal installation of the innovation. Its chief drawbacks are expense, severe logistical problems, the risk of highly visible failure, and the probability of low-grade but widespread complaints. The risks can be reduced considerably by careful planning.

Pilot trials would appear to be best for elaborate, expensive innovations demanding a high level of skill; temporary adoption would appear to be best for innovations which are scheduled for widespread adoption, when practice in a new kind of instructional skill is more important than the success of the specific innovation.

Richard Hooper

III:3 Educational technology in the USA—a diagnosis of failure

Educational technology is one of the innovations that has failed to penetrate the American educational system to any significant degree. The diagnosis of this failure identifies a whole range of interlocking causes, including the inertia of the educational system itself, the posture of the educational technologists pushing the innovation, the absence of a viable theory of learning, the fear of comprehensive curriculum change. Strategies for successful innovation need to map out the many causes of resistance.

The newer technologies are failing to penetrate the American educational system. But the cries of frustration . . . seldom lead to any real diagnosis of the failure. There is, instead, a tendency to gloss over innovations—such as teaching machines and instructional radio —that have gone awry. . . .

A major obstacle to the introduction of technology into education is the inertia of the educational system itself. There are few incentives for teachers to change their methods, and educational institutions seem to be designed to resist change. Schools and colleges too often take on the outward appearance of innovation, but not its substance. The educational bureaucracy neutralizes innovative ideas with apparent ease. Each new technology intent on transforming educational procedures soon finds itself the one that is being transformed.

This inertia is fed by the strong antipathies to technology, found both inside and outside education. Many people, rightly or wrongly, see technology of whatever variety as a threat. . . . The technology of polygraph tests, computerized data banks, miniaturized bugging devices, invades our freedom and privacy. Before the advent of the videotape recorder, the only way of judging a teacher was on the basis of examination results, what students said about him, his be-

Audio-Visual Communication Review, vol. 17, no. 3, 1969, pp. 245–264. Reprinted by permission.

havior at faculty meetings, and a rare personal visit to watch him teach. Teaching has always been an intimate and unrecorded process. Technology—the recording medium—must be a threat.

> It is quite predictable . . . that any new means of moving information will alter any power structure whatever. . . . innovation threatens the equilibrium of existing organizations. (McLuhan, 1964, p. 91)

The educational system is a labor-intensive industry built around the live teacher. The power of many universities resides with the faculty as opposed to central administration. This power alignment is threatened by the introduction of capital-intensive technology. Departmental chairmen face some loss of sovereignty because of the high capital investment in a technological system. The problems of technical compatibility with television or computer equipment cannot be solved if the purchasing decisions are made independently of each other. The autonomy that faculty enjoys in the matter of textbooks may prove a poor model for the selection and use of a sophisticated educational technology. Technology is resisted in education because it builds up new power centers and weakens traditional ones. . . .

Media discrimination

> . . . a curriculum is a thing in balance that cannot be developed first for content, then for teaching method, then for visual aids, then for some other particular feature. (Bruner, 1966, p. 164)

The average curriculum supervisor, department head, or subject matter specialist makes content decisions that are already, without his being aware of it, affected by two factors : the live teacher and the printed textbook. The decisions are in fact made on the assumption that content will be carried via the printed word and the teacher's mouth. A split—very harmful to educational technology— has opened up in education. On the one side there are the pure content decisions which on closer analysis are anything but pure. On the other side there are the secondary decisions dealing with the so-called newer media—films, audiotapes, television. An unfortunate (and false) polarization has taken place around *content*, which means the traditional way of doing things in the classroom, and quite separate from it, *media*, which means anything new.

The word *medium* is as often misused with regard to meaning as it is with regard to grammar (medium-singular; media-plural). The two major media of educational communication—teacher and book —are seldom called *media*. Thus when educators discuss the media available to solve an instructional problem, if they do at all, decisions about the strategic use of the teacher and textbook are seldom made on the same level or at the same time as decisions about teaching aids, machines, and technical assistance. . . .

This discrimination against the newer media is enshrined in the organizational structure and functioning of many school district administrations. In an affluent school district on Long Island, for example, the power flows down from the assistant superintendent for instruction through the directors of elementary and secondary education to the curriculum supervisors and on into the schools. The audiovisual department is a service agency off to one side, like the kitchen, maintenance, and janitorial staff. Major decisions about courses and textbooks are made in this school district by curriculum supervisors with groups of teachers, *without reference* to the audiovisual coordinators. In fact, the two groups are not really on speaking terms. Audiovisual people are not even invited to participate in the summer workshops when new course guides are designed.

The newer media are not present in the inner sanctuary of curriculum decision-making. They are consulted, if at all, after the key decisions have been made. Television, film, programed texts remain afterthoughts. . . .

Thus educational technology ends up doing little else but perpetuating the traditional system of education. It is an abiding irony of the newer media that despite their ability to revolutionize and upgrade the quality of education they can by the same token prolong and mirror what is already going on in school. Programed instruction is a very useful and efficient way of dumping more information into children's heads. Computer-assisted instruction may actually *increase* the amount of drill and practice in the classroom. Closed-circuit television might be the worst thing to happen to colleges at a time of bursting student enrollments. Instead of the crisis forcing faculty and administration into retooling the whole system, television has made it possible to solve the problem of large classes in an age-old way. The lecture as *the* staple medium of college communication could now be set fair, thanks to television, for another hundred years. . . .

The image of the media people is on the whole poor. According to a professor at a big midwestern university, 'Media people should be kept on the periphery. They are not qualified to make teaching decisions. They are tradesmen, with a parochial view and vested interests too strong. They are often very unimaginative.' Audiovisual specialists have on more than one occasion been called 'the dregs of the teaching profession'. The audiovisual coordinator is still associated with the ex-football coach who carries 16mm projectors, buys overhead projectors, fixes plugs, and runs a film library. Audiovisual men are indissolubly linked, in the minds of most teachers at all levels, with programed instruction and television specialists whether the latter like it or not.

Media man's image is not helped by a number of entrepreneurs in the ranks. They are the bandwagoneers of education, practiced in the art of grantsmanship. They are the first to jump at the newest ideas and put in a research proposal to the Office of Education. Federal legislation and commercial encouragement have led to a Klondike media rush. Programed instruction people, while exhorting education to espouse the new science of learning, rush to press with unscientific, unvalidated, and skimpily written programed texts. School superintendents can make their names with innovation. A year or two later they move on, leaving another technological graveyard behind them. Education despite its inbred conservatism—or because of it?—is very prone to fads and fashions. There is a special breed of opportunist consultant who caters to this market. Computer-assisted instruction is the latest fad in a long line. Some most unqualified people are climbing on its back, goading it forward with cries of 'systems analysis'.

It is obviously impossible to say how much of this generally negative image is justified. Much of it is a hangover from the past and a convenient excuse for the educational establishment to do nothing. But the complaint, for example, that media people are obsessed with gadgetry is not ungrounded. . . .

Media people have been accused, often with good cause, of getting overinvolved with public relations. Too many media conventions and media journals degenerate into platforms for PR statements about innovations by men and women who have strong vested interests in their success. This had led to a fool's paradise of media innovation. The *real* problems are not being sufficiently reflected in the published statements and so new projects too often start up on rather shaky ground.

Much criticism of media people revolves around the question of their motives. The entrepreneurs apart, there seem to be too many cases of conflicting loyalties. Are the audiovisual coordinators really in the business of improving the quality of instruction, or are they just empire-building? Are television people interested in helping the teacher widen the range of his or her resources, or are they primarily interested in 'selling' television? The two are not necessarily compatible.

Divided and conquered

Media people have consistently failed to work together and deliver a concerted attack on traditional education. An instructional television expert from Pennsylvania was flown to the West Coast to do a consultation job with a state education department. The top audiovisual people in the department, with whom he had appointments, kept him waiting in the outer office and then refused to see him at all. Among the learning psychologists a running fight has developed between Skinnerians and Brunerians, thus postponing the important task of trying to fuse the discovery method with programed instruction to get the benefits of both. The powerful curriculum reform group, Educational Development Center, which is of Brunerian persuasion, makes no use of behavioral technology.

The myriad national associations, such as DAVI, NAVA, NAEB, NSPI, have tended to intensify the conflict between the newer media. 'Objective' studies of educational needs, undertaken by national associations, have led on occasion to a glorified product promotion of the particular association's own medium. At the local level there is also separatism and conflict in the organization of media. Each medium, especially at college level, builds up its own empire independently of the others. At the University of Texas at Austin for example, the television and audiovisual services operate as two autonomous units.

Such philosophical and administrative apartheid is blocking the way to progress. It postpones the day when the communications functions of an educational institution can be planned on a more comprehensive basis. Attitudes and professional affiliations have rigidified in the 20 years and more since the media revolution began. Terminology like *audiovisual* has set hard. New ways of thinking and new ways of using a rapidly changing technology are in a sense held back, inhibited by a frozen terminology. Existing media organizations, with few exceptions, do not seem to want to reconfigure themselves.

Media-ocrity

> It must . . . be said that most (not all) of the pictorial and recorded material made available to classrooms is on the level of the textbook—i.e., it is relatively uninteresting, relatively uncivilized, and directed at establishing values and achieving objectives rather than at revealing the complications and fascinations of reality. (Mayer, 1961, p. 383)

The single and most obvious factor in the slow advance of educational technology is poor software. Commercial interests tend to avoid the more uncertain area of software production. The gadgetry passions of teachers and audiovisual coordinators are profitably exploited. Machines have appeared on the educational market long before appropriate materials were made available for them. This happened with language laboratories and much of the initial enthusiasm was lost. . . .

The design of good instructional materials is inhibited by the absence of a viable theory of learning. Progress with educational technology is closely linked to progress with understanding the basic processes of education. Much of the research into learning and audiovisual communication has been contradictory. Even where behavioral objectives have been properly defined, 'The awful truth is that we have little idea of how to develop instructional conditions to meet these specific objectives' (Barson, 1965, p. 86). The lack of clear guidelines and the conflicting nature of many research theories have given educational administrators another convenient excuse to do nothing. They have also led to frustration: 'At one time or another, radio, motion pictures, filmstrips, TV, language labs, and teaching machines have been hailed as the saviors of education. So have large classes, small classes, seminars, tutorials, independent study, years abroad, work-study programs, mid-winter reading periods, and year-around operation. None of these is either as bad as detractors assert or as good as zealots claim. Lacking an adequate theoretical framework in which to place these innovations, the pendulum continues to swing wildly from euphoria to cynicism' (Gustad, 1964, p. 38).

But even where good research has been done, the results have seldom been incorporated into the design of software. This lack of link-up has a number of causes. First, it costs money. The sort of pretesting and revision which is necesssary if research is to be designed into materials, has often been avoided by, for example, commercial firms. 'Faced with field reports on their programs, they tried to avoid expensive revisions. The incarnation of programs in programed books tended to harden the form at the moment when it should have been most flexible and most responsive to test findings and new technical developments' (Schramm, 1964a, p. 102). Dr. Douglas Porter of the Office of Programed Instruction at Harvard has done a survey of 350 commercially produced college-level programed courses. Despite the fact that scientific validation is one of the major planks in the programed instruction platform, less than 10 per cent of the courses possessed evidence that the materials had been validated with students. ...

Accessibility

A major complaint, especially from teachers, about the newer media centers on the question of accessibility. Given the existence of good materials, can they be got at and used? A West Coast teacher described her experience: 'I have to order the films I want a school year in advance. Usually I end up getting a quarter of the ones I ordered—and then they come not at times when I wanted them.'

The new media—both hardware and software—have persistently failed to make themselves easy to use. Microfilm reading machines are classic examples of design incompetence. The secondary school teacher with one free period a week does not have time to go searching for a projector. ...

Localism

One of the obvious phenomena of recent American history is a realignment of power between local, state and federal interests. In education the change has been dramatic over the last decade. The federal government has grown into a major force as a result of recent legislation, such as NDEA and ESEA. State education departments have emerged out of the wilderness to become increasingly powerful, many of them getting involved in statewide television and telecommunications networks. On the local level, the one outstanding fact is the continuing decrease in the number of school districts as a result of consolidation.

Yet despite this realignment there are still many places where the effective use of educational technology is being strangled by the big hands of localism and parochialism. This will become more troublesome as the more sophisticated and extensive technologies develop —computer networks, information retrieval systems, and multipurpose telecommunications grids.

Behind, and reinforcing, the localism there are whole series of academic attitudes. They are most visible at college level but have counterparts right down through the educational system. 'Institutions, and departments within institutions, cling to cherished institutional images of themselves. These images make it difficult for members of an institution to admit the possibility of high levels of competence in the instruction of other institutions and departments. Autonomy for the college, in particular, and even sometimes for the lower schools, is a familiar aspect of the American educational scene. His training and experience make the teacher see himself as an independent leader of a group of students' (Erickson, 1964, p. 177).

Educational autonomy can be healthy—as with the good teacher ranging out far beyond the syllabus and dogmas of the bureaucracy. It is vital to much of the research work carried on at universities where the researcher should not be just reacting to the needs—often short-sighted and utilitarian—of society. But educational autonomy is a negative force if it reinforces those aspects of localism that are causing either no use or poor use of the newer media.

Localism—in the sense of local production and/or local organization—has, of course, a number of advantages for the growth of educational technology. 'From an educational point of view, there appear to be many advantages in a close link between television programmes and local school systems. Such integration makes it easier to ensure that the programmes correspond to the needs and curricula of schools or colleges which utilize them. Classroom teachers can participate in determining programme schedules and may directly influence the programme from week to week. . . . Television frequently proves particularly valuable in providing materials of a purely local nature, and for which neither films nor textbooks are available' (Cassirer, 1960, p. 93).

Localism can allow educational technology to be developed close to, and responsive to, the real problems. It may help the newer media to break into the inner sanctuary of curriculum decision-making. Probably one of the reasons why educational films have slipped into the enrichment-supplemental role is that the majority were produced and developed on their own, separate from any comprehensive curriculum development. Where the newer media are designed locally there may be rather more opportunity for them to be integrated into the *core* of the instructional system.

Locally produced materials have the advantage of space and time relevance. The general problem of town planning, for example, can be anchored to the particular town where the learner is living. Similarly time relevance is possible with a locally produced television lesson on current affairs which builds on something in the local paper's morning headlines. Much of education is criticized because the reality outside the classroom and the reality inside barely overlap.

Unfortunately, for every advantage that localism brings with it, there seems to be a disadvantage. Technology, to be really effective, demands two things: large resources in time, money, and manpower for development and production, and a large population for distribution. The costs of developing computer-assisted instruction are so high that accessibility by many students must be guaranteed if it is to be even remotely cost effective. Films, using expensive techniques such as time lapse and high speed photography, must have promise of wide use to make economic sense. The sort of curriculum reforms undertaken by Chem Study, the Educational Development Center, or the Oakleaf project in Pittsburgh, are regional and national in perspective. Television and radio as instructional strategies make more and more sense, the larger the audience.

Localism is a threat to a technology which must have economies of size. The autonomy of the teacher, the cherished image of the institution, too often conflict with the pressing need to pool resources and exchange materials. Schemes such as the Texas Educational Microwave Project (TEMP) have all but foundered on these rocks. There is probably no major university in the United States using videotaped lectures or lecture segments produced at another university. Dozens of series on accounting, politics, physical education, are being produced locally and most are unable to exploit the full potential of the medium. Educational broadcasters complain constantly of lack of resources. But there have been resources running into millions of dollars. The trouble is that, thanks to localism, these dollars have in the main been poorly invested. Instead of going into regional production centers, they have been scattered across hundreds of separate studios which now stand idle uncomfortably often. 'There is great economic waste in the present development of instructional television for public school education, with almost every school group which is currently involved in television producing all of its own programming. Our schools do not each produce, separately, all their own textbooks, but utilize those that are produced and distributed nationally or regionally. The time must soon come when our schools can satisfy their needs for the instructional resources they use via television distribution facilities without each separate school having to duplicate what every other major system in the country is also doing' (*The Financing of Educational Television Stations*, 1965, p. 148).

The ecology of education

'Too many of our efforts to improve the curriculum have been based on a limited attack. . . . Thus, we undertake to improve Ninth Grade General Science or American History in the Senior High School or Arithmetic at the Fifth Grade level and so on. Many of these efforts have been productive but, as changes are made at any one level or stage of the continuum without making relevant changes at each of the preceding or following stages, the inevitable result is confusion, needless repetition, regrettable gaps and either boredom or discouragement. The curriculum may be likened to a spider web. It is impossible to disturb any single strand or spoke of the web without shaking the whole web. The attack, to be really effective, needs to deal with the entire range and continuum of content from first grade through elementary, junior and senior high school and, certainly, the undergraduate school' (Nelson, 1961, pp. 58–59).

The fear of comprehensive change, and the refusal to undertake it, are basic to the failure of educational technology. The educational establishment is willing to make one change but when this change starts to demand other changes, the cut-off point is quickly reached. '. . . programmed instruction . . . was coming along fine until someone started actually using programs; then the pall effect and the discomfort in changing administrative procedures to accommodate the new medium made it quite unacceptable except of course, for the usual "enrichment" programs which are so necessary in modern education' (Taylor & Williams, 1966, p. 109).

The fear of anything but marginal change has led programed instruction, television, and audiovisual materials into playing a marginal role. It has led to innovations being pasted on to the outside of an educational institution: when the grant money runs out, the innovation is carefully peeled off without damaging the structure, and thrown away.

Education's lack of interest in comprehensive planning and reform is reflected in (caused by?) its budgeting procedures. 'The existing budget and budgeting procedures,' writes Werner Hirsch (1964) in *Program Budgeting*, 'are so patently uninformative that they conceal most of the needed insight. Many old-timers are quite comfortable in such a situation, which makes it difficult for any operation to be judged and evaluated seriously' (p. 153). Educational burgets reveal how much was spent on teachers' salaries, television equipment, heating—that is to say on the *objects* of expenditure. They do not reveal how much was spent on reaching a given level of reading competence with fifth graders, or on driver education—on the much more important *objectives* of expenditure.

Traditional budgeting methods obscure the necessity of developing specific objectives, and thus the necessity to analyze the best ways of achieving those objectives. The consistent absence of any but the vaguest and most ambiguous objectives is right at the root of education's troubles. The costs and benefits of the newer media are not measured against other systems' performance in doing a particular job. So it is difficult for any innovation to prove itself. The teacher, the textbook, the thirty-students-to-a-class are seldom analyzed. They are constants around which any innovation must wind itself.

The decision-making process that leads to the purchase and utilization of educational technology is of poor quality. Machinery is installed for the wrong reasons and without adequate planning. School systems invest in highly expensive dial access retrieval equipment but allocate no resources to teacher training or software production. Money is made available to buy or hire films, and project them, but it is not around to free the teacher to preview and plan their use. New school buildings are erected to house audio-visual facilities and then it is discovered that there are not enough power outlets and the floor-to-ceiling window wall lets in too much light.

Educational technology is caught up in a series of vicious circles which can only be broken by a comprehensive attack on all fronts. Probably the most vicious of circles has to do with the training of administrators and teachers. Few colleges of education *require* their students to take courses in educational technology. And so another generation of teachers goes out into the schools unequipped to deal with, and probably antipathetic to, technology. They were taught without educational technology as children, and were taught to teach without technology at college. The sins of the fathers are—yet again—visited upon the children unto the third and fourth generations. . . .

Conclusion

Educational technology will remain on the periphery without resources unless educational administrators—and the civilian administrators above them, for example, school boards—give it top-level commitment. Without top-level commitment there will be no favorable climate in which change can happen and no favorable organization of time, space, and money inside which the teacher may be able to make the change.

Educational technology will begin to have a significant, and hopefully beneficial, impact on education only when all the many interlocking problems of change have been squarely faced. Much more is needed than odd bursts of enthusiasm for a piece of technology here or an innovative idea there. The piecemeal approach must be discarded. As Julius Stratton (1964) has said, 'We indulge excessively in uncoordinated conferences, surveys, and studies that on the whole are highly unproductive. Our ailments are vast and complex, and they will yield only to planned, collaborative attacks focussed on clear objectives and leading to concerted action' (pp. 20–21).

References

Barson, J. *A procedural and cost analysis study of media in instructional systems development*. East Lansing, Mich.: Michigan State University and US Office of Education, 1965.

Bruner, J. S. *Toward a theory of instruction*. Cambridge, Mass., The Belknap Press of Harvard University, 1966.

Cassirer, H. R. *Television teaching today*. New York: Unesco, 1960.

Erickson, C. G. 'The administrator, educational problems, and instructional television.' In Diamond, R. M. (ed.), *A guide to instructional television*. New York: McGraw-Hill, 1964.

Financing of educational television stations, The. Washington DC: National Association of Educational Broadcasters and US Office of Education, 1965.

Gustad, J. 'On improving college teaching.' *NEA Journal*, 1964, vol. 53 (3).

Hirsch, W. Z. 'Education in the program budget'. In Novick, D. (ed.), *Program budgeting*. Rand Corporation, 1964.

Mayer, M. *The schools.* New York: Harper & Bros, 1961.

McLuhan, M. *Understanding media.* New York: McGraw-Hill, 1964.

Nelson, L. W. 'Implications of research for curriculum change.' In *Newer Educational Media.* Pennsylvania State University and US Office of Education, 1961.

Schramm, W. 'Programed instruction today and tomorrow.' Reprinted in *Four case studies of programed instruction.* New York: Fund for the Advancement of Education, 1964.

Stratton, J. A. 'The MIT 1964 commencement address.' *Technology Review,* July 1964.

Taylor, C. W. and Williams, F. E. (eds.). *Instructional media and creativity.* New York: John Wiley, 1966.

John Nisbet

III:4 Curriculum development in Scotland

The pattern of curriculum development in Scotland is different from that of England. The work of the Consultative Committee on the Curriculum—the Scottish equivalent of the Schools Council—is described, and its manner of operation. The activities of curriculum working parties in various subject areas are outlined. The Schools Council approach to curriculum development—definition of objectives, design of materials, trials in schools, evaluation and feedback—has not been widely applied in Scotland.

'The danger of making comparisons is that one easily falls into the trap of exaggerating differences. Examiners, with their fondness for the "compare and contrast" type of question, know only too well what ingenuity can be used in discovering distinctions where none exist. Similarities can be overlooked because they are too obvious. ... The temptation is not merely to describe the differences which exist but to try to explain them.'[1] The pattern of curriculum development in Scotland is certainly different from that in England, and it is tempting to explain the contrast in terms of differences, in both size and character, between the educational systems of the two countries. Scotland is a small country, with only some 3,180 schools supported wholly or partly by public funds. Its educational system is more tightly knit: over 98 per cent of children attend the public schools (in the literal and Scottish use of the term). The smaller unit can function on a less formal basis, for consultation takes place between people who know each other and meet together frequently. In consequence, some changes can be introduced quickly and easily. Revision of the secondary school mathematics curriculum in Scotland began in 1963; in 1969 over 70 per cent of schools are being examined on the new syllabus, and in 1970 the figure will be 98 per

Journal of Curriculum Studies, vol. 2, no. 1, 1970, pp. 5–10. (Published twice-yearly by Williams Collins Sons & Co. Ltd.) Reprinted by permission.

cent.[2] Another consequence is that the process of change is seldom adequately documented, so that it is difficult for those outside the system to know precisely what has happened. Two recent publications have helped to fill in the details of recent developments. In *Scottish education looks ahead*,[3] the Senior Chief Inspector has outlined the machinery of change in Scottish education, and two members of the inspectorate have described the changes in English and mathematics. The *First Report* 1965/8[4] of the Consultative Committee on the Curriculum gives a comprehensive review of the whole range of curriculum development in Scotland, and provides an opportunity to make comparisons with the Schools Council report, *The first three years*.[5]

The Consultative Committee on the Curriculum is the Scottish equivalent of the Schools Council. In both Scotland and England, a considerable amount of work in curriculum development was under way before any formal national co-ordinating body was set up. But whereas the Schools Council was established with a large measure of financial and administrative independence, the Scottish Consultative Committee is a committee of the Scottish Education Department, with the Secretary of the Department as its chairman. 'The Consultative Committee, as an advisory body with no executive functions, has no staff of its own and secretarial services are provided by officers of the Scottish Education Department. The work of enquiry and curriculum development has been carried out almost wholly by H.M. Inspectors and teachers in schools, colleges of education and universities.'[6] Perhaps appropriately, the Scottish arrangement would appear to be economic of funds. Costs are absorbed by other parts of the educational system, but if they could be separately accounted, it seems likely that the total cost of curriculum development in Scotland would fall well below the traditional eleven-eightieths, which used to serve as a basis for the ratio of Scottish to English expenditure on education. Whereas the report of the Schools Council lists research projects costing a total of over two million pounds, the report of the Consultative Committee does not mention money at all.

The twenty-four members of the Scottish Consultative Committee on the Curriculum are 'appointed as individuals—for their personal knowledge and experience—rather than as representatives of particular organizations'.[7] However, it is not by chance that nine of the members are teachers in schools, together with one from a technical college and one from an art college, while four are from the inspectorate and two are officers of the Scottish Education Department (the Secretary and one under-secretary). The Principals of three of the ten Scottish colleges of education are members; in Scotland, the colleges of education are financed directly by the Scottish Education Department. The other four members are: a director of education, a professor of chemistry, a professor of French and a banker. The Committee is thus very much an organ of the central authority in partnership with the teachers. At least the teaching profession cannot complain of over-representation of outside interests or of domination by the universities. For its independence and freedom of action, the Committee must rely on the independence of mind of its members, and on the frequent and consistent disclaimers by the Scottish Education Department of any wish to encroach on the teachers' freedom in curricular matters. 'The Committee's terms of reference require it to maintain a general oversight over the school curriculum, both primary and secondary; (and) to draw the attention of the Secretary of State to any aspect of the curriculum, whether general or particular, which seems to call for consideration by specialist bodies. . . . Neither the Secretary of State nor the Scottish Education Department has any direct responsibility for the school curriculum. Education authorities . . . acting with the advice of the heads of their schools and their teachers, decide what shall, or shall not, be taught in their schools . . . and it is for them to decide whether or not to accept any advice which is offered to them.'[8]

But the essential guarantee against interference by the central authority is the method of working which the Committee has adopted—the small working party, comprising a majority of practising teachers and inspectors, with college of education lecturers and occasionally a university teacher or other adviser. In 1955 the first working party on this model was set up to review the curriculum of the senior secondary school. The recommendations of their report in 1959 led to the introduction of the Ordinary grade in the Scottish Certificate of Education in 1962. Previously, memoranda of advice on the curriculum had been drafted by the inspectorate—for example, *The primary school in Scotland* (1950), *Junior secondary education* (1955) and a series of papers on individual secondary school subjects issued between 1950 and 1961. This was the basis also of the memorandum, *Primary education in Scotland*, which was published in 1965. Increasingly, however, the working party structure has been favoured, and more than twenty such groups have been formed in the past ten years.

A description of the work of one such group is given by A. G. Robertson,[9] formerly H.M.I. and chairman of the Mathematics Syllabus Committee from 1963 and 1968. The appointment of the Mathematics Syllabus Committee followed from a report by a previous Departmental committee on mathematics, which had reviewed recent changes in university honours courses in mathematics. The new committee was given both a broad remit and a precise task: 'to review the school mathematics syllabus and to initiate in a number of schools experimental work on the introduction of certain aspects of modern mathematics.' The committee comprised fifteen principal teachers of mathematics in secondary schools, two principal lecturers in mathematics from colleges of education and four inspectors; later, three university lecturers were added to the membership. In April 1964, twelve months after its formation, the committee published draft syllabuses for the O grade in mathematics of the Scottish Certificate of Education. An experimental text with teachers' notes began its trials in fifteen pilot schools in session 1963–4, and the following session forty-five other schools joined in the experiment, thus involving a total of some seven thousand pupils. Seven books were planned to cover the three and a half years of study to O grade. Book I was written in the spring of 1964, printed in the summer and used in the experimental schools in the autumn. The remaining books were written in quick succession, two more being added eventually to take the course up to Higher grade (Scottish fifth year of secondary school). In-service courses and the supply of appropriate equipment to schools were also organized. Robertson[10] describes the task involved:

'At any one time from 1964 to 1968 then, the committee was revising one book, testing the subsequent book in the series, and writing the one to follow that. Most chapters for the experimental book went through three or four draft stages before being accepted by the group as a whole. The committee met about six times each year, held several two-day conferences, and worked through sub-committees from time to time. Debate and discussion were often strenuous, sometimes heated, but rarely acrimonious; the endpoints in the syllabus construction and associated writing were invariably compromises between the various extremes and shades of opinion. A reasonably close liaison between the Syllabus Committee and the sixty schools was maintained over the years by means of visits, conferences, questionnaires, newsletters and correspondence.'

The resulting series[11] has had international success, special editions being prepared for Australia, South Africa, Holland, Germany, Sweden and Norway.

A number of working parties on this pattern had been set up before the appointment of the Consultative Committee; others have been appointed since. Some deal with subjects in breadth, English, science, classics, art, physical education; others with specific aspects, decimal currency and the metric system, computers and the school; others again with specific applications, modern studies for non-certificate classes, an integrated science syllabus as a common course in the first two years of secondary education.

In the field of English, a more extensive network of activities has been established. The co-ordinating body is the Central Committee on English, appointed in 1966 with eleven members (four school teachers, two university professors, two college lecturers, two local authority advisers and an inspector as chairman). Their remit is to 'promote research and development in the teaching of English at all levels'. The Central Committee has seventeen local development committees, which in turn have set up study groups to deal with particular aspects. To improve communication and act as a clearing house and resource centre, the Centre of Information on the Teaching of English has been established in Moray House College of Education, Edinburgh, with college staff serving on a part-time basis. This Centre issues regular newsletters, one of which provides a detailed description of the Central Committee's activities.[12]

It will be clear from this account that the various working parties and committees differ among themselves in their organization and procedure, so that it is difficult to write in general terms about curriculum development in Scotland. In some subjects, physics, chemistry and mathematics, for example, syllabuses have changed substantially—and, most would agree, for the better. Curricula in other subjects, such as geography, have been changing without the aid of any formal curriculum development organization. New ideas have been put forward in classics and English : whether these will affect the content of teaching in schools seems to depend on the content of future S.C.E. examination papers more than on the persuasion of teachers. In other subjects, working parties have not yet had time to produce reports. But the production of reports is only the first step in the process of curricular change, as the *First Report*[13] recognizes. 'There must be some follow-up locally and nationally, if in the end the work of teachers in all parts of the country is to be influenced and, the Committee hopes, improved, by the changes and developments proposed.'

Curriculum development, however, is slow in arousing genuine involvement of teachers, though Scotland is not unique in this problem. Perhaps the Scottish educational pattern is too authoritarian at heart, so that it is unrealistic to expect teachers to show initiative or to do anything other than wait for a strong lead from the centre. With the concentration of effort in the hands of small working parties, one looks in vain for growth at the grass roots. Provision for discussion and development of the reports issued—through local groups in teachers' centres and through in-service training—is still far from adequate. Also, some of the reports are of a kind which is hardly likely to stimulate discussion. Built up from the experience and considered opinion of practising teachers, they can readily encourage the best of current practice. They can also too easily slip into the hortatory style of *Suggestions for teachers*, or lay themselves open to criticism that they are just the old 'projects and activity' in a new glossy wrapping. The experimental sequence of defining objectives, designing appropriate materials and method, trials in schools, evaluation and feedback, has not been widely applied in Scotland. The Schools Council type of project has been adopted by the English Committee, but not by the others. The working party procedure keeps our feet firmly on the ground, and there are few in Scotland who would object. Nevertheless, there is a danger that a group of busy practical people may be too unreceptive of unconventional ideas which, though unpractical, are often a stimulus to re-thinking about important fundamental issues and are effective at least in provoking controversies and starting discussion.

The major achievement of the Scottish Education Department so far in this area has been its success in starting up the process of curriculum development, without arousing uneasiness or discontent among the teachers. In so far as teachers are aware at all of what is going on, they seem to welcome their new role of partnership with the inspectors and the colleges of education in this task. Some of the criticisms which have been made above must ring a familiar note to English readers. But those who know the Scottish system will recognize that the procedure which has evolved is peculiarly well suited to the Scottish situation. Educational problems know no frontiers, but educational institutions are not exportable. The Schools Council structure is probably too cumbersome for a country with one-tenth the population of England; and one cannot imagine the Scottish working party of twelve to fourteen members (the average size) being acceptable as a nationally representative group in England.

Curriculum development in Scotland is practical and down-to-earth; its reports are economical of words; and the provision is relatively inexpensive—three characteristically Scottish virtues, or faults?

References

1 G. S. Osborne, *Scottish and English schools* (Longmans, London, 1966), p. 307.

2 J. Nisbet (ed.), *Scottish education looks ahead* (Chambers, Edinburgh, 1969), p. 87.

3 *Op. cit.*, pp. 1–10, 59–73, 74–90.

4 Scottish Education Department, *Consultative Committee on the Curriculum: First Report 1965/8* (H.M.S.O. Edinburgh, 1969).

5 Schools Council, *The first three years* (H.M.S.O., London, 1968).

6 *First Report 1965/8*, p. 6.

7 *First Report 1965/8*, p. 5.

8 *First Report 1965/8*, p. 5.

9 *Scottish education looks ahead*, Chapter 6.

10 *Scottish education looks ahead*, pp. 80–81.

11 *Modern mathematics in schools* (Chambers, Edinburgh).

12 W. A. Gatherer, 'The Central Committee on English: a report' (*CITE Newsletter*, vol. 1, 2, pp. 3–5, May 1968).

13 *First Report 1965/8*, p. 6.

J. Banks

III:5 Curriculum developments in Britain, 1963–8

The Schools Council approach to curriculum development projects is traced through the various stages—from the feasibility study, through the development stage to the selection of pilot schools, the design of evaluation instruments, the diffusion of the innovation through more schools and the commercial publication of the curriculum materials.

This paper is an attempt to distil from the Schools Council's curriculum development activity in the last five years some ideas about the nature of development projects.

There are two good reasons for trying to do so. In the first place, the techniques and processes that have been used need to be more widely understood, particularly by those who may engage in curriculum development in the future. Many people, in different parts of the education system, have to work together with a common purpose if development is to be successful. A greater degree of mutual understanding of each other's rôles is therefore very desirable. Secondly, there is no doubt much that is imperfect in the way that development is organized and the promotion of debate or research aimed at improving it needs to be informed by an account of present practice.

How do projects begin?

The germ of a project is, naturally, a feeling that something is wrong with a particular part of the curriculum. Probably this feeling is expressed by teachers—indeed by a minority of teachers. But their being a minority is not so much a disqualification as, one may

Journal of Curriculum Studies, vol. 1, no. 3, 1969, pp. 247–259. (Published twice-yearly by William Collins Sons & Co. Ltd.) Reprinted by permission.

hope, a reflection of their perceptiveness, either in seeing the need, ahead of their colleagues, for the curriculum to be modified to take account of changes in society's requirements of the schools, or, maybe, of their perceptiveness as teachers in the sense of having something fresh to contribute to theories of how we teach.

Common-sense requires that some means be used to find out whether their 'hunch' (for it is really no more than that) genuinely reflects what society at large does wish of the schools, and by society one means particularly parents and employers rather than just teachers. The first stage of a project is therefore likely to comprise a 'feasibility trial'. Over a period of a year or two the ideas put forward to constitute a new curriculum are critically assessed by discussion with other teachers (both specialists and those with a general perspective); with teachers in the post-school stages of education; with employers; and in the country at large with any group of people whose judgement and experience in that field are likely to be informed and relevant. An untidy process, perhaps. But adequate, in the early years of systematic curriculum development, when there is ample scope for improvement.

Teachers, of course, are not the only source of new ideas about the curriculum. Initiatives have come too from academics with a progressive interest in school education. Some would perhaps argue that too many of the universities' contributions come from those whose goal is to get more of their own specialist learning into school education, without due regard to its durability or worthwhileness. But so far, development in Britain has been less fraught with problems of this kind than it was in the early years in the U.S.A.

The feasibility study is, ideally, entrusted to the person who, if feasibility is established, will be responsible for the ensuing development project. One could go further and say that it is unlikely that a feasibility study will be of great value in the development stage to a director who did not himself carry out the study. The point here is the crucial rôle played by the director in a curriculum project; the more the project is concerned with fundamental changes in education, the more the director's whole personality is engaged in putting it into effect—his views on the fundamental nature of education, his feelings about teachers and children, and his assessment of social need. Hence the difficulty in asking someone to execute a prescription resulting from someone else's exploration of feasibility. Hence, too, the need for committees or institutions to resist the temptation to try to define closely the nature of the development to be attempted, and then to find a director to undertake it—a sequence of operations sometimes strongly urged by curriculum theorists.

Much time and energy may have to be spent on trying to find the right person to direct a feasibility study. One of the difficulties of those engaged in organizing curriculum development in its early years is the lack of an adequate information network about good potential directors. It may often seem that all that is available is an old-boy network competent to identify not so much those who are genuinely progressive as those who have come to be thought so by echoing the views of the curricular establishment. The key to success lies in encouraging teachers who have progressive ideas to have faith in them, and to identify themselves by articulating them.

Formulation of the development project

At the end of the feasibility study one would expect to have not just a statement of educational objectives pertinent to the area of the curriculum under study formulated in general terms (in other words the sort of educational maxim that nobody in their right mind could possibly object to), but rather an attempt to state the specific objectives in view in terms which ultimately will be amenable to validation by research in some form. It is to be feared that any study which is not specific at this stage about its objectives, or hypotheses, will either result in the director spending the first years of his project in trying to hammer them out, or, maybe, even the whole period of the project. Or it may even be that they will never be hammered out at all, and the whole exercise will be incomprehensible and fruitless—if not positively harmful by virtue of the disrepute it brings upon the curriculum development process in general.

The difficulty of securing such a statement should not be underrated. The putative project director is being asked to make a declaration of faith—in himself, in a philosophy of education, in children, in the educational system, and last but not least, in teachers. To make it is to take the gigantic step from being a progressive teacher to being the standard-bearer of progressive development—in other words to be elevated to a pinnacle from which the fall looks only too easy and disastrous. What reason is there, after all, to suppose that the forces in favour of change in education will make it feasible for the director to make a perceptible dent on the system as it exists, on people and institutions dedicated to preserving their specialist parts of the educational process, and so many others lacking the professional self-confidence to act on their convictions? As in any situation where the aim is large-scale change, the battle is for the hearts and minds of the less-well-off, whether it be economically, professionally or personally. The director's act of faith in addressing himself to the less competent and poorer qualified section of his profession is generally not well regarded by the educational establishment. Or, if it is well regarded for its intentions, it is poorly regarded for its feasibility. So many have so little confidence in the teacher as a professional. Perhaps less is heard now than a few years ago of the desirability of making the products of curriculum development 'teacher-proof', i.e. suitable without any contribution from the teacher, for use in the school. But there are still those who think head teachers incapable of controlling school expenditure, or teachers at large incapable of taking charge of their own training. Such people do not make the director's task easier.

The director can, perhaps, comfort himself, in his exposed position, with the reflection that the content and quality of the curriculum are of much less importance to the editors of the national press—and, probably, to school governors and education committee members—than, say, the number and quality of the lavatories, and the organization and nomenclature of schools. So, when his public declaration is made and his feasibility study conclusions published, it is not very likely that much attention will be paid to them in proportion to their significance. What is less fortunate is that it is equally unlikely that the less qualified members of the teaching profession will read his conclusions; getting the message across to them is one of the major tasks ahead of him.

The rôle of the sponsoring central agency, the Schools Council (now that the Nuffield Foundation is not sponsoring any new work in this field) is restricted in the feasibility stage to providing contacts and sources of information to the investigator. Once the feasibility report is presented, the Council's specialist subject committees and its general curriculum committees must make up their mind whether a good case for setting up a project has been made out. Relevant criteria here are not only the obvious ones such as cost and ability to plan, but also whether there is evidence of a capacity to communicate with the kind of teachers to whom the project is directed, and whether there is a realistic sense of what can be achieved in changing educational patterns within a project time span of say three or five years.

Development begins

Once approval is given, the director's first task is to collect a writing team. All too often he is aware of people with a distinguished teaching record but not so sure whether they can write good teaching material for other teachers. Many of those who have proved ability to write are likely to have been signed up by publishers already, and as the director will not be able to offer them more money to work for him—secondment at existing salary, with a small honorarium, being the usual terms he can offer—he is dependent on the attraction of working full-time in a national project, and the chance of getting a better job (and more publishing contracts) when the project is over. Some will be put off by the comparative insecurity of a three-year contract, compared with staying put and (perhaps) picking up a headship. In time, however, the fact that most project members do improve their prospects, and many (ironically) never teach in schools again, will help to change this—one hopes, for the better.

The director's next tasks are to plan and start the writing programme; to find trial schools; to plan systematic evaluation of the new materials in the trial schools; to find, through the Council, a publisher; and to devise appropriate training through which to introduce the trial school teachers to the new materials.

In planning a project programme, timing is important, and difficult. It could be said, as a general rule, that the greater the curriculum gap—i.e. the greater the difference between the subject as currently taught in schools and the new development of it as conceived by the project director—the longer the development project will have to be from start to finish. This is particularly important in the initial period. Novel, inter-disciplinary projects which have complex timetabling demands for a school, require longer warning from the team to their trial schools if they are not to be unduly put upon. In other projects, the experimental nature of the director's ideas may be such that he wishes to have them validated in a very few schools, before launching out on a wider front. A very few teachers known to be interested and favourably inclined, may be asked to run a pre-trial with a few pieces of material. All this may require an extra year, and may mean that large-scale trials of materials do not begin until year three of a project, and that subsequent stages of a project have to be taken more gently too.

The selection of pilot schools usually begins soon after the project starts. The Council's help is available here: a letter to all education authorities is normally sent out, describing briefly the aim of the project, and its organizational and financial implications for schools and authorities (e.g. the setting up of teachers' centres for support, where they do not exist already) and asking for the names of any schools interested in participating. (Independent schools are also invited to participate, through their associations, though very few have, so far.) A description of the project is sent at the same time to agencies with a supporting function for schools, i.e. colleges of education, university institutes and departments of education and, where necessary, colleges of further education.

What happens when these letters are received by local authorities probably varies widely, and would repay further study. The variables are likely to include the size of the authority, the expertise or confidence of its staff in curricular matters, the nature of teacher/l.e.a. relations in the area, the local financial situation, and so on. Certainly some authorities consult teachers and heads about participation in a project in detail; others pass on very little information to the schools, and appear to designate trial schools without much consultation even with the teachers who will take part in the project, if that school is ultimately chosen.

It is of course anything but certain that a school put forward by an authority will in fact be chosen to act as a pilot school, since so far being a trial school has been a major attraction both to schools and their authorities, and only a few are needed for each project. This may well change, as more projects are set up, and spread into more schools. In selecting trial schools, the Council's aim, in consultation with the director, is to build up a sample comprising roughly a cross-section of educational conditions in the country, with a reasonable geographical distribution, and with the schools grouped in clusters.

What determines how many? To answer this, it is necessary to establish first that the function of the trial school is primarily to help the project team, rather than to help the school (though it is to be hoped that the latter will be achieved too). Certain demands are made of pilot schools which are not made of other schools later in the project; for instance, that they should use the materials as the project team intends them to be used (not piece-meal or mixed up with other course material). And, once committed, they must undertake to see the project through. They will also be asked to provide the project team with a good deal of information about their experience in using the materials, and to report on the results, good or bad, as they go along. From the team's point of view, there is obviously a limit to the number of schools from whom they can assimilate detailed information of this kind, and indeed there is a limit to the number of schools that they need to give the materials a valid testing. Thirty is generally regarded as ample for this purpose.

Against this must be set another factor, that if these trials go well, the project team will want to involve a further wave of schools in the following year. So the better distributed and thicker on the ground the pilot schools, the more expertise there will be in different parts of the country with which to prime the second wave of schools in the following year. Pilot schools, in other words, do have a rôle as demonstration units; their teachers have a rôle as demonstration teachers, if and when they can be spared to assume this function.

While this operates in favour of having a larger number of trial schools, the balance, it might be said, is held by finance. It has been Council policy so far that trial material should be provided free to the participating trial schools, i.e. at the expense of the development project and therefore of the Council. Some projects are cheap in this respect, mathematics for instance. Others are extremely expensive, particularly science and modern languages. Obviously, where trial materials are going to prove costly, the number of pilot schools has to be limited.

Once the trial schools are selected, it is usual for a short conference to be held at which the project team, the director in particular, meets the l.e.a. staff who will be responsible for the support of the pilot schools locally. They are a crucial link. Their goodwill, on which may depend continuity of staffing in the school and the supply of small sums of money to support the pilot trial, is essential. In cases where the l.e.a. inspector/organizer—or, much more exceptionally, a Chief Education Officer—has had the time and expertise to involve himself closely in a project, and has developed a commitment to it, the increase in effectiveness of the project in the classroom has been dramatic. But as projects increase, faster than local authority inspectors, and as reorganization makes additional demands on their time, the chances of this happening decrease.

The l.e.a. contribution to the project is one of many kinds of external help which a project school depends on. Nobody involved in educational innovation would doubt that the dice are heavily loaded against any change taking place in the school, and that all possible kinds of support need to be given to the teacher in a classroom who wants to institute change. Hence the conception of the project, which is in effect an organizational amalgam. Its central component will be new teaching material (books, reference material, library resources perhaps, film material, film services, tapes, slides, equipment, and so on). Next in importance are purpose-designed courses, some annual, some local on a weekly basis, aimed at explaining the philosophy behind the materials, and providing opportunities for 'playing out' the new rôle required of the teacher in a supportive group situation, in a teachers' centre. Here there will be opportunities for mutual encouragement and reinforcement, and exchanges of views between experimenting teachers. The next essential is the organizational support that flows from the commit-ment of the head and the local authority to a nationally spot-lit experiment, requiring them to help the project in small but crucially important ways on the spot (such as providing small sums of money). Then there will be a need for a new examination, perhaps even a new kind of examination, suited to the new kind of curricu-lum. A project must also include a psychological 'life-line' of sup-port if things seem to be going seriously wrong, stretching from the teacher in the classroom, through his colleagues at the teachers' centre, through their liaison officer with the project to a member of the project team, and to the director himself in the last resort. And finally, the project depends also on those who can help the schools locally—and are increasingly willing and able to do so—those in university education departments, and institutes and colleges of education. Their accessibility and sympathetic understanding of the teachers' difficulties are potentially a great asset.

The training component

Generally in the months before the trial schools begin to use the materials, some (or in some cases all) of the trial school teachers attend a one-week briefing conference, mainly staffed by the project team and led by the director. This is the occasion when the first attempt is made to 'convert' teachers, some of whom may not come in a sympathetic frame of mind, to the desirability and practicabil-ity of the new curriculum. It is of course a crucial occasion in any project, and is the forerunner of many such meetings, as the pro-ject spreads out (assuming it is successful) in successive years to larger and larger numbers of teachers. It is a particularly testing time for the team—and the director in particular—in that for the first time he faces the objections, raising from pedagogical through psychological to practical and organizational, which will come up time and again in differing forms as the project progresses. Often the very nature of a trial school's rôle has to be carefully explained, because many teachers are still deeply conditioned to expecting to be told what to do, and some come to briefing conferences expecting to be handed out a finished product, with the instructions accompanying it. Obviously this conception has to be removed before progress can be made.

These meetings are greatly helped if the project team have got ready in time for them a reasonable sample of the trial teaching materials the teachers are expected to start with in the autumn. This usually presents difficulties, but it is clearly of considerable importance. Other points which regularly occur at these meetings are the organization of the support life-line from the teacher in the classroom to the project team; how much money each authority has agreed to allow each trial schoolteacher for the project; and how the teacher's progress in using the materials is going to be assessed, i.e. what kind of evaluation of the results of the experiment is being organized.

These meetings usually take the form of reproducing, or simulating, at the adult level the relationship between teacher and pupil envisaged by the project in the classroom. The significance of this is that the shift aimed at by the project is in any case a shift in the rôle and attitude of the teacher, rather than a change to new content. It may well be that the project aims at both; but it may also be true that, in reality, changing the content is only a vehicle for trying to deepen teachers' understanding of the teaching process.

The function of the new teaching materials developed by the project is however not an unimportant one. It could be argued that there is a tendency for directors who omit to produce an adequately specific statement of their project's aims also to tend to the belief that a project can be effective without producing teaching materials. One might suggest an explanation of this; it is difficult to translate into guidance material for teachers a concept which you have not formulated sufficiently precisely yourself. In more personal terms, any project team who believes that specific educational ideas can be transmitted by word of mouth (by means of courses) from team to teachers (and by those teachers to other teachers), and that this will yield results which are significantly comparable with their own original intentions, are almost certainly in for a rude shock. If it were possible to organize educational innovation in this way, the whole conception of 'package' curriculum development—centring a complex of pedagogic and organizational support round a collection of printed material—would be unnecessary. The temptation to take this wrong turning is perhaps all the stronger in the present phase of British educational innovation, when, as we have noted, the importance of *what* you teach is being de-stressed, and the importance of *how* you teach it exalted. Some people are perhaps misled by this to thinking that if teachers are 'on the right wavelength', i.e. they sustain an interest in a project's philosophy and (highly generalized) goals, then progress is being made. But the flaws are two-fold; first that only the ablest teachers will be able to translate these goals into something specific in terms of teaching their own pupils, and it is not the ablest who most need help; and secondly the healthy desire of teachers to see some results from any curriculum development activity they engage in will gradually put paid to any project which views its task in this way.

Checking up on results

The next question the project must answer is whether the materials, and the total project 'package', are in fact achieving in the class-room the results they hope for. In other words, they must establish some form of 'concurrent' evaluation, to collect evidence, stage by stage, about their materials' effectiveness. There is still plenty of room for debate and experimentation about the means of doing this. Schools Council practice, gradually developing, is to assign a part- or full-time evaluator to each development team; this is a person who is envisaged as being sympathetic to, but independent of, the development team members. His sympathy is needed to enable him fully to understand what the team is aiming at; his independence to permit him to challenge the formulation of objectives, and to demand that they be refined (or abandoned) with a view to achieving ultimately, as we noted earlier, some formulation of the project's purposes which are amenable to research evaluation. In projects which are mainly concerned with pupils' acquiring skills or knowledge, this may be fairly straightforward. But, happily, curriculum innovators, like teachers, tend to be more concerned with the less measurable outcomes of the educational process, like social adjustment, or creativeness. Other means than objective testing need therefore to be found for assessing the effects of the project. Experimentation so far extends to the collection of teachers' own assessment of changes in their pupils, and to some extent to the observation of them by competent outsiders such as local and national inspectors; shortly it will include also the collection of video-tape recordings in selected trial schools. Apart from tests, questionnaires and recordings, the collection of the trial school teachers' opinions through annual meetings organized by the project is a fairly frequent feature. Such meetings in any case foster the feeling of 'togetherness' which is a noticeable and probably important part of the early stages of a project, when the feeling of mutual support (and hence willingness to 'have a bash' regardless of the possibility of failure and loss of face amongst one's colleagues) is all important. (It is worth noting that team teaching is sometimes defended on this same score—that teachers feel less acutely the shame of failure if they are sharing responsibility for a lesson, rather than carrying it undividedly themselves; and hence there is a greater willingness to experiment.) A little, but not much, has been done to collect pupils' opinions about a new curriculum; and there may also be a case for finding out what parents think too.

Development leads to diffusion

There is no need here to go into detail about the functions of the project team in the mid and latter years of the project's life—the continuing process of preparing fresh material, of revising and restructuring in the light of 'feedback,' and of preparing it for publication. But something must be said about the development of a strategy of diffusion—the steps that must be taken to ensure that the stream of innovation does not disappear into the sand when the team's products are published, and made available to teachers at large.

In nearly all the projects sponsored by the Schools Council, the schools originally put forward for participation in a project but not selected as pilot schools, have been included in a 'second wave' (sometimes called second phase, or large-scale trial) following on a year behind the pilot schools. The logic of this is that, if the new curriculum is reckoned successful on the evidence of the pilot trial and its evaluation, and diffusion of it on a country-wide basis seems desirable, the process of diffusion will be greatly facilitated by bringing a fairly large number of schools into contact with the project before the materials are published. Without such a stage, the transition from say 30-40—or even 100—trial schools being involved to a proportion of schools in all parts of the country—say 5 or 10,000 teachers—suddenly wanting to start using the materials at publication date, can cause an awkward hiatus. A well-planned project will be prepared to provide courses on the scale that they are desired at the time of publication, and subsequently. This means that it will have planned sufficiently well in advance to see that course tutors and directors are available all over the country to provide such courses locally, as the need for them arises. Hence the need for an intermediate stage, between pilot trial and general participation.

Some of these second wave schools may also be invited to report on their experience with the materials. And useful lessons can be drawn from their experience in other ways; they are, for instance, being offered a curriculum which has to some extent been 'proved' (in the trial schools), but they are being offered it with rather less detailed attention and support from the project team than had the pilot schools. There is therefore something of a test here of the effect of transmitting the new curriculum in a more broadcast fashion, through the agency of people who were not directly involved in its original formulation. Misunderstandings and omissions which are exposed at this stage can therefore, hopefully, be rectified, so that the same mistakes do not occur on a larger scale later on when publication takes place and many more teachers are introduced to the project. At this time, it is not only a question of involving more schools, but of bringing in the institutions who are concerned with training. A year or two before publication begins, a major effort must be made by the project team to see that this is done. This is not a case of organizing a once-and-for-all programme of courses. Diffusion is a slow and complex process, which is likely to need careful planning and support over perhaps five (or more) years. The project team will have already gathered experience about the kind of courses which are effective in introducing the new curriculum. But now the different needs of specialist teachers, headteachers, teachers' centre leaders and local authority organizers will all require detailed and different treatment. The Schools Council has recognized its own responsibility in this stage of a project, and undertaken to continue projects in existence to meet the need for a continuing central 'inquiry' point, and stimulus to ensure that these needs are met. But so far, given that so few projects have reached this stage, there is no experience of, for instance, how best to meet the specific needs of headteachers, although experimentation is beginning. The Council has also recognized that it must take the lead in promoting greater communication in the fields both of in-service training and initial training—communication between the Council itself and the potential providers of courses about its own perceptions of future needs arising from each project, and communication between the providers so that each agency is helped to see its own rôle more clearly in relation to those of others.

Final evaluation

Lastly, what check is there that projects do achieve on any scale the results that they hope for? Or that they do not achieve harmful and unforeseen side effects? Equally important, what evidence will be offered to the teacher who asks for guidance in choosing a curriculum for his pupils, between project A and project B?

Inevitably, the Schools Council, only four years old, has not much to contribute here yet. The only major thrust in final evaluation so far is the large-scale attempt to assess the effects of introducing French into the primary school curriculum, undertaken by the National Foundation for Educational Research. But the Council has recognized its responsibility in organizing final evaluation, and a few strategic ideas are taking shape. First, in a field where the tools, let alone experience, are still lacking, it has commissioned research to produce some of the necessary measuring instruments. Second, there is a recognition that in this area it does not pay to use half-measures; if studies of the effects of curricular change, using social science investigation methods, are to pay off in terms of results, considerable resources are needed, given the number of variables which surround the teaching situation. This implies that depth studies in a few settings, rather than a collection of selective information from many schools, may be the strategy to be adopted. It also implies, however, that all those who are interested in any way in studying the outputs of the school system will need to club together if the necessary resources are to be found for such major studies to be launched. Here, as in other areas of its work, the Council may provide the right forum for working out such strategies, and for contributing from its funds to a common programme. It cannot, and should not, go it alone.

Denis Lawton

III:6 Preparations for changes in the curriculum

The design of curricula to meet the requirements of the raising of the school-leaving age must be seen in the context of the continuing disagreement about the aims and objectives of secondary education. Hirst and Bantock are quoted as examples of this conflict of views. Before examining some specific suggestions that have been made about the curriculum for school-leavers, Lawton identifies three main social pressures behind the movement to raise the school-leaving age—economic, ideological, and secular/rational. Among the curriculum ideas for school-leavers examined are the Newsom and Crowther reports, Schools Council Working Paper No. 2, various Schools Council projects, as well as local curriculum developments via teachers' centres.

Nearly all industrial societies have committed themselves to a policy of universal secondary education, but none has yet completely solved the problem of what to include in this universal programme. Additionally, most countries are pressing ahead with proposals for extending the period of compulsory education without waiting for a satisfactory answer to be given to this problem. The reasons for the widespread uncertainty are that the problems involved in providing secondary education for all are extremely complex.

In this country it is sometimes said that the struggle is between the *elitists* and the egalitarians, but this is really a vast over-simplification. The recent Black Paper has made very clear that there are many kinds of *elitists*; similarly, among those who think of themselves (or who are thought of) as egalitarians there is no total agreement on policy. For example, one of the goals of compulsory education is universal literacy, and most educationists as well as most of the population would agree on this as a goal. But even at

From 'Preparations for changes in the curriculum' by Denis Lawton in Tibble, J. W. (ed.), *The extra year*, Routledge & Kegan Paul Ltd., 1970, pp. 97–116. Reprinted by permission.

this level there is no total agreement. At least one Professor of Education, Geoffrey Bantock, does not hold this opinion. In his book, *Culture, industrialization and society*, he quotes with approval the statement made by D. H. Lawrence that 'The great mass of humanity should never learn to read and write—never'. Bantock justifies his support of Lawrence in this respect by saying the vast majority of the population have a culture which is non-literary in its origins. This folk-culture has been partly destroyed by the process of industrialization, but, according to Bantock, the urban proletariat are still not capable of benefiting from the 'high culture'. He goes on to support his opinion by describing some of the failures of popular education. Bantock is certainly right in claiming that no one has solved the problem of what to include in the curriculum for the majority of the secondary-school population—let alone how to teach this. His solution is, however, a non-answer, and seems to fall into the trap of saying that if we cannot go back to merry England, where the peasants were happy and creative in their own simple way, at least let us stay where we are and avoid slipping further down the slope towards egalitarianism. This is an extreme view of a curriculum, or, rather, a non-curriculum, for secondary education, but a number of people would share the opinion that it is a waste of time trying to *educate* 'the masses' : 'Instruct them in useful skills by all means,' they might say, 'but be realistic and don't try to aim too high!' This is the implication contained in many unsolicited testimonials for secondary modern schools : for example, one from Quintin Hogg :

> 'I can assure Hon. Members opposite that if they would go to study what is now being done in good secondary modern schools, they would not find a lot of pupils biting their nails in frustration because they had failed the 11 plus. The pleasant noise of banging metal and sawing wood would greet their ears and a smell of cooking with rather expensive equipment would come out of the front door to greet them. They would find that these boys and girls were getting an education tailor-made to their desires, their bents and their requirements.' (*Hansard*, 21 January 1965, p. 424, quoted in J. D. Koerner 1968.)

Such advocates of secondary education might want equality of educational opportunity (weakly defined) so that bright children get a chance of advancement, but they would not really want 'education' in its true sense for all pupils, or they might not think it a realistic goal.

At the other extreme we have those who deny innate ability altogether. According to them, everything is due to environment. Therefore all the school has to do is to provide an enriched or compensatory environment and all children would educate themselves. Somewhere in between these two extremes there are those who recognize the existence of innate differences, but who suggest that they can be greatly modified by environmental factors, and who say if you believe in equality and democracy you must provide an opportunity for *every* child to achieve a satisfactory basic minimum education and at the same time allow plenty of opportunity for every child to go on as far beyond that basic minimum as he or she is capable. The argument about the raising of the school leaving age is really a question about 'Can we do this for *most* children by the age of 15?' There is also a less open question: 'Is it worth trying to do this for *all* children?'

Changes in the curriculum and other kinds of preparations made for the raising of the school leaving age must be seen against this kind of lack of consensus about the aims and objectives of secondary education. Another, very different, kind of *elitist* attack on our present provision of secondary education might best be represented by the American educationist, J. D. Koerner, who dislikes the British emphasis on equality of opportunity (especially comprehensive schools), but also criticizes the low level of education which we seem to have in mind for the majority of our secondary-school pupils. Koerner gives us a very perceptive analysis of a situation in which teachers and educationists generally lack clarity about what they think secondary education is for. At the end of his book, Koerner sets out a series of alternative goals: education as an instrument of social change; as an arm of the Welfare State to be a child-minding institute; schools as job-training centres; or schools which will initiate pupils into the basic subjects of human knowledge. His analysis is that most schools seem to be going in the direction of non-academic life-adjustment courses or vocational training rather than true education. His advice would be to make our pupils work harder, raise their levels of aspiration and introduce them to real knowledge. This is a perceptive analysis, but seems to confuse the issue by implying that this can be achieved without our having to modify the present highly selective system. Most sociologists would see the kind of curriculum reform that Koerner wants as an inextricable part of a general reform of secondary education.

A point of view in some ways similar to that of Koerner, but expressed cogently in philosophical terms, has been put forward by Professor P. H. Hirst. Hirst agrees that education is primarily concerned with the transmission of knowledge, and that knowledge consists of a number (seven or eight) of distinct and autonomous forms of knowledge. Hirst's major contribution to the raising of the school leaving age issue is his insistence that if we accept an egalitarian view of education, and if we are really committed to equality of educational opportunity, then it follows that an attempt must be made to initiate *all* pupils into forms of knowledge and understanding. Some will undoubtedly achieve greater understanding than others, but all pupils must be led towards the same objectives. The method of teaching pupils may be different according to their level of ability or aspiration, but the forms of knowledge which are the educational objectives must of necessity be the same for all pupils.

This would seem to be a strong argument against some of the so-called Newsom Courses which are referred to later in this chapter, but it should not be seen as an argument in favour of extending the traditional grammar-school curriculum to all pupils of all abilities (which was the implication of the Koerner argument). There is no great degree of correspondence between the traditional grammar-school curriculum and Hirst's seven forms of knowledge. If Hirst is right, therefore, there is a need for all secondary schools to re-think their total curricula.

This range of opinions regarding the 'problems' connected with raising the school leaving age makes it necessary to analyse very carefully both the background to the problem and the present situation before attempting to evaluate some of the proposals which have been put forward for a curriculum for the final year at school. That is, we must try to clarify the issue in question before pronouncing on the kind of courses which some may want to provide.

What are the social pressures behind the movement to raise the school leaving age? I have suggested elsewhere (Lawton, 1968) that the social pressures most powerfully exerting an influence on schools and school systems can best be divided under the three headings of Economic, Ideological (the move from an *elitist* towards an egalitarian society) and Secular/Rational (the move away from Christian values and ways of thinking to more secular/rational views).

The economic pressures

In relation to this particular issue of the raising of the school leaving age, the economic argument is probably the weakest of the three. It is, of course, true that as the process of industrialization continues, and as such factors as automation become more widespread, there is a declining demand for unskilled and semi-skilled manpower and a corresponding increase in demand for more skilled workers of many kinds. It has been argued that the need is not only to produce technicians rather than operatives, which will involve a general raising of levels of achievement, but also to produce workers who are more flexible, who have been taught general principles rather than specific skills, so that they can readily abandon jobs which become redundant and obsolete and apply themselves to new industrial skills and techniques.

All of this would seem to be beyond question, but it is not in itself an entirely convincing argument for raising the school leaving age. It could be argued that from a purely economic point of view it would be more efficient to change the kind of teaching that pupils receive up to the age of 15 and to make even greater changes to the kind of training in apprenticeship, etc., that youngsters now receive having left school—less of the 'sitting next to Nelly' kind of practice, but more general technical education, including maths and science. In addition, it would be necessary to expand the training which young people now receive (only 40 per cent of 15-year-old male leavers now enter apprenticeship schemes of any kind). From an economic point of view this alternative proposal might be theoretically desirable; whether it is a practical possibility, given existing resources for industrial training, is another matter. The evidence provided by the extremely disappointing results so far of the Industrial Training Act might make one more optimistic that schools could adapt to change more effectively than industry.

Ideological pressures

One of the major preoccupations of sociologists since the war has been to document the difference between the *ideal* of equality of educational opportunity implied in the 1944 Act and the *reality* of what actually happens in schools. This gap between the opportunities available to middle-class pupils as compared with the children of manual workers has been shown to exist at all levels from the age of 5 to university entrance, and the problem could perhaps best be summed up in the words of the *Crowther Report*, which suggested that the education received by the majority of the population was 'inadequate both in its quality and in its duration'. This is an important point of view, since it emphasizes that *two* changes are necessary if the school leaving age is raised—*quality* and duration. Simply to extend the duration without improving quality might be worse than useless. This warning was uttered in 1965 by Lionel Elvin: 'There are experiments in some schools, often showing enterprise and imagination. But by and large we have not thought this problem out, and we have not deliberately trained teachers to do it. If the higher school leaving age comes into effect before we have done so the result will be not merely wasteful, but disastrous.'

There is, however, another interesting gap which is as important as the social-class gap referred to in the paragraph above. This is the gap between the attitude of official Reports like Crowther and Newsom and the views of those at local level who are responsible for making changes. Perhaps this point can best be made by historical reference: the ideological contrast between mid-nineteenth century and mid-twentieth century is a sharp one. The nineteenth-century view of society was still unself-consciously hierarchical and *elitist* rather than democratic; the great nineteenth-century Commissions and Enquiries on education, such as the Newcastle Commission or the Taunton Commission, saw nothing wrong with the notion of different kinds of school, different qualities of education with quite different curricula to correspond to the different social classes in society. Today we have by no means achieved equality, but it is now the official policy established by the 1944 Act, and has even been interpreted by Plowden as the need for *positive* discrimination. My point here is that although this is now official policy, and although few people publicly quarrel with the principle, in practice many people concerned with education—for example, teachers, head teachers, administrators, local government officials and elected representatives—only pay lip service to the principle, and beneath the surface may still retain an *elitist* attitude on questions of educational provision. This may be expressed in a reluctance to provide new school buildings in slum areas or to provide recreational facilities for the youth service at anything like the scale thought to be minimal for universities and colleges of education, or, perhaps most importantly of all, it shows itself at secondary level in a reluctance to think of a curriculum which would be real education rather than mere containment.

A related point is that education for working-class so-called non-academic 14–15-year-olds is often seen as a means of education for citizenship or training for democracy. The danger here is that unless this objective is seen as part of a programme of *education* (i.e. real understanding of the problems, which would necessitate an initiation into the social sciences, such as economics, political science, sociology), a civic approach to secondary education becomes no more than indoctrination or manipulation.

On the other hand, a well-reasoned argument in favour of raising the school leaving age could be based partly on the 'explosion of knowledge' view, and partly on a sociological view connected with the failure of the policy of parity of esteem. The 'explosion of knowledge' view would simply say that if we really want pupils to understand the world in which they live in a mathematical way, a scientific way, etc., then this simply cannot be done by the age of 16—especially when much of the thinking required must be of an abstract nature, probably beyond the level of many 14–15-year-olds.

The second argument, regarding the failure of parity of prestige in secondary education, would link raising the school leaving age to the more general problems of secondary education and recommendations for comprehensive schools. Olive Banks, in her book, *Parity and prestige in English secondary education* (1955), made the point very clearly that in a society which accords differential prestige to the products of two different kinds of school, then automatically the schools themselves are accorded different kinds of esteem. This is part of the argument for comprehensive school systems, and it would also apply to those pupils aged 15 to 16 who in the past would not have been classified as academic : if we accept the principle of equality, not only must they have the same kind of curriculum, but they must also have an adequate amount of time to mature and master the curriculum. This would also relate to the Crowther statement regarding greater *quality* as well as duration.

So far the argument has been idealistic and theoretical rather than practical. This is inevitable : if we believe in equality of opportunity, then it is the task of teachers not to waste time arguing 'when' or 'whether', but to find out *how* to achieve this goal. There is no reason to think that this kind of education is beyond the capacity of the majority of the population. This view has been accepted in an unquestioning way for far too long.

The secular/rational pressure

In his contribution to *Schools Council Working Paper*, No. 12, Professor Sprott connected the growth of rationality with concern for people (which I have considered above separately as part of the ideological change). I would agree that these two aspects of modern life are closely connected, but not that they are identical, and I would prefer to analyse them separately. I would also want to stress the change from a religious to a more secular society. For good or ill, people are less influenced by Christian doctrine, and many people have suggested that it is important that a rational basis for morality be provided in schools. The really important change in objectives in education here is that we can no longer believe it sufficient for young people to be obedient and to conform to laws and rules; if they conform they must do so for the right reasons (i.e. rational ones), and occasionally we might even approve of their non-conformity if this is also based on rational decisions. Part of the difficulty of living in a pluralist society is precisely that a number of choices have to be made regarding behaviour in politics or morals and that, even if religious issues are at stake, decisions should be taken on rational lines.

If one important objective in secondary education is to acquire a rational basis for moral decision-making, then this is quite clearly a powerful argument for keeping pupils at school until they have reached the stage of maturation which will make this kind of learning easier or even possible. The work of Piaget, Kohlberg and others suggests that 15 is a dangerously early leaving age for many young people in this respect.

Once again, however, it must be stressed that this is not simply a question of maturation. There is no reason to believe that rational thinking will simply develop with increasing age; it must be taught. This ought to give us a considerable help in deciding the content of the curriculum for the 15–16-year-old pupils (see later references to the work of Wilson, McPhail and Stenhouse).

With that general background in mind, we might now examine in some detail some of the specific suggestions that have been made for a programme for the school-leavers.

The *Crowther Report* was of course not only concerned with 15-plus leavers. It was also concerned with sixth forms of grammar schools. The 'leavers' were divided into two groups by the *Crowther Report*: the minority who would proceed to some form of further education, and the majority who would not. The Crowther recommendation was that the school leaving age should be raised from 15 to 16, and that the extra year should be at school. Presumably members of the Committee were thinking that the curriculum for the extra year should resemble the ideal four strands that they envisaged as the Further Education curriculum : (1) to help young people find their way about the world; (2) moral values; (3) education for leisure; and (4) education in a narrow sense—vocational and intellectual. In retrospect, perhaps the most striking fact about Crowther is the complacent attitude towards the grammar-school curriculum, especially the sixth form curriculum, which is more specialized than anywhere else in the world. The opportunity for making a significant contribution to curriculum development was sadly missed on this occasion.

The *Newsom Report* took the analysis of 'secondary education for all' one stage further by widening the definition of secondary education. It suggested that so-called extra-curricular activities should be considered an essential part of school. To enable these to be incorporated, they suggested an extension of the school day. This might be regarded as a very important reform, but it has an fact received very little support from teachers or administrators.

As a document on the curriculum suitable for *Half our future*, the Report is a peculiar mixture of optimism and traditional stereotyped thinking. On the one hand, the Committee recommends that all pupils should have more and better science teaching, and should have the opportunity of learning a foreign language (probably the least important aspect of the high-prestige grammar-school curriculum); they also had some extremely useful and sensible suggestions to make on English teaching, as well as on 'practical subjects'; on the other hand, whilst recognizing the need for young people to understand their own society, the remedy suggested seemed to be a re-vamped version of history, geography and R.I. rather than any new ideas about incorporating the social sciences. The greatest shortcoming of the *Newsom Report* was, however, that it lent itself to being interpreted as an argument in favour of the outward-looking, life-adjustment courses which I have criticized earlier. . . . The fact that so many schools have simply opted for 'Newsom Courses' for non-academic 'Newsom' children is in itself a condemnation of the fact that the *Report* did not take a more positive line on a curriculum, not for 'Half Our Future', but for 'All Our Future'.

Schools Council Working Paper, No. 2, *Raising the School Leaving*

Age: A Co-operative Programme of Research and Development, is in many respects a much more revolutionary document than either Crowther or Newsom. *Working Paper,* No. 2, suggests that

'The possibility of helping the pupils who are the concern of this paper to enter the world of ideas, to use powers of reason and to acquire even the beginnings of mature judgment, may seem to contradict the experience of many teachers. Indeed, it may carry an almost revolutionary ring to some, and this accounts for the tentative character of many of the ideas put forward in this Working Paper. It is often said that these pupils are not interested in ideas; they cannot handle abstractions; they cannot verbalize; they make choices by comparing immediate satisfactions; they are only interested in people and concrete situations. It is just these assumptions which the raising of the school leaving age gives all in the sphere of secondary education the opportunity to challenge. For the more able pupils, now staying on voluntarily in increasing numbers, the fifth year has revealed powers which many did not suspect. When, for some 60% of the pupils, schooling stops often before the fourth year is out, and before a sufficient maturity is reached, possibilities for development may be undiscovered. This is the basic assumption which the *Newsom Report* asks us to make when it calls for a change of heart in our attitudes towards the slower learners. In thinking about what is desirable, and practicable, in developing new curricula and courses for the young school-leaver, the standpoint of this Working Paper is thus that some existing assumptions, though soundly based on current experience, may be invalid in the situation which would follow the raising of the school leaving age. There is evidence from Further and Adult Education, and from the experience of those few schools which have successfully held appreciable numbers of the less able pupils for a fifth year of secondary education, that doors can be thrown open where current experience of a four-year course might suggest that they must remain closed. There is also evidence from primary education that practically all pupils can acquire insights into abstract ideas, and a capacity to work with them (particularly by oral means), if doors are opened through the use of teaching methods which build on the pupils' present experience and supply new forms of experience which help them to discover for themselves the powers of their own minds.'

The *Working Paper* did not, however, simply express pious hopes
about what might be achieved. It went on to make positive suggestions about what the curriculum should include. It suggested that
the curriculum should possess organic unity, and that the organizing
principle most likely to provide a sound basis for development was
the study of man, and of human society, human needs and purposes.
The suggestion was that subjects like English, geography, history
and religious education which had previously been studied in isolation might now be combined into a humanities course which would
deal with men and women in relation to their environment, their
communities and their own self-knowledge. This did not appear to
be a recommendation for any kind of life-adjustment course, but
rather for bringing economics, sociology, psychology, anthropology,
etc., to bear on problems of the modern world. The complexity of
the task here was recognized and it was therefore decided that the
Council would offer its support to a feasibility study financed and
organized by the Nuffield Foundation. The study was designed to
discover how far it would be possible to offer the schools organized
forms of help in tackling the problems of new humanities courses.
The terms of reference given for the feasibility study were:

'The team should assume that the Headmaster of a comprehensive school (which draws boys and girls from both town and
country areas) has asked for help. He is concerned about the last
year or two of work for those who do not take O level, and is
particularly aware that some of his problems will grow more
acute in five years' time when the school leaving age is raised. His
school is adequately equipped with modern aids, and (more important) has members of staff in the departments of English, R.I.,
history and geography who would be prepared to co-operate in a
new scheme which is more relevant than present courses to the
needs and aspirations of pupils of average and below-average
ability. One-third of the weekly time-table could be made available for this new course; some of those who took the course
would attempt C.S.E., but many would not. Several neighbours,
including a social scientist, might give help on a part-time basis,
and the school is willing to consider flexible arrangements for out-
of-school work, including projects and assignments based on other
institutions.
The team are asked to advise such a Headmaster whether a
curriculum-development group could produce materials that

would help these teachers to mount a worthwhile course; they should indicate what form such a course and such materials might take. The main question will concern what attitudes, experiences, skills and knowledge are important in adult life, to society as well as the individual. In their study of this question the team should consider in particular: (a) what is likely to be of interest to boys and girls (and therefore conducive to a 'learning experience') during the final years of secondary school? (b) what can be discovered from successful courses of this kind that have already been tried out (not only for pupils of this level of ability, but also in sixth forms and further education colleges), apart from the fact that the teachers of them may be especially gifted? (c) what can be learnt from the failures of past attempts in this field, and from justifiable criticisms (by young people themselves, employers or others) of what the schools now provide?'

There were elements of ambiguity in this brief, but much of the *Working Paper* does contain sound educational ideas. Unfortunately, the translation of the ideals of *Working Paper, No. 2*, into reality in the form of *Working Paper, No. 11*, is much less satisfactory. This paper, *Society and the young school leaver*, has been criticized so severely that the tendency now is to ignore it completely or to assume that it has been completely superseded. There is a great deal of poorly-thought-out material in the paper (much of it of the life-adjustment kind), but it is not completely without merit. For example, one of the four suggestions on how an area of inquiry might be developed (in the Appendix) is much superior to the other three. The main criticism has been that such projects as the 97 'bus are really 'soft options' rather than alternative approaches to acquiring forms of knowledge. John White, for example, in an article in *New Society*, criticized such approaches, not only because they did not clearly have any worthwhile knowledge content, but also because they appeared to him to be forms of indoctrination—encouraging young working-class pupils to accept their lot in life rather than to rebel against them. Many other educationists were equally unhappy about the kind of inter-disciplinary work of a low intellectual level suggested in *Working Paper, No. 11*; and the follow-up study financed by Nuffield and Schools Council directed by Lawrence Stenhouse has taken a very different line of approach to that set out in the *Working Paper, No. 11*. The view adopted by Lawrence Stenhouse and his team working on the Humanities Curriculum Project will be discussed in some detail below.

Out of the rather confusing array of opinions, recommendations and suggestions contained in the above official and semi-official documents regarding the raising of the school leaving age, four main curricular problems emerge in a fairly unambiguous way:

1 *Vocational requirements of an extended course:* the need to present more opportunities to more pupils to acquire greater knowledge and understanding, especially of science and technology.

2 *Social:* to extend pupils' ability to understand the political, economic and sociological issues of their own and other societies.

3 *Moral:* to reach a rational basis for moral decision-making.

4 *Recreational:* to equip all pupils with the means of enjoying the non-vocational aspects of adult life, and also to regard education as something which does not end at 15 or 16, but which should continue throughout life.

To achieve all of this would be a very tall order indeed, but a number of preparations have been made to incorporate at least some of these goals or objectives into the curriculum. These will be described in the next section.

Some of the preparations have been made on a one-year or two-year basis, others—more realistically—represent a tendency to re-think the curriculum for the whole secondary-school age-range, and are set out as from eleven to sixteen projects. It should perhaps be stressed that this is not an exhaustive list, but only a few significant examples:

1 Vocational

(In the sense of acquiring real knowledge about science and technology rather than job training in the sense condemned by Koerner above.)

(a) Mathematics for the Majority: a Schools Council Secondary School Mathematics Project. Directed by Philip Floyd, University of Exeter.

This project aims to meet the mathematical needs of pupils of average and below-average ability aged 13 to 16. It is concerned with the production, trial and dissemination of teaching materials, presented mainly through a series of guides for teachers. The aims of the project team are:

1 To provide pupils with experience of mathematical situations, to encourage powers of judgment and the exercise of imagination.

2 To give pupils some understanding of the mathematical concepts which underlie the numeracy required for everyday affairs.

3 To remove barriers isolating mathematics from other areas of the curriculum and other interests of the pupils.

4 To enable pupils to appreciate in some measure the order and pattern of their environment.

The secondary mathematics project will not be completed until 1973, but before the school leaving age is raised a number of pilot schools will have reported back, and materials and ideas will be available to schools throughout the country. It is as yet too early to make any assessment about the final results of the project: it has been received with enthusiasm by many teachers but detailed results are not yet available. Perhaps even more important than the result, however, is the aim. The stated objectives of the project clearly set out the principle of teaching real mathematical knowledge by new methods. It is not a 'watered-down' sort of mathematics designed for the less able to play with; it is a genuine form of knowledge and understanding.

(b) *The Applied Science and Technology Project* (Schools Council Project Technology). Directed by Mr G. B. Harrison, Loughborough College of Education.

The goal of this project is not to introduce technology as a new subject on the time-table, but to encourage schools to foster an understanding of technology and to encourage a creative attitude towards it. The overall objectives of the project are expressed as: 'To help all children to get to grips with technology as a major influence in our society and, as a result, to help more of them to lead effective and satisfying lives.'

This is perhaps a very good example of a merging of the educational needs of individual pupils with the economic needs of society. *Schools Council Working Paper*, No. 18, specifies the four man-power needs that were the concern of the project in the following way:

1 A sufficient proportion of able pupils choosing scientific and technological careers.

2 An adequate supply of candidates to train as skilled technicians.

3 Administrators and managers with sufficient technical and scientific understanding and knowledge.

4 A working population more prepared and able to learn new skills as the older ones become obsolete with advances in science and technology.

These are clearly seen as manpower needs, but they are not in any way in conflict with educational objectives. 'The first of these manpower objectives is more likely to be achieved if pupils receive a longer period of broad education and if this reflects better the fundamental interaction between disciplines.'

Sixty schools were initially studied at the pilot stage, some based on technical or handicraft departments, others based on science departments, still more operating on a basis of interdepartmental co-operation. One very encouraging feature of the work is the participation of girls in the pilot programmes.

This project is not, of course, designed exclusively for the raising of the school leaving age, but it does have clear relevance to it.

(c) Science for the Young School-leavers. The Nuffield Science Teaching Project. Directed by Mrs H. Misselbrook, Chelsea College, Centre for Science Education.

This programme is specifically concerned with pupils of average and below average ability aged 13 to 16. The project sets out with the purpose of putting right one of the criticisms made of school science in the *Newsom Report*: 'Too much of the tradition of science teaching is of the nature of confirming foregone conclusions. It is a kind of anti-science, damaging to the lively mind, maybe, but deadly to the not so clever' (para. 423).

The answer, however, was seen not in terms of any kind of interest-based project, but carefully structured experimentation: 'Pupils who are not high-flyers will need considerable help in posing the questions to be asked if their inquiries are to meet with adequate success. This means, for example, that the use of open-ended experiments will probably need to be carefully regulated if confusion and depression from an apparent lack of clear progress and achievement are to be avoided.'

The project team spent a good deal of time on consultation and discussion of the ideal curriculum and eventually selected eight themes, and have indicated the principle ideas and areas of knowledge with which these themes are concerned. The eight themes are:

1 Interdependence of living things.
2 Continuity of life.
3 Biology of man.
4 Harnessing energy.
5 Extension of sense-perception.
6 Movement.
7 Using materials.
8 The earth and its place in the universe.

II, III, IV Social, Moral and Recreational

(The non-vocational aspects of the demand for the raising of the school leaving age.)

(a) The Nuffield Foundation and Schools Council Humanities Curriculum Project. Directed by Lawrence Stenhouse, Philippa Fawcett College, Streatham.

Some reference has already been made to this project, which is probably the most ambitious and highly organized research specifically designed to cope with problems of raising the school leaving age. It should be stressed, however, that the materials referred to below are not necessarily limited to 'average or below-average pupils'. The project refers back to the para. 321 of the Newsom Report in explaining the purpose of the team: 'To set a class to study a carefully defined problem in human conduct and human relations into which boys and girls can project themselves and work out the various implications of different courses of action—this is realistic teaching.'

An introductory leaflet about the project also refers back to *Schools Council Working Paper*, No. 2 (*Working Paper*, No. 11, is discreetly ignored): 'The problem is to give every man some access to a complex cultural inheritance, some hold on his personal life and on his relationships with the various communities to which he belongs, some extension of his understanding of, and sensitivity towards, other human beings. The aim is to forward understanding, discrimination and judgment in the human field.'

The way in which the team is tackling this very interesting but very difficult task is to try to develop pupils' understanding of a number of 'controversial areas of universal human concern'. The controversial issues are approached through a technique of discussion which:

'enables the pupils to take responsibility for their own learning and which protects them from the bias of the teacher; the teacher acts as an impartial and neutral chairman in handling controversial value issues with the group. The pupil's understanding of the issues is given substance and extended in a consideration of a range of "evidence" which is fed into the discussion.'

The materials are designed for the 14–16-year-old age-group (of average and below-average ability without serious reading difficulties). In addition to printed materials there are audio tapes of original material, some of which also appear in printed form. Experimental materials have been tried out in thirty-two pilot schools as well as a number of other educational establishments. Extensive evaluation has been carried out by an independent evaluation officer (Barry MacDonald).

By the time the raising of the school leaving age is effected, materials published by Heinemann Educational Books Ltd. should be on sale to schools wishing to join the experiment. Some training is, however, necessary for teachers.

Nine areas have been selected for experimental study:

1 War and society.
2 Education.
3 The family.
4 Relations between the sexes.
5 Poverty.
6 People and work.
7 Law and order.
8 Living in cities.
9 Race.

Collections of materials will probably be published in the order given above.

An interesting feature of this project is that a complementary Roman Catholic project directed by Mr Tony Higgins at St Mary's College, Strawberry Hill, Twickenham, is investigating the implications of the project for Catholic schools.

b) *Schools Council Integrated Studies Project.* Director, Mr Bolam, Keele University.

This is a four-year project (1967–71) to examine how broad an application the humanities as a whole can have to the needs of secondary-school pupils, and to explore the possible value and means of integrating various subjects in this field. Materials will be produced and tested in 250 schools. This is not designed specifically for the average and below-average pupils aged 14 to 16, but is designed for the whole of the secondary-school age-range and ability-range.

(c) The Farmington Trust Research Unit on Moral Education. Directed by John Wilson at Oxford.

The research unit was set up in October 1965 to conduct research on the topic of moral education. Apart from the Director, who is a philosopher, the unit has two Research Fellows, Norman Williams, a psychologist, and Barry Sugarman, who is a sociologist. The work is expected to continue for at least ten years. The first publication of the Farmington Trust is the work of this research unit, and is a book with the title *Introduction to Moral Education*, published by Penguin Books. This does not set out to provide a curriculum on moral education for secondary-school-leavers, but it does contain a wealth of very important ideas and research, as well as some practical suggestions for the school and for teachers. It should certainly be read by all teachers concerned with the education of 14–16-year-old secondary-school pupils.

(d) The Schools Council Moral Education Project. Directed by Mr Peter McPhail, University of Oxford Institute of Education.

This research project is quite independent of the Farmington Trust Research Unit, but obviously maintains close contact with it. It is designed to study methods of teaching moral education in schools and providing supporting material for the moral education of young school-leavers.

It would be unfair to give the impression, however, that the only kind of preparations that have been made for the raising of the school leaving age are those national projects supported by the Nuffield Foundation or the Schools Council. One of the tasks assigned to the Schools Council when it was first set up in 1964 was to make preparations for the raising of the school leaving age, and the Council has devoted a great deal of its resources to this end. But many more local projects have also been launched, some of them with great enthusiasm and encouraging results. This kind of curriculum development at grass-roots level was, of course, encouraged by the Schools Council itself, especially in *Working Paper* No. 10, *Curriculum Development: Teachers' Groups and Centres*, which set out guide-lines for local groups of teachers.

In 1967 a Working Party in Oxfordshire (Chairman, Mr John Hanson, Communications Centre, Gosford Hill School, Kidlington, Oxford) produced a report on 'Non-Academic Education, 14-16'. The Working Party had looked carefully at the *Newsom* recommendations and others, and had designed a curriculum for the 14-16-year-old pupils of average and below-average ability. Some of this curriculum would not be immune to the Koerner criticism about life-adjustment courses quoted above, but it also contains some good materials dealing with 'Man in Society' which would be excellent at any level.

Another, very different, area in which a teachers' centre has been the organizing machinery is in Newham. This may not be typical of teachers' centres, but it is a good example of one. Here the Teachers' Centre's 'leader of curriculum studies' is the extremely energetic Ernest Millington, who keeps in close touch with every secondary school in the area, runs courses and stimulates new thinking. One of his methods is a monthly bulletin, in which he describes interesting new courses outside and inside the borough, especially those which might help pupils learn about their own environment and their own wider society. In this case (and in the case of many other teachers' centres) the organizer sees it as part of his function to keep alive and even to intensify the interest that had originally developed regarding the raising of the school leaving age—this despite the fact that the Government postponed the date. Millington describes this part of his job in these terms :

'In January 1968 the Government postponed the raising of the school leaving age until 1973. We are now in the era of R.O.S.L.A., contemptuous initials for a cynically deferred education project. Immediately we were faced with the relaxation of tension. Sighs of relief were heard throughout the land. Instead of a universal determination to use the opportunity of a further two years for research and development, in some quarters much of the steam went out of the campaign and some schools lapsed back into apathy, whilst others, not in this authority, reaffirmed the prescription, 'The mixture as before, but with much tougher discipline'. Our job in the Teachers' Centre became more demanding, since the activists of the regular Curriculum Study Group had not only to press on with those aspects of development which would affect the 'reluctant heroes' of our 1973 compulsory extra fifth forms, but struggle throughout our deliberations to maintain the impetus and keep the spirit of excitement and adventure on the move. It gave us what we most urgently needed : time not only to try out new or re-vamped courses, but opportunity to examine experimental work going on throughout the country. It enabled us to take a long and searching look at our objectives and at the underlying psychological and social reasons for the problems.' (Extract from *Project: The Newham Curriculum Development Bulletin*, No. 6, June 1969).

I would have no hesitation in saying that the development of teachers' centres throughout the country has been one of the most important educational innovations in recent years, not only in regard to the raising of the school leaving age, but for curriculum development as a whole. Unfortunately, there are still some L.E.A.s who seem reluctant to encourage teachers' centres more actively by providing the money and resources to allow them to operate with maximum efficiency.

Conclusion

It would seem to be quite clear from the above description of various kinds of preparation that one-year courses are at best useful temporary measures designed to rectify previous deficiencies in the curriculum. For many years to come some schools will have to undertake such salvage operations; in the long run, however, there is no substitute for a re-thinking of the entire secondary school curriculum. The raising of the school leaving age should therefore be seen not as one isolated problem, or a gap to be filled, but as part of a complex of reform measures. The complex will include, for example, how to organize comprehensive schools so that they do not become grammar and secondary schools under a single roof; how to unstream schools and yet preserve opportunities for individual fulfilment at the highest possible level; how to cope with the explosion of knowledge by a policy of adequate coverage, plus a balanced curriculum; how to avoid early specialization; how to organize sixth forms in order to cater for pupils who are not only destined for higher education and for whom A level courses may not be entirely appropriate. This may seem to be an enormous set of problems for schools to solve, but taken together they may even be seen as more manageable than if attempted one at a time. Piecemeal reform almost inevitably results in fragmentation of the curriculum, whereas the indications are that what is really required in English schools in the 1970s is far-sighted, long-term planning which would give the curriculum some kind of logical structure and unity.

References

Books and Papers

Banks, O., *Parity and prestige in English secondary education*, London, Routledge and Kegan Paul 1955.

Bantock, G., *Culture, industrialization and society*, London, Routledge and Kegan Paul, 1968.

Elvin L., *Education and contemporary society*, London, C. A. Watts 1965.

Hirst, P. H., 'Liberal education and the nature of knowledge', in *Philosophical analysis and the nature of knowledge*, ed. R. D. Archambault, London, 1965.

Koerner, J. D., *Reform in education*, London, Weidenfeld and Nicolson 1968.

Lawton, D., paper given at N.F.E.R. Conference, *Into Work*, July 1968.

Sprott, W. J. H., 'Society', in *Schools Council Working Paper*, No. 12.

White, J., 'Curriculum Reform', in *New Society*, 29 April 1968.

Reports, etc.

H.M.S.O., Crowther Report, *15–18*, 1959.

H.M.S.O., Newsom Report, *Half Our Future*, 1963.

H.M.S.O., *Schools Council Working Paper*, No. 2, *Raising the school leaving age*, 1965.

H.M.S.O., *ibid.*, No. 11, *Society and the young school leaver*, 1967.

H.M.S.O., *ibid.*, No. 12, *The educational implications of social and economic change*, 1967.

H.M.S.O., *ibid.*, No. 18, *Technology in schools*, 1968.

G. W. Bassett

III:7 Modern developments in primary education in England

This overview of innovation in English primary education begins by pointing up three key features of the changes that have taken place: the move from formal lessons to more informal and individual learning activity, the attempt to relate learning to the pupils' environment, the recognition of the need to interrelate curriculum changes with methods of teaching and testing, school organization and school architecture. Bassett then examines a number of specific innovations in the area of curriculum: the unified curriculum, the Initial Teaching Alphabet, Nuffield Mathematics, Nuffield Science, the teaching of French.

There is considerable ferment in primary education* in England. The publication of the Plowden Report is both an expression of it and a further powerful stimulus to it. The most prominent activities are those that involve the curriculum, organization, and teaching methods in the primary school. ...

There are general features of these changes which may with advantage be stated at this point. They will help to bring out the significance of specific innovations.

First, there is evident a resolute attempt to interpret education in behavioural terms. This emphasis on nurturing the personal growth of individual children has shifted attention from formal lessons to the more frequent use of informal activities in which the children, individually or in groups, pursue their tasks. Teaching by guiding and stimulating the pupils has tended to supplement, and often replace, teaching as formal class instruction.

Second, there is a resolute attempt to relate the curriculum to the pupils' environment, to make clear the point that subjects are ways

Bassett, G. W., *Innovation in primary education*, John Wiley, 1970, pp. 27–42.
Reprinted by permission.
* The term 'primary' refers to the age range 5–11 years. It is usually divided into two stages, 'infants' (5–7 years) and 'junior' (8–11 years).

of ordering the environment, and of guiding new studies of it. By using subjects to explain, describe, and show appreciation of the environment, children learn to use mathematics, science, geography, art, English, etc., rather than just to learn about them. With this need in mind for children to use subjects, rather than to memorize factual content, there has been a searching re-examination of traditional curriculum statements. Most of these statements dealt with selected results, rather than with the basic concepts, structure, and methods of the subject. This re-examination has produced surprising revisions, particularly in science and mathematics.

Third, the interdependence of different innovations is being more thoroughly recognized. Changes in curriculum, in methods of teaching and examining, in school organization, and in school buildings, are all interrelated—and, by reinforcing each other, they make a greater mobilization of resources possible.

With these guiding statements in mind we may pass to a description and appraisal of the new practices. ...

Curriculum

There are no legal provisions governing the content of school curricula in England, except that the school day begin with an act of worship, and that religious education be given.* It is the responsibility of the individual school to provide a curriculum which is suitable for the age, ability, and aptitude of the children. What influences there are towards uniformity are the more informal pressures of professional opinion with which the school is in contact through publications of various kinds, in-service courses, and the visits to the school of advisers and inspectors. The examination which was taken at the end of the primary school (in the child's 12th year) and used as a basis for selection to different forms of secondary education did provide, in part, an unofficial curriculum for the upper classes of the primary school. But with the increasingly widespread introduction of a comprehensive system at secondary level, the need for the 11 + examination is less apparent, and many authorities have abandoned or substantially modified it. The head of a primary school in England, then, is unusually free from direction from outside his school, and is in a very privileged position in being able to deter-

---

* There are provisions which allow non-attendance at these according to freedom of conscience.

mine what is taught in his school. Undoubtedly some heads do not use this freedom very adventurously, but on the whole it does result in a programme which varies from school to school. This fact should be borne in mind throughout this chapter: it will help to explain how some of the measures described here which involve choice based on children's interests or teachers' judgment can be achieved.

Prescribing a subject in a curriculum may mean a number of quite different things. The subject may be merely named and the details left to the professional judgment of the teacher, or the actual topics to be taught may be set out, and even the order in which they are to be done. The ultimate in course prescription yet devised is the Skinnerian programmed text. The question of the degree to which the structure of a subject is inherent, and is not open to children or teachers to vary, is an important one. Clearly the more prescribed a curriculum is, the less freedom of choice there is for children, and the more does the speed-of-learning dimension come to the fore. The less prescribed it is, the greater is the possibility that individual differences in other respects than in speed of learning will show up.

I. The Unified Curriculum

The unified curriculum is put first in this list because it is perhaps the most thoroughgoing departure from conventional school practice. It also illustrates well how difficult it is to separate the categories of curriculum, method, and organization in describing some school practices, and also how old a new idea can be.

A generation ago, the 1931 Hadow Report on the Primary School included this famous sentence, 'The curriculum is to be thought of in terms of activity and experience rather than of knowledge to be acquired and facts to be stored.' This concept has been both the hope and the despair of educationists who have struggled to make it a reality. Perhaps the posing of 'activity and experience' and 'knowledge to be acquired' as alternatives has led to misunderstanding. What really are being contrasted are 'active' and 'inert' forms of knowledge, a distinction that every teacher readily understands, but does not always adequately guard against. The unified curriculum is an attempt to express the curriculum in terms of activity and experience rather than in terms of subject matter to be learnt.

In trying to describe it one can only list a number of general features and make a number of explanatory comments; inevitably an idea like this takes on a different character according to the teacher using it.

(i) A substantial part of each day's work is devoted to projects, centres of interest, topics, units, studies, activities (however they may be named).

Examples of them are endless. One can start with a topic almost anywhere where interest and attention are captured, and follow it in all sorts of ways. Some of them will lead to complexities where children get out of their depth. But this is valuable. All too often with nicely ordered knowledge to be taught we give the impression that there is always an answer, which is in the book, or in the teacher's head. Three examples only are given (two of which were observed by the writer): the idea is a familiar one to most readers, and does not need labouring.

(a) *A study of time* (9–10-year-olds). This required a great deal of reading which has involved mathematical–astronomical–scientific–geographical ideas, a good deal of historical research (clocks through the ages), much writing (describing construction details, functions, origins, etc.), a great deal of calculating, experimenting, constructing, inventing, drawing.

(b) *A study of printing* (8–10-year-olds). This began with art and handwork, making designs, cutting them in various media (wood, linoleum, etc.), and printing them onto paper and materials, and led to a considerable amount of historical, geographical, and scientific study.

(c) A top junior class (11-year-olds) became interested in the problem of measuring the area of an awkwardly shaped field at the back of the school. The problem stimulated much learning about surveying and triangles. From surveying, interest passed to navigation. For one boy the work on navigation took the form of a story of encounters of pirate ships and men-of-war, and involved a great deal of calculation, history, geography, and English (example taken from Plowden Report, p. 199).

(ii) Projects may arise from something done or said by the teacher, or by a child; but in either case they are *accepted* by the children.

(iii) They may be pursued by a whole class, a group within the class, or an individual child. Commonly a group is involved, and individuals work on different aspects.

(iv) They may be pursued for varying parts of the school day, and for a varying number of days and weeks. Some pupils may use the greater part of the day, others a morning or an afternoon, depending on what other jobs have to be done. The teacher's 'control' of this kind of situation is very subtle and skilled indeed, and requires an intimate knowledge on his part of each pupil.

(v) While there is no timetable in the ordinary sense, there usually are some fixed commitments because of the use of common facilities such as the hall for dancing and movement, and, in some schools, the outside part-time specialist coming in to teach French. As will be pointed out later when the French course is being described, where class teachers are not qualified to teach French, use is made of part-time teachers. Criticism of this arrangement is often heard in those schools where a unified curriculum is used, because of the break in the unity. There are also commitments in the sense that the teacher has a general plan of what he wants to achieve, and commitments for individual children whom he knows need special work; but his route to these goals is not a fixed one.

(vi) Children improve in their effectiveness in working in this way by practice in it. Many of the 10- and 11-year-olds observed had never known any other way of working, and were quite skilled in using their time effectively. The presence of a visitor in the room, claiming the whole of the teacher's attention, made no observable difference to their absorption in their tasks.

(vii) As a concluding comment we may state the values which supporters of the unified curriculum claim for it. Most prominent among these are the educational experiences afforded the pupils: the pursuit of a significant task with interest and zest, the practice of a number of important intellectual skills (collecting evidence, analysing, reasoning, etc.), presenting results in writing and a mathematical form, increased self-reliance and responsibility, increased clarity of the meaning of subjects (mathematics, history, etc.) in the examination of the environment.

Less importance is attached to actual factual material learnt than to skills, insights, and attitudes. Because of this, the supporters of the method are not disturbed by the criticism that the knowledge gained by pupils may be somewhat unsystematic and fragmentary.

II. The Initial Teaching Alphabet (i.t.a.)

The Initial Teaching Alphabet is an alphabet devised by Sir James Pitman, consisting of 44 characters each with a constant sound. It is made up of 24 of the existing Roman letters (each being given a constant sound), and 20 new characters. The 44 characters cover all the sounds in the English language.

The 24 existing Roman letters are as follows: a (as in apple), b (as in bed), c (as in cat), d (as in doll), e (as in egg), f (as in finger), g (as in girl), h (as in hat), i (as in ink), j (as in jam), k (as in kitten), l (as in lion), m (as in man), n (as in nest), o (as in on), p (as in pig), r (as in red), s (as in soap), t (as in tree), u (as in up), v (as in van), w (as in window), y (as in yellow), z (as in zoo). Note that q and x have been dropped.)

The 20 new characters are as follows:

ɑ (as in father),   æ (as in angel),   au (as in author),   ᴄh (as in chair),
ɛɛ (as in eel),   ie (as in tie),   ŋ (as in king),   œ (as in toe),
ω (as in book),   ꞷ (as in food),   ou (as in out),   oi (as in oil),
ɼ (as in bird),   ʃh (as in ship),   ӡ (as in treasure),   ᵵh (as in three),
ᵭh (as in mother),   ue (as in due),   wh (as in wheel),   ᴢ (as in is).

Note that many of the additional i.t.a. characters, for example:

ᴄh, ɛɛ, ʃh, ᵵh, ou, au,

closely resemble the traditional digraphs. Lower-case and upper-case letters in alphabet have the same shape: they differ only in size.

The alphabet has been designed to assist children by eliminating the following inherent difficulties of traditional orthography:

(i) Some of the letters represent a variety of sounds. For example, a has a different sound in each of the following words: all, any, want, am, mate, rather. In each of the following words o has a different sound: do, one, gong, go, women.

(ii) The same sound is spelt in a variety of ways. For example, the sound i (as in bike) is spelt differently in each of these words: height, eye, buy, by, bye, guide, island, sign, lie.

(iii) There is great variety between the appearance of lower-case, capital, and script forms of the letters. Pitman has pointed out[1] that the traditional alphabet has not 26, but 66 characters: e.g., A, a, *a*, B, b, *b*, F, f, *f*, etc.

As will be clear from the description of i.t.a. given:
(i) Each letter has one sound only,
(ii) Most sounds are spelt the same way, and
(iii) Each letter has only one shape, upper- and lower-case letters differing only in size.

As a medium for learning to read (assuming that the learning of the additional characters is not a great burden), there appears to be *a priori* evidence that the Iinitial Teaching Alphabet has a clear advantage over traditional orthography.

But a host of questions spring to mind.
(i) In fact, do children learn to read faster with i.t.a.?
(ii) How is comprehension affected?
(iii) How will spelling and writing be affected?
(iv) How do children transfer to traditional orthography (t.o.)?
(v) Is this a scheme mainly for backward readers?
(vi) Most children do learn to read using traditional orthography, so why bother?
(vii) Are there sufficient supplementary reading books in i.t.a.? And does one have to provide sets of reading books and library books in both t.o. and i.t.a.?

Undoubtedly there are more questions than completely satisfactory answers to cover the widely varying conditions, and the many countries, in which English is learnt as a native tongue, but there are preliminary answers to most of the obvious ones, and they do give some assurance to the half-hearted.

A major experiment with i.t.a. was undertaken by the University of London Reading Research Unit (in charge of Dr J. Downing), in association with the National Foundation for Educational Research, with financial backing from several sources including the Ford Foundation. In its report[2] it made the rather unusual provisions of critical evaluations of the results by twelve independent educationists from Britain, Australia, Canada, and the U.S.A. The results gave favourable support to the experimental group of children using i.t.a. as compared with the control group using t.o. The number of children used in the experiment is not large, but the results appear to be quite positive.

Three findings from this research do not need further elaboration and are reproduced below in graph form, A showing progress in reading the basic reader series used in the experiment as the criterion of reading success, B showing a comparison, using comprehension as the criterion, and C showing a comparison of the experimental and control groups with regard to spelling.

This statistical statement may be supplemented by some comments of the Chief Education Officer for Southend, Donald Bartlett:[3]

'What results does Downing obtain? Are they borne out by the opinions of the practising teacher? Are they of value to the teacher not using i.t.a.? . . . The results . . . may be summarized briefly as follows. Can children learn to read more easily by i.t.a.? Results show that they can do so, whether judged on accuracy, speed, or comprehension. Can they transfer their training to reading in traditional orthography? Here there was shown to be a setback on transfer. After transfer are reading attainments in t.o. superior to what they would have been without the intervention of i.t.a.? The results show that the experimental group achieved scores in t.o. superior to those of the control group by the beginning of the third year. The fourth question is concerned with the

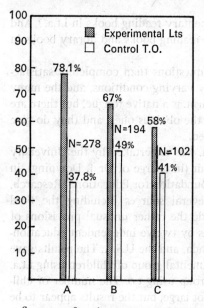

A. *Progress in reading Basic Reader Series*. Proportions completed the Series and advanced beyond. After 2 years at school.

B. *Comprehension in reading in t.o.* (Neale Analysis Test). Proportions having a comprehension-age equal to and higher than their chronological age. After 3 years at school.

C. *Spelling in t.o.* Proportions having a spelling-age equal to and higher than their chronological age. After 3 years at school.

fluency of written compositions with i.t.a., and the results show that the written compositions of i.t.a. pupils are longer and use a more extensive vocabulary than those of their counterparts using t.o. Spelling attainments are the subject of the last question, and here again those children who had started with i.t.a. proved better in t.o. than the control group of children. . . . These results are remarkable by any standards and show to the inquirer that i.t.a. is worth its place in the schools. The results which indicate regression at the transfer stage will cause comment particularly from teachers using i.t.a. Many have not found this at all to the degree indicated and notice little setback except for hesitancy on the part of the child for a few days.'

Dr W. D. Wall, the Director of the National Foundation for Educational Research, surveying the evidence in the London study, was moved to comment as follows.[4]

'We are justified in concluding that the irregularity of English spelling is a cause of difficulty in learning to read for children between the ages of five and seven. It is, too, justifiable to add that i.t.a. itself simplified the learning task significantly.'

Other evidence is not so favourable to i.t.a. A three-year i.t.a.–t.o. study was recently completed in England by Terence Swales at Reading University. He concluded,[5]

'Children taught by i.t.a. for three years were neither superior nor inferior in reading achievements to those taught by t.o. from the outset. . . . i.t.a. produced neither more nor less backward readers than t.o.'

American research studies, supported by the United States Office of Education, have not established any superiority for i.t.a. Mazurkiewicz[6] reported in 1965 that at the end of the second year of his experiment, when most students would have transferred out of i.t.a., there was still very little difference in reading achievement between the i.t.a. group and the t.o. group in their scores on the California Reading Test.

The weight of recent evidence seems to be leaning towards the conclusion that there is very little difference in their reading abilities between children taught in traditional orthography and those who first learn the initial teaching alphabet.

Research results are of course subject to evaluation according to the methods used. Devotees of i.t.a. may take the view that research findings which do not establish the superiority of i.t.a. are a poor compliment to the quality of the research done.

Adopting a more objective view, it can be said that in experiments with large numbers i.t.a. is at least as good as t.o. as a medium for teaching reading. This in itself is a rather remarkable result. Perhaps in the hands of some teachers, and for some children, it may prove to be superior. Each year something of the order of six million children in the world begin to learn to read in English. Improvement in methods of teaching reading is obviously a field of immense importance.

Whatever its merits, a striking feature of i.t.a. is its rapid rate of adoption, considering the notoriously slow pace at which innovations in education usually occur. It was introduceed to a handful of British schools on an experimental basis in late 1961. By mid 1966 it was being used in 1,765 schools all over Great Britain and in many more than this in the U.S.A., had spread in a limited way to many other countries, including New Zealand and Australia, and had been experimented with for the teaching of illiterate adults and of English as a second language. An i.t.a. foundation was set up in England by Sir James Pitman in 1962, and in 1965 an American foundation was established at Hofstra University, Hempstead, New York. Publication in i.t.a. has spread to thirty-five publishing houses, who have published among them seven beginners' reading schemes, three remedial reading schemes, and some three hundred supplementary reading books in the new medium.

III. The Nuffield Mathematics Project

The Nuffield Mathematics Project, sponsored by the Schools Council and financed by the Nuffield Foundation, was set up in 1964. Its establishment marked a ferment in the field of mathematics teaching which had been growing since the end of the war, and which was the subject of the first curriculum bulletin issued by the Schools Council.[7] The major pressure was obviously the nation's need for mathematicians, but the educational question was not just one of numbers of students. There was a growing realization that school mathematics courses were encumbered with a good deal of material that not only was of little value in itself, but also produced unsatisfactory attitudes among the children. There was also a clearer recognition that, although the problem was with secondary-school and university-level studies, the reform of the content and spirit of the subject in its introductory phase gave the best promise of improvement. The Mathematics project was aimed at this introductory work, but, in setting its age range at 5–13, and thus bridging primary and secondary education, it sought to ensure that a course was not abruptly altered at the point of transfer to secondary education after a promising beginning.

In the short time since it was set up the Mathematics Project has counted the following achievement to its credit.

(i) It has involved a great many schools, teachers, children, parents, administrators, and mathematicians in an approach to learning mathematics from the tender age of five through to thirteen which is so different from the arithmetic to which everyone had become accustomed as to be understandably called the 'new' mathematics.

(ii) It has stimulated a flurry of interest and concern that has sent teachers, inspectors, administrators (and, in many cases, parents) back to 'school' to ensure that they, as well as the five-year-olds, understand the new ideas.

(iii) It has produced ideas about concrete material for assisting the development of mathematical concepts that have produced such a volume and variety of improvised 'equipment' (pots and pans, sticks, marbles, scales, shells, etc.) as to change the appearance of the classroom.

(iv) It has produced a number of draft publications embodying the progress of its thought for comment and criticism, and, more recently, a number of 'permanent' publications which represent milestones in the development of the teaching of mathematics in Britain, and which undoubtedly will exercise an influence for some time to come.

The books are *I do and I understand*, an introductory book; *Teachers' Guides*, which cover three main topics—Computation and Structure, Shape and Size, and Graphs; *Weaving Guides*, which are single-concept books giving detailed instruction or information about a particular subject; and *Check-up Guides*, which will provide checks on the child's progress. The task of evaluating success and progress in a course such as this is an unusual one. We can gauge progress when the criteria are number of sums right, or speed of working on assigned tasks, but progress in such matters as interest, originality, and depth of insight is an unfamiliar object of measurement. The check-up guides are being prepared by a team from the Institut des Sciences de l'Education in Geneva under the general supervision of Jean Piaget.

(v) It has, while giving such an authoritative lead in a new venture, with great wisdom stressed the view that the books should not be looked on as guides to the only 'right' way to teach in mathematics, and that development from work in the guides is more important than the guides themselves.

It is difficult to decide whether to include a description of Nuffield Mathematics under the heading of curriculum innovation or methodology. The title of the key volume, *I do and I understand*, gives pride of place to the way in which the subject is learnt. It is dedicated to Jean Piaget, the Swiss psychologist, whose ideas of cognitive development have so strongly influenced it. Its chapter headings carry on the methodological orientation of the title, as can be seen from these examples:

Chapter 3   How children learn
Chapter 4   The significance of language
Chapter 5   Learning through discovery
Chapter 6   The use of the environment
Chapter 7   Problems of organization with the school
Chapter 8   General problems of class organization
Chapter 12 Evaluating progress

Its stated aim (in a general introduction) is 'to devise a contemporary approach for children from five to thirteen. The stress is on how to learn, not on what to teach. Running through all the work is the central notion that children must be set free to make their own discoveries and think for themselves, and so achieve understanding, instead of learning off mysterious drills.'

It should be stressed that the Nuffield material is not a syllabus for children to follow, nor is it a textbook. It is addressed to teachers, and aims to create a universe of discourse for them, richly illustrated with the kind of examples that teachers appreciate (namely, actual children's work) but not in the form of a set of models to follow. Mathematics is presented as an important way in which primary-school children may order their experience, and effectively communicate with one another and with their teacher, in a meaningful language involving words, symbols, pictures, or diagrams. Their growth in proficiency in using the medium is closely related to their experience, and to other school tasks, and to their wish to communicate. No ready-made problems are presented. Rather they are expected to arise out of the children's own interests, out of the tasks in other 'subjects' which are being pursued, and, of course, as developments of mathematical work going on. Many children become intrigued with mathematics as a 'pure' study, and spend a good deal of time working at such things as number series, sets, magic squares, and the geometry of unusual shapes, often with a sophistication that confounds our earlier notions of what children can understand.

The spirit of this approach is one that teachers of infant children find familiar. The change for them is mainly in the kind of material needed to enrich the classroom, and in the challenge to their own mathematical insight. For other teachers, habituated to the sterner realities of the mathematical world of 8–11-year-olds with its endless sums (whether in honest form or disguised as 'problems'), the difficulties of encounter and reconciliation are greater. There are promising signs that the number of teachers who see the point of the 'new' mathematics is increasing rapidly. Since it is in essence an approach, an understanding of the rationale which underlies mathematical operations, rather than a body of mathematical facts, it is bound to fail if the teachers do not appreciate this.

Characteristically, the Plowden Committee end their discussion of primary mathematics teaching with a reminder of the generative and regenerative power which must always come from the teachers, and this is a convenient note on which to end this section.

'It happens that our inquiry has coincided with a period of change in the teaching of mathematics, and we have been privileged spectators of it. While it must be evident from our remarks that we are full of enthusiasm for what we have seen, and of hope for the future, we must emphasize that the last thing we wish to see is a hardening of the new approach into an accepted syllabus supported by textbooks, workbooks, and commercially produced apparatus, and consecrated by familiarity. The rate of change must obviously slow down, but the initiative must remain firmly in the practising teachers' hands.[8]

IV. The Nuffield Science Project

The revision of the primary science course has many of the same general features which have been described in connexion with mathematics. These are summarized in the following six points.

(i) It was undertaken by a national committee sponsored by the Nuffield Foundation. There was close association with schools, and each step was taken only after satisfactory 'field' trials.

(ii) It takes the environment as its starting point and focus of attention. Previously in primary-school science attention was limited to biological phenomena. In this new approach, biological and physical phenomena are used, and the idea of the relatedness of science is brought out.

(iii) It advocates a discovery approach with great freedom in the type of topic selected, and in the depth and range of ideas invoked as the investigation proceeds.

(iv) Its deliberations cover children with an age range bridging primary and secondary years, from five to thirteen.

(v) There is stress on the link with other subjects, especially with mathematics and history, and on the skills of expression in written and diagrammatic form.

(vi) The materials produced are not intended to be followed by teachers as a syllabus, but rather to assist an understanding of the new approach, and to help by suggesting the type of investigation likely to be successful with children and the type of equipment that might (at least to start with) be acquired.

The keeping of animals, fish, birds, and other pets in school, and the study of the botanical environment (often with the aid of horticultural or agricultural plots), the keeping of weather records, and similar projects, have been an accepted part of primary-school science for many years. These activities are now extended to include phenomena that might be classified as falling within the scope of physics, chemistry, geology or astronomy; and simple apparatus such as magnets, cells, basic chemicals, are provided. Observations, measurements, experiments are supplemented by science from history, or contemporary description. History is full of exciting science stories, many of which cannot be, or should not be, repeated. They may be too expensive (the conquest of space for example) or too dangerous (the conquest of dread diseases for example).

Interesting as the facts of science may be to primary-school children, the importance of the study lies in the influence it can have on their maturing mentality. The scientific knowledge gained by the age of 12 amounts to little in comparison with what has to be learnt; and it is likely that much of it will be modified later. But the attitudes engendered, and the intellectual skills associated with the methods which science uses, can have an enduring value, carrying the student on to more mature studies in the subject, and transferring more generally to other studies.

Pervading all the observing, experimenting, constructing, speculating, testing, and recording that go on in the pursuit of primary-school science is the practice of the important intellectual skills that underlie scientific thinking: accuracy in observation, precision in the handling of evidence, hypothesizing, and generalizing.

For those who are going to use science professionally this introduction in the primary school may well be crucial. But the scientific method, being applicable to many kinds of problems, is relevant to everyone. All need to be able to distinguish fact from opinion, to know what evidence is and what the weight of evidence is in a particular situation, and to know when doubt is called for, even if it cannot always be resolved. All need to catch some of the scientist's passion for seeking truth, and, because they have done so, to be impatient of careless or imprecise observations or inferences that lead to error or half-truth, and to abhor procedures which lead deliberately to error.

The chief concern of education is with the establishing and disseminating of truth. In this it finds itself in collision with anti-educational exploitive influences, concerned with securing some personal or group advantage. If, in our schools, our children can be taught more effectively to think like scientists, to be touched with their scrupulous regard for truth, and to be made more sensitive to humane values through humanistic studies, they will be less tolerant of exploitation than many of their elders at present seem to be. A course in science which has behavioural objectives of this kind, and is not content merely with presenting scientific facts, may not be so new; but it is a novelty if taught well enough to succeed. It is too early yet to say whether this kind of success is being achieved in English primary schools. After all the idea that *everyone* should be able to think for himself, and to apply rigorous tests to distinguish fact from opinion, is new in any society.

V. The Teaching of French

Most commonly in England the learning of a foreign language used to be regarded as a task for the secondary school, although some private preparatory schools did begin it earlier. Now there is a widespread acceptance of the idea that it is better to begin it in the primary school, and use the language as a means of dealing with ordinary situations, as one uses the mother tongue.

The commonest language taught is French, partly because France is England's nearest neighbour (although one suspects that this reason is something of a rationalization), and partly because there is a tradition of French teaching in England, and more teachers of French are available.

Not that teachers are available in adequate numbers. On the contrary, the average primary-school teacher does not have the competence needed, and a great deal of the effort involved in introducing the subject has gone into providing emergency courses for teachers. The result is that part-time teachers, often with a background of secondary-school teaching, have been employed.

There are a number of courses in vogue—*Bonjour Line*, a course on filmstrip made for the Ministry of Education in France, *Parlons français*, a course on moving film made in the U.S.A., and *En avant*, the Nuffield course. The French and American courses have the advantage of being first in the field, but it is expected that the Nuffield course will gain in popularity, and to a degree displace the others.

En avant is a five-year introductory course, bridging the primary and secondary years. It is designed for pupils in the last three years of the primary school (9+, 10+, 11+) and the first years of the secondary school (12+, 13+). Its objectives are to teach pupils to speak, read, and write French, to introduce them to French customs and institutions, and to widen the general educational experience of the children. It is arranged in four stages, stage 1 being completely oral, stage 2 introducing some reading and writing, and stages 3 and 4 developing reading and writing and leading to composition. For each stage an appropriate teacher's guide and supporting materials are published (or are to be published). For stage 1, for example, the material is as follows:

(i) Teacher's book. This contains the text and the teacher's notes for twenty lesson units with suggestions for exploitation of the material presented. The full text of all the recorded material is included. The book also contains an introductory unit, a list of French names and of classroom phrases, and an index of the vocabulary and sentence patterns which occur in these units.

(ii) Flannelgraph figurines in colour. These sheets of figurines which are to be cut out depict the objects and people which occur in the stage 1 lessons.

(iii) Flashcards, printed in two colours—two sets numbering twelve and ten cards respectively. The first set depicts animals and the numbers 1 to 12, and the second illustrates the verbs of action included in the first 20 lessons.

(iv) Tape recordings. Twelve tapes (at $3\frac{3}{4}$ i.p.s. half track). These are made by native speakers, male and female, adults and children. They include the presentation of sentence patterns and vocabulary, songs and exercises, etc.

(v) Three films (sound, colour, running time $7\frac{1}{2}$ minutes). These are regarded as ancillary, but are closely linked to the course, and use the structures and vocabulary which it introduces. They depict the adventures of three puppet characters, Boupah, Nigot and Fléon.

The text and tape recording of the sound track of the films can be purchased separately. Instructions are also provided for making the puppets and a puppet theatre.

The Nuffield course is a notable contribution to the teaching of modern languages in England, expressing in a practical way ideas about introductory teaching which have been gaining currency there and elsewhere for some years. It is hoped by many, however, that it will come to assume a more background role than at present, and that as teachers become better qualified in foreign languages (including ones other than French) they will follow a particular course less and less, and take advantage of ideas in the existing courses to develop their own. The 'step by step' presentation of these courses, with controlled vocabulary and sentence structure, represents a formalism from which the primary school in other aspects of the curriculum has been freeing itself. The recent change in mathematics teaching was a major step in this direction in a subject which has been noted for its fixed sequential treatment. It would be something of a regression if foreign-language teaching, transferred from the secondary school, brought back with it a formal approach to its teaching.

Concluding note on developments in the curriculum

It is perhaps not surprising that, when so much attention has been given in the last decade to mathematics and science, it is these subjects that are so prominent in the reform of the primary-school curriculum.

But there is a great deal to admire in other aspects of the curriculum. One may mention especially the greatly increased output of children's writing obtained by associating it with many activities in the curriculum, and the environment studies in social studies. The work in English is likely to be further stimulated as the Nuffield programme in linguistics and English teaching comes to completion and begins to exert its influence. This project was set up in September 1964, and based on the Communication Research Centre, Department of General Linguistics, at University College, London; it is due to complete its work in 1970.

In the development of physical and art education since the war many of the modern concepts of primary education have been successfully incorporated. The individual creative expression of children in pictorial art, in crafts, and in movement and dance, and the linking of this with speech and drama, literature and music are particularly admirable. The work is impressive, however, rather than new, and is not listed among recent innovations.

References

1 Sir James Pitman, *As difficult as ABC: the case against the traditional orthography as a learning medium.* Pitman, London, 1966.

2 J. A. Downing, *The i.t.a. Symposium.* National Foundation for Educational Research in England and Wales, Slough, 1967.

3 Comments on the i.t.a. Symposium (mimeographed).

4 *Ibid.,* p. 164.

5 Quoted in 'Initial Teaching Alphabet: a look at the research data', *The Educational Magazine,* Melbourne, Feb. 1968, p. 43.

6 *Ibid.,* p. 43.

7 'Mathematics in Primary Schools' (*Schools Council Curriculum Bulletin No. 1*), H.M.S.O., London, 1965, Revised 1967. The approach in this bulletin emphasizes exploratory methods rather more than the Nuffield scheme does.

8 Central Advisory Council for Education (England) *Children and their Primary Schools,* H.M.S.O. London, 1967 ('Plowden Report'), p. 239.

Eric Midwinter

III:8 Curriculum and the EPA community school

*The director of the Liverpool Educational Priority Area
Project, Eric Midwinter, argues for a new sort of
curriculum in the community school more in keeping
with the social role of the community school. This social
purpose must become implicit in the curriculum. One of
the problems with changing the curriculum is that,
because of massive changes in teaching method over the
last twenty years, educationists think that the revolution
is over. Much of that revolution has overemphasized
method and done little about changing content. The
community-oriented curriculum in the EPA school has
three advantages—children will do better in traditional
skills because these skills will be geared to their
experience; the child is dignified by the curriculum dealing
with his world and not evading it for the 'cowsheds of
rurality'; parental involvement would be increased. Eric
Midwinter concludes by describing the steps that the
project has taken to implement a locally based,
community oriented curriculum.*

The underlying national theme of the EPA project is the Community
School, recommended in the Plowden Report as especially needful in
Educational Priority Areas. The major task of the project is the pilot
testing of approaches in community schooling with a view to suggesting a national policy on the subject. The Community School has
as many different definitions as there are people opening their
mouths on the topic, but most of them tend towards an 'open' as
opposed to a 'closed' school, with more intensive usage of plant by
the community in evenings and during holidays and usually some
pattern of parental participation in school-life. This is surely welcome and the EPA project has worked hard in these fields. But one
might also wonder whether the curriculum needs some reappraisal.
There is a danger of the Community School being the same package
as before, albeit with the knots and wrapping paper a little easier to
untie. Is there, in fact, a case for the Community School having a

Liverpool Educational Priority Area Occasional Papers No. 6, 1970. Reprinted
by permission.

community-oriented curriculum, suited to the aims of community education?

The Community School is normally seen as a method of achieving harmony between school and community, but it could go beyond that. As well as providing a means, it could suggest an end. In the EPA the fundamental need is for communal regeneration and for the resolution of the dreadful social ills that beset the inhabitants. Eventually, this should mean some form of self-regeneration as the people involved set about solving these problems. The pouring in of palliatives, in resources or services, from outside is not sufficient; indeed, without the active and vital participation of the local inhabitants such interventionist policies lose much of their point. The transference of social and educational problems to new housing estates emphasises this. A natural aim, then, for the Community School might be the education of children to be the next generation of parents, voters and citizens in the neighbourhood, in the hope that they will conceive of creative responses to the pressing needs of the downtown and other disadvantaged districts.

A negative illustration is provided by the planners' lip-service to consultation. They may knock on the door of a client for rehabilitation or decantation and ask what sort of home and environment is required. What is the unfortunate interviewee to say in answer to this? What, in too many cases, he could say is something like: 'I was never educated to listen to that kind of question nor to articulate responses, technical or creative, to it'. He might well add: 'If you would ask me to repeat the symptoms of the Black Death, recite "Cargoes" or write an essay on the Masai Tribe, I should be happy to oblige.' The Community School presupposes a social role for education and, in turn, this might equally apply to the curriculum. In Educational Priority Areas, if not elsewhere, the important issues are social and not, basically, literary or numerary. The school could attempt to help by placing a larger emphasis on social education and a corresponding smaller emphasis on 'academic' education, the inverted commas reminding one that social education can be as intellectually and spiritually rewarding as conventional scholarship.

Herein lies the essential difference between community education and compensatory education. The latter assumes the correctness of a uniform system and merely attempts to lubricate it where, as in EPA's, it seems a trifle inefficient and rusty. This is fine, but the net result is the provision of educational passports out of the area for a few more lucky winners, the ones who, as they say, have the potential to stay on for further education. No one would begrudge them the chance, as long as it is recalled that this does no more than dilute the majority. In 1991, according to the planners, there will be 90,000 people living in the Liverpool EPA; as many again will have been ferried out to the redevelopment estates on the outskirts of the city. The children in our primary schools will, by then, have children at primary school. Community education in the EPA's need to give urgent priority to these and their peers elsewhere.

This social purpose must become implicit in the curriculum. One difficulty is that, so extensive and successful has been the massive modification of method in the schools over the last twenty years, that many educationists think the educational revolution is past and over. There has not, unhappily, been a similar radicalism in content and wonderfully colourful methodology has disguised the old hatted sterility of much of the substance of education. The prime example of this is the teaching of French. In the spacious days following the Cobden–Chevalier Treaty, a wing-collared clerk scratching a few words of French was something of an asset for a merchant house trading with the continent. The 1904 Memorandum on Secondary Education sustained the idea and imbued it with its own strange brand of academic respectability. Supported by the recruitment of French graduates who were blooded by this system and justified on the ludicrous grounds that our halting endeavours to transcribe sentences like 'summon the postillion; my grandmother's ear-trumpet has been struck by lightning' somehow strengthened international understanding, the confidence trick boomed. French eventually moved into the primary school, presumably to fit children for more energetic construing at the secondary stage. The hardware was moved in. Records, tapes, earphones, language labs and a sizeable load of other technical equipment was deployed, giving the subject a trendy modish air. It became the vogue to teach French and the Plowden Report smiled approvingly. Despite the fact that five times as many people go to Spain as France for their holidays and that we run the risk of turning out children illiterate in two languages rather than in one, we insist on the most specious grounds on teaching the subject. Princess Margaret opened a primary school in Barrow-in-Furness a year or so back and during her visit to its large French set-up 'at no time', according to the *Guardian*, 'did the children speak a word of English'. Trad meets Mod; the outmoded Edwardian discipline is saved by the technological mechanics of today and the whole ghastly mix up to what might be called the *chef d'oeuvre* of irrelevancy.

Most other subjects in some (not, of course, in all) places could similarly be assessed. With the onset of the white-hot technological era, for instance, Science has had a face-lift and the jars of Bottogas have been appearing in Junior school classrooms. The water-filled milk-bottle, containing straws adorned with pieces of plasticine, has replaced watercress on blotting paper, and, lo, the scientific salvation of the nation is nigh. Yet it still seems to dwell in the dreary Edwardian world of museum mustiness with its tedious series of wrongly-called 'experiments' on matters resolved a million times over. Tunes change but melodies linger on. Given the massive factor of perpetuation in education, teachers sometimes discover themselves transmitting an artificial heritage, the one, in fact, transmitted to them. There is bric-à-brac of this and that, bits and pieces of history, shreds and patches of geography, dribs and drabs of scripture, bubbles and squeaks of science, odds and sods of maths, poems and stories, a ragbag of shoddy oddments with little meaning outside the school. It's not only remote and sterile, it tends to be backward-looking and romanticist. It is romanticist about the dainty twee Victoriana of poesy and the country city teachers, for instance, are occasionally heard saying 'some of the children in my class have never seen a cow', as though the cow has some especially bovine godlike quality or as though its modern existence is so delightfully pastoral. All the more praise, then, to the hundreds of city teachers who withstand the heavy pressure of the unwritten conventions of the timetable and struggle manfully to get to grips with the valid educational problems around them. This is the optimistic note. There seems some awareness among head teachers and teachers that the common curricular round might not be admirably suited to the EPA.

It is time, perhaps, to look closely at subjects as such. The lengthy debate between informal and formal protagonists, the former with their heads blinded in the clouds, the latter with their feet clogged on the ground, has been reminiscent of the Lilliputians divided into Large-enders and Small-enders with no one bothering about the egg itself. Never mind a 'new' approach to maths. Can maths be justified in its own right and, if so, can it be justified for every day of the school year? Even the purported 'integration' of subjects can mislead. What price the eight-plus centre of interest on monasticism, hopeful of drawing religious education (the monkish virtues) history (the middle-ages) geography (Northumberland) English (a day in the life of a monk) and art and craft (drawings and models of monasteries and/or their inmates) into epistemological harmony? This can compound the felony. Having decided on a topic outside, at any reasonable level of accuracy and meaning, the conceptual grasp of the child, one ends with a series of third-hand exercises in support of a theme only open to second-hand consideration.

Many curricular activities are justified in terms of the 'interest motif', but interest is method, not aim. The child assuredly needs to be interested if he is to be educated, but the reverse is not always true. Surely it is the task of the teacher to make dull old ditchwater sparkle like champagne, having decided that dull old ditchwater requires investigation. Everything should and can be 'interesting'; what is necessary is a vigilant inspection of the content to ensure that it has social purpose. It is also argued that the inculcation of 'skills' is of greatest import and transfer of training is still accepted *sotto voce*, e.g. the logical thought one needs for life can be learned from mathematics. Leaving aside the inadequate correlation between first-rate mathematicians and high-grade lives, what is wrong with learning it from life! If all these 'skills' are so essential in life, why are not life-themes more frequently used to exercise them.

Reading offers an instance of this. The range of approaches and the acrid debate over the pros and cons of each reading mystique is quite phenomenal, so much so that reading has come to be regarded as an end rather than a means. It matters not only how children read, but what and why they read. As the coincidence of the rise in public education and in popular literature suggests, reading can be a soporific and not a stimulant. We may even be preventing some people from purposive action because we give them the escapist tranquilliser of a bad book. There is no reason why reading, like writing, number, creativity and everything else, shouldn't be geared to the child's growing awareness of his reality.

Here, therefore, is a major task for the community school, both at primary and secondary level. A principle goal might be the familiarization of the child with his immediate environment, in all its moods and manners, warts and all. Schools have occasionally rejected this—sometimes on 'compensatory' grounds—preferring to cosset the children with the consolations of suburban culture, attempting (in the kindest and most well-intentioned fashion) to give the children a taste of life on the other side of the tracks. Attractive though this is, it has certain defects. In offering an alien clime for an hour or so a day, it risks socially schizophrenic children and it does nothing to help the children who must perforce remain in the neighbourhood. When this approach is aligned with the pyramidal educational system, with everyone entering for the same prizes but with only a few winning them, it adds up to a training for frustration which might possibly be one of the causes of social unrest today. One sometimes hears teachers talk of broadening the children's horizons, when, in effect, they are doing no more than temporarily exchanging them. This duality of approach and content amounts to the same weakness—the consequence of forcing the academic pace is to reduce the realism of the curriculum, just as the pressing of a foreign cultural norm also dilutes the immediacy of the child's education.

Conversely, if we were to concentrate on the everyone who will be a citizen-parent, as opposed to the someone who will be a college student and if we were to concentrate on the many who are called as opposed to the few who, with their 'O' level certificates brandished like visas, are chosen, it might be a more productive assignment. Social education—the exercise of social skills on related social materials—would take precedence and, in the visionary longterm, new concepts of city life might emerge. Even in the shortterm one might, in A. H. Halsey's compelling phrase, 'raise the heights of their dilemmas'. Only on a thorough grounding in and understanding of their situation can one hope to develop the abilities to perceive exactly what is amiss and how it might be righted. It is not so much moving from the known to the unknown as making the known more knowable.

This does not mean a dogmatic assertion of any ideology. If anything is dogmatic, it should be the assertion of tolerance and open-endedness. The teachers' role would become more one of guide in the art of choice and taste; less of mentor in prejudged standards and valuations. Many teachers would agree that studies should be locality based; in some degree it is merely the 'child-centredness', beloved of the educational psychologists, while many see the commonsensical point of using easily sought and convenient resources. It is this possible change of social attitude that will, if accepted, impose most strain on teachers, for the teacher, traditionally, has been a mainstay of the *status quo* and a guardian of society's customs and mores. It would take years of arduous and genuine soul-searching for teachers to agree that openmindedness and relative value-systems and extreme toleration are or should be the finest hallmarks of a free and democratic society. The teachers' conventional support of certain established planks may have to be lessened, as they endeavour to conduct an objective examination of the issues facing people today in the city centres. This might include a questioning of, say, the viability, of local government procedures or the validity of social and cultural standards. If teachers are to teach children to stand on their own feet, they must expect to have their own toes trodden on occasionally.

The community-oriented curriculum has three possible subsidiary advantages, beyond the prior, long-term hope for a higher level of civic participation. First, it is likely that, given a socially oriented content, children will do as well and probably better in traditional attainments, simply because the exercise of their reading, writing and so on will be directly geared to their experience. This answers a much-pressed criticism of social education; that is, the suggestion that 'academic' prowess suffers. Second, the child is dignified by the acceptance that education can be about him and his environs, that he is an historical character in a geographical situation with social, spiritual, technical and other problems facing him. The ceaseless wandering off to the cowsheds of rurality or the poesy of yesteryear can be a constant reminder to the child that 'education' is, by implication, not of his world. Third, parental involvement and support for curricular enterprises would probably be enhanced by a socially relevant curriculum, in that their own experience, occupations, insights and so forth would be material evidence. The mysteries of the school would be, in part, replaced by a substance well-known to the parent.

Two strong arguments against the community-oriented curriculum must also be met. One claims that a downtown curriculum for downtown schools helps create a ghetto or some kind of proletarian enclave. This puts the question in reverse. Does anyone doubt that social polarisation exists and that, be the borderlines blurred, unequal circumstances have created massively unequal lifechances? If this is so, a uniform educational system might well be drawing a curtain of normalcy over the gross inequalities of life. It might be fairer and more honest, in brief, to tell the children the truth and help them face up to the reality constructively; it might, conceivably, be more encouraging for teachers to embark on such an enterprise rather than constantly to submit themselves to immaterial standardisations. Admittedly, this is a harsh doctrine. Superficially it may appear to run counter to the grand concept of equality of opportunity—but this is not so; rather does it insist that the only chance of producing equal opportunity is by differential or discriminatory treatment. Here it meets the twin grand concept of the realisation of best self; it is an attempt to allow each child to realise his most fruitful potential. Socially, it is a pretence to assume that this can be done by 'equal', that is, uniform, educational treatment.

The other argument is that a downtown curriculum for downtown schools indicates a second-class sort of education, a reversion to the Victorian two-tier system of one education for the rich and one for the poor. It is argued that this teaches the child to accept his lot patiently and, by concentrating on his environment, fails to thrill him with the stirring challenge of fresh horizons, such as a lesson on the climate of New Zealand or the armour of the New Model Army. It is right to be suspicious, for it was a long uphill struggle earlier in the century to establish education for all at all levels. Indeed, this is the ideal that informs the community school approach. This approach accepts the ideal, but points out that, implemented as a system, it has failed to work, simply because social background has proved so crucial an element in educational performance. And those who think the community based curriculum is a recipe for resignation have totally missed the point. By stretching the children, intellectually and creatively, on the social issues that confront them, one hopes to produce adults provoked and challenged into a positive and constructive response.

In short, it is an outward looking attitude not an introverted one. It is intended that, from the stable base of an understanding of his own locale, children can look outwards to wider frames of reference. A mastery of the immediate situation is surely the most practical means of fitting children for adaption to other situations. It is a question, then, of exercising social skills in viable and immediate content. Heaven knows one would not begrudge the children reading a fascinating story of long ago and far away or travelling out for joyful days in the woodlands and pastures. But let us not beatify this as some kind of 'cultural enrichment' which will transfigure the children. The majority of EPA children will live in their present neighbourhoods or on the redevelopment estates; this is the chief likelihood for which we must educate. A coachtrip to the seaside or a gambol in the fields does little to redress the present inadequacies of children's preparation for their often grim destiny. A day in the country is a welcome holiday not a social solution.

So much for the fine talk. What steps have we taken on the project to explore the possibilities of a locally based curriculum? Frankly but predictably, this is one of the slower and more laborious aspects of the project. The schools have co-operated freely, and, considering what must have appeared a rather harebrained analysis, bravely. Most of the project schools have undertaken the exploration of a curricular element, attempting to assess its relevance to the modern life of the urban child, and college of education teams have assisted most energetically in these investigations. The slowness of results forthcoming is relative to the quicker turnover of, for instance, home and school activities where results are immediate and obvious, be they for good or ill. It is in the nature of curriculum development to be a lengthier process, involved, as it must necessarily be, with the educative evolution of the child. This is even more accentuated when one is not initially concerned with short-term pay-off like reading age or writing ability, but with the child's capacity for social adaptation later in life. Further, the teacher would be right to approach wholesale reappraisal warily, knowing that the children could be the critical sufferers if things went adrift. Nor would it be reasonable to expect teachers, trained and experienced in one set of methods and approaches, suddenly to adopt a different set on the say-so of any crank who happens on the school. Put another way, the theories that project directors must perforce peddle automatically come into contest with the practical realities of the school situation and the Liverpool Project team is immensely appreciative of the kindly and encouraging fashion in which the schools have given them house-room.

Perhaps our social environment probes are the most straightforward examples with which to begin. There are five of these. Two of them examine with immense detail and care some immediate social agency such as the school itself, the church, the street or the shops. This is in part a physical examination, searching out the minutiae of fabric ostensibly well-known to the children and drawing on varied media to represent it. Another investigates the cultural and literary heritage of the area, looking critically, for example, at the differing religious sects and other institutions around about or recreating, verbally and dramatically, local life and stories. Another bases its local studies on features like street surfaces and furniture, derivation of street names and changes in building usage. An infant school utilises the everyday festivals like Guy Fawkes Day or Pancake Tuesday as foci for its work and parents are invited in to find enjoyment and instruction in the outcome. All these explorations add up to a distinctive and vigorous investigation of many facets of the locality. The manhole covers, the Victorian lamposts and pillar-boxes, the types of windows, grids, hydrants and paving-stones—all these give the primary child the chance to get down to a well-founded knowledge and awareness of his environ.

Creative expression is another modus operandi. The group in question choose a theme, such as 'occupations', 'streets', 'money', 'transport' or 'the city'. The children apply all creative media, verbal, oral, dramatic, artistic in two and three dimensions, musical and dance, to a representation of the theme, flexing their creative muscles on matters native to them, learning to conceive of responses to immediate issues. In another school a whole range of recreational activities are aimed at offering a breadth of possible leisure oppor-tunities for the children both now and in the future. These run from film-making and gardening to fishing and ice-skating. The relevancy of animal/plant studies is raised in another school, where, against the background of a well-stocked animal room, the possibilities are explored of children in highrise dwellings finding pleasure and value in smallscale home experiments with bulbs or larvae.

We have two infant number projects, attempting to improve the pupil's grasp of mathematical concepts with a utilitarian base like area or money. We have done a little work with junior language kits constructed around local features like the docks and another group have composed and gathered together a series of local folk-songs. This amounts to a dozen or so miniature probes. Unfortun-ately, because of organisational difficulties, the language work we had planned in an infant school collapsed and left us without any direct linguistic exploration, but, by and large, we had been able to commence in a minor key, an across-the-board sounding of the normal curriculum.

It would be folly to pretend that in a few short months the results have been startling. It took the first year of the project to complete a reconnaissance, negotiate college linkages and fields for curricular activity and navigate our way through the early weeks of difficul-ties. Only by and during the second year of the project (that is, the academic session 1969/1970) was the curricular work in any way structured. Even then it was, on the whole, framed thematically and in half-termly phrases. Flexibility was maintained. These probes sometimes went on much longer than had been expected if teachers adjudged them fruitful. No attempt was made to institute formal evaluation mechanisms, not only because of the fluidity of the activity and the concentration on a strategic frame rather than tactical detail, but also because the outcomes watched for were not the traditional ones. We were not primarily interested, for instance, in reading age, intelligence quotients and other attainments. We were anxious to maintain an open observation of the general reaction to these activities and our interpretation of them will be founded on the consensus of the carefully prepared reports of heads, teachers, tutors and students. As in many other aspects of the project, we are looking for hypotheses which might, in the future, be subjected to more puristic scrutiny.

Several teachers and others, of course, find little of value in the exercise, because (as we would agree) it is not by any means novel or because (as we would agree) it bears too little relation to the conventional school timetable. Others press, with respectable reasoning for a blitz on language and reading, while others see the work as pleasant but diversionary. So let there be no mistaking that we do not present a united front. Nonetheless, many seem agreed that two minor outcomes are evident. The first is that, through the introduction of student teams and the consequent improvement of the adult–child ratio, the children have shown some general educational betterment, measured not just in terms of the actual field investigated but more in terms of the broader social relationships established. The second is a general acceptance that, whatever else, language and communications generally have been uplifted, and, given the disappearance of our one language exploration, that comes as something of a relief.

It is fairly obvious that the mounting of student teams and possibly the introduction of fresh stimuli and equipment has been the major cause of this, but we do feel encouraged to add a third minor outcome, albeit a negative sounding one. The utilisation of immediate resources has not, at least, created any problems of indiscipline, of time-wasting nor, more significantly, of a decline in traditional standards. There have been isolated complaints that this kind of socially-based work robs time and energy from 'bread and butter' subjects, but, all in all, many teachers appear to conclude that, whatever else, it doesn't make any difference. Some go beyond this healthy teaching reaction and positively affirm that locality-based work does add that extra dimension of stimulation and value for the child. We are inclined to argue, therefore, that if reappraisal content does not critically impede the conventional educational development of the child, it might as well be included. The child might as well exercise his skills on locality-based materials in the hope that, overall, social awareness and purpose might be generated. Whatever our somewhat theological faith in the community curriculum, it would, on the available evidence, be unfair to go further than this rather wishy-washy conclusion. We are inclined toward the opinion that we have tried out several curricular pointers that could, without let or hindrance, be profitably drafted into the normal primary school syllabus.

The general nature of the project's curriculum work may be best described by what is perhaps our most picturesque illustration. A junior school undertaking a maths project decided to simulate a moderately-sized supermarket in a large, vacant domestic science room. With the help of the Tesco company, a dozen or so other firms and the enthusiastic collections of the children, this supermarket was established, complete with genuine shelving stacked with dummy packets and products, a till, baskets, and shoals of new decimal coinage. 'Chatty Stores' is now an excellent teaching aid for the school and it splendidly demonstrates the integrated character of a well chosen centre of interest. The money studies are an obvious starting-point, with role-playing, stock-taking, porterage and other adjuncts. A considerable amount of allied maths has been undertaken, chiefly based on surveys of local shopping provision and habits, simple market research, household budgeting and a host of other pointers. In turn, many of these lead to meaningful social studies; for instance, a graph showing the types of shop in the vicinity may lead to the question, why are there eight chip shops and no banks? The whole social and economic issue of shopping is open to examination and it is one, of course, of great import in the children's lives. There are art and craft possibilities—window dressing, trading stamps and so forth—and moral educational themes like shoplifting, advertising and smoking may be pursued. One could continue taking off layer after layer of potential teaching resource, all of it geared to a relevant and significant simulation all of it interflowing without too much 'subject' division and all of it delighting the children with its real-life pleasure. In a word, 'supermarket' could become a subject in its own right.

We have certainly examined the curriculum in breadth, if not in depth, from the standpoint of locality. One reaction is fairly common. As might be expected in the excellent primary schools where we operate, the integrational fluidity, mentioned specifically with regard to the supermarket, is pretty much a constant feature. Although one school might begin with creative expression and another with animal and plant life, the overflow into all other curricular realms has been deliciously encouraging. We receive reports of children's language benefiting from the maths project or of attractive creative work emanating from an environmental exploration. The chief approach is thematic: one creative expression approach has been based on 'the street': one social environment approach was based on 'the street': the point of entry was different but the overall product differs only in mild emphasis. This feature is impressive enough to tempt one to go the whole hog and recommend that the timetable be jettisoned in favour of community themes to be pursued as widely as possible. This may be a little too highflying at the moment. The set pattern of reading, maths, physical education, religious education and the like will not be dislodged quite so simply.

As a basis for negotiation, one might suggest the compromise of half the sessions (say, two mornings and three afternoons) being devoted to social education for the junior child. One bids so high not only because of the urgent importance of such work, but because the social or communal centre of interest can embrace all other curricular forms. Beyond that, it does not embrace them merely; it enlivens them with immediacy, so that the child can master the 'skills' of reading, talking, writing, number, physique, movement, art, music, drama, religion and all the rest in an exercise of relevant utility. Pick your theme. Draw up, in consultation with the children, your flow-diagram of the points of interest and concern that commend themselves as natural and spontaneous manifestations of the theme. Organise the work-load accordingly and programme the production so that it has some pattern or notion of ensemble, in order that, eventually, the entire group will witness and benefit from the final outcome.

The implication here is that, by seven or eight, if not before, the primary child is ready to examine his community thoroughly. Some teachers argue that it is too early and that it is better left to the secondary school. Granted, the secondary school should do likewise at a higher and more sophisticated level, but the irony is that this method is more easily implemented in the primary school, where happily, the fits and starts of the secondary school timetable do not incommode the regular and natural commission of project-style work. But apart from the freer and less artificial clime of the normal primary school, some people underrate the social capacity of junior children in Educational Priority Areas. One never ceases to be amazed at their resilience and aplomb, at the mature manner they cope with social situations and problems that might test the emotional and intellectual stamina of many an adult. To us, some of these responsibilities thrust on small children seem appalling and, occasionally, teachers see the school as a respite from such tribulations and a temporary five-hour shelter from the cold blasts of reality. This can be being kind to be cruel. It would be kinder to help them withstand these circumstances and it is certain that it is rarely too early, in terms of the children's experience, to commence social enquiry of the type now suggested.

Many teachers, encouragingly, are persuaded of the need for a community oriented curriculum, but two objections are paramount. One, already referred to, is the question of attitude, of whether teachers should (whatever their own especial beliefs, which need not, of course, remain hidden) attempt to impose and set particular value-systems on children. This is highly controversial country and one could not expect teachers—for that matter, parents—to shift—their traditional ground sharply or swiftly. Unluckily, it is a truism to state that we are unlikely to obtain informed, constructive and articulate social criticism if we are overcircumspect about encouraging it in schools.

The other problem is more humdrum and less fraught with philosophic and moral subtleties. It is the question of resources. Education is privately serviced and, inescapably, the publishers of books and other teaching aids must sell their wares both at Land's End and John O'Groats. So much of our teaching material is thus rendered neuter, abstract and 'national'. It is this which is in part responsible for the perpetuation of content which teachers often realise is either irrelevant or divorced from the children's reality. This applies not only to history and geography but to 'readers' which so often dwell in another world amazing to behold. Teachers, therefore, quite fairly argue that it is difficult to base teaching on Liverpool 7 when the available materials deal with Francis Drake, pygmies and Janet and John. Educational theorists would reply that teachers should prepare their own resources—but teachers would remind educational theorists that forty or more children won't fend for themselves while this is being accomplished. EPA teachers devote long and arduous hours to their tasks and, while many perform miracles of creation in terms of materials, there is a limit to this. Moreover, the teacher might justly add that, if community-oriented studies are our idea and one we make such a song and dance about, we could at least offer some concrete examples.

This we are endeavouring to meet with the production of teaching kits called 'Projectors' a generic label for a very varied assortment of bits and pieces, culled from the work on the project, and put into some form of order for all the Liverpool EPA schools. Two already published are *Social Environment in the Downtown School*, a packet of teacher-centred suggestions on using the immediate environment and, *Down Your Way*, a large, well-illustrated workbook for junior children, leading them to examine the roads and buildings in their area more thoroughly. Two others are in production. One is called *Home-School Horse-Sense*, an advisory wallet arising from the parental links developed by the project but including a certain amount of advice on curricular activities related to this theme. The other is an educational game, *Streets Ahead*, designed to strengthen social awareness; it can operate at three levels, the development of buildings, shops, houses and other social institutions, the uses and issues arising from the usage of these social agencies, and the assessment by children of other pupil teams' efforts in these fields. We entertain high hopes of the enjoyment and value to be found in *Streets Ahead*. Two others are at the planning stage. One of these is an individual set of maths equipment for infants and the other is a 'scouse' language kit for the four-to-six age-range, drawing where possible on the local sub-culture. Others contemplated include material dealing with creative work, localised 'readers' and local folk-music. A couple of barriers face us; money and time. There is no need to elaborate on inadequate financing, while lack of time is an obvious handicap; in puristic terms, some of these notions of language kits and games need years of time and hundreds of pounds to resolve the snags and polish the corners. All we are claiming, then, for these 'Projectors' is that they are the kind of community-based teaching aids that a teachers' resources centre might produce for its clientele. They are pilot examples—like practically everything else in the project—of what could be accomplished, rather than finished answers to the problem.

It will be a long, maybe a never-ending haul. There are, nonetheless, good signs. Progressive primary school method of the controlled enquiry and discovery brand is ideally suited to the content here delineated. Carried to its logical conclusion, 'discovery' could lead to the open-ended attitude to social investigation that may be necessary. The operation of the pedocentric or child-centred approach has meant a considerable amount of 'localisation' of the curriculum and we do feel, on the project, that we have opened up the area of relevant content still further. Sometimes teachers say 'this is all very well, but you can't do it until you've dealt with the basics'. Our ambition is to make social environmental or community study one of the 'Basics'.

Index

502

Katona, G., *cited* 319
Katz, E., *et al.*, *quoted* 380
Kekewich, Sir George, *quoted* 31
Kelsall, K. K., *cited* 22
Kerr, John F., 116, *178–199*
Khrushchev reforms, 1958, 84
Kircher, Everett J., *quoted* 357
Knowledge, 174, 190, 239 *et seq.*, 268
et seq., 362
classification, 192, 281–284
Koerner, J. D., *cited* 445, 446
Kotschnig, W. M., *cited* 30

Laban, Rudolph, *cited* 261
Lancaster's mutual system, 23
Language, 257
Lawrence, D. H., *quoted* 253
Laybourn, M., *cited* 212
Learning ability, 47
Lamm, Z., *cited* 163, 165
Lawton, Denis, *444–464*
Learning activity, 143
experiences, 136, 143, 154 *et seq.*, 193
Research & Development Center, Pittsburgh, 345
theory, 121, 136, 154, 299–319
Leavis, F. R., *cited* 251
Lester-Smith, W. O., *quoted* 23, 58
Levin, Kurt, *cited* 392
Liberal arts colleges, 19, 113
Liberal education, 42–43
Life adjustment courses, 103
Lindvall, C. M., 351
Linguistic differential, 95–100
Lionberger, H. F., *cited* 383
Liverpool Educational Priority Area Project, 483–498
Local change strategies, 399 409
Localism in educational technology, 417 *et seq.*
Lowndes, G. A. N., *quoted* 28
Lynn, R. & Gordon, I. E., *cited* 156

'MPIR' sequence, 202
Maccia, Elizabeth, *cited* 170, 182
McGee, R., *cited* 379
Mack, E. C., *cited* 25
McLuhan, M., *quoted* 412
McNicol, Harry, *cited* 221
McPherson, J. A., 70
Madras system, 23
Management process cycle, 124–127

Maritain, J., *cited* 243
Mathematics Syllabus Committee, 427
Mazurkiewicz, A. J., *quoted* 473
Mayer, M., *quoted* 416
Mead, Margaret, *cited* 230
Measurement, 157
Mechanics Institutes, 45
Medawar, P. B., *quoted* 183
Media, 194, 262, 299–319, 412 *et seq.*
mass, 255
Melton, A. W., *cited* 302
Meredith, G. P., *cited* 153
Merritt, John E., 116, *201–215*
Midwinter, Eric, *483–498*
Miel, Alice, 122, *cited* 184, 356–367
Miles M. B., *cited* 381, 382, 386, 392, 393
Miller, N. E., *cited* 303
Millington Ernest, 462
Mini-school, 109
Modern Mathematics in schools, 427
Modern school, 49 *et seq.*
Modes of thinking, 240
Moore, W., *quoted* 375
Morant, Sir Robert, 27
More, Hannah, 24
Morell, D. H., *cited* 176
Morris, J. M., *cited* 57
Morris, R., *cited* 196
Mort, P., *cited* 383
Motivation, 82, 140, 202, 304
Movement education, 261
Multiple chance principle, 93
Musgrove, F., 118, *cited* 155, *216–231*

National Association of Educational Broadcasters, *quoted* 420
National Association of Schoolmasters survey, 57
National Science Foundation, 381
National Union of Teachers: Kent County Association survey, 58
Neill, A. S., 4, 109
Nelson, L. W., *quoted* 420
Network analysis, 124–127
'New-Fist', 7 *et seq.*
New Zealand, 95–100
Newcastle Commission, 1858, 24, 449
Newcomb, T. M., *cited* 220
Newham Curriculum Development Bulletin, *quoted* 462–463
Newman, Sir Henry, 64
Newman, J. H., *cited* 219